LAW, LITERATURE, AND THE TRANSMISSION OF CULTURE IN ENGLAND, 1837–1925

For my parents, Armin and Geneva

Law, Literature, and the Transmission of Culture in England, 1837–1925

CATHRINE O. FRANK
University of New England

Routledge
Taylor & Francis Group
LONDON AND NEW YORK

First published 2010 by Ashgate Publishing

2 Park Square, Milton Park, Abingdon, Oxon OX14 4RN
711 Third Avenue, New York, NY 10017, USA

Routledge is an imprint of the Taylor & Francis Group, an informa business

First issued in paperback 2016

British Library Cataloguing in Publication Data
Frank, Cathrine O.
Law, literature, and the transmission of culture in England, 1837–1925
1. English fiction – 19th century – History and criticism 2. Wills in literature
I. Title
823.8'093554–dc22

Library of Congress Cataloging-in-Publication Data
Frank, Cathrine O.
Law, literature, and the transmission of culture in England, 1837–1925 / by Cathrine O. Frank.
p. cm.
Includes bibliographical references and index.
ISBN 978-1-4094-0014-1 (hardback: alk. paper)
1. English fiction—19th century—History and criticism. 2. English fiction—20th century—History and criticism. 3. Law and literature—Great Britain—History. 4. Wills—Great Britain—History. 5. Wills in literature. 6. Inheritance and succession in literature. 7. Inheritance and succession—Great Britain—History. I. Title.

PR878.L43F73 2010
823'.8093554—dc22

2009047678

ISBN 978-1-4094-0014-1 (hbk)
ISBN 978-1-138-26055-9 (pbk)

Contents

Acknowledgements

My thanks go to Laurie Mathes, Bethany Kenyon, Brenda Austin, Sharon Eckert, and all the librarians at the University of New England for their diligent and expert assistance, as well as to Maureen Quinlan and the reference librarians at Maine Law, and the respective staffs of the Library of Congress, the British Library, and the Public Record Office in London who helped me gather primary materials.

I am grateful to The College of Arts and Sciences of the University of New England whose junior research leave provided valuable time to complete this project. My colleagues in the Department of English and Language Studies at UNE have supported my work in various ways, through conversations, attendance at talks, participation in conference panels, and general encouragement. My thanks to them. I would particularly like to acknowledge Matthew Anderson whose collaboration on other projects has been an invaluable part of my intellectual and professional growth. Anything I've noticed about the relationship between law and religion in Chapter 5 has been enhanced by conversations with him.

Thanks go as well to Ann McClellan for years of conversation, camaraderie, and support, including trans-Atlantic talks about Virginia Woolf. My conclusion is better for her having read it first.

This book has been a long time in the making, and it might yet be a collection of stuffed and still-expanding files were it not for the interest and support of Ann Donahue, Whitney Feininger, Kathy Bond Borie, and India R. Tresselt at Ashgate Publishing. My thanks to them. Portions of the introduction and Chapter 6 were previously published and are reprinted here by kind permission of the following: portions of the introduction appeared in Frank, Cathrine O. "Of Testaments and Tattoos: The Wills Act of 1837 and *Mr. Meeson's Will* (1888)." *Law and Literature* 18 (2006): 323–41. Chapter 6 is an expanded version of Frank, Cathrine. "Fictions of Justice: Testamentary Intention and the (Il)legitimate Heir," originally published in *English Literature in Transition* 47.3 (2004): 311–30.

I come from a family of English majors and lawyers (with an errant Political Science degree snuck in), and my childhood living room was a scene straight from the end of Bleak House, its floor often strewn with "masses of papers," some of which came to comprise my own file of so-called "importancies." My mother's reading lists of Victorian novels led me to literature instead of law, but this book is a natural outgrowth of those early connections, and so I dedicate it to my parents, with thanks and love.

PART 1
Writing the Will

Introduction
Novel Bequests

> The ownership of a thing cannot be looked upon as complete without the power of bestowing it, at death or during life, at the owner's pleasure; and all the reasons, which recommend that private property should exist, recommend *pro tanto*, this extension of it.
>
> J.S. Mill, *Principles of Political Economy* 1848

> Goodness only knows what novelists and dramatists would do without wills.
>
> L.S. Lewis, "Some Peculiar Wills" 1897

Victoria began her 64-year reign as Queen of England in 1837. In the same year, a new statute was enacted that gave the last will and testament the shape it essentially still bears in England and in the United States today. The Wills Act of 1837 repealed hundreds of years of testamentary law and made the will a distinctly modern document. Bringing together the older forms of devise and testament (forms used for the disposal of real and personal property, respectively), it created a single legal will to serve as the mechanism for expressing and enacting the testator's newly expanded power (Ritchie 21). As a specifically written document, one whose authenticity was declared in writing by testator and witnesses alike, the will provided a permanent, visible record of the writer's worldly goods, and of the writer.

The will's new documentary status brought with it a new rhetorical function. Like the birth and marriage certificate, the written will is a legal register of identity. It comes into existence through the would-be testator's interaction with legal codes governing the inheritance of property—and with the lawyers who understand them. This professional intervention in private will implies that the individual's social self does not exist prior to such engagement with the law, yet the will is generally understood, after all, to be an expression of the individual's personal volition, an imperative originating with the private property-owner and delivered to future generations via the law. These opposing functions suggest a paradox of the will: it is at once a testament to private, autonomous character and a bureaucratic tool of legal identity. In this sense, the legal document has a metaphysical counterpart—the will in will—which raises the important questions, first, of how much control any individual has in the construction of his own subjectivity, and, second, how much pressure such a legally sanctioned identity must exert on his beneficiaries' own powers of self-definition.

These conflicting attitudes towards subjectivity were a consequence and expression of the transformation of "character" into a distinctly modern, capitalist "identity."[1] The last will and testament acknowledges, even creates, the desire to control one's own property, but the legal regulation of individual will through laws of inheritance, and the rise of legal professionals to mediate the individual's relationship to the law, emphasize the turn towards bureaucracy. So the self-possessed testator—full of plans, confident in his powers, and certain he has character—comes to the law for the services it provides. The documentary registration of persons, however, is a mechanism of social order, which, if not divorced from ideas of the individual's human personality or agency, nevertheless seeks to reframe, redirect, or curb and control it. Subjectivity understood in these terms as identity is inseparable from the legal structures that enable it, and so the testator's disposal of property becomes a convenient way for the State temporarily to delegate a power that finally supports its own social organization, values, and authority. Looking at the will, the overlaps and the conflict between these ideas of personhood become clear. Though the dominance of either model shifts over the course of the nineteenth century, both models also co-exist throughout it as different concepts for the same physical person. The private individual and the public subject are different ways of looking at the same figure, that is: as one's self-image versus the image as refracted through a legal lens, and, as we will see, through literary ones as well.

The written will became a means of making people legible as legal subjects and in this sense participated in a shift towards identity, yet by emphasizing conscious volition, it appealed to ideas more properly associated with character.[2] Intention assumes moral agency, desire, and an ability to act upon both that defines character, and testamentary rights express a legal and cultural endorsement of this idea of subjectivity. However, the formalization of intention through the 1837 Act, and the solicitor's similar transformation of the testator's instructions into his will, together participated in what Ronald Thomas in his study of forensic sciences has so usefully described as the "institutionalization of the textual construction of identity" (60).

As a document whose most obvious legal purpose is the orderly transmission of goods, the will aligns this social identity with materialism. In the early modern period, the consolidation of land was the principal determinant of one's social identity, security, and power. When Lear, for example, divvies up his demesnes *before* his death, he relinquishes the foundation of his identity as ruler of both a kingdom and a family, which is most forcibly signaled by his loss of sanity (a king's public figure being the essential part of his private character). The shift

---

[1] Ronald R. Thomas in his work on nineteenth-century detective fiction and the forensic sciences follows Benedict Anderson's argument that changing modes of political organization necessarily lead to altered ideas about the people living in these newly imagined communities. The movement from character to identity is symptomatic of the "nation's" transformation into the "State" or the "bureaucratic system of order and enforcement that governs the individual impulses within the nation" (11).

[2] Thomas links specific forensic technologies (such as the polygraph and mug shot) to the shift towards "identity" insofar as they transform people into texts and make them "legible" for others; see 17.

from feudalism to more modern, capitalist economies certainly did not eliminate the importance of landed property, but the proliferation of goods came to provide additional means for assessing one's self and worth. The mass of goods that litters Belinda's dressing table, for instance, and her horror of the forfex that cuts her lock, her principal asset, links what in Pope's poem is the commodification of the body with the idea that the measure of one's self *is* one's property. Similarly, Hareton Earnshaw is dismayed to find that the beggar-boy his father brings home has broken a coveted violin, thereby signifying for him the orphan's threat to the material integrity of his possessions and, consequently, of his identity as future master of Wuthering Heights.

The altered sense of public and private spheres and the related concepts of personhood adumbrated in these examples were among the many changes worked by the revolutions of the eighteenth and early nineteenth centuries. Instead of their separate but equal relationship in the eighteenth century, the private became qualitatively superior to the public in the nineteenth century with industrial capitalism and the reformulation of secularism. Capitalism created private selves and outward signs. It created a chaotic public world from which people needed protection and which redirected their energy inward towards control of the domestic sphere where, as Allan Sennett explains it, "order and authority were unchallenged, security of material existence could be a concomitant of real marital love, and the transactions between members of families would brook no outside scrutiny" (20).[3] Its methods of mass production also emphasized material goods and contributed to the fetishization of commodities that endowed them with human characteristics and made them signs of their owner's personality as well.

Commodity fetishism is but one expression of nineteenth-century secularism. In place of sacred mysteries, things were endowed with meaning. They were no longer defined by their place in an overarching natural order, but carried their meaning inside them. This principle of "immanence" became the basis of knowledge in secular society, which rendered all external appearances intrinsically significant, or at least assumed that they might be (Sennett 21). To speak of personal possessions documented in the will is, in this sense, to speak of goods in which more than material value inheres. Secularization also mystified the human subject by replacing his will to believe in God with a will to believe in himself (Sennett 150). Personality can thus be understood as the principle of immanence applied to individuals in parallel to the similar fetishization of commodities. How can we know the strangers among us? If phenomena must be apprehended in terms of one's

---

[3] Sennett notes the way eighteenth-century structures survived into the nineteenth century and provided ballast amidst otherwise bewildering changes (141). For example, eighteenth-century belief distinguished "civility" from "nature": "While man made himself in public, he realized his nature in the private realm" (18). If this belief in the private as a place of self-realization persists in the nineteenth century and is paired with that sphere's increased self-jurisdiction, then any external interference, such as a lawyer's scrutiny of one's private will, would be felt as a challenge to one's rights and authority. This is the conflict between the testator's sense of character and the legal community's perception of his identity.

sensory experience of them, then one answer is that people too must be equated with the "immediate impressions" they make, or their personality (Sennett 151). Citing Carlyle's focus on costume in *Sartor Resartus*, Sennett notes that "appearances in the world are not veils but guides to the authentic self of the wearer" (153). In the legal world, the will was not merely a list of property but a "speaking likeness," as one solicitor of the time put it, of the testator (B.B. West 33).

In the burgeoning capitalism of the nineteenth century, then, the will—that catalog of one's possessions and expression of a right in things—became synonymous with a sense of personal agency and selfhood. As J.S. Mill clearly states in the passage that opens this study, the capitalist institution of private property logically demands that ownership include, first, the right to dispose of property, and, second, that individual "pleasure" be the guide of that disposal. In the epistemological context of empiricism, the will that expressed these rights itself became the empirical register of identity, a legalistic fetish in which intention and personality were immanent. It was (and is) a document that survived the testator, one that preserved the goods with which he identified, whose resonance for Victorian culture especially rested in the uncertainty of what lay beyond the material world. Anny Sadrin makes the point specifically for Charles Dickens's work that "if essence and existence are to be reconciled in a worldly society, man must *have* in order to *be*" (4). If one was what one had, then the individual could in a sense outlive himself as long as his pleasure continued to govern the goods comprising that identity; the will sought to provide just such a mechanism of control.

This desire for a concrete index of identity was particularly acute in the nineteenth century for a variety of reasons but notably because of the uneven value for empirical ways of knowing. The material world was expanding: through the mass production of goods at home, but also through means as various as scientific discovery and imperial conquest abroad. Charles Lyell's *Principles of Geology* (1830–33), for example, announced the astonishing discovery of pre-historic remains, which proved, he argued, that although *human* history was brief, the world was old, and the Victorians were consequently so far removed from its real origins as to make it nearly impossible to trace the human connection to them or, worse, to imagine themselves as being exempt from its cataclysms. In response to this specter of oblivion, the Victorians "reconstituted themselves as origin," writes Gillian Beer, and busily set about documenting themselves both for their own psychic relief and for posterity (85). In this climate, the written will provided just such a traceable origin for individual identity because it was literally a physical document—a legal fossil—that provided evidence of the testator's possessions, those observable markers of his social existence over which even the dead hand could arguably maintain control.

The correlation between the will and empiricism is sufficiently, even suspiciously, neat and thus raises the question of what happened to the document when the epistemological value of empiricism was challenged. Victorian constancy to the doctrine of "seeing is believing" was not uniform throughout the century. If reliance on the ability of appearances to convey an object's essential meaning was challenged by a growing sense that the observable was not, in fact, one-dimensional (and that the viewer's efforts to identify the True or the Real might therefore be inadequate), access to the unobservable posed still greater challenges. Material expansion was matched by growth in areas not of themselves available to sensory apprehension. The inner workings of the mind, for example, was a subject of intense interest to Victorians of all stamps, and, as Lisa Rodensky notes in her work on criminal intention, the "possibility of getting access to the interior self" (9) occupied psychologists and philosophers like Bentham to lawyers and writers of fiction. As James Fitzjames Stephen lamented, however, "Every word which describes the operation of the mind, is a metaphor, taken from some external objects" that therefore eludes the essential (qtd. in Rodensky 9).[4] The only means outside of fiction of representing interiority and, indeed, of conceptualizing it in the first place was through inference from the physical world (Rodensky 11).

The effect of this shift in empiricism on the documentary will highlights the importance of the imperative will. One response to the challenge was a determined insistence that meaning could, or had to, be located on the surface of things because the alternative was too unsettling. Another was the open acknowledgment and investigation of this epistemological and ontological conflict that informs those Victorian novels that took the legal will as their subject. At issue here is the constructed nature of both meaning and identity, the role of desire and volition in that construction, and the extent to which identity and meaning (both individual and cultural) were negotiable. Victorian novels that self-consciously tackled these issues, acknowledging empiricism's sway to the extent that it made a worthy subject of debate, presage the urgency of those issues at the turn of the century when empiricism's viability as a mode of knowledge had become far more suspect.

The oblivion that empiricism sought to avoid erupted, virus-like, in invigorated form throughout the century and peaked, if not in *fin de siècle* attitudes of degeneration and decline, then certainly in August 1914 with the war that would obliterate a generation. A particularly striking example of the effort to repress the unknowable appears in *The Times* published immediately following the Queen's death in 1901 ("Queen Victoria's Descendants"). Victoria's family tree is depicted and, while it identifies her many offshoots, it tellingly omits any record of her own descent. Victoria is posited as origin, an entirely self-evolved or fully formed queen from whom all Europe emanates. The significance of the representation lies both in its impulse to make of the Victorians a cultural *Ursprung* just as its chief symbol, Victoria herself, passed into the oblivion of death, and to highlight the degree to which such representations are clearly willed. (Obviously, the queen's pedigree is easily, indeed, necessarily traceable.) The Edwardian novel offers a similar paradox. Notoriously concerned with inheritance, the early twentieth-century novel shows very little interest in the attested, written will, and one has to ask why, just when the usefulness of such a concrete marker of generational transition would seem to be highest, the document fell out of representational favor.

---

4 The passage Rodensky cites is in an unpublished letter among the Stephen papers at Cambridge University Library.

The answer lies in the connection between realism as an empirical mode of representation and the decline of faith in that mode of knowledge that led ultimately to more abstract, modernist attempts to represent the Real. Turning their attention away from the external markers privileged by their realist Victorian forbears, modernist writers opted for depictions of an internalized subjectivity or consciousness as the more authentic expression of real experience. Where the documentary will provided an eligible rhetorical strategy in realistic Victorian novels for discussing the formation and transmission of individual and cultural identity, it was because of empiricism's indebtedness to materialism, which, in the new century, was supplanted by a more general interest in inheritance and the sometimes liberating, sometimes threatening dissolution of Victorian identity. Of course, the importance of goods in and of themselves did not wane with the century, as the "Forsytism" of Galsworthy's *Man of Property* (1906) (the first novel of *The Forsyte Saga*) attests. However, their centrality as reliable indicators of the True or the Real was problematized in Edwardian novels in which the imperative will—the self-conscious, metaphysical attempt to define one's self and embody and convey that concept—stepped forth in more meaningful ways. Put differently, the "end" of Victorianism and the rejection of empiricism required the development of a new subjectivity and, indeed, of alternative methods of defining one's self and one's culture. These methods are traceable in the novelistic bequests of the Victorian and Edwardian periods.

The nineteenth-century investment in empiricism and the birth of the modern legal will specifically as a document coincide with the rise of the realist novel as the literary vehicle that represents, even documents, culture. It seems less necessary now than it may have been 20 or even 15 years ago to defend the realist novel from those views which cast it as a hopelessly unreflective, mimetic representation of an uncontested reality, but at the risk of belaboring the point, evaluations of that kind severely underestimate the degree to which the Victorians actively interrogated, criticized, and negotiated the foundations of their cultural beliefs and practices. That this image of the Victorian novel was created by modernist authors (and perpetuated by postmodern theories more sympathetic to their methods) helps to explain its persistence, but, as George Levine reminds us, the two periods differed chiefly in the *means* of representing reality, insofar as neither contested the idea that a reality did exist to represent (4).

Of course, these means are so apparently different that the question of just how one gets a modernist out of a realist has to be asked; when considering a literary genealogy, how does one get from Eliot or Trollope to Woolf? The short answer is via the Edwardians. I will be concerned with the reciprocity primarily between the realist novel's use of the will, its negotiation with legal culture, and the construction of Victorian cultural identity, and so I do not propose a full-scale study of modernism's response. Rather, I pay particular attention to novels of the post-Victoria, pre-war period as products and producers of an interstitial time in which authors oscillated between old and new values, as well as old and new methods. Periodization is of course a mercurial if not an arbitrary activity, and there is something to the idea that the Edwardian era was not recognized as such until after the war (Thale 41). However, when Edmund Gosse felt compelled to chronicle his relationship with his father, when Galsworthy and Bennett were writing novels specifically about the "passing of an age," when Forster actively, though not sanguinely, struggled to "connect" two eras, it becomes clear that writers of the period were very much aware of the passage of time, of their role as inheritors of a culture, and of their role as novelists seeking to depict this new and amorphous reality.[5]

The testamentary novel marks the nexus of the literary and legal concern with identity and inheritance and more than warranted L.S. Lewis's observation, "Goodness only knows what novelists and dramatists would do without wills." In order to understand the rhetorical value of the documentary will in Victorian novels, one has to read legal wills, whose objectives the novel appropriated. Moreover, those wills have to be read for their own imaginative response to the prospective dissolution of identity threatened by the death of the body. Relying on Geertzian "thick description,"—that method of "seizing upon an event or anecdote ... and re-read[ing] it in such a way as to reveal through the analysis of tiny particulars the behavioral codes, logics, and motive forces controlling a whole society" (in Veeser ix)—I take the will as just such an anecdote. To read nineteenth- and early twentieth-century wills, statutes, case law, and legal texts governing inheritance and the composition of wills is to encounter questions about how wills are formed, who writes them, what they are meant to accomplish, how they enter the social register, and what happens when they are contested.

In both law and literature, authorial intention has been a guiding, albeit much contested, principle. Belief in this agency is a crucial facet of understanding the will and the novel; it is akin to the realist's belief that language, though limited in its ability to capture reality, is nonetheless the going principle that makes shared meaning possible in the nineteenth century. That said, the contours of agency remain notoriously imprecise. Rather than attempt a definitive explanation as to whether or when it takes shape, the question should be why the idea of agency was so important, what purpose it accomplished or need it satisfied for the Victorians (and for us), and thus why a sense of the will as an unmediated statement of its author's desires is so powerful. In this sense of the will as a negotiation between the self and social system, it can be read as a rhetorical strategy that enables a particular conception of one's metaphysical subjectivity, which, as a strategy, also changes when the governing practices do.

---

[5] In my approach to realism, I borrow Levine's proposition that it "posits 'mixed' conditions" (4), namely, that in its attempt to represent human experience, the novel engages with the contemporary non-literary discourses that enable and inform it. David Lodge suggests similarly that realism is "the representation of experience in a manner which approximates closely to descriptions of similar experience in non-literary texts of the same culture" (25). This isolation of the "manner" or conventions of realism and their indebtedness to non-literary forms is analogous to Stephen Greenblatt's theory that meaning develops out of the interrelationship or "circulation" of discourses and of the material practices informed by them (in Veeser 13).

To map this change, we can imagine an arc from an empirical, one might say formalist, conception of the will (as formulated by the Wills Act of 1837) to the 1925 Administration of Estates Act alongside a second arc from the realist to the modernist novel. Both of these arcs originate from a point where, as has been suggested, material forms possessed meaning, and language was representational and referential.[6] In the will, this reference was to property but, importantly, it was also to the moral will of the testator, which could make sense only if people were understood to possess character. Character was an essential aspect of the novel, of course, and the relationship between the two expanding professions of law and literature became a competition over the representation of subjectivity, of character and states of mind as expressed in actions and written forms.[7] Maria Aristodemou in her study of the fictionality of law grants literature the remedial function of exposing legal discourse's "repressed rhetoricity," thereby returning us "to a time before existing practices, begun as myths and plays, became law and started to take themselves (extremely) seriously" (20–21). While Aristodemou's history reaches back to the ancient world and classical literature, the early nineteenthcentury affords a similar opportunity for re-thinking legal practice and the legal professional. As staunchly as the "discourse of custom" was invoked by aristocratic elites as a safeguard against the dangers of reform, the common law was nonetheless countered both by democratic and utilitarian appeals to develop a

---

6 John McGowan refers to the debates of the empiricists and the romantics as a heritage which offered the Victorians two models for knowing: the representational and the revelatory. The first is mediated knowledge in which nature and mind meet through the word. The second is unmediated; the mind can apprehend nature directly through the physical senses or through intuition. The Victorians used both models, which indicated differing attitudes towards reality (even for a single author over time), rather than the single vision with which they are usually attributed. In this context, the writer is responsible for explaining how he or she arrived at knowledge because that explanation would serve as a model for readers of how they could do the same (2).

7 Recent studies in the field of law and literature have moved away from a narrowly comparative model that typically enlists one discipline to play up the shortcomings of the other in favor of a more conscientious analysis of what constitutes the legal and the literary. They should be more self-aware about how they distinguish between the two, whether in terms of their professed cultural functions—the goals of law and of literature—or in the sense of how each discourse operates, its attitudes towards and uses of language. On this view, cultural studies would seem to obviate the problem of determining whether law and literature studies should emphasize the points of similarity or departure between them, since in the truest sense of interdisciplinarity, law and literature would be recognized more as circulating discourses than practices competing for institutional prominence and support (even if professional rancor has been said to characterize their history with one another). For this work see Julie Stone Peters, "Law, Literature, and the Vanishing Real: On the Future of an Interdisciplinary Illusion"; Anthony Julius, "Introduction" to *Law and Literature* (Freeman and Lewis); Guyora Binder and Robert Weisberg, eds., *Literary Criticisms of the Law*; Jane B. Baron, "Law, Literature, and the Problems of Interdisciplinarity"; Dieter Polloczek, *Literature and Legal Discourse: Equity and Ethics from Sterne to Conrad.*

more systematic code of law (Barrell xv–xvi, 141). Indeed, it is during the reform movement that the law assumed many of the forms recognizable to us now, not least among them that of the powerful lawyer. There were of course influential lawyers and changes in law before the nineteenth century, but the point here is to recognize the links between industrial capitalism, the emergence of a professional class, and mass literacy and book production, all of which gathered momentum in the early 1800s and placed both law and literature in a period of flux rather than stasis. Following these arcs, one starts to see a divergence between the ongoing commitment to the empirical and formal in laws governing inheritance and to an increasing commitment to consciousness in literature. These are broad swathes, indeed, but they make the point that when the possibility of moral agency was questioned in the last quarter of the century, law itself became more deterministic (documenting, organizing, identifying people so as to manage them) whereas literature went further into the mind in an effort to represent individualized responses to this world.[8]

Looking at the figures of the testator and the heir opens up a discussion of how each one comes into a sense of self, as a desiring legal subject competent to enact his will in the world, or as a subject dependent on another's will (whether benefitted by or deprived of an inheritance). As characters in the novel, these two figures provide models of the kinds of subjectivity available to readers in the real world, but the novel also created a reading experience that allowed its audience to engage in their own imaginative self-fashioning.[9] It is true that average Victorians, whether they were reading the novel or simply living their daily lives and being in the world, were explicitly and often tacitly submitting to authority.[10] However, knowing this, we can think about the opportunities for agency and the sense of possibility each of those experiences—either of the lawyer's office or

---

8 Literature's exploration of the mind is not a forensic exercise in the sense of providing legal evidence or the materials of scientific proof. I am sensitive to the possibility that by exploring the mind, or trying to know and reproduce a state of consciousness, literature might in fact appear invasive. My sense of this desire to know how people are constituted—or at least of the literary project of representing character—is that it is more neutral: if not categorically benign, it can provide an opportunity for author and reader to engage in a process of self-knowing played out in the register of the imagination.

9 For discussion of the constitutive power of legal language, see the foundational work of James Boyd White in *The Legal Imagination* and *Heracles' Bow*. See Robin West's assessment of White's textual communities in "Communities, Texts, and Law." For analysis of legal language's rhetorical powers, see Richard H. Weisberg, *The Failure of the Word* and *Poethics*.

10 As Robin West explains, people submit not only to law's commands; they also importantly grant moral authority to law that can undermine attempts to critique it (*Narrative*). Like West, Maria Aristodemou turns to the literary precisely because unlike the legal imagination, which insists that its creations are "natural, inevitable, and [able to] provide … all the right answers" (2), fiction, even when it "appears to be inevitable" (1), neither forgets it is a fiction nor asks its readers to do so (18).

the particular novelist's creation—was likely to promote. And we can think about how literature revised legal texts and reinserted imagination into an increasingly rationalistic legal system.[11] What did the reader's world look like from a legal point of view as compared to a literary one? What can we as readers learn about Victorian culture by seeing the interaction between these two world views, and what can this history mean for us as we consider the ways we ourselves are in the world as desiring individuals and as legal subjects?

Writing the Will

Part 1 focuses on the testator and the figure he made in popular periodicals and legal texts and in the novel. Chapter 1, "Writing the Will: Victorian Testators and Legal Culture" begins with a discussion of the will's place in the Victorian cultural imagination. Contemporary accounts of "curious wills," of the compulsion to write them, and of their frequent literary representation linked law and literature as subjects of everyday, popular interest and consumption. Far from being beyond the average individual's sphere of activity, they in fact provided two of the most influential arenas in which individual and institutional authority met in the creation of persons and culture.

Focusing primarily on the law's particular conception of the individual's relationship to and motivation for belonging to a society, I briefly discuss property's role as the marker of individual identity. If, as political and legal theorists argued, the protection of property is the chief reason for submitting to government, then the legal system that regulates property perforce regulates individual autonomy. In this context, the will functions in a contractual sense as an expression of the testator's right to control his property, but inheritance laws also shaped those rights so as to uphold a particular model of social organization. The potential conflict between these two authorities becomes clearer when read in terms of the Wills Act

---

[11] Literature in general shows readers cracks in a confident legal mien, but Aristodemou links realism to the law's confessional failures so that realism becomes literature in denial—literature, like law, in its repressed state. Indeed, realism appears to be the only form of literature, which does want its readers to forget that it is fiction. "It is realism in literature, empiricism in philosophy, and positivism in legal theory," she writes, "that, by identifying the knowable not only with what is observable but more damagingly 'with all there is' that have the effect of flattening our experiences" (26). But this view of realism depends on a sense of representation as mimesis for its own sake, a multiplication of existing circumstances for further consumption rather than realignment or critique, that underestimates its achievement. Aristodemou prefers fantasy, in contrast, because it approaches the world as potential rather than completion. However, the closure that realist fictions offered, the possibility that knowledge was available to all, the solace that events had discernible causes and good behavior would be rewarded, and the view that happy marriages could be achieved—these are fantasies. And this should not suggest an impoverished Victorian imagination as much as a desire for control and for outcomes that were not uniformly available in lived experience. Moreover, much of the inequality of opportunity results from social organization and policies that reading fiction, including realism, reveals.

of 1837, which gave priority to the testator's intentions, and the magazine articles and legal manuals imploring the solicitor, for instance, to curb the testator's will. The actual conflict, as many of these articles warned it would, can be seen in the litigation surrounding poorly made wills, and so I turn to case law to illustrate more specifically how testamentary rights were construed in the law.

Following discussion of the Wills Act and its impact on the nature of the document, the wills of several Victorian novelists exemplify the power of possessions to shape the testator's self concept, as well as the testator's own power to shape the lives of his beneficiaries through control of the goods he bequeaths them. They also illustrate the will's narrative potential. In *An Autobiography* (1883) Anthony Trollope famously compared the novel-writer to a "shoe-maker" and "tallow-chandler" (81), claiming that all professional enterprises entail methodicism and depend on discipline. I would add to Trollope's list the writer of wills, but, rather than moving as Trollope does from literary professionalism towards other jobs analogous to it, I address the question of how writing wills is like writing novels. In this way, the chapter concludes by examining the content and structure of the will in terms of what it offered the novelist for his fictional writing.

Moving from the testator in the Victorian legal world, Chapter 2, "Writing the Novel: Victorian Testators and Literary Culture," looks at the figure he makes in the novel. Like a testator writing himself into posterity, the novelist shares with fathers and with law the power to will the behavior of his literary children.[12] However, like the testator he worked within particular conventions. Backed by empiricism, the realistic novelist seeking to "represent" his world could select no more comprehensive document than the will to do so. Essential Victorian themes of death, money, inheritance, and marriage all coalesce in the will. However, the Victorians were attempting more than the "copyism" with which Hardy charged them ("The Science of Fiction" 262). Seeing in the will the collision of materialism and subjectivity, personal determination and social, legal codes, Victorian writers isolated it because it combined the metaphysics and the materiality of both sides in the debates on realism and idealism: namely, whether the novel should explore character or develop action, whether it should emphasize metaphysical thought about the way the world ought to be, or whether it should focus on depicting the world as it is. Where law governed the real world, the novelist who appropriated and revised forms like the will could present an alternative world in which it might be constructed differently and might mean something different. By presenting a new worldview, the novel could reveal not so much the fact of the will's constructedness (although this alone would be much) as the process through which it came into being as well as its effects. In this way, literature uses the law to expose the false inevitability of particular legal ways of ordering the world, which could work to show literature's equal and sometimes more "equitable" ability to define subjectivity and organize social experience.

---

[12] See Deirdre David's discussion of Dickens and the "powers of the omnipotent novelist" (74).

The Victorian novel is littered with wills, tucked away in its bedsteads, cupboards, and chests but always emerging. Ever attuned to the getting—and keeping—of property, the Victorian testamentary novel was especially intent on the testator whose identity it linked directly to the possession of great wealth or to a great plan not yet brought to fruition. And because he is old or ailing and particularly conscious of his mortality, the novels frequently focus on characters in the process of drafting their wills. Chapter 2 begins by providing brief analyses of certain novels because of the developmental trajectory of the will's usefulness that they make visible. *Wuthering Heights* (1847) displays a conflict between Brontë's romantic emphasis on the individual's primacy in interpreting reality and oneself, and her recognition of the growing importance of the material world as an intermediary of meaning. This conflict translates into a series of "splits" in the text itself: Cathy's divided desires between her romantic impulses and her material ambition, Heathcliff's manipulation of property to satisfy a desire for revenge that does not change with his social standing, the text's own conscious use of realist tools and material metaphors to satisfy more romantic aesthetic aims. All these serve to show how the will in both its senses, as desire and as document, combine elements of the aesthetic debate. Collins's novels in the sixties, especially *The Woman in White* (1860) and *The Moonstone* (1868), discuss the failings of male testators; Lady Julia Verinder shows far more sense than her late husband, for example, when she gives her solicitor power to write her will, not least because she is a woman and ineligible for inheriting the property outright, but because her husband's indifference to the law has left substantial loopholes that the legal professional must correct. Here the realist novel's use of the legal framework points out the way that the lay person's testamentary intention is actually limited and that real authority, whether appropriately or not, resides in the law and its representatives.

George Eliot's *Middlemarch* (1872) uses Featherstone's and Casaubon's wills to separate the effectiveness of legal forms—the fact that wills make things happen—from the particular intentions they encode. The story of Featherstone's will becomes a legal fable in which the testator who cries wolf, by tampering with his wills, receives the rational punishment of getting just what he asked for, even though legal justice in this case seems more accidental than deliberate. If this ending is a comic one, Casaubon's is the tragic alternative insofar as it precipitates the very outcomes it sought to prohibit. His will is a breach of consensus that destroys the ostensible union of husband and wife by binding Dorothea to a promise of whose nature she remains ignorant. It creates a view of her that no one who knows her finds credible. It transgresses the agreement made before marriage as to the nature of her proposed settlement and reveals an abuse of language in the sense that the will is used to keep secrets, to punish, and humiliate—all in a perfectly legal and effective form. Dorothea's rejection of her husband's will is justified for Eliot by this breach in the same way that the novel's worldview can be rejected when it imposes on rather than engages the reader.

In these examples, the novel focuses on the testator, but where there is a testator there must be an heir. The remainder of the chapter looks to Dickens's *Our Mutual*

Friend (1865) for an extended analysis of the different public identities John Harmon, Sr. creates for himself through his three different wills. It also examines his son's response to his father's dictates in order to explain how Dickens provides in this one novel a model for the transition from the Victorian to Edwardian era. John Harmon's different identities and Dickens's revelation of them involve his readers in a process of discovering just how much agency one really has when confronting the law of the father and of the legal system. Like the novel itself, John's disguises are symbolic devices for negotiating his relationship to the world that are successful in the degree to which they represent not merely what is, but engage the fictional individual and the audience in an examination of what might be. By thus depicting the will in its creation and in its implementation, *Our Mutual Friend* exemplifies the realist principle of consensus. However, if John Harmon ultimately comes round to his father's plan for him, the same cannot be said for the success of all wills.

Proving the Will

Part 2 shifts attention from writing the will to its implementation, from the testator to the heir whose inheritance of property brings with it an identity that to varying degrees proves burdensome. Chapter 3, "Victorian Daughters and the Burden of Inheritance," focuses on women as beneficiaries in order to examine the way that inheritance laws and the married women's property laws in particular—laws developed ostensibly to "protect" women's property—in effect deprived them of it. When applied to women, the claim that property has ontological significance in the Victorian period suggests that because married women could not legally control property, they could neither write their own wills nor control their own identities in the most obvious and powerful ways available to men or single women. Starting with the appearance in 1856 in *The Westminster Review* of both the Law Amendment Society's report on the married women's property laws and George Eliot's essay "Silly Novels by Lady Novelists," in which Eliot calls for realistic reform of the novel, I suggest that both law and literature required reforms that would support the consensual view of legislation and of reading. The laws relating to women's property were failing to gain the support of the women whose social identity they determined, that is, in the same way that the novel was called upon to offer a view of the world in which all readers could actively partake. Like the law, the novel required new endings that did not equate fictional success with the marital unions that in the real world signaled loss of control.

Following discussion of the history of the reform movement and the state of women's testamentary capacity, I turn to three novels in which the woman as protagonist offers the woman as reader an opportunity to re-imagine her relationship to property. By actively relinquishing an inheritance, the heroines of *Little Dorrit* (1857), *Felix Holt* (1866), and *The Woman in White* (1860) choose not to identify themselves in terms of their possessions. By giving up property, they simultaneously exercise the power of disposal so important to the concept of ownership, while promoting the view that self-possession can be defined in non-material terms. The inheritance plot's trajectory of uncovering character thus becomes the novel's formal critique of the (legal and literary) marriage plot's "covering" of its female characters. In *Little Dorrit*, for example, Dickens creates several sub-plots in which the consensual process of creating and reading fiction is illustrated so as to provide clues as to how the reader should understand Amy's rejection of her fortune. Money has always cast her in fictions woefully unlike her sense of the real and contrary to her personal volition. Only without money can Amy marry Arthur Clennam. When she denies the existence of Gilbert Clennam's will, destroying it at the moment she and Arthur agree to marry, she creates a new fiction in which her will is the one fulfilled. Similarly, Esther Lyon finds herself the subject of two different narratives in *Felix Holt*, neither of which she constructed. She is both a minister's daughter and the heiress to a massive estate, but the split plots of the narrative give Esther a choice as to which story will gain her consent. Like Amy Dorrit, Esther can either give up her property and marry Felix, or keep it and marry Harold, but at no point does Eliot suggest that Esther should retain the property *and* her single status. As unsatisfying as Esther's options and ultimate choice may strike modern readers, the point seems to be that Esther has a choice at all and that she opts for personal fulfillment that also benefits a community over a solitary existence amidst her fortune that essentially benefits no one.

The Woman in White, in contrast, is one of few novels to give a central place to the single woman who remains single. Laura Fairlie is the passive victim of all sorts of impositions: her fortune makes her susceptible to the likes of Percival Glyde, and her marriage results both in fraudulent and wholly legal "deaths." As an example of the heroine of traditional marriage plots, Laura is presented as a pathetic and ineffectual counterpart to the vibrancy and ingenuity of Collins's real heroine, the single Marian Halcombe. Unwilling perhaps to depart entirely from the traditional marriage plot, however, Collins splits the sisters' narratives. By making Marian instrumental in Laura's union with Hartwright, he satisfies the desire for a marital conclusion and domestic stability in which, significantly, Marian shares without needing to give up her single status or finding it somehow unfulfilling.

The appearance of the woman testator in the early twentieth century is a mixed blessing. On the one hand, the legal reforms enacted throughout the end of the century make their way into Edwardian novels in the shape of women who at last are capable of exercising the rights held for so long exclusively by men. However, the majority of those novels in which the woman's will appears treat it much as they do that of the male testator's: as a starting point for a discussion invested far more in the beneficiary than in the means through which the will comes down to him. It is as if women arrive at a point in the novel that it is no longer desirable to occupy, no matter how important those changes proved to be in the legal world. In this sense, the work begun by these Victorian wives and daughters marks the beginning of a process carried on by Edwardian sons. Like the Victorian women who changed the basis of identity from fortune to fulfillment and upset the primacy of possessions, Edwardian men shifted their attention from the testator and his literal will to the concept of inheritance and their own metaphysical will to define themselves. Chapter 4, "Edwardian Sons and the Burden of Inheritance Redux," reverses those characterizations of the Victorian period as a cultural childhood leading to a more thematically and structurally mature twentieth century and raises the question as to how effectual the sons' wills were in countering their Victorian fathers'.

In many respects, novels of the Edwardian period, which tackle the themes of intention, inheritance, and identity, describe the testator's will similarly to the Victorians. This is especially true of Theo Pontifex's "shake of the will" in Samuel Butler's *The Way of All Flesh* (1903), but Butler's novel, completed in 1873 yet published 30 years later, serves as a transitional text in the move from era to era that resonates, as Anthea Trodd has it, with the "parricidal" values that inform more properly Edwardian writers (53–5). Embedded within the nineteenth century, it confirms that use of the written will is a peculiarly Victorian strategy whose values, though they resound in the twentieth century, are significantly muffled by the more imperative, abstract will. The elderly Forsytes in Galsworthy's *Saga* (1922) of the same name, for example, dominate the first volume. Originally published in 1906 as *The Man of Property*, it is told from the mixed perspectives of two generations so that the legal document (that Old Jolyon lovingly reads and that Soames Forsyte would write if he could) represents an old ethos that has been diminished in the new era. With only the briefest mention of the legal will in *Clayhanger* (1910), Bennett portrays Darius Clayhanger's stultifying influence on his son and Edwin's reluctant fascination with his father's decline and his cognate assumption of authority. And in a single stroke in *Howards End* (1910), Forster has Henry Wilcox destroy the will in which his ailing wife bequeathed her home away from the family and to a woman who would much better understand its meaning.

Each of these examples suggests that testators of the twentieth century continue to exercise their wills but with two stylistic differences: the novels' narrative stance tends to favor the rising generation in terms of presenting the story primarily from their perspective, and they rely less on the documented will for their rhetorical punch. In the first instance, the testamentary generation is posited specifically as Victorian. Its presence serves as a springboard for investigating the consciousness of its heirs and for marking the novel's inward turn towards subjectivity. In an inverse relationship to a legal turn towards externalized identity, this consciousness signals the declining value of empirical or material representative modes in the movement towards modernism, which renders the literal will an obsolete rhetorical device.

Bracketing the chapter with Bennett and Woolf's debates about the state of the novel, I suggest that although the endings of these novels offer an equivocal picture of the relationship between Edwardian sons and their Victorian fathers, they *start* from the assumption that those sons have wills of their own, which they are entitled and expected to exercise.[13] This expectation in itself is a departure

---

[13] Like Anthea Trodd, I argue that Butler's and Gosse's "sons" are more successful in repudiating their fathers' designs than are Galsworthy, Bennett, and Forster (48–58). Soames Forsyte's new methods for acquiring Victorian status markers backfire and leave

from the treatment of women in Victorian texts. But like their Victorian sisters, the Edwardian novelist sought to change the literal shape of the novel so as to accommodate new kinds of stories. These twentieth-century novelists who tackle the constraints on individual subjectivity match these themes stylistically by referencing their literary fathers' legal wills then relegating them to the background as they test new ways to represent their experience. And in this they are like the modernists, who in Woolf's terms sought to depict the "semi-transparent envelope" that is Life "with as little mixture of the alien and external as possible" ("Modern Fiction" 124), in this case the literally external identities of the documentary will.

Contesting the Will

The final part turns to those instances in which the will is actively contested or where there are difficulties in construing and implementing authorial intention. In each chapter, a Victorian text raises a particular legal issue that impinges on the laws of inheritance and reveals the way that the freedom of testation offered by the Wills Act is always contingent on a wider network of law. The potential constraint of the testator's volition in these novels introduces a latent conflict between legality and justice, which is picked up in the Edwardian novels paired with them.

Chapter 5, "Broken Trusts: *Cy Près*, Fiction, and the Limits of Intention," examines two forms of trust: the legal arrangement at the center of Trollope's *The Warden* (1855) and the trust established between Edmund Gosse's parents in his autobiography *Father and Son* (1907). Though of different genres, each text's successful rendering of its subject depends on its ability to represent intention and thereby to frame subjectivity as an internalized experience. In both works, the individual is confronted by institutions—Septimus Harding by the Church, the Law, and the Press; Edmund Gosse by his parents and a set of conflated religious and legal determinants (as well as the conventions of biography)—that systematize from the outside the possibilities for defining personhood. In contrast, both Trollope and Gosse look to fiction as a tool, albeit differently employed, for extricating individual subjectivity from these frameworks.

The realist novel must involve its audience in the process of establishing meaning, which Trollope's novel does by presenting a legal difficulty—that of determining testamentary intention in the case of a charitable trust—which his readers, as much as his fictional lawyers, must interpret. Declining to decide whether Hiram's will has been legally or illegally administered, Trollope draws attention instead to the liabilities of interpretation as a process. He turns away from the law's employment of its own fiction, here the mechanism of *cy près*, towards

him unfulfilled (although Old Jolyon comes to adopt his son's more modern thinking); Edwin Clayhanger becomes his father in essential ways and in spite of efforts to the contrary; and the swaggering Henry Wilcox, rich in money but morally bankrupt by novel's end, ultimately cedes control to Margaret Schlegel, while his son is jailed for an outrageous abuse of moral authority that results in Leonard Bast's death.

the novel's ability to represent characters' intentions directly and thereby to provide a more authentic representation of subjectivity through literary fiction. Where Trollope's Victorian novel focuses on the literal will and the trust established by it, Gosse inflects the trust with a doubled meaning in his Edwardian text. Within the autobiography itself, trust operates as a "solemn charge" laid on Philip Gosse by his dying wife to raise their son (249). What in Trollope was a literal will becomes in Gosse a bond between his parents that in its religious and legal fundamentalism bans imagination from his spiritual upbringing, the object of the trust.

Trollope's abandonment of final judgment nonetheless raises the disturbing possibility that a testator's intentions, try as the law may to affect them, may not always be discernible in his text. By focusing on the will, Trollope conforms to Victorian convention, but by raising doubts of its efficacy he foreshadows Gosse's endeavors to define himself in terms of consciousness. Rejecting the "iconoclastic literalness" (78) of his parents' generation, Gosse looks for more imaginative and abstract ways to articulate his "innate and persistent self" (168). Describing the book as "the record of a struggle between two temperaments, two consciences, and almost two epochs" (35), Gosse's adherence to the concepts of transition and inheritance mark his Victorian literary heritage, but the primacy of his own subjectivity, as the protagonist of his book and as the touchstone of his narrative approach towards "facts," make him a pivotal figure in the move towards modernism.

The final chapter, "Fictions of Justice: Testamentary Intention and the Illegitimate Heir," focuses on "bastardy" as another legal fiction, used in the novels both to critique the concept as such and to question the legitimacy of the legal system, which either curtails testamentary freedom (exercising too great authority), or which can be manipulated in such a way as to nullify its popular authority. Turning again to Trollope, I read *Ralph the Heir* (1871) and *Mr. Scarborough's Family* (1883) as two different ways of working out the tensions between kinds of property, models of ownership, and the kinds of legal subjectivity they imply. Both novels offer conservative and liberal views of the individual's relationship to landed property: the former advances the idea that land represents the nation (in the same way possessions represent familial identity) and as such is meant to be preserved for its own sake; the latter assumes that the land is a private possession in which the owner has a personal right. And both show unwillingness either fully to succumb to tradition (especially when as in *Ralph the Heir* excluding the illegitimate son works against preservation of the estate), or to subvert it, as Trollope's rejection of Mr. Scarborough's maneuverings suggests.

Trollope's ambivalence on these points is echoed in Forster's *Howards End* (1910) where legality as such is put aside in favor of more spiritual and theoretical definitions of legitimacy that make his novel a stylistically modernist tribute to traditional cultural values. By allowing Ruth Wilcox's feudal conception of her house as a symbol of England's better past to be the arbiter, rather than any legally ratified will, of its own proper transmission, Forster prioritizes the desiring will over its legal expression. The eligible "adopted" heirs, Margaret Schlegel and her technically illegitimate nephew, are determined by their attitude towards property.

They become cultural stewards in ways that recall the past, yet which are made possible in the novel by Forster's modernist preference for the abstracted will.

I conclude with a brief look at the historic, legal, and cultural ascension of modernism. In Lytton Strachey's biography *Queen Victoria* (1921), he describes the dead queen in terms that by then were decidedly Victorian. She was, he writes, a "tenacious woman, hoarding her valuables," one "who would not lose one memory or one pin," and whose debilitating devotion to the past and its emblems gave way in her old age to an "egotism" that at last "proclaimed its rights" and to a "force of character … [that] imposed itself absolutely upon its environment by the conscious effort of an imperious will" (385–6). The biography appeared at a time, after the war, when Victoria and her ethos might seem so far removed from daily experience as to enable a final, formal dismissal of both. However, even if Strachey intended no eulogium, the *Trauerarbeit* of finally laying Victoria to rest was one that Strachey found extremely difficult to execute because, as Jay Dickson explains, he "was being overwhelmed by his subject, and becoming himself subject … to her will" (34–5), a will he himself praised. As a Victorian testator, Victoria is a maternal example, like Ruth Wilcox, of the woman whose imperative will presides over a changing generation.

This view of Victoria as woman and testator is one that the legal system had slowly come to apply to all women throughout the latter half of the nineteenth century. In the same way that the laws governing trusts and illegitimacy hampered the testator's freedom, the laws of primogeniture and entail remained an obstacle to women's inheritance and freedom of testation, as Vita Sackville-West's loss of Knole famously made clear early in the new century. But in the same year *Mrs. Dalloway* appeared, The Administration of Estates Act abolished primogeniture and marked a legal revolution of Victorian, indeed, medieval practices. I conclude with a reading of *To the Lighthouse* (1927) as Woolf's revision of *Mrs. Dalloway* and with it the effort to oust the dead queen.

Virginia Woolf, perhaps the most pointed advocate of a new literary creed, published *Mrs. Dalloway* in 1925, yet even in this thoroughly modernist novel, Woolf is in some ways little better able than Strachey to depose Victoria. Like the aging queen hoarding her pins, Clarissa Dalloway hoards her memories, dedicating herself to the party, her tribute to past beauty, over which she reigns. For Peter Walsh, the "terror" and "ecstasy" of his modern experience, the desire to leave the party and the fear of doing so, lodges in Clarissa herself for, like Victoria, "there she was" (194). (If the past tense of that final word implies a narrative time beyond the novel's end and hence Clarissa's—and the queen's—inability to stop time, Woolf would try again two years later with Mrs. Ramsay and make this point more clearly.) Nevertheless, as a literary venture, *Mrs. Dalloway* is all consciousness. The subjective experiences it offers are all actuated by the same occasions, uniting her characters almost in spite of themselves in much the way that Woolf's generation was united by their compulsion to respond to Victoria even as they designed a new literary legacy.

Chapter 1
Writing the Will: Victorian Testators and Legal Culture

In 1890 a writer for *All the Year Round* observed:

> By the year 2000, if we can trust Mr. Edward Bellamy's "Looking Backward," wills will be curiosities of an extinct phase of civilisation for in his 'Utopia' no one will possess any property to bequeath. In the meantime, however, every reasonable person will make his or her last will and testament at the very earliest moment after becoming possessed of anything worth disposing of. And by making it, we mean getting it made, for there seems to be a fatality about making one's own will, to which even lawyers themselves fall victims. ("Wills: Old and New" 178)

Post-millennial readers know that Bellamy was wrong, but from the writer's perspective, it seems that the prospect of even another hundred years would be inadequate to dislodge property from its place as the key-note of social organization and personal ambition. Indeed, his wry note that "in the meantime" the act of acquiring property should almost immediately prompt thoughts of its disposal suggests that will-writing is something of a compulsion and that the history of troublesome wills will continue to pose thorny legal questions for the foreseeable future. For with the acquisition of property comes a sense of individual rights and duties pertaining to it.[1]

Property is the focus of an economic and psychological investment both prompted and perpetuated by the link between ownership and domestic comfort, social standing, familial welfare, and fundamental egoism. The credo that one is what one owns implies that the control of property during one's lifetime is an essential component of personal subjectivity and social identity, which the controlled testamentary disposal of property will preserve even in death; as Charles Cutler remarks in *The English Illustrated Magazine*, "The character of a man is usually stamped on his will" (171), right along with the goods it catalogs. But the practical dimension of this continued existence, the legal fulfillment of the

---

[1] This sense depends largely on the view of property one takes. The "doctrine of absolute possession," for example, gives its owner "rights to" a thing; it is his alone to manipulate irrespective of other concerns either for the thing itself or with others' potential interest in it (Nunokawa 77). Most clearly connected to portable or personal property, this view differs from an older conception, typically relative to real property, that ownership entails obligations. Here "ownership" is more properly understood as stewardship, or the maintenance of house and land for its own integrity as for that of future generations of the family, for instance.

testator's desire, was apt to suffer in direct relation to his proprietary sense and to his active role in "making" a will. The writer for *All the Year Round* comments that among the many purposes Blackstone attributed to the will, its chief object was "to prevent strife and confusion" (178) among those who stood to inherit, but if the testator's personal interest is counted among those "other purposes," it is easy to see why "a counsel practicing in the Probate Court probably considers that they [wills] were primarily intended to create instead of prevent" discord ("Wills: Old and New" 178). Thus, the writer advocates a more passive role for the testator, one in which his desire is framed and mediated by the legal profession. Such intervention may raise doubts, however, as to exactly whose character is "stamped on [the] will": the testator's or the law's? Any simplistic notion of the legal instrument as a direct expression of its testator's desire and intentions must itself be tempered by the understanding that when the private will takes a public form, it becomes subject to the higher will of the law.

The purposes of the will and the uses to which it is put, the right way to make (and not to make) one, its meaning for the testator, and its effect on the heirs was a much-discussed legal issue in the nineteenth century, but as a process in which "every reasonable man" (and, after 1882, every reasonable woman) could expect to be engaged, will-writing occupied the popular imagination as well. Articles like the above that go on to catalog examples of "curious" wills frequently appeared in magazines of the century and catered to the public interest in Midas-like testators, mercenary heirs, twists of fate and eccentric or secret practices. Part of the reason for this interest lay precisely in the private dimension of the will. Although the proven will would be in the public domain, the will is also a statement of the author's personal, private desire. It records a unique relationship between possession and personality that literally effects the fortunes of those to whom property is or is not bequeathed and which, as B.B. West lamented in 1893, can give a funeral "the odious quality of an antechamber to a lottery office, at which the company at once hope and fear to learn the result of a turn of the wheel of fortune" (130). Dry and matter-of-fact as many wills prove to be, the *idea* of a will nonetheless focused the voyeuristic imagination.

L.S. Lewis calculated on this interest when he invited readers of *The Strand Magazine* to accompany him on a private tour of "the vast vaults and strong rooms beneath the Probate Registry" ("Some Peculiar Wills" 441). "In spite of the ever-present gloom and dust," he enthuses,

> The great spirit of romance pervades the great subterranean chambers we are considering. Millions of wills, going right down through the ages! The system of arrangement is absolutely perfect. Shakespeare's will is as readily produced as is that of the lowly Cockney who died the other day. (441)

It is not simply the wills themselves that are so intriguing (though Lewis will give descriptions and photographs of some of the most "peculiar," such as the will in rhyme or the will in shorthand), but their very aura that excites interest. They exist in a world of Victorian gothic—a "subterranean" world of "gloom and dust," stretching "right down through the ages," but also one of perfect "arrangement"—and they exude a sense of "romance." The style alone of Lewis's account of Somerset House is enough to situate the will as a subject of literary interest, but he in fact opens his article with the question that forms the epigraph of this book: "Goodness only knows what novelists and dramatists would do without wills" (441). He frequently reminds readers that literature has adopted the will for its own use because it is both a character in private dramas as well as a narrative form itself.[2] "The will stories buried away in the dark vaults of Somerset House," he writes, "would enable novelists to turn out stories until the Greek Kalends. Only one has to do one's own delving in this extraordinary place—as Miss Braddon frequently does, by the way" (446). References to Shakespeare and Braddon, like the reference to Bellamy, further illustrate the point that the legal last will and testament is equally a "will story." Even William Hazlitt, in his much earlier criticism of will-making, drew attention to its imaginative aspects. Give the accumulation of wealth the "privileges of an abstract idea, so that the project has the air of a fiction or of a story in a novel" (116), he wrote, and it will appeal to the testator's imagination, to his projection of a future, posthumous self.

In this chapter I discuss these "will stories" in terms of both the legal and symbolic function the will served, of its narrative potential, of its "authors" (the testator, the solicitor, and the novelist alike), and of the reasons it should have remained so prevalent in fiction as to be considered by today's critics a "tiresomely conventional" device in Victorian and Edwardian plots (Schor 136).[3] I begin by discussing the will's interest for a broad Victorian readership as a subject both of curiosity and critique, a document of practical importance as well as cultural significance, whose contours were shaped by writers for the popular press as well as by legal professionals and legislators. A reading of the Wills Act and Victorian

---

[2] For instance, Lewis recounts the story of an 1801 will written by an apothecary who had contracted the plague while stationed in Egypt. The will was sent by letter to a surgeon bound for England, who immediately copied it and placed the original in a "bottle of spirit" for fear of infection. When the will arrived in England and was decanted, it was discovered that the print had been entirely effaced by the alcohol, so that the surgeon's copy had to be accepted for probate instead. Similar stories such as that of the nobleman's will that was discovered in the leg of an old bed (that leg then being produced as evidence in court), or the will in verse variously position the will as a literary form as well as a suitable literary subject.

[3] Hilary Schor, in her reading of *Little Dorrit*, apologizes for the novel's interest in the will by pointing out that the story's unconventional characters are what prevent its use of the will from turning it into an "utterly conventional" novel, one in which the will marks a clumsy Gothic interruption of otherwise realist narratives (136). In a note to the chapter, she refers to a general critical "dismissal" of wills, basically because they had become boring and predictable plot devices (225 n.10). Certainly in this study, the prevalence of wills is a boon, rather than a bore, insofar as the will marks a point of common interest and even competition between law and literature where the function and goals of both institutions and their texts are at stake.

case law follows, and I conclude by forecasting the way the legal conceptions of character—or, more appropriately, identity—opened law more generally and the will specifically to the uses to which realist novelists put it.[4]

Reading the Will: Curious Characters in the Periodical Press

Lewis could rest assured that his guided tour through Somerset House would find a wide audience. Indeed, Charles Draycott, writing in the same year, also commented on the appeal of Somerset House, particularly the tendency of its wills "to reveal many curious phases of human nature" and, so, to speak to a diverse readership:

> As a matter of fact, abundant instances of the broadest humour, the most extradordinary caprice, the most ridiculous farce, and the most malevolent spirit are to be gleaned from the documents storied up in Somerset House; and today, as in the past, eccentric will-makers, judging from the cases continually coming to light, are probably as busy and numerous as ever. (66)

These "storied" wills filled Victorian papers and magazines and shared their pages with essays warning of the dangers of intestacy alternately with those criticizing too much freedom of bequest. Others lamented the will's degenerate state, its fall from the lovely language of former years into the coldly bureaucratic, "simple" idiom of modern law, while others still extolled the antiquarian value of wills for the insight they provided not only into "strange manners and customs long passed away" ("Wills" 410), but also into the "true character" of men ("Extraordinary Wills" 162). And in addition to these entertaining snippets and more polemical analyses, readers could expect to find ample advice for how they, too, could—and should—execute a will, prove a will, and otherwise enter into the "perilous science" of will-making ("Wills and Will-Making" 6). But why so *much* and so varied an interest? What shape did this "curiosity" take and what did readers gain from their inquiry?

---

4 I have chosen to look at the wills of the same Victorian authors whose books appear throughout this study as well as those of the Edwardian writers' fathers, but I attempt very little psycho-biographical reading of them. The potential for this sort of reading, to draw causal connections between the subject of the novels and the content of the will, is clearly nascent, especially in my discussion of the Edwardians' response to their literary fathers. But I do not avail myself of the tools of psychoanalytic literary criticism, preferring instead a largely historical investigative mode. Thus, my reasons for choosing authors' wills are largely pragmatic: rather than wading through the "millions of wills going right down through the [Victorian age]," which L.S. Lewis observed, to choose authors' wills was the more expedient route. Although from time to time the suggestion of a connection between particular novels and the will has proven irresistible, I leave any biographical explanation of the nature of the bequests themselves to another and look at the wills primarily for what they can say about the historical relationship between the individual testator and the legal institution, for what they offer by way of analogy to the writing of novels, and to the picture of Victorian culture their relationship creates.

How should we understand the tension revealed in the press between the will as a legal instrument about which readers were routinely told they needed practical knowledge, and the will as a concept, a right or freedom, subject to critique?

Any number of reasons for this interest can be inferred from the periodical press, especially after mid-century, but what is perhaps most telling about the cultural significance of the will is that while articles about it were of course varied to suit a publication's particular audience, *all* audiences were interested. *The Leisure Hour* and *Once a Week*, *Household Words*, and *The Spectator* published pieces on the will alongside the *Quarterly Review*, the *Contemporary Review*, *Temple Bar*, and (in America) *The Green Bag*, that "Useless but Entertaining Magazine for Lawyers." The will was a focus of professional and popular interest, of political, economic, and philosophical importance, and, not insignificantly, it was a source of great humor, entertainment, and sometimes poignancy, its gravitas as an expression of human nature and human relationships underlying even the strangest bequests.

Reading about wills thus could prompt solemn reflections on one's own duty, and there was certainly much written on this score, but a more basic effect, especially of reading about "Strange Wills," "Extraordinary Wills," *Ancient, Curious, and Famous Wills*, "Testamentary Curiosities" and other products of "Whimsical Will-Making" was the way it confirmed for its audience a version of reality and of itself. These particular articles, written between 1860 and 1898, share a generic quality that structured the reading experience: they begin with reflections on the will as a powerful mechanism—"What a remarkable document a will is [...] it speaks, and people hearken; it commands, and people obey; law supports and enforces its wishes; no power on earth can alter it" (Baring-Gould 233)—and then catalog malicious, farcical, or otherwise eccentric uses and abuses of this power. Yet they all assert that the will is essentially an expression of the "heart" and "motives" of the testator (232); even if readers were to spend a year "amongst the wills," suggests an unsigned piece, it would be time well spent: "you would not only obtain a deal of valuable information, but get a good insight into human nature also; for a man's will is a kind of mirror in which you may see his peculiarities" ("Wills and Testaments" 721). So, for example, S. Baring-Gould regales readers of *Once a Week* with the Biblical bequests of Adam and Job, with animals that received legacies—or, better still, with animals that left legacies such as M. Grunnius Corocotta Porcellus, a pig—with bequests to establish strange charities and still odder instructions for the division and bequest of internal organs (234). One might well ask exactly what sort of comment on human nature and on reality such wills were making: by displaying the peculiarity of other men—those removed by history, culture, or class—these wills bound Victorian readers together in normalcy, rationality, and perhaps in middle-class economy.

The "perhaps" is significant, for this strangeness extended to readers' contemporary world as well, particularly in terms of class. "There are few things more toothsome to newspaper readers than the small paragraphs headed 'Wills and Bequests,'" wrote a contributor to *Chambers's Journal of Popular Literature, Science, and Art*, "for we all of us like to know how rich our neighbors are, and how they dispose of their wealth, when they are no longer able to enjoy it themselves" ("Wills and Testaments" 721). Such weekly "Wills and Bequests" columns, which appeared well into the twentieth century in *The Illustrated London News*, kept readers apprised of the size of their neighbors' fortunes or their debts, the appointment of executors and the disappointment of heirs, so that even the commonplace will was made the subject of general gossip ("The Degeneracy of Wills" 46)[5]. George Sala jokingly called the *ILN* "an estimable journal evidently on excellent terms with the Court of Probate" (328), but well-off readers might scan its pages in satisfied contemplation of their own reflected plenitude, enjoying the staidly pleasurable security of a well-regulated transmission of property. Others might feel the *frisson* of a glimpse into the private lives of the newly deceased and know that, whether they managed their money well or badly, all were equal in death.

Eccentrics and millionaires notwithstanding, the wills cataloged in the press further unified readers in so far as they showed more or less average people writing them at all, and in this they offer an important indicator of the changed times and an explanation for the fascination with a range of wills. Writing in a more serious vein for the *Quarterly Review*, A. Hayward compared past- to present-day wills in "Wills and Will-Making: Ancient and Modern" (1860). Beginning with a review of two collections of largely royal wills (one compiled in 1780 by John Nichols, Printer to the Society of Antiquities, and another *Testamenta Vestuta* published in 1826 by the barrister Nicholas Harris Nicolas), the essay ends with liberal references to Lord St. Leonards's recently published *A Handy Book on Property Law* (1858). Hayward moves from an almost chronological recitation of the royal wills collected by Nichols and Nicolas to an advice manual on how to make wills, interspersed along the way with summaries of legal history, methodological reflections on cataloging wills, and praise for their historiographic value for "the legislator, moralist and divine" alike (425). In effect, Hayward brings the collection and study of wills up to date: from the will as curiosity or artifact to the will as a contemporary and practical legal instrument, from the will as the purview of kings and nobles to the will as the responsibility of modern legal subjects. As he explains, a collection of "modern wills" could evoke "a livelier and more rational interest" than royal testaments if it focused on the "magnates of intellect, the great writers, thinkers, and orators" (446)—an Enlightenment document more than an edict of Divine Right.

[5] The subject of the publication of wills or details as to estates in the national and local press was often a topic of discussion in parliamentary debates of the 1950s. Niall MacDermot, MP for Lewisham, North, called their publication "an unwarranted interference with the privacy of the individual in a matter which is essentially personal and private" (HC Deb 28 Nov. c. 767). However, Major Hicks Beach from Cheltenham, a practicing lawyer, argued that publication had sometimes led to the discovery of subsequent wills (c. 759), and, more to the point in his view, publication of the details of great estates provided a service to the people who could see the inequities of estate tax, or the siphoning off of monies for the government to use as revenue instead of paying down national debt, for example, or investing it for the public, its real beneficiaries (HC Deb 08 May c. 782).

Writing many years later, Virgil M. Harris, a lecturer on wills at the St. Louis University Institute of Law, framed his book *Ancient, Curious and Famous Wills* (1911) as an opportunity to redress what to him was the surprising fact that "no one in America [had] seriously undertaken the collection of famous and curious wills" (vii).[6] Harris's prefatory remarks convey his sense of working within a well-established genre of will-writing, but even his initial emphasis on the "famous and curious" gives way, as does Hayward's, to an appreciation for the will as what might be called the apotheosis of middle-class individualism and consumption: a solemn document whose importance derives from its imbrications of the very private dimensions of individual character with the maintenance of a social economy founded on property, and whose public effectiveness requires the assistance of legal professionals. And what's so interesting about the writing on wills in this period is that in spite of the "great men" approach found in Hayward and Harris, both make way for the possibility that other, more truly average citizens could also generate curiosity. Hence *Chambers's Journal of Popular Literature, Science, and the Arts* could locate its "Testamentary Curiosities" in the wills of John George of Lambeth or George Watts of Stoke-Bishop (curious for their vengeance and generosity respectively), or in wills as relatively recent as 1810 or 1814 (422–3). As was true for novel writing, will writing in the nineteenth century showed signs of realism, of shifting from the epic to the everyday, from the typological to the characters of ordinary people living in familiar times and places.

Reading about the will provided before all else lessons about character and identity, the self in both its private dimensions and in its role in the legal and cultural domains. Commentators and essayists emphasized testamentary character—not so much the dispositive "I" of the professionally drafted will as the moods and motives of the individual person for whom the composition of the will was to be an occasion for reflection on life, property, family and friends, interests and passions. Hayward remarks that "In their wills, *few men can keep up an assumed character*. Whatever dash of satire or hypocrisy there may be in the preamble, the dispositions at all events, are sure to tell us what was nearest their hearts" (emphasis mine 425). Harris insists that "the subject of wills is not so prosaic as might be supposed" (viii) precisely because they reflect "as a mirror"—that image of literature's realist enterprise—"the customs and habits of the times when written,

---

[6] The omission might be explained by what one writer, signing himself "Exchange," had to say in an issue of *The Green Bag* (1898): noting that in England "a man's last will and testament is regarded as a very sacred thing," he observes that in America "there is a strong, though perhaps latent, sentiment in favor of setting aside provisions in a will that are manifestly absurd or unjust. This largely explains," he continues, "why there are so many attempts in the United States to set aside wills, and why so many of these attempts are successful" (163–4). There is equal interest in the self-determining individual here, but the comments show an American preference for the wills of the living and a rejection of the English desire to extend that control beyond death. The cultural divide adumbrated here obscures, however, the way that English fiction, for example, adopted this present-focused preference for the heir's or legatee's self-ownership.

as well as the characters of the writers." He emphasizes the point by reference to a recent editorial in the *North American Review*, worth quoting at length:

> [T]o read [a will] is to come very close to the spirit of the man who wrote: to know his treasures, to understand his feeling toward men, and to measure his fitness for adventures among the seraphic and angelic beings. The words a man desires to have read when he lies dumb, the gifts he leaves, the grace with which he gives, all these lay bare the spirit, the heart of disposition, as few other things can. For a will is that which is to live after one, and it is written knowing that no wound inflicted can be remedied, no neglect repaired. How egotism, or miserliness, or conceit, or self-satisfaction can shine out in a will. How little exalting it is in most cases to read wills, and how often they turn us back to the authoritative statement, that it is easier for a camel to pass through the eye of a needle. (1–2)

The reviewer here clarifies the specific pressure points that the will touches: it is one's hand, one's voice, one's "posthumous self," but it is also an intention—instructions for a will—that, like the camel and its needle, must navigate the narrow avenues of law before it becomes a will in fact, however contorted by the passage it may be. Thus, readers were encouraged always to moderate and control their impulses, to learn from examples of badly behaved testators both the moral hazards of using the will as a weapon and the potential harm to one's vanity of leaving any other than a rational, compassionate, and well-prepared will for posterity's contemplation, for though we may "weep over the loss of our relative," nonetheless, "we quarrel over the division of his property" (Sugden 155).

This assumption that character is made manifest and permanent in the will grounds concepts of testamentary intention and hence the relationship between the desiring subject and his legally constructed identity. (One might also reverse the locution: the idea of intention depends on assumptions about character and the meaning of legal subjectivity, the responsibility for any action, lawful or unlawful, making sense only when people are understood to be both rational and effective, capable of reflecting on their desires and deciding how to act or refrain from acting.) The testator conceives of the will as an expression of his desire and control (certainly of property but also of his mortality); the lawyer and the courts explain their intervention in the will, not as a complication of intention or interference with the testator's rightful actions, but as the mechanism for bringing that intention to fruition by guiding the document through the law. In short, however it may appear to a layperson, case law and legal manuals reflect the legal assumption that intention should be ascertained and fulfilled.

This apparently shared investment notwithstanding, however, many essays reveal the distance between the testator-to-be and the legal professional. To the degree that the testator identified with his documentary will—in other words, to the degree that he conceived of the written will as a direct and effective statement of his desiring will—so was he less likely to see the need for legal help, and in a sense, this belief is reasonable. After all, readers were regularly told that the will was a mirror reflecting character. However, character and intention are not altogether static, and the will was just as likely to be a snapshot capturing the testator's mood and intention, for good or ill, at the moment of writing. Sons and even wives cut off with shillings, restrictive conditions on inheritance, ridiculous bequests to immortalize the testator have all been given legal effect, so readers were shown. However, the problem urged on them from a legal perspective was that while the self-authored will could indeed be made to take effect, very often the effect intended was not achieved—so complex was testamentary law, even practicing lawyers had been known to leave bad wills—or the intention itself was inconsistent with the testator's general character, his rational and more dispositive, "sound" frame of mind. Relatedly, the testator himself might not in fact know his own mind. He might be fully competent, but age or illness or external influences might leave him uncertain about what his actual desires are (Harris 6). For these and other reasons, much of the writing on wills went beyond exempla of the curious will to urge timely and well-considered action paired with professional assistance.

Let a testator be as clear as possible about his own intentions, he did not possess sufficient legal knowledge to frame his will so as to effect them, nor did he necessarily want to make his will. Writing the will was an act of self-determination, but it was hard to think about dying and maintain that sense of control. Viewing the will as a "death warrant" (Hazlitt 114) or, only marginally better, a trip to the dentist—"Mr. Paterfamilias seems to have as much dread of making a will as of having a couple of back teeth taken out by an unskillful [sic] apprentice" ("Wills and Testaments" 722)—testators postponed writing it, since "when everything is ready signed and sealed, there is nothing farther left to delay their departure" (Hazlitt 113). But Edward Sugden, Lord St. Leonards, scolded readers for waiting too long, claiming that to put off making a will "evinces either cowardice, or a shameful neglect of your temporal concerns" (133). First, then, property-owners had to be impressed with the necessity of confronting their mortality, a task approached through appeals to egoism and duty, explanations of the effect of intestacy (whether the disappointment of legitimate family interests or the unintended benefit to the State into whose "coffers" "large sums of money are swept every year" from the estates of intestates "who have left no heirs-at-law or collateral kith and kin" [Sala 334]), or, worse, of the benefit bad wills brought to the legal profession itself. The typical mistakes are quite specific:

> If you wish to leave a legacy to the legal profession, nothing is more simple to effect: make your own will; make use of a few ambiguous expressions; place your signature to the will in a remote corner; practice a little unmethodical madness when you are signing your name; use strange words; and go out of the broad highways of legal phraseology, and, depend upon it, if the lawyers don't come in for a large slice of your property, the fault will not be your own. ("Wills and Testaments" 723)

Though "some noodles" may use the "sixpenny printed form," it's nothing more than a "penny-wise and pound-foolish plan" since not making a will or making one badly could cost testators much more than a solicitor's fee (722).

The picture to emerge from these pieces, especially given their time period, is the way the legal profession, its documents and their functions, and consequently its conceptions of personhood were being reframed as a specialized science rather than a discourse of letters. As early as 1865, readers of *The Leisure Hour*'s regular column "Hints on Legal Topics," were warned that will-making in particular was a "perilous science," which the author, "speaking in the interests of the client, and not in that of the lawyer," advised them not to undertake "without the aid of a solicitor" ("Wills and Will-Making" 6).[7] Joseph Sutphen, writing for *The Popular Science Monthly* in 1883, wondered whether it were possible to write an incontestable will. Sutphen's question is a perfectly reasonable and much-repeated one that arose from the quantity and costs of litigation, which over the years had resulted in numbers of testators' intentions being overturned. "Like surgery, law is a science," he declares; "The unscientific man may with equal propriety endeavor to amputate his own limb as draw his will. In each case he has ventured upon a field in which he had neither knowledge, nor experience, nor skill. He may succeed, but every probability points to a fatal result" (529). Sutphen does not contest the symbolic significance of the will, much less the practical desirability of making one, but he insists that men have mistakenly equated the antiquity of will-making, and hence their familiarity with the concept, with an understanding of its rules and methods, its specialization within legal practice brought home to readers through analogy to medical practice.

This emphasis on the practical, technical knowledge of law persisted even when attention shifted from the would-be testator towards the will's executor. Rich and poor alike could benefit from basic knowledge of "How to Prove a Will," for example. Although admittedly "amongst the gloomiest topics" to make its way into the popular press (the essay appeared in *Chambers's Journal* in 1886), the writer excuses its presence on the grounds of usefulness—providing the "best and cheapest method of proceeding" (299)—for his readers. So much is familiar in the rhetorical stance taken by these "how-to" pieces. Of greater interest in this essay is its attempt to pit the secularized system of modern Probate against the abuses of the Ecclesiastical Courts, while retaining the sense of a spirit of law that, although decidedly not religious, is not entirely positivistic either. This tension is particularly clear for the wealthier classes who look to the reading of the will as a compensation for their emotional loss: "Constituted as men are, it is very certain that the distribution of property amongst survivors forms a not inconsiderable item on the alleviations provided by Mother Nature for the pain of inevitable losses by death" (299).[8] Why is it "Mother Nature" who alleviates the loss; why not Law? This metonymic

7 In a very brief article, the author poses a series of questions to guide the reader, beginning with the desirability of making a will at all and progressing through the designation (and definition) of heirs, the wording of the will—including another admonition to "eschew all printed forms" (8)—and concluding by emphasizing the centrality of proper execution through reference to a number of cases brought before various Lords Chancellor over the years.

8 The article's appeal to the poorer classes is less sentimental: they can learn how to take out letters of administration on intestacies or to gain title to a small estate without having to pay high fees, which would have been unavoidable under the old Diocesan courts.

slide from law to Mother Nature naturalizes law without returning it to God's law. The article creates a new mythos of law that links it at once to pagan symbology and to the natural sciences in contrast both to purely secularized, utilitarian bases of man-made law and the overtly Christian emphasis on natural law that came of the Ecclesiastical court's jurisdiction over such social relationships as marriage, birth, death, and wills. In short, it attempts to humanize law without being religious, to preserve the will's significance as the posthumous embodiment of a loved one and yet enable it to be verified and implemented by scientifically following a series of steps so simple as to be outlined in two pages of a popular magazine.

If law in the latter half of the century was to be understood increasingly as a new science, it was a mode of order and organization that had evolved organically and in conjunction with other new social sciences. But law's professionalism depended on an increasingly bureaucratic conception of identity, one that permitted greater efficiency in managing people, but one that also meant a loss in terms of character.[9] *Temple Bar* showed little sympathy for those lamenting the loss: "Those who never cease to regret what they call the good old times may usefully reflect on the condition of society in days when a portion of a subject's goods was obliged to be given to the Crown or to some royal favourite, in order to preserve the testator's family the secure possession of the remainder" ("Wills" 412). In the writer's view, in other words, ownership followed a progressive model. In spite of rising socialism (or as a warning against it), individual property rights had become more secure by 1894 when the essay appeared, and readers inclined to resist reform should consider whether they'd like the State to tax their property, for example, through death duties. This conception of the individual pitted against the State, so the article goes, demands a mediator—the legal professional—to protect the testator's rights in property.

Judging from *The Spectator*'s examination of "The Degeneracy of Wills" (1900), however, mediation by a professional class of interpreters robbed the will of its style, the testator of his voice, and the legatees of the need for patience or decorum. The "old-fashioned will"—meaning those that retained the formal influence of the Ecclesiastical Court's jurisdiction through inclusion of an opening prayer or the "fine introspectiveness of the preliminary recitals" (46), for example, possessed "a distinct element of picturesqueness" and of style completely lacking in the modern will:

> [T]he present-day will has come to be on the whole a prosaic and business-like performance; it has been pruned of much of that pleasing and useless verbosity with which its forerunner was adorned; its language is now what the esoteric body which holds the key to such mysteries is pleased to describe as "simple"; and although the bewildered testator may not always recognise his "instructions" when put into their scientific dress, he will confess at any rate that it has but little charm in the way of literary graces. (46)

---

9 See Martin Wiener, *Reconstructing the Criminal Character* 174, 337–8.

In this passage, style has become science, and the art of the will, its literariness, has been sacrificed to the business of disposing of property in this new "less spacious age." No lay-man, including the testator, can understand the language of the modern will without expert help and in this sense is alienated from what even the writer for *Temple Bar* asserts the study of wills—that "rare opportunity for stripping off the mask"—should reveal: "the real affections and wishes of men" ("Wills" 410). Instead, the modern will supplies a new, bureaucratic mask. As if in adherence to the many adjurations to acquaint oneself with the practicalities of will-making issued through these essays, "the modern will-maker" no longer considers that "the real business of the will was to inform his executors of his bodily and spiritual condition," nor does he think of his will as a "final message to the world" (46–7). Instead, he "sink[s] into the commonplace all at once" (46) in a bid for brevity that also infects the ceremony of reading the will at which those assembled to hear it learn about the legacies instead of reflecting on the deceased.

There is clearly a spiritual/secular divide at work in these differing conceptions of the will—between the sort of practical hermeneutics of the will as it was under the Ecclesiastical Courts and the market-influenced, rights-oriented approach to the will assumed by modern Probate. This conflict is one way of expressing the point that in the legal sphere subjectivity was increasingly understood and deployed as identity, a designation placed on the individual by institutional bodies such as the State, in this case in conjunction with the law and in accordance with new narratives of social organization. Character remains largely as a form of moral, even specifically religious, atavism.

The Spectator's observation that the old will possessed "literary graces," however, could remind readers that if law had lost its religion, the novel had not. If they wanted to find a version of the will that retained the curiosity of all those oddities circulating in the press, or one which relied on conceptions of character the reader was more likely to desire for himself (that is, the image and experience of the self-determining individual), they could turn to the literary will, the surrogate for a lost spiritualism and a new psychology.

The literary will is the subject of the next chapter. This chapter, so far, has shown that the last will and testament was for the Victorian reader a subject of intense, far-ranging interest. It was an artifact that turned the national registry into a museum of human nature and cultural history. Yet it was also a modern legal document, reformed in the Victorians' own age, to reflect utilitarian values for the preservation and seamless transmission of property, on the one hand, and to expand notions of the individual as a self-determining moral agent with authority to act on his intentions, on the other. Practical advice on how to make a will directed towards a popular audience assumes that many more people had property to dispose of and denotes widespread support for the freedom of bequest in line with this notion of the autonomous individual. It would be wrong to assume, however, that freedom of bequest—in the specific shape it took in England in the nineteenth century—was universally admired or condoned. This next section considers the origins of testamentary freedom, its role in the social contract, how it was framed specifically in legal manuals, as well as the nature of its popular critique for that same lay-audience of modern, would-be testators.

Writing the Will: Documenting Desire in the Legal System

The will is a doubly empirical record: a catalog often of material possessions and a physical document that strives to create the permanent communicability of intention through writing. The will's essential graphicness, a condition formalized by the Wills Act of 1837, is telling for a variety of reasons. First, it coincides with the movement towards codification and statute law advocated by Jeremy Bentham over the "unwritten" traditions of common law. His utilitarian preference for the "plain language" of a discernible body of laws over common law and its "legal fictions" was informed by empiricist impulses, more precisely, the ability written laws would give judges to reach better interpretations of legislative intent since the specific law makers and their cultural context could be known (Barrell 141, 131). In this context, writing the will became a verifiable form of witnessing (even distinct from the required witnessing of its execution), and the document itself evidence of intention. Of course, the dispositive or testamentary "I" was a persona constructed in many cases by a solicitor—the civil law's analogy to representation by counsel in the criminal trial—but this management of the testamentary narrative varied over the course of the century and in relation to the value of subjective and objective epistemologies, the value of facts and the modes of construing them, and the value for individual autonomy in a socially-deterministic world. Although the legal and lay communities disagreed over the best way to frame the testator's intention, legal manuals describing his moods, case law construing his meaning, and novels conveying his thoughts reveal just how much the testator felt freedom of bequest to be a right and a sign of ownership. Thus, the will provides an important index for changing conceptions of human subjectivity and their representation in law and in literature.

As a "testament," the will calls forth many of the same values associated with "testimony" at trial. Indeed, the *OED* gives the root of testament as *testari* "to be a witness, attest, make a will." However, attention to the will challenges the implication gleaned from recent studies of legal and literary structures that criminal law influenced literary practice more than any other branch.[10] The most influential of these studies linking legal to literary representation is Alexander Welsh's *Strong Representations* in which he confronts the epistemological problem of how to establish the truth about events, which no one can describe at first hand (and about which testimony might in any case be misleading). Basing his argument in the rules of evidence, he charts a shift from eighteenth-century models of eyewitness testimony towards narratives of circumstantial evidence, or "strong representations," as the more reliable form of determining fact and as the only form capable of establishing facts as to "things not seen" (6). In fiction as in the law, he argues, it was the method of narration, more than any particular

---

[10] Several critical works have taken the trial as a legal analogy to and model for developments in the novel. See especially Alexander Welsh, *Strong Representations*; Jan-Melissa Schramm, *Testimony and Advocacy*; Lisa Rodensky, *The Crime in Mind*; and Jonathan Grossman, *The Art of Alibi*.

"facts," that signaled truth; thus, the novel turned its attention away from characters and witnesses towards the disinterested narrator, who like the lawyer, became a "manager of evidence" (35). This emphasis on objective, impersonal constructions of fact lasted until mid-century when "stories of experience" re-emerged in the context of new "subjective epistemologies" (199). Testimony returned as the primary means of representing individual points of view as being themselves kinds of knowledge whose credibility lay solely in the manner of their presentation (200–201).

Attention to the function of the will, however, complicates claims for the diminished importance of testimony (and the attitude towards human character suggested by suspicion of it), as well as the chronology and duration of these attitudes.[11] In particular, Welsh's contention that the importance of circumstantial evidence did not diminish until the middle of the nineteenth century has generated considerable disagreement about when facts lost their persuasive power.[12] To focus for a moment on the issue of dates is no idle exercise in periodicity. It is important

[11] Welsh anticipates such objections in his turn, again, towards Bentham: although false testimony might be given or fallacious narratives constructed, the internal weaknesses of the latter will lead to their deconstruction (40). But concerns about bias raise the question of why first-person testimony should be distrusted in the first place. The epistemological stakes of the debate as to facts is further complicated, in other words, by attitudes towards witness (and professional) character. The demotion of witness testimony raises the professional's power to represent events and intention and ultimately to do justice. The argument in favor of this shift is that the managers of evidence, as professionals, are interested only in justice, whereas witnesses, let alone defendants, are motivated by self-interest. See also Ronald Thomas for changing conceptions of character 11, 63; Schramm 140–44; and Weisberg's introduction to *The Failure of the Word* 1–9 for the argument that the adversarial nature of the trial that emerges in the 1830s created interested lawyers as well, since defense counsel had to decide whom it served: the interest of the courts, the client's interest, professional self-interest, or justice.

[12] Recent studies describe the relative importance of first-person witness testimony and third-person narration of facts thus: Jan-Melissa Schramm cites the Prisoners' Counsel Act of 1836 (when narratives of the accused felon's intention were brought in to counter the prosecution's narratives of fact) as the legal system's acknowledgement that facts and inference were too complex and too prone to bias respectively to function alone as indices of the truth. Lisa Rodensky focuses on an enlarged mid-Victorian period (1837–1880s) in order to draw attention to the third-person narrator, dominant in high realism, whose direct access to interiority circumvented the need for legal professionals (22). By providing access to characters' intentions, these narratives intensified legal debates about the relationship between criminal intention and criminal acts, but they also show how literature began to test circumstantial evidence by circumventing the inferential method well before mid-century. In contrast, Ronald Thomas's work on forensic science and detective fiction relies on Welsh's dates. Where Welsh marked the 1850s as the end of "stories of things not seen," Thomas argues that the detective in fact embodied forensic technologies that enabled him to transform characters into texts and to see more clearly signs that were always present to the discerning eye, thereby "filling in the blanks of a broken story" (4), just as circumstances had supplied links in a chain of evidence.

because it influences the conclusions we can draw about Victorian epistemology, the will's particular function, how we can understand the novel's representation of it, and hence literature's varied role as an ethical supplement to law, or an adjunct to its disciplinary mechanisms, or the means of testing reforms yet to be enacted by law.

The self-evidence of facts may well have been viewed (by the legal community at any rate) with suspicion long before the 1850s, but circumspection is very different from wholesale dismissal of the persuasiveness, if not the truth-bearing status, of the material world. Bentham's value for a code of statutes and the graphocentricity of the Wills Act are but two examples to suggest that in the 1830s empiricism, even if expressed as a banal but utilitarian value for record keeping, still made sense. Beyond this sort of proto-bureaucratic obsession with forms, moreover, the very concept of the nineteenth-century will was grounded in there being a first-person narrator—the subjective "I"—whose state of intention created an occasion for writing in the first place. The "will speaks" in legal terms from the moment of the testator's death (its function and temporal orientation both being prospective, even as the testator assumes a reflective stance), but it only acquires its language when the subjective "I" gives his instructions and allows his intentions to be framed by law, transforming him into the testamentary or dispositive "I." Making the will a written document thus linked together contrary forces: it assumed that language—specifically written language—could make meaning and intention both palpable and retrievable, but it also complicated the idea of the intentional subject by blending first- and third-person testamentary voices, that is, the testator's and the law's. Making the will a written document provided a permanent record of intention and in this respect resonated with empiricist impulses, but by complicating the idea of whose intention was being made concrete, it contributed to a climate of skepticism about the relationship between surface and substance.[13]

The will also invited discussion of the law's assumptions about individual moral agency and of the relationship between creating rights and protecting them. Indeed, it was crimes against property and their "unsystematic and often reactionary" punishment (Polloczek 107) that called forth Bentham's reformist energies and brought property law, criminal law, legal fictions, and moral agency together. As one of the three basic rights outlined by Blackstone (his *Commentaries*

[13] In this regard, the Wills Act provides a means in the probate courts of countering the untrustworthiness of "fact" and the difficulty of interpretation that concerned the criminal courts. For example, although in criminal trials no act could be considered criminal without proof of criminal intent, yet the law could only determine intention through inference from fact and through a lawyer's incomplete access to his client's mind (Rodensky 23–4). Victorian commentary on *mens rea* conveys a persistent desire for visible effects to reveal their invisible causes (the same desire to be seen in natural religion and in the physical sciences that motivates a searching after origins), while at the same time highlighting the possibility that experience of the one may not lead to certainty about the other. Forensic technologies were developed precisely to address this problem by "render[ing] visible and measurable what had previously been undetectable" (Thomas 6), but the Wills Act had rendered intention visible when it mandated that the will become a written document some two decades earlier.

a target of Bentham's zeal), property and the laws designed to maintain it should be considered as seriously as procedures in criminal law for what they contribute as a model for the Victorian novel to the one suggested by procedures in criminal law. Indeed, to shift to the literary register, the desire for empirical certainty helps to explain why Victorian novels of mid-century and later continue to be interested in material facts and effects even if acts of observation or interpretation replace simple acceptance of them. Indeed, the point is less that facts have become altogether inaccessible than it is that their increasing complexity requires better skilled observers and interpreters—the novelists—to see them.

The last will and testament is a specific instance of the way individual and institutional authorities engage one another. In his *Second Treatise of Government* (1689), John Locke raised the question as to why anyone would submit to government: "If man in the state of nature be so free [...] if he be absolute lord of his own person and possessions, equal to the greatest, and subject to nobody, why," he asked, "will he part with his freedom? Why will he give up this empire and subject himself to the dominion and control of any other power?" (75). The answer, he conjectured, was that the ability to "enjoy" this right was "very uncertain and constantly exposed to the invasion of others" attempting to enjoy the same rights for themselves. The primary reason for submission, then, was the "mutual preservation" of what he generally terms property, or the "lives, liberties, and estates" of all who by "common consent" enter into civil society (75). William Blackstone seconded Locke's views in volume one of the *Commentaries, Of the Rights of Persons* (1765), naming the right of property the "third absolute right" (134) after those of "personal security, and personal liberty" (136). Blackstone constantly reminds his readers that property rights are purely social in origin, as opposed to the natural prerogative envisioned by Locke, but he nonetheless agreed that it counted among "those civil advantages, in exchange for which every individual has resigned a part of his natural liberty" (134).[14] Jeremy Bentham, although typically at pains to distance his ideas from Blackstone's, also viewed the right to property as a purely positivist rather than natural construction (both the "right" and "property" as such being fictions) (III.218).[15] However, because property was a useful concept for securing one's labor,

[14] For both, this exchange is largely a matter of reason. Locke theorized that even the state of nature was governed by "natural law" or reason (4); it simply made sense to protect oneself and to use the reason that, literally, God had given one for this purpose. Blackstone inverts this order: civil rights, in the sense of those rights upheld by law, are "sacred and inviolable" (I.135), not specifically because they come from God, but because they seek to maintain "the peace of mankind" and avoid "endless disturbance" (II.11). Blackstone affirms that because "the universal law of almost every nation" makes some provision for the disposal of property by will, for example, then that right is *ipso facto* a "kind of secondary law of nature" (II.10).

[15] "The word right, is the name of a fictitious entity: one of those objects, the existence of which is feigned for the purpose of discourse, by a fiction so necessary, that without it human discourse could not be carried on" (from *A Fragment on Government*, III.218). All references are to the Bowring edition and are cited as volume followed by page number.

Bentham argued that the rights and liabilities pertaining to property could serve the utilitarian function of promoting pleasure and dispelling pain for the greatest number of people only when it had been formally "secured" through legislation and extended to more people so as to prevent "disappointment" (Polloczek 91–2).[16]

From its inception, then, the concept of property was considered either a natural right or a component of social liberty and was thereby intimately linked to issues of individual autonomy. By consent, the individual relinquished some of that autonomy to the State in the expectation that he would be protected. Yet he retained a great deal, too, so the law, which had established the legal right to and protection of property in the first place, was often felt to infringe upon individual desire. The right of testation itself was introduced in order to minimize the discord that resulted when property was devised or bequeathed according to prescribed inheritance patterns (Blackstone II.12). Emphasizing the "pleasure of the deceased," the new rules for disposing of property were nevertheless so often confounded by other testamentary laws that they seemed to emphasize the legal profession's prerogatives rather than the testator's (II.13). In this sense, the legal last will and testament, "emphatically stile[d]" a will because it purported to convey its testator's volition (II.12), might be understood as yet another legal fiction.

In his discussions of the "original contract," Bentham had declared the "season of fiction" to be at an end (I.269), but his antagonism to legal fictions specifically was aroused by punishment of crimes against property (Polloczek 106). Bentham's attention to property and his sense of the abuse of legal fictions as an abuse of private citizens usefully translates into the specific problematic of individuals' expectations regarding their property and the legal community's own conflicting interest in self-maintenance and professional aggrandizement. Legal fictions are "procedural devices" that allow the court to establish jurisdiction, to circumvent old and more complicated procedures, and to broaden the application of particular "remedies" without requiring or resulting in any substantive change to the law as would occur under legislative reform (Stone 128).[17] But this very avoidance of

---

16 Paul Kelly identifies two basic principles in Bentham's theory of justice: "security-providing" and "disappointment-preventing" (in Polloczek 78). The first determines the "pattern of expectations" secured through legislation, and the second seeks to negotiate existing expectations while trying to institute different rules that would support utilitarianism. At bottom, Bentham felt one had to support only those "established rules and practices" that in their turn supported the expectations which would lead to the greatest utility (90). If property, albeit a fiction, creates expectations regarding one's own labor and its products, then maintaining property may serve to "maximize" utility for the greatest number. Only the legislator is able to achieve this effect, and only the legislator can extend access to property—expanding security—while at the same time establishing punishments for infractions—preventing disappointment. Stephen Munzer writes, "If, as Bentham maintains, utility is the presence of pleasure and the absence of pain, then *ceteris paribus* utility will be promoted by securing persons' expectations with respect to the things they possess" (in Polloczek 92).

17 In "A Fragment on Ontology," Bentham developed a theory of fictions in philosophic and linguistic analyses of inference as a mode of identifying and acquiring knowledge about

legislation disturbed Bentham because it signaled judges' usurpation of legislative authority under the guise of doing justice, the complication of what could be a much simplified procedure, and mystification of legal practice (Bentham VII.283–7). William Blackstone had assured readers of his *Commentaries* that the use of legal fictions was always guided by principles of equity; however, his promise that they would never "extend to work an injury" (III.43) raises the questions of whether they really worked any good and, if so, for whom. Bentham's utilitarian response showed that it created the "greatest happiness for the greatest number" of legal professionals interested in conserving common law. By stealing power from the legislature, pocketing fees from the additional legal labor, and then hiding their practices in the complexity of legal procedure, lawyers and judges became swindlers at work in their "justice shops" (Bentham VIII.285).[18] From this viewpoint, the new Wills Act confirmed and extended proprietary "rights" even as its requirement of written testaments created work for the emergent legal profession by playing upon clients' expectations regarding their property and their ability to further secure it through their wills.[19]

The concept of individual rights in things poses a challenge, however, to certain legal understandings of the individual's role. J.S. Mill in his *Principles of Political Economy* (1848) argued:

> The ownership of a thing cannot be looked upon as complete without the power of bestowing it, at death or during life, at the owner's pleasure: and all the reasons, which recommend that private property should exist, recommend *pro tanto*, this extension of it. (224)

---

those things that are not "perceptible" to the senses (VIII.195). He distinguishes between "real entities" and the "fictitious entities," or names and concepts, by which we commonly know them (VIII.196–7). In simplest terms, Bentham shares skepticism about the relationship between fictional signs and the real things they signify. In spite of this separation, however, linguistic fictions are necessary for communication and, on that basis, their use should not be discredited. When they outlive their original uses (as in the original contract) or are put to unethical purposes, then must they be recognized as fictions and their use discontinued.

[18] Henry Maine cautioned against taking Bentham too seriously, urging readers to resist "the ridicule which Bentham pours on legal fictions wherever he meets them. To revile them as merely fraudulent is to betray ignorance of their peculiar office in the historical development of law" (26). However, Pollock notes that even Maine's account fails to make explicit the reason for fictions: "the desire of obtaining a speedier or more complete remedy than the strictly appropriate form of procedure affords" (396).

[19] Bentham does, however, distinguish between legal and other kinds of fiction on the basis of their intended uses: "Fiction, in the logical sense, has been the coin of necessity—in that of poets, of amusement—in that of the priest and the lawyer, of mischievous immorality in the shape of mischievous ambition" (VIII.199). If legal fictions are a means of privileging the institution over the individual, literary fiction emphasized the concept of individual rights in things. It certainly "amused" through its portraits of self-important lawyers and bureaucratic idiosyncrasies, but it also explored the relationship between personal volition and its public expression as a process.

Echoing Blackstone, Mill's analysis places the "owner's pleasure" ever further forward as a defining element of private possession.[20] But while the emphasis on private possession and individual rights stressed the centrality of the individual in nineteenth-century social theory, the legal system retained a more broadly based and contradictory concept of social organization. The law's continued adherence to "Patria Potestas," or the concept that the head of the family was not merely an individual but a representative of a social corporation (P. Milton 51), brought it into conflict with the social preference for individualism.

Henry Maine expounded the concept for English readers in his classic study *Ancient Law* (1861), specifically in his focus on testamentary succession. The will, he explained, was an instrument for disposing of an inheritance, an inheritance a type of "universal succession," and the latter the assumption of a "university" or bundle of rights and duties that "comprise the whole set of legal relations in which each one of us stands to the rest of the world" (172–3). Whether this transfer was achieved by will or by intestacy had no bearing on the heir's legal character, since he "became instantly clothed with [the dead man's] entire legal person" (175). But if this "primitive" Roman form of inheritance was also the most "durable" (175), how then, asks Maine, did inheritance become the purview of a testator's volition, and what did this change mean for the will as the instrument of transfer (173)?[21] Like Blackstone, Maine returns us to a time before there was any such concept as modern testamentary capacity, when the rights of the heir (restrictive as it might seem to a modern heir to be clothed in the legal person of the deceased) were considerably broader than the testator's whose entire identity was "swallowed up in his family" (177).

Even apart from its value for understanding the legal origins of the preference for testamentary intention over more prescriptive modes of passing on rights and obligations—rights which allowed for the control of property but did not make property their principal focus—Maine's history is important as a study in method. (Frederick Pollock considered him to have done "nothing less than create the natural history of law" [xiv], in fact). Instead of taking the law at face value—assuming that "prima facie impressions" reveal what law is and what it has always been (169)—Maine advocates a view of law as an evolving, social institution with distinct phases, traces or whole tracts of which remain in contemporary

---

[20] Dieter Polloczek reads the same passage as being Mill's acknowledgment that "the desire to bestow is at the heart of the human drive towards self-extension" (164), yet Mill "does not explore the question as to whether there inheres in the power to bestow a compulsion to do so." L.S. Lewis's comments at the opening of this chapter answer this question in the affirmative, as do most of the Edwardian novels discussed in Chapter 4.

[21] Maine's dates are descriptive rather than precise: the universal succession is a concept of "primitive jurisprudence" or the "ancient law of Rome" (177), whereas "later Roman law" and "modern testamentary jurisprudence" prioritize the testator's intentions. In his notes to the 10th London edition, Pollock cites Henri Auffroy, an authority on French medieval law, who places the "triumph of individualism" and the "personal volition" of the head of the family in the Roman empire (426).

usage without being fully understood. One of the more insidious versions of this tendency is the assumption that the essential qualities of a will (for example, its revocability, its secrecy, its effectiveness at death) are in a sense not socially derived but "attached to it by a Law of Nature" (170). Locating the origins of this idea with seventeenth-century jurists, Maine quickly constructs a genealogy that shows the persistence of this idea even as it disproves its basis in an "original instinct and impulse" shared by all nations (171). Although enlisted as an example of the merits of an historical sensibility, Maine's brief mention of Enlightenment jurists serves as a useful reminder of the centrality of ideas regarding individual rights, to say nothing of the fiction of the social contract by which man elected to leave the state of nature for civil society. Maine may not have agreed with the premise of their theories in respect to testamentary law (seeing in that law a distinctly Roman influence), but he would certainly have admired the way philosophy and morality provided theoretical foundations for law in contrast to a modern, instrumentalist, "empirical pursuit" of law (170).[22] Indeed, his point is to understand how the will—which "next to the Contract, has exercised the greatest influence on transforming human society" (188)—became linked with individual prerogatives and acquired its function as "the instrument by which the intention of the testator is declared" (172), as opposed to its quasi-sacred reference to the family.[23]

Of particular interest about Maine's findings, however, is the way they reprioritize the relationship between the individual and the family by showing how the modern primacy of the individual—understood as the "natural person" and "normal unit of legal institutions" (Pollock 426)—is actually an inversion of the ancient primacy of the family—understood as a corporation—of which the patriarch is no more than the "public officer" or temporary representative of a body that would never die because its rights and responsibilities always survived and were transferred to a new head (Maine 178–9). In other words, the nineteenth-century extension of individual identity to a corporation reverses the Roman transfer "by a fiction" of the attributes of the family to the individual (180). Why does the corporation "return" at this point in time? What does showing Victorian jurists that the corporate family is really the historical unit of society mean for testamentary law specifically? And what does it mean to call this transfer a fiction?

Maine said that law is a stable body that is slower to change than are social needs and attitudes, but in "progressive societies" the general good depends on how readily and how nearly the differences between law and social feeling can be

22 For a description of the nineteenth-century aversion to principle (including Pollock's own), see Gordley (216); note, however, his skepticism about the connection between legal "will theories" and the general philosophical emphasis on individualism (214–15).

23 The viability of both wills and contracts depends on a concept of the intentional subject, that autonomous individual who can act and be held responsible for acts. Maine is very clear about the specifically social value of both, calling them the "two great institutions without which modern society can scarcely be supposed capable of holding together" (197). For more on the "Early history of contract," see Chapter 9 of *Ancient Law*. For the "will theory of contract," see Charles Fried.

ameliorated (23).[24] Nowhere does Maine suggest that the will of the testator ought not to dictate the disposal of property; rather, his express purpose is to understand *how* "the relation of man to man substituted itself for the relation of the individual to his family and of families to each other" (180). A perhaps unintended effect of his comparison, however, is to show testamentary law moving in advance of that social opinion which still held to the primacy of individual volition. That is, his analogy of the individual to a corporation sole and the family to a corporation aggregate could make sense to a legal community (Pollock suggests as much), but it also helps to explain the growing tension between social ideas about the individual and a legal reliance on corporate identity or, at a minimum, the tendency in the latter part of the century for relationships between individuals to be supplanted by relationships between institutions impersonating them and acting on their behalf.[25]

Of course, given the contradictory emphasis in social discourse on both the family unit and the expansion of individual rights, legal rules must inevitably have lagged behind some needs even as it attempted to meet others; there's nothing new in that. Two apparently contrary responses ensued: the extension of testamentary powers concomitant with expanded notions of legal subjectivity (itself dependent on expanded property rights), and the continued emphasis on the well-being of surviving family and heirs. The result is maintenance of the testamentary privilege, on one hand, paired with sufficient legal influence to curb its excesses and benefit the heirs on the other. Maine's analysis of the Roman fear of intestacy—or "passion for testacy" (212)—is instructive on this point. Testation was only permitted originally when there were no heirs (blood or adopted) to inherit the family, not as an opportunity to disinherit or to divide an inheritance (211). However, the reason testation came to be so much preferred to intestate succession was because it allowed the testator to provide for his family in contrast to rules of succession that actually made him disinherit those he might be assumed to "esteem" the most, for example, emancipated sons who were no longer considered members of the Family (212).[26] In this conflict between legal and affective notions of the family, Maine sees a very early instance of a disjunction between law and social feeling,

[24] One way to align the two is through legal fictions. Since universal succession was meant to "eliminate the fact of death" from the continuous existence of the bundle of rights and duties of the *patria potestas*, it must be the legal fiction noted above.

[25] Although Pollock allows that the comparison may be "helpful to English students," he grants it no authority for expressing actual Roman attitudes (427). "We are not meant to take this statement [that the patriarch was "managing director" of a corporate family] as if a definite legal doctrine of persons, much less artificial persons, was to be ascribed to the patriarchal stage of society" (426). In contrast, modern corporations still rely on the individual as social unit, but they assume a "collective personality": "a group of men acting in a common interest or duty and behaving like an individual."

[26] He asks: "What was the Family? The law defined it one way—natural affection in another. In the conflict between the two, the feeling we would analyse [the abhorrence of intestate succession] grew up, taking the form of an enthusiasm for the institution by which the dictates of affection were permitted to determine the fortunes of its object" (248).

and thus an occasion for applying a legal remedy. Of these remedies, legal fiction is the earliest and most rudimentary, followed by equity and legislation (24). So, while it may be possible to think of the testamentary power (what Blackstone said in law was "stiled" a man's will) in its earliest form as a legal fiction, it is more likely to have served an equitable function.[27]

Maine's curiosity about the "horror of intestacy" was piqued precisely because the Roman tables of succession so closely resembled modern ones.[28] If testation was meant to protect the family, then the last 200 years of possessive or proprietary testation—with its reliance on liberal notions of property as a right in things—had been out of sync with the conception of ownership as stewardship and hence discordant with the idea of testation as an exercise of duty, not the enjoyment of individual privilege. In this regard, Victorian legal manuals were quite correct in their efforts to guide and modify vindictive, overly assertive, or even ignorant testators to consider the needs of the family and to frame their wills accordingly.

However, the law certainly played its role in helping to create and sustain this type of legal subjectivity through freedom of bequest. The Will's Act was more than a mere tool for further entrenching traditional legal discourse. It revised the law and contributed to a concept of modern individuality that was intimately linked to the material possession of goods and the assumption of agency. Moreover, as a legislative act it performed that remedial function Maine described as being the advanced society's most sophisticated means of keeping pace with prevailing social attitudes. At the same time, it is important to recognize that even if the law was something in which every gentleman should be conversant, a legal professional mediated most contact with it. Blackstone decreed a knowledge of the law "the proper accomplishment of every gentleman and scholar; an highly useful [...] part of liberal and polite education" (I.6). Every man, even those of "inferior condition" (II.7), should be familiar with the laws that define his rights under and duties to society, but especially "gentlemen of independent estates and fortunes; the most useful and considerable body of men in the nation" should understand their relationship to the law. Though they may not be expected to comprehend all its complexities, particularly in the matter of last wills, "yet still the understanding of a few leading principles [...] may form some check and guard upon a gentleman's inferior agents, and preserve him at least from very gross and notorious imposition." (Bentham took a different view: "Put into the hands of your sons the *Commentaries* of Blackstone? Send him to attend the courts at Westminster? For learning jurisprudence, yes: but for cherishing in his bosom

27 Maine's explanation that "the characteristic of the family is transferred *by a fiction* to the individual" suggests the universal succession is that fiction, since its function was to "eliminate the fact of death" from the maintenance of the family rights and duties. The idea of the House or gens is also a fiction insofar as it extended the Family to anyone bearing the same name, on the assumption that they shared a common ancestor (193).

28 See Maine's discussion of Praetorian jurisprudence as compared to the Roman Civil law (213–16). The former recognizes and inserts more classes of relatives into the latter.

the principles of veracity, of sincerity, of true honour? Stay till you have made your daughter get by heart the words of Piron and Rochester" [VII.287].) Though Blackstone implies that such knowledge can protect the testator from inept or dishonest agents, he recognizes nonetheless that the laws of inheritance are too complex to be confronted unaided. A brief survey of solicitor's manuals reveals the legal head-shaking of countless professionals burdened with cleaning up the mess into which testators had brought their families through the erroneously held belief that they knew the law and could write wills on their own.

It also has to be noted that testamentary right was subject to critique, and not exclusively by the disenfranchised who might have admired the right more had it extended to them. J.S. Mill had argued that freedom of testation was a logical and necessary extension of the concept of private property, whatever view one took of the institution, but when private property came under attack at the end of the century, testamentary freedom shared in the criticism. Implementing a new utilitarian test of private property, Lady Cook commented on the solidity of English notions regarding property in general: "We are so accustomed to modern notions of property with its individual rights and customs that we are apt to regard them as of almost sacred and indefeasible origin" (187), but, she asks, "Do the various rules which govern it promote the greatest happiness of the greatest number?" Her answer, of course, is that they do not. England's insistence on absolute freedom of bequest, and its maintenance of primogeniture in particular, make it anomalous among modern nations, but England has only to consult its own history to find better, more equitable conceptions of property, ones that expressed principles of "justice and decency" and that did not disregard the "natural claims" of family (200), or the "civil and natural obligations" English law ought to resume (202).

Cook (the American-born Tennessee Claflin: one-time spiritual medium, Wall Street broker, and Viscountess, who with her sister Victoria Woodhull was an active advocate for women's rights) locates this history prior to the Conquest, before English law was adulterated by the "Norman iniquity" (200).[29] Other critics of freedom of bequest looked more favorably on the Continental law and its reliance on the Roman civil code. T.C. Fry, Doctor of Divinity and Head of Berkhamstead School, cited the French *légitime* in particular as a model that balanced some testamentary freedom with a more equal distribution of capital and was morally and logically superior to the obstinate English insistence that "a man has the right to do what he likes with his own" (190). This maxim was the bedrock of the Englishman's identity—"his very position as a social unit of personal importance seems built upon it"; "it is a right about as sacred to the average Briton as the *patria potesta* must have been to many Roman fathers"; "it is English all over" (190)—but as Fry points out, there is no moral foundation for this emphasis on

[29] Assuming that Cook's scapegoating of the Normans extends to modern French law, it may explain why she takes her examples of more communal forms of property from Muslim law rather than from the civil codes cited by her contemporaries. For more on Cook herself, see her obituary in *The New York Times* ("Lady Cook Dies" 13).

individual right over social welfare; the power is an outgrowth of "the supremacy of male legislators with a property qualification" (192). From this position, and like Cook, Fry tests the "ethics" of wills, arguing in the end for the claims of the community and for measures that, while they would not abolish freedom of bequest, would create ways of ameliorating its negative impact, for example, by introducing a sliding scale of inheritance tax (what he calls a "'quasi-betterment' fund") or a limit on the size of any one legacy (198–9).

The arguments here in favor of more communitarian rules for the distribution of property are all part of the rising socialism—or in Fry's case of Christian socialism—of the late nineteenth century, a movement which met resistance from obvious proponents of private property such as the Liberty and Property Defense League, as well as from those who remained skeptical about outright socialist doctrine. Historian I.S. Leadam, writing for the *Contemporary Review*, took these contradictions head on in "Freedom of Bequest" (1888). Groups like the LPDL were right to argue that restrictions on testamentary freedom were restrictions on the concept of private property, but Leadam objects that this conception is only of recent origin ("less than two hundred years") when the "keynote … in law as in philosophy, was individualism" (116).[30] English caution paired with the "independent growth of [English] law"—meaning presumably its insular reliance on common law in contrast to the civilian code—has meant that the national temper "still adheres to the extremest limits of individualism" and hence so do many English institutions (117). But individualism, for Leadam as for the others cited here, is inadequate to the needs of families and, by extension, those of the social body; it was even out of step with other areas of law in which "the newly vitalized principle" of the interdependence of the members of the polity had emerged.

This conflict returns us to the issue of what the will signified in Victorian culture. What was it meant to perpetuate: a specific system of legal, social, even economic organization in the family, or a specific bureaucratic identity, or personal character? In what sense had the relationship between individual and family described by Maine finally become inverted so that the family was merely an extension of the testator's individuality? Was the circle turning again? To what extent did the possession of commodities as opposed to land alter the basis of identity and extend it to those of erstwhile "inferior condition"? When the time finally came to write the will, how was the testator's own sense of volition aided or impeded by law? Had the legal language, interpreted and applied by legal professionals, established the place from which the testator could speak and the nature of what could be said in such a way that it constituted testamentary volition, or was that desire and identity already in place prior to engagement with the law? How much negotiation was permissible

---

[30] Leadam cites a series of statutes—the Irish Land Acts, the Factory Acts, The Education Acts, and the Married Women's Property Acts—as signs of "solidarity," that "ugly word" of Comte's which, like Bismark's "blundering and half-hearted" "semi-Socialistic schemes" (117) he nonetheless borrows because of their principles.

or desirable? And what opportunities for agreement and engagement does the will offer its writers and readers that can form the basis of its interest to the novelist?

The erosion of property in land as the principal foundation of one's social identity coincided with industrialization, imperialism, and the rise of commodity culture. Capitalism thus exerted a sort of leveling influence in which a newly consolidated middle-class imbued goods with personality and let those goods represent their "selves"; if they didn't make their possessions, the money they earned symbolized their labor and, expended on things, their right to that property. But this further privatization of property could entail a change in the relationship between people as well by isolating family units and turning their focus inward. The *noblesse oblige* of the landed aristocracy had either to be dispensed with or replaced with social programs administered through the State or by private philanthropic societies. In short, private property encouraged an individualistic, rights-oriented understanding of ownership that, as we have seen, gave more property to more people but also made them responsible only unto themselves.

This new, propertied individual was still viewed in relation to broader categories of organization such as a family, a social class, a nation and even an empire, but the nature of its engagement with those larger entities, whether determined by science or God or left to human agency, was a subject of ongoing debate still based on a presumption of selfhood in competition with the bureaucratic reduction of persons into identities. These concepts of personality in property, human character and agency, and a legal identity in property come together in the last will and testament, making it a central document in Victorian culture.

Reading the Wills Act: "Will Stories" and the Legal Narrative of Identity

The Wills Act gave statutory shape to these concepts in the first year of Queen Victoria's reign and, like the queen, it provided a conceptual anchor throughout an otherwise tumultuous age. But as a youthful Act, its mission was to change the old, which it did by merging the devise of land (the will) and the bequest of chattels (the testament) into a single document (*Halsbury's Statutes* 203). It further distinguished itself as a modern act by repealing some eleven earlier wills statutes going as far back as Henry VIII's reign. In a culture obsessed with origins (Beer), this deliberate break with the legal past would have the dual effect of simplifying the law in practical terms, and, in symbolic terms, of making the Victorians the source of this particular relationship between the individual and property.

Totaling 36 sections, the Act describes the forms of land tenure and the kind of property that can be willed; the age, gender, and marital status of would-be testators; the method of executing and attesting a will (as well as who may or may not attest) and the exceptions for military personnel; the actions that revoke a will and those, such as crossings-out or interlineations within the document, that will not; from what point the will is considered to "speak"; how trusts will be arranged, and what will be meant by words such as "child" or "issue."

(Great Britain "Wills Act of 1837").[31] Maine observed that the will's secrecy, revocability, and posthumous operation were its most familiar, modern traits (169), and indeed each one is allowed for, if not required by, the Act. Secrecy, for example, is not a necessary aspect of the will. Section 13 emphasizes proper execution as the key to validity; it does not call for secrecy so much as dispense with the need for "any other publication thereof" than the two witnesses' signatures. Revocation, in contrast, is both an action to be consciously undertaken by the testator and an effect of a change in his or her condition. That is, an existing will would be revoked only by properly executing a new one, by a written statement of intention to revoke, or by "the burning, tearing, or otherwise destroying [the will] by the testator, or by some person in his presence and by his direction, with the intention of revoking the same" (Wills Act s. 20). If the testator married, however, it would be revoked automatically. And the new Act made no change as to when a will took effect (after the testator's death and after the will had been duly proved). Rather, it marked a change in how the will would be construed: instead of applying only to property possessed by the testator on the actual date of execution, wills made after the Act would be considered "to speak and take effect as if it had been executed immediately before" the testator's death (Wills Act s. 24).[32]

For James Traill Christie, commenting on the Act in 1857, the third section (in conjunction with s. 24) affected the greatest overall change precisely in the degree to which it "enlarge[d] the power of the testator" (162). By allowing a will to encompass all the property a testator would have at his death, "notwithstanding that he may become entitled to it subsequently to the execution of his will," it removed both the necessity of having to draft a new will whenever new property was acquired and with it "one of the most frequent causes for the failure of wills taking effect" under the old law (162). In essence, it gave greater scope to the testator's intention *as such*—the intention to devise real estate, rather than to the precise real estate in question—and it sought to secure that intention and act upon it.

It was the will that encoded intention, and by and large no alteration in the testator's circumstances could be taken by the courts to imply any change in his intentions and therefore as cause to revoke the will (Wills Act s. 19)—no circumstance, that is, except for marriage. Prior to the new Act, marriage *and* the birth of a child would require a man to draft a new will (marriage alone being insufficient cause for a new will presumably because a wife was provided for through the right of dower). For women, marriage alone sufficed. The Act of 1837 might appear to

31 Subsequent references to the Wills Act will be to Wills Act, followed by section number.

32 In *Bullock v. Bennett* (1855), Lord Justice Turner held section 24 of the act to mean that the will speaks "in reference to the real and personal estate comprised in it" at the time of the testator's death, not in reference to the objects or recipients of those gifts (285–6). Because the testator did not republish his will after his daughter's third marriage and in spite of his tacit approval of it, she remained disqualified to inherit by that marriage as laid out in the existing will.

have equalized the requirements for husbands and wives. Christie calls it a "most important and most judicious" change that places the wills of both men and women "on the same footing as those of women made before this Act" (173–4). However, this understates the dramatic difference between men and women's testamentary powers. After January 1, 1838, a man's marriage, like his wife's before it, would indeed occasion a new will, but now marriage constrained her right to leave one at all: "no will made by any married woman shall be valid," reads the statute, "except such a will as might have been made before the passing of this Act" (152).[33]

Inasmuch as the testator's intentions were more heavily emphasized under the new Act, it might surprise a modern reader that his familiar assertion of sound mind was not. For all the care that's taken about how to execute and attest the document—those acts that conclude a will—little is said there about the disposition of the testator as he contemplates, frames, or otherwise begins it. Although many forms of expression recommended by solicitors (a formal clause of attestation, for example) are not in fact required by statute, much is still assumed. "Every person" may dispose of property by will in the terms laid out in the Act, but that person must be of sound mind (*Halsbury's Statutes* 153). Not surprisingly, wills written during a bout of insanity would not be valid (*Palmer and Brown v. Dent*),[34] but even partial unsoundness of mind might be acceptable as long the testator's general faculties remained unimpaired and no particular disposition seemed directly related to the malady. In *Banks v. Goodfellow* (1870), the testator John Banks had been "confined as a lunatic" for a period of time in 1841 and continued to suffer occasionally from delusions until his death in 1865 (549). (Banks believed that he was being harassed by "devils and evils spirits," in particular by a man called Featherstone Alexander, a former acquaintance who, though long dead, continued to bother him and whose name alone could pitch Banks into "a state of violent excitement.") At the Cumberland Spring Assizes, Justice Brett directed the jury to consider whether Banks "was so far master of his intentions, free from delusions, as would enable him to have a will of his own in the disposition of his property, and act upon it" (550).

---

33 I cannot speak as to what married women of the time before the passage of the 1837 Act might have had within their power to bequeath, but as is clear from the beginning of this Act's influence, married women in the nineteenth century, especially those of the poorer classes, had almost no rights over property. The provision here that a male testator's will would be understood to include all property in his possession at the time of death, for example, was not extended to women until 1893. Christie himself observes that the sweeping statement made in section eight immediately raised questions since it appeared to contradict other sections, but the best he can suggest, even in 1857, is that lawyers be especially careful in how they execute wills until some clearer legal decision could be reached.

34 Joseph Palmer made a second will shortly before his death in which he attempted to bequeath more property than he actually owned and to give it to nieces and nephews whom he could no longer properly describe, notwithstanding their close acquaintance. The legatees agreed not to support the second will, and probate was given to an earlier one in which they were correctly named.

In that case the jury found for the defendant, but a new trial was ordered, and Chief Justice Cockburn reframed the question as what *degree* of unsoundness would incapacitate the testator (555).

Cockburn's decision is interesting both for its consideration of contemporary ideas regarding the "unity and indivisibility" of the mind as well as the moral responsibilities that belong to freedom of bequest.[35] Bringing the two together, he arrives at a measure of the minimum mental powers required in a testator:

> If the human instincts and affections, or the moral sense, become perverted by mental disease; if insane suspicion, or aversion, take the place of natural affection; if reason and judgment are lost, and the mind becomes a prey to insane delusions calculated to interfere with and disturb its functions, and to lead to a testamentary disposition, due only to their baneful influence—in such a case it is obvious that the condition of the testamentary power fails, and that a will made under such circumstances ought not to stand. (*Banks* 565)

Affection is rational. Banks's will benefited his heir-at-law (meaning that even if he had died intestate, the law would have given his property to her) and, as Cockburn notes, "was yet rational in this, that it was made in favor of a niece who lived with him and who was the object of his affection and regard" (571). According to this formula, the many testators who ignored affection, or made their wills a tool of revenge, would seem still more unsound—read as unnatural—than those whose bequests were merely weird or eccentric.[36]

Broadly speaking, however, soundness of mind referred more to the particular frame of mind—the sound *disposing* mind—than to its general health or stability. Sir J.P. Wilde, considering the proposition that a will might be valid even if the testator were not aware of its actual contents, commented on the consequences of such a holding:

35 "In our day the doctrine has sprung up of the unity and indivisibility of the mind, but the ground on which insanity should cause incapacity appears to have been overlooked in the reasoning on which it is founded." That reasoning includes a lengthy consideration of the "moral law" which frames the testator's responsibility and his family's reasonable expectation that he will provide for them after his death (563). To the degree that moral responsibility is emphasized, a case might be made for the more prescriptive patterns of the civil code, but English law puts no limit on this freedom because it assumes that human nature and the testator's intimate knowledge of his family can be trusted to better distribute property than any "stereotyped and inflexible rules of a general law" (564). Although Cockburn seems especially solicitous for the family's well-being, he also recognizes the will's usefulness as a tool for the aged to secure his family's help and attention in the event they did not reciprocate those feelings as fully as they might.

36 Cockburn also compares Banks's temporary delusions to other "defects of intelligence," for example, advanced age, physical infirmity, even "want of intelligence due to defective organization," and concludes that Banks's will must be held good since in these other examples, "if there be sufficient intelligence to understand and appreciate the testamentary act in all its different bearings, the power to make a will remains" (566).

> the most important of these is, that it would no longer be necessary to show that a testator was, in the old language of the law, of 'sound mind, memory, and understanding.' These words have been time out of mind held to mean sound disposing mind, and to import sufficient capacity to deal with and appreciate the various dispositions of property to which the testator was about to affix his signature (*Hastilow* 68).[37]

Hastilow v. Stobie (1865) was concerned with whether a will, albeit duly executed, could be considered valid, for example, if a lawyer drew up a will, which the testator signed without reading. Both the defense and Wilde cited Henry Swinburne's dictum that a testator may not give his testamentary power to another—what would amount to ceding his will and abdicating intention—"for as thy soul is not my soul, so thy will is not my will, nor thy testament my testament" (Swinburne). Wilde, perplexed by an idea that ran so far counter to the "natural and popular idea of the nature of a will" (*Hastilow* 67), further mused on the farce and contradiction it would introduce into this branch of law: if the "mental act of disposing" could be delegated, then the "sound disposing mind" would be a useless requirement, better replaced by a robust capacity to trust. "Nor would it be easy to acquit the law of an absurdity," he adds, "in requiring of a testator a capacity to understand an instrument, the contents of which it did not require him to know" (68).[38] In both these cases, the natural is rational and vice versa. The Wills Act enlarged the testator's powers on the related assumptions that he knew best how to dispose of his property and that he would be guided by "natural" feelings of familial love and duty, not that he would gain the power and casually transfer it to another.

The proposition Wilde had to consider was first introduced by Sir Cresswell Cresswell, and although Wilde noted that he must only have entertained the idea in the abstract (not having ever laid it down in a decision), Cresswell had presided over *Sefton v. Hopwood* (1855) in which he gave a far more liberal interpretation than either Wilde or Cockburn of the rational basis of the testamentary power and its scope: a testator "must have what old lawyers called 'a disposing mind'; he must be able to dispose of his property with understanding and reason" (*Sefton* 580). So much agrees with Wilde's opinion. But Cresswell continues:

> That does not mean he should make what other people think a sensible will, or a reasonable will, or a kind will, because by the law of this country, a man has absolute dominion over his own property, and if he being in possession of his faculties thinks fit to make a capricious will, a harsh will, or cruel will, you have no right to set it aside on that ground, for that would be interfering with the

37 The case revolved around the two wills of Vincent Phillips. Hastilow was executor of a second will, Stobie of the first, who pleaded that the later will was invalid because, among other reasons, the testator was unaware of its contents when he signed it (4). The case before Wilde was to decide whether the substance of this plea was good; Wilde held that it was.

38 See also *Earl of Sefton v. Hopwood* (1855) on the related issue of undue influence. J.A. Hamilton, in his entry on Cresswell in the *Dictionary of National Biography* refers to it as one of the "great will cases"(73).

> liberty which the law gives him, that would be to make his will for him and not to allow him to make his will. (580)

Removing both reason and affection from the testator's state of mind, Cresswell focuses exclusively on legality and right. No criticism of the testator's morality or even common sense can countermand his will, so strong is the law's commitment to his intention. For Swinburne and Wilde, no one can make a man's will for him and still call it his will; for Cresswell, neither can the law.

To secure and confirm this intention, section nine of the Act stipulated that henceforth no will (except for those written by soldiers and mariners who understandably might not have access to a lawyer) would be valid "unless it shall be in writing" and "signed at the foot or end thereof by the testator, or by some other person in his presence and by his direction." By affixing his name to it, he claimed the will as his own, making it an original and unique expression of his desire.

Furthermore, to prevent frauds or forgeries, this act of signing had to be witnessed; the testator's signature "shall be made or acknowledged by the testator in the presence of two or more witnesses present at the same time" who in turn "shall subscribe the will in the presence of the testator." But where was the end of the document, really? What did "presence" mean: mental presence, being in the same room, being in separate rooms (or even buildings) but within sight of one another? Could an illiterate man execute a will, or a blind man witness it?[39] Would simply saying that the document was a will count as "acknowledgment?" One of the earliest authorities, *Casson v. Dade* (1781), held that although the testatrix Honora Jenkins remained in the carriage outside her solicitor's office while the will was being attested inside, the fact that she could see her witnesses through the windows of her carriage and those of the lawyer's office satisfied the Lord Chancellor that her will was properly attested.[40] J.P. Wilde was still more generous in *Smith and Smith v. Smith* (1866): although the witnesses could not see the attestation clause nor any of the will itself (because the testatrix Maria Smith had covered the whole with blotting paper), nor did they even know it was a will they were signing, the will was valid because the witnesses had seen her writing something, which the court presumed to have been her signature. "If the court were to hold that it [the attestation] is not [sufficient]," said Wilde, "it would invalidate a great many wills" (*Smith and Smith* 146).

[39] Edward Burtenshaw Sugden (Lord St. Leonards) explains that witnesses must sign where it is *possible* for a testator to see them; the testator is under no obligation to prove that he did, however. Venting his dissatisfaction with Parliament's inattention to this aspect of the law, Sugden notes, "Even in the case of a blind man, he is treated as if he could see for the witnesses must sign where, if he enjoyed the organs of sight, he could see them" (142). But see also Dr. Wambey's argument for the defendant in *Hastilow v. Stobie*: "By the 71st rule (1862) the registrars are forbidden to grant probate of the will of a blind or illiterate person, unless satisfied that it was read over to him before execution or that he had at such time knowledge of its contents" (66).

[40] Jenkins was "asthmatical" and the lawyer's office was hot. She and her witnesses returned to the carriage where she executed the will, which they took back indoors to attest.

Stricter interpretations did sometimes prevail, of course, and confirmed the necessity of having both genuine intention and proper form. Wilde himself had commented in an earlier case on the "enormous weight which attached to the document itself as evidence of the *animus* [*testandi*] with which it was made," yet even a duly executed and witnessed codicil, if intended as a sham—"in reality the offspring of a jest or the result of a contrivance" (*Lister v. Smith* 288)—had no testamentary substance.[41] Conversely, intention could be well established, but if the form were not adhered to, the will would fail. Mary Gunstan's will of 1881 was not granted probate because it appeared that she had not signed it in front of the witnesses. Sir J. Hannen reluctantly held that the will was not properly executed because the testatrix "had not followed the excellent advice [...] of employing a professional man who would have seen everything done properly" (*Re Gunstan's Goods* 104).[42] His decision was upheld on appeal with similar expressions of regret that this "mere accident," this "want of form," should invalidate a document clearly meant for a will (107). But Jessel, Master of the Rolls, asked the central question: "what is in law a sufficient acknowledgment under the statute?" Lord Justice Brett concurred, "One must feel distressed at the result that the disposition of her property which this lady intended to make must depend upon the accident of putting a piece of blotting paper a quarter of an inch higher or lower" (111). Nevertheless, "we have to consider here an enactment of a statute, in which there is no elasticity." Adhering to the letter of the law, their decisions emphasize the unity of content and form, the acts of signing and witnessing and the written form essential to their authenticity. Lord Justice Holker explained that "Although the words of the statute are, 'such witnesses shall attest the will' and not 'the signature,' it seems to me that it amounts to the same thing, for when the document is properly signed or acknowledged in the presence of the witnesses, it becomes a will" (116). Without the proper forms, it remains in legal terms a mere "document," no matter how fully the testator believed it to be her will.

This insistence on testamentary intention suggests that character-driven ideas of subjectivity based in the Enlightenment theories of reason and responsibility persisted well into the latter half of the century. The anxiety about authenticity and the desire for empirical, documentary forms that could or would confirm it certainly informed the Wills Act itself, but they were also carried forward by legal decisions that strictly interpreted the Act. Even the first of its only two nineteenth-century amendments, which responded to "great evils" that had arisen from the "strict manner" of implementing the original (Christie 167), reiterated as it refined

---

41 Wilde was especially concerned about admitting testimony as to intention: "The momentous consequences of permitting parol evidence thus to outweigh the sanction of a solemn act are obvious. It has a tendency to place all wills at the mercy of a parol story that the testator did not mean what he said" (288).

42 Gunstan's lawyer wrote out an attestation clause which she then copied into her will. The question for the appeal was whether the presence of this clause could supply the gaps in the witnesses' depositions, that is, that it demonstrated the will had been acknowledged as one in their presence.

an obsessive regard for documentation.[43] Lord St. Leonards (otherwise Edward Burtenshaw Sugden), who ushered the amendment through Parliament, observed of section nine

> The first alteration of the law made hundreds of wills void; they were, when attempted to be proved, carried away in basketfuls as valueless, simply because the testator's name was directed to be signed at the foot or end of the will, [...] so that at last it rather required a carpenter to measure the distance in each case than a judge to decide upon the application of the Act. (Sugden 135)

Yet all of these instincts—the idea of character and its expression and verification in the formal will—also explain the potential disagreement between the testator and the solicitor writing his will. As Joseph Sutphen had remarked, the idea of the will was so familiar that many people thought they knew what making one entailed (529), but this familiarity also translated into a popular assumption that freedom of bequest meant an unrestricted right. Although Cockburn and Cresswell present two very different images of the testator's liberty and his use of it, the picture to emerge time and again from the practical legal books is one of solicitors policing abuses of power, reining in wayward testators, and educating the ignorant.[44] Thus, although the Wills Act was one of the most consistent pieces of Victorian legislation, its complexity was such as to make Blackstone's old advice about seeking professional aid seem altogether reasonable, especially when one considers the network of inheritance laws (the women's property laws or the laws of trusts and "bastardy," for example), which established their own prohibitions that even a validly executed will could not surmount.

The Lord Chancellor followed his work on the 1852 amendment with a "handy" book designed to address just this feeling that the laws had become too complicated for the responsible man of property to address competently. Hailed in the press and the courts alike, Sugden's *A Handy Book on Property Law* (1858) performed the astounding service of condensing "all the Property Law in England" into a series of letters and collecting them in a "pocket" volume ("Lord St. Leonards' Handy Book on Property Law" 190).[45] Extolling its value for

---

43 The Wills Amendment Act, 1852 declared a signature valid only if it appeared "at or after, or following, or under, or beside, or opposite to the end of the will" regardless of "the circumstance that a blank space shall intervene between the concluding word of the will and the signature" (Christie 168).

44 These are differences in interpretation, certainly, attributable to the differences in the judges themselves, but coming later, Cockburn's decision resonates with some of those family values so apparent in Maine, in the Christian Socialism of Fry, and in the radical politics and feudal history of Cook and Leadam respectively—with an emphasis on collective identities and duty to others.

45 Concluding his decision in *Allen v. Maddock* (1858), T. Pemberton Leigh remarked that although he could not base a legal decision on a popular work, nevertheless, he and the other Lords Justice could observe that "(in a work which, though it professes to be written only for the un-learned, may often be consulted by the most learned with advantage) Lord

all readers regardless of class, the reviewer in *Blackwood's Edinburgh Magazine* declared it "law for the million" that nevertheless did not encourage men to become their own lawyers—"which would be simply giving every man a fool for a client"—but provided general knowledge and advice to "inspire him with a prudent self-distrust, put him upon inquiry, and arm him with weapons against fraud and over-reaching" (190). A Victorian Blackstone in this regard, Sugden prefaced his letters with a brusque address to readers in which he enumerates their complaints—"You complain to me, that although utterly ignorant of law, you are constantly compelled to exercise your own judgment on legal points; that you cannot always have your solicitor at your elbow"; or that "you cannot readily comprehend your solicitor when you seek his advice" (Sugden 1)—and identifies their needs as the occasion for his book:

> In short, you want a form of familiar letters, what is now so much in vogue, a work upon an interesting subject calculated 'for the million,' upon whom I should be but too happy to assist: such a work, whilst it imparts knowledge, may, perchance, beguile a few hours in a railway carriage. I have in my youth and in my manhood written much for the learned in the law; why should I not, at the close of my career, write somewhat for the unlearned? (2)

Setting aside the former Lord Chancellor's rather optimistic vision of his book's chances in the railway market, as well as his sense of *noblesse oblige*, what is more important here is his incredulity that readers "are even at a loss in giving instructions for [their] will, and wholly incapable of making the most simple one for [themselves]" (1). He therefore devotes three letters to testamentary law: to the timely observance of testamentary duty, to the desirability of intestacy over a bad will, to methods of revoking and reviving wills as well as the nature of certain dispositions, but especially to the "all-important point" of complying with the statute in executing and attesting it (135).

Though addressing his comments to a lay audience, Lord St. Leonards was not alone in observing the gulf between the average testator's understanding of his will and that of the legal community. In *The Practice of Wills and Administrations* (1860), George S. Allnut directed himself to a legal audience and commiserated the unnecessary work created by testators who believed they could untangle the network of laws on their own:

> Endeavoring to exercise the right of ownership over [his property] after he shall have ceased personally to enjoy it, [the testator] seeks to fetter his gift with conditions and limitations, of the effect of which he is so ignorant, that it often appears as if he had intentionally obscured his meaning, if, indeed, he may be said to have had any meaning at all. "Testators," recently observed an eminent judge, "seem inexhaustible in their devices for puzzling courts of justice." And thus it

---

St. Leonards treats as clear, a point which, from its extreme importance, their Lordships have thought it advisable to examine at so great a length" (770), that is, whether a duly executed codicil could incorporate an improperly executed will.

> will continue to be, so long as persons without any knowledge of the legal effect of their words and intentions, prepare their own wills, or entrust the preparation of them to individuals as ignorant upon this subject as themselves. (2)

Allnut does not quite condemn the testator's desire to maintain control of his property, but his contempt for their mismanagement at the very least underscores the felt strength of testamentary prerogative against which legal professionals had to contend. He thus seeks to alert practitioners to the obstacles they will face when drafting a will and to the right way of handling them. "The first duty of the solicitor, when called upon to prepare a will," he writes,

> is not only to draw it as to effect the testator's intentions *as nearly as the rules of law will permit*, but to explain to the testator himself the ultimate consequences of his wishes being carried into effect, and advise him to adopt a better course, if such should appear necessary or desirable. *A solicitor is not to be a mere instrument to do whatever a testator may request*, but there devolves upon him in this matter an important moral duty; he is bound to be an advisor for the *benefit of the testator's family*, or for that of any other intended objects of the testator's bounty. (emphasis mine 3)

The competent professional will recall that a will is the legal representation of a testator's intentions rather than a direct statement of them. Moreover, he will remember that those intentions need to be brought into conformity with the law. For Allnut, the lawyer simultaneously serves two functions: he performs a "moral duty" by reminding the client of his own obligations, and he reshapes and articulates his client's intentions.

Personal ignorance of the law was not the only problem to beset the construction of wills, either. B.B. West pinpointed various testamentary "moods" for their disruption of the desirable, dispositive mind. In *Wills and How Not to Make Them* (1893), he comments on the "angry testator" in particular, noting that "somehow, whenever a man of means flies into a passion, it is the most natural thing in the world for him to go and make his will [...] when morally he is incapable of performing the task rightly, he rushes to its discharge" (32–3). Anger is only one of the many "multifarious moods" to have negative consequences for the contemplated heirs, and by West's account the complete absence of personality, if possible, would be most desirable.[46] "As things and lawyers are," however, "[the testator] is rarely permitted to keep his own individuality sufficiently out of his will. Wherever it appears," he observes, "it is almost sure to show itself in

[46] In his chapter on "Multifarious Moods," West explains: "I am not now complaining that a man radically wrong-headed and perverse, is, according to the orthodox doctrine of will-making, lawfully entitled to realize his obstinate folly. That result, if absurd, is yet consistent with the view of English jurisprudence that a will is the expression of a man's volition. Irrational as the action of that volition may be, when a will duly reflects that, its legal end, it may be admitted, has been substantially reached. The misfortune is, that in a multitude of instances, a testator's true volition cannot be ascertained" (73–4).

the wrong place. But, necessarily, the more of it that there is, the more calamitous must be the consequences" (32). In other words, as a legal document the will would be far better if it at least reflected less of any particular mood since these are changeable and therefore a faulty gauge of the more general testamentary volition. Assuming the lawyer's point of view, West does not condemn the profession for enacting a client's desire, but he does blame them "for the fostering of the fallacy that a will is the reflection of the testator's character, which leads a man, when he chances to be at his worst, to imprint on his property a very ugly speaking likeness of himself for the contemplation of posterity" (33). This reform would be possible if two simple principles were borne in mind: that because "all testators have, on the surface or beneath, a vein of lunacy" every will should "be regarded as instructions for a will rather than one itself" (130).

West's and Allnut's frustration, like that found in essays and law reports of the era, reveal the testator's feeling that his personal identity and desire were intimately tied to this act of proprietary control, on the one hand, and the law's equal conviction on the other that this was often lamentably so. More specifically, they reveal the legal professionals' competing attitudes towards their own obligations that are based on attitudes about their clients: they acknowledge the testator's character and attempt to reshape it into the bureaucratic function of identity, yet their reductive approach to personality here is offset by concerns for the ethical treatment of the family and heirs. Their professional management nevertheless marks one step in the transformation of moral agency into legal identity, the new testamentary persona encoded in the will. This creation and registration of identity in the will reminds us that documents exist in a metonymic relationship with the body; they provide for a "textual construction of identity" (Thomas 60) that makes the legal subject knowable, verifiable, and manageable. The will, however, encodes internal qualities, states of mind, and character. His intentions ventriloquized by the legal professional, the testator acquires a new identity, recorded in his will, and legitimated by law. It is impossible to say whether an individual's sense of self existed prior to this engagement with social structures, or if the law provided the framework for that sense in the first place. What is clearer, however, is that the will was at once a social, legal document—real sheets of paper cataloging real material possessions—and an expression of abstract desire, personality, and character, which conjoined the ontological and epistemological concerns that were central to Victorian cultural debate.

As mentioned at the outset, some of the wills I read here are decidedly un-dramatic and betray a conflict neither between the writer and the legal institution, nor between the testator and the heir. The author of "Extraordinary Wills" remarked that if a will proved dull indeed, it was simply because most people were themselves rather boring—"It is true that there is nothing especially noteworthy about an average will, but that is because there is nothing especially noteworthy about the average man—yet even those wills make 'an unconscious revelation of character'" (162). In 1883 Philip Gosse, for instance, left a single paragraph in which he bequeathed an absolute legacy to his second wife, invested a portion of the estate, and settled the remainder on her for use only during her life and, after her death, entirely on his son, Edmund. Enoch Bennett's will is even shorter. In two sentences, he leaves everything to his "dear wife Sarah Anne," and nearly 20 years later in 1890 merely adds a codicil appointing his sons, Arnold and Francis, co-executors. Their wills, like large sections of many of the others, follow the prescribed forms and leave little room for ambiguity as to intention or for the authorial "personality" dreaded by legal professionals.

Others, in contrast, are far more personal and evince a sense of compromise between formal, legal requirements and the testator's desire. Many of the wills, especially those (like John Galsworthy III's) covering large estates or making a wide variety of bequests, are full of lengthy, complex passages, passages in which every eventuality (for instance of there being a single or multiple executors or of the types of investments that can be made) is laid out and repeated. Their grammar is perforce almost impenetrable and yet absolutely necessary in the eyes of a legal professional that would avoid ambiguity. But out of this labyrinth of legal language, the voice of the testator does emerge and nowhere more strongly than in Dickens's will. After several passages that dispense with what is essentially the business of the will, Dickens shifts the tone of his address in order to make far more personal injunctions that are worth quoting at length:

> As I have here set down the form of *words which my legal advisors assure me are necessary to the plain objects of this my will*, I solemnly enjoin my dear children to remember how much they owe to the said Georgina Hogarth and never to be wanting in a grateful and affectionate attachment to her, for they know well that she has been through all the stages of their growth and progress their ever useful, self-denying and best of friend, and I here desire simply to record the fact that my wife since our separation by consent has been in the receipt from me of an annual income of six hundred pounds while all the great charges of a numerous and expensive family have devolved wholly upon myself. (emphasis mine)

Most of the will up to this point is straightforward. Few adjectives color its directions. One can infer from the bequests themselves the regard in which Dickens held his various heirs, but in the case of his "dear sister in law" Georgina Hogarth, to whom Dickens left an £8000 legacy, all his "personal jewelry," all "the other familiar objects from [his] writing table and [his] room" and all his "private papers whatsoever and wheresoever" with which "she will know what to do," Dickens departs from his reserve and expresses a "grateful blessing" to "the true and dearest friend man ever had." If for the most part these early sections may be styled the legal component of the will, Dickens himself comes further to the fore in an express statement that he has "set down the form of words which my legal advisors assure me are necessary for the plain objects of this my will" following which he seems to have followed no other advice but his own desire. Giving instructions for his funeral, for example, he "emphatically insist[s] that [he] be buried in an inexpensive, unobtrusive and strictly private manner," and that "at the utmost not more than three plain mourning coaches be employed and that those who attend my funeral wear no scarf, cloak, black bow, long hatband or other such revolting absurdity." Images of Sarah Gamp, Mr. Mould, and the preparations for Anthony Chuzzlewit's funeral at which "feathers waved, horses snorted, silk and velvets fluttered" (*Martin Chuzzlewit* 385) inevitably intrude, but the poignancy of his wish in the end to be treated as a private citizen discourages clinical analysis. Resting his "claims to the remembrance of my Country upon my published work and to the remembrance of my friends upon their experience of me," he adds,

> I commit my Soul to the mercy of God through our Lord and Saviour Jesus Christ and I exhort my dear children humbly to try to guide themselves by the teaching of the New Testament in its broad spirit and to put no faith in any man's narrow construction of its letter here or there.

As a man contemplating death, Dickens advocates freethinking and an attention to the spirit of religious teaching that might equally apply to the spirit of legal edicts that are distorted by the "narrow construction of its letter" to which legal practitioners may sometimes subject it. He works with the law so that his financial objects may be achieved, but he orders his heirs in ways that carry the moral obligation of a deathbed request.

In this latter portion of the will, Dickens develops a testamentary persona with definite opinions as to what is seemly, giving explicit instructions for how he is to be treated, leaving a lesson to his children on how to conduct their lives, and making his own humble appeal to God. Samuel Butler's will is on the whole far less solemn, but it nonetheless develops a character, or gives the picture of a man, that can be inferred from the kinds of goods he bequeaths. Indeed, the preservation of the goods seems to be the chief means by which he is to be remembered, since Butler requests that his body be cremated and that his "ashes shall not be preserved." For example, to his clerk Alfred Cathie he leaves a £2000 legacy as well as his

> furniture (except my carved oak family linen-chest), clothing, household effects, and my watch and chain and plate (except the two large "S.B." spoons and also except my drawings, pictures, and books) and all my photographic cameras and all other my photographic materials and apparatus and articles used for photographic purposes.

He allows Cathie to keep any negatives of his own family and directs that he may have "any two negatives of me which he may select but not any copyrighted negatives nor copyrights in negatives." From this the reader learns that Butler was something of a professional photographer. We know, too, by a bequest to Henry Festing Jones of "all my interest in all musical compositions upon which we may have been jointly engaged and all copyrights and manuscripts and stocks of all such works as have been published in common by us," that he is also an accomplished composer. Select pictures, named by title and price paid for them, he leaves to various friends; others he allows to be destroyed or sold. And all his "unpublished manuscripts [...] three volumes of notes and sundries [...] letters and letterbooks and all copyrights of my unpublished works" go to his literary executor Richard Streatfield of the British Museum. The overall image is of a renaissance Victorian, multi-talented and professionally active in several artistic fields, and the number and extent of his bequests reflect this interest in the arts and the priority he placed on them. The annuities he establishes for Cathie and for the artist Charles Gogin, for instance, were to take precedence over all other bequests, including those made to his sister-in-law and nephew. And like Dickens, Butler made his will the occasion for expressing gratitude towards those who helped him during his life, as did Jason Smith to whom Butler leaves the picture "Heatherley's Holiday" in "grateful acknowledgment of valuable assistance given during my many years of poverty." For Butler as testator the objects he leaves behind are emblems of his accomplishments. Their disposal in the legal document, the precedence they take in the order of bequests (the real estate and so forth coming last), and the particularity of their description, emphasize their importance as attributes of his character that he would see maintained.

For Dickens and Butler both, the will serves as a vehicle for developing a testamentary and a private persona. In Dickens's will Georgina Hogarth is the "true and dearest friend man ever had;" his wife, whom he never once mentions by name, is a woman who takes his money but implicitly shirks her maternal duty, leaving it for her sister to fulfill and Dickens to finance.[47] For Butler, Alfred Cathie is a valued assistant. Whatever "character" the testator develops for himself, he also attributes a character to his heirs and through the disposal of property influences their future identities and relationships. In some instances the influence is largely beneficial. George Eliot's will, for example, (which is marked on the form as "Probate of a Married Woman's Will" and bears the name Mary Ann Cross) states from the outset that through "two several indentures," including one between herself and her husband, a variety of real and personal property had been settled "in trust for myself for my separate use for life and after my death in trust as I should by my last will and testament appoint." Further, the proceeds of the "exercise of my literary skills" had been agreed to be her separate property. The will is very careful to document Eliot's right as a married woman to leave one at all. Having thus invoked the right, Eliot grants several substantial annuities to women, again, being careful to specify that they shall be "for the sole and separate use of the respective annuitants free from the control, debts, or engagements of any husband and without power of alienation during any coverture."[48] As a woman of property and thus enjoying certain social freedoms, Eliot must remain alert to the women's property law that dictated her legal identity and that in 1880, when the will was written, had still to undergo its most significant reforms. The advantages she had, she also made available to other women through her will.

---

[47] See Fred Kaplan's biography of Dickens for discussion of Dickens's separation from Catherine and the campaign against him and Georgina (376–96).

[48] For interpretations of "sole" and "separate use," see *Thornton v. Bright* (1836), *Reid v. Reid* (1858), and *Lewis v. Mathews* (1866).

Anthony Trollope's bequests to his sons, though apparently made in a spirit of equity and generosity, nonetheless leave an opening for conflict between them that in a novel would surely be exploited. On the death of their mother, Trollope's two sons were to divide the estate "share and share." The oldest son, Henry, had been made literary executor and given outright his father's "library of books and pamphlets for his own use and benefit," valued at £1000. The younger son, Frederick, owed his father £4000. Both of these sums were to be considered when calculating the share each son was still due, but Trollope directed that if Frederick's loan was outstanding at the time of his death, and if the amount owed exceeded the share that he could take, then he was to be freed from the debt and, in any case, released from paying interest on it. In short, it was possible that the bequests would not be equal. The gross value of Trollope's personal estate was nearly £26,000 so, on the face of it, it seems unlikely that a conflict between the two would have developed. But the larger point is that Trollope's efforts in his will to be fair and to remove the financial burdens his sons might bear nevertheless turn his parental decree into a legal order for how they must relate to one another.

John Galsworthy's stance towards his property and his sons' inheritance is a forceful example of whose interests the will is made to maintain, as well as of the character it establishes, even by implication, of those set to inherit. Thirteen pages long, including 22 clauses and 4 distinct codicils, and disposing of an excess of £110,000, Galsworthy's will is the sort which Old Jolyon Forsyte could contemplate with pride. Especially interesting is the provision Galsworthy makes in respect of his sons. Having left all his children annuities as well as shares in the residual estate, he adds that if any son "shall charge or incumber any annual sum [...] or his contingent or expected share," or if he should become bankrupt or cause the money to vest in someone other than himself, then the gifts "in favor of such son respectively shall absolutely cease and determine in like manner as if such son had died at the time when such cause of forfeiture occurred." Galsworthy is clearly interested in preserving the estate. The suggestion that any son of his might live on his expectations, that is, be so undutiful as to look forward to his father's death and, further, to assume for his own use what is by no means his property, is enough to render him dead in the eyes both of the father and of the law.

Whether this came to pass (an event I have not tried to discover), the point is that the will is the legal vehicle for preserving the testator's possessions, his control over them, and transitively his control over his heirs. Like God, who knows what humanity's fate will be yet leaves each individual free to fall, the testator provides for a situation that the heir, in ignorance thereof, may stumble into for, as we have seen, there is no legal requirement that the contents of a will be made known prior to its probate. The will is valid, and it may be perfectly just, but in any case, the legal language that has created a position from which the testator can speak (and Galsworthy is himself a lawyer) also enables him to determine what it is possible for his heirs to have and to be. Their consent to this fact is compelled rather than asked. No retort is possible, and their agency that was free when the will was written is constrained when it is read.

In addition to charting a relationship between the private person and the law, and to creating personae for testator and heir alike, the will can then also be an occasion of suspense. Certainly, as B.B. West observed, the reading of a will was often, if inappropriately, a suspenseful event for those asked to attend. It can also be the subject of suspenseful narrative, as the many examples of case law and, of course, of novels written about wills will attest. But the document itself is also a narrative (more obviously in some instances than in others) that follows a dramatic arch, building suspense as it progresses. The formal boundaries of the will are standard: first, the principal actor introduces himself and appoints his executors; last, the will ends with a reaffirmation of its intentions and the invocation of witnesses. What falls between these brackets in the sense of order seems for the most part a matter of the testator's preference. Some wills, like Gosse's and Bennett's, are sheer climax, so to speak. They simply convey the bequest with neither introductory comment nor reflective peroration. Others, like Wilkie Collins's, busy themselves with smaller details, setting a scene as it were, before making its greatest revelations.

Collins's voice is so present in his will—a man contemplating his surroundings as he writes—that it is possible to forget that the moment of writing is passed, the speaker a living voice no longer. He begins by giving instructions for his burial at Kensal Green and, like Dickens, specifies that "no scarves, hat bands, or feathers shall be worn or used." Preferring a less ostentatious funeral, he directs that on "a plain stone cross" nothing should appear but "the inscription which my executors will find written and placed in the same envelope occupied by this my will." The allusion to this other document that exists outside the boundaries of the formal will heightens the effect of Collins's living presence in the sense that it shows him engaged in other activities even as he writes the will. (It also raises the legal question of whether the letter is thereby incorporated in the will, becoming another testamentary instrument but one written without the restrictions of legal form.) This sense is further augmented by his careful descriptions of the personal effects he bequeaths. For example, in a gift to Caroline Elizabeth Graves, then living with him, Collins specifies that she have

> my gold studs and gold sleeve links and the furniture in her bedroom and the furniture and effects in the backroom on the ground floor next to the dining room (excepting only the iron safe now standing in the said back room and securities for money, cash, pictures, prints and books) in my dwelling house 90 Gloucester Place aforesaid.

The passage is an odd mixture of the legal and the highly personal. It conveys a visual sense of things as they are and where they are, of Collins's mental eye roaming over his familiar objects, as well as a sense that none of this arrangement will change even after Collins is no longer there to survey it.

His presence as narrator, though palpable, is only one part of the literary quality of his will. After disposing of his books and pictures, he makes several legacies. His relationship to most of these legatees is carefully delineated: to his "late mother's sister[s]" Mrs. Dyke and Mrs. Gray and her daughter Marion a £20 annuity, to Holman Hunt the portrait he made of Collins's brother Charles. Then to Martha Rudd, he leaves £200 before going on to several lengthy sentences disposing of his real estate. But Martha Rudd, living at such and such an address and "passing under the name Mrs. Dawson," returns later in the will as the beneficiary of a trust. If the alias were insufficient cause for curiosity, the names of her three children—Marion, Harriet Constance, and William Charles—lend a clue to the mystery. At this point Collins reveals the relationship he seems to have obscured: "And I hereby acknowledge the said three children as my children by the said Martha Rudd" and "for the better identification of the said three children" gives their dates and places of birth. The remainder of the will focuses chiefly on the trusts for his now formally recognized daughters and draws to an orderly conclusion. However widely known the relationship between Collins and "Mrs. Dawson" may have been, its treatment and position in the will, the precedence it did *not* take in the ordering of Collins's books and shirt studs, makes the document read like something of a mystery itself.[49] The strong narrative presence of the testator, the attention to the physical details of the house, and the specificity with which other relationships are described offset the initial ambiguity around this central relationship. Collins's will, perhaps more than any of the others, has the makings of the best "will story," not only in terms of its substance, but in the way it subtly presages the coming revelation so as not wholly to surprise the reader.

In Collins's and Dickens's wills especially, the use of aliases, the revelation of unconventional behavior, or a barely suppressed conflict lend dramatic energy to a supposedly staid, official legal document. Great fortunes, illegitimate children and the suggestion of undutifulness in others, estranged wives, and pleas to God are the extravagant components of the will that fit it for sensational fictional use. But even the more homely wills of moderate figures like Gosse and Bennett are recognizable in the realist novels of "things as they are," of those which depict the common man enjoying a legal right to dispose of his hard-earned property and exercising a moral duty to care for the family he leaves behind him. Though the wills are a terminal point in the stories that inform them, they are a beginning for the novels about them.

Because the will is, finally, a means of conveying property, it deals in the material things that were so important to the object-laden descriptions of realist fiction, but those possessions had tremendous symbolic potential even in the will as expressions of the taste and status of the person who owned them. Whether one argues that the fact of ownership made those goods subject to the possessor's will, or that the possessor's will in a thing (his or her ability to control it) constituted the basis of ownership, the material object was intimately linked to that person's autonomy and sense of self. The last will and testament, as a document, thus

---

[49] See Chapter 1, "The Will," of William M. Clarke's *The Secret Life of Wilkie Collins*. Clarke comments that Collins "had planned his will with as much care for detail as he had always given to his most complex plots" (4)—Caroline and Martha were given separate, private readings of the will—but which nevertheless failed to have its intended effects (6, 8).

conjoins the testator's metaphysical ability to enact desires with specific material objects. Standing in as testaments to the owner's control, those objects themselves also became the means by which the testator controlled other people. To control things is to enlarge or restrict the agency of those to whom they are bequeathed; thus, the will could express the testator's character even as it impinged on the identity of his heirs.

The testator's control in the will parallels the novelist's control of his narrative. Both confront the conventions of their discursive form: the testator negotiates the law (and those legal co-authors who monitor and shape his language,) just as the novelist navigates contending theories of his art and the variety of techniques at his disposal. As the next chapter will show, these theories were widely debated throughout the century but were fairly consistently divided between the idealist's interest in metaphysical contemplation of how things should be and a realist commitment to deriving meaning from the experience of reading about things as they are. Anxious to guide the readers' thought, the idealist author interposed himself in the narrative in ways that are analogous to the testator's own narrative presence in the will. That is, the testator has a conception of how the world should be after his death. He becomes his own first person narrator and, by constantly asserting himself, dictates how the will should be read.

If the writing of the will depends on certain consensual values (the significance of property, the right to dispose of it, for example), its reading is a decidedly non-consensual mode. The narrating testator speaks to the reader in the most didactic of tones, unlike the realist author whose narrator largely absented himself from the textual world and left the reader to engage with its protagonist and draw conclusions based on their shared experience. However, if we think of the testator as the protagonist of his will, then Dickens's decision to "rest his claims to the remembrance [...] of [his] friends upon their experience of [him]" is in some sense akin to treating his life like a closed book whose meaning his friends are now free to determine. Collins's few hints as to the identity of Mrs. Dawson and her children permit the reader to piece together knowledge on their own before the testamentary Collins-narrator confirms it. In these ways, the will can be said to invoke certain consensual principles of reading, even as it directs the actual auditors gathered to hear it.

Through its content and its form, the will offered nineteenth-century novelists a model of the very issues they faced when debating the merits and aims of their art. The documentary will modeled the author's role in relation to his text by showing how the testator's volition had to be framed in terms of legal conventions. It created a narrator with lessons as well as things to impart. It brought those things together and linked them to ontological questions of how one comes to be, to metaphysical inquiries into human agency, and to epistemological interrogation of how we know and understand reality. It created an audience whose apparent passivity raised the question for the novel of how much input that audience should have in the creation of their own worlds. Indeed, the ability to contest a will or appeal a legal case shows that the law is regularly used to alter rather than endorse the testator's text when its readers cannot accept a particular "will story."

In short, the will's combination of metaphysics and empiricism, those poles of the Victorian idealism and realism debates, made it precisely the sort of "real" document the novel needed in order to define its social function.

Public interest in the realist turn of wills reached its height, not surprisingly, late in the nineteenth century, when the number of wills on record in Somerset House would have increased and when the novel had established its dominance of the literary world. In this context, the will could offer both a subject and a reason for realist narrative fiction. When law was unable to keep pace with changing social needs (and therefore required legal fictions, or equitable or legislative remedies to bring it in line), or when law defined its role as a restraint on social change in the interest of preserving traditional social institutions, it created an opportunity for literary fiction to do in the domains of culture what law could not or would not do: instead of lagging behind law, in other words, fiction could run ahead in an imagined projection of social alternatives and a deeper study of individual subjectivity.

Chapter 2
Writing the Novel: Victorian Testators and Literary Culture

H.B. Finlay Knight published his first of only two novels called *A Girl with a Temper: A Romance of the Wills Act* in 1892. Its title suggests a children's tract on the perils of misbehavior more than a three-volume novel, but the narrative reveals a sensational story about the proper drafting and execution of a will that defies legal and literary genres. Knight's novel makes use of plot elements typical of the sensation novel: enforced marriages, disappointed lovers, suppressed identities, inheritances lost and regained. It is more interesting, however, for its mixture of these conventions with prosaic accounts, even author's footnotes, explaining the legal mechanism of bequeathing and inheriting property, the location of Somerset House, and instructions for how to consult "proved" or probated wills. This incongruous pairing of romance and bureaucracy—or, more particularly, the sense of romance *in* bureaucracy—nonetheless illustrates how the will functioned within and alongside the development of the realist novel.

Knight, himself a barrister, numbers among the many forgotten authors of the Victorian era, but what is notable about Knight's contribution is his sense of what literature and the law might share. In a long eulogy to "the ghosts of Temple Gardens" (258), he names some of his own authorial benefactors. He describes that "sacred earth, which the democrat Dickens has dared to defile with the presence of his puling Pinch and his parvenu Pip," where "Johnson pondered over his ponderous paragraphs and prepared them for the press" and, added to these literary (and alliterative) figures: "where Coke mused on Littleton, Williams on Executors and Chitty on contracts; where Smith lingered over leading cases, and Byles displayed the true inwardness of Bills." Knight positions his novel as a contemporary addition to this literary and legal history, which begs the question as to why a fledgling novelist like Knight should feel there was a viable market for a novel about wills in the first place.

The will often enters the novel as a finished document, one that emerges from time past in order to resolve disputes or clarify uncertainties in the story's present and thereby allow the narrative to conclude. Wills of this stamp have so often appeared in fiction as to cast a certain banality or predictability over such plots (Schor 136). However, the Victorian novel features to a more remarkable degree wills that are the *source* of dispute and uncertainty, wills that *create* conflict and narrative, in spite of their declared legal purpose of smoothing the transfer of property. This difference between the function of wills within literature and between literary and legal representations of the will signals a broader sense of what it represents than is suggested (or even substantiated) by legal discourse.

Victorian novels are indeed peopled by testators for whom the literal prospect of death, the dissolution of the body, prompts the writing of a will in order to prevent a similar dissolution of property, since to keep property intact is to retain one's personal integrity. At death, the testator is transformed into his testament, and through that document's metonymic relationship to his individual character and agency, the will extends beyond death the control he exercised in life and therefore extends himself. The legal document thus performs a regulatory function that, while extolling the powers of the testator, limits the beneficiary's powers to act and calls for ingenious ways on his (or her) part to circumvent legal dictates to become a self-determining individual.

To contemplate the will only as a finished document, however, is to underestimate its rhetorical significance. Freedom of bequest may broadcast the "owner's pleasure," but the process of drafting a will affords an opportunity for both legal and literary writers to define individuality and allocate agency. Where legal texts approach the testator with caution, even suspicion, and advise solicitors on how best to press their clients' intentions into a legal mold, the novel dramatizes conflicts between the private man and his legal advisor, or between the individual and a society underwritten by law. By depicting those aspects of individual character that overflow the legal mold, the novel has a choice to make: it can expose the way a unified legal persona is fabricated at the cost of its more humanistic elements, or it can participate in that constriction. Put differently, where the law uses legal fictions as the least disruptive method of adjusting to changing social needs (unlike recourse to equity or new legislation, a way of adapting law while maintaining fidelity to the forms and mores of the legal past), literary fiction could look behind, ahead, or all around itself, declare itself a fiction and yet offer a realistic view of the world, tell readers how things are and how things ought to be. It could create affective support for the status quo, or be the engine of criticism and change. In either case, the novel's attention to and uses of legal forms provide a way of making sense of the vexed idea of realism and the functions of both law and literature.

Law's and literature's common investment in subjectivity, agency, and their expression in the material world—their internal struggles over how to administer or represent these principles—places legal and literary discourse in conversation and even in competition. The cultural complexity to emerge from this dialectic highlights the role literature plays in shaping culture, certainly in shaping later readers' perceptions of the Victorians and their novels. The legal will and its various manifestations in literature thus provide a new index for understanding the function of the novel and its part in the formation of socially cognizable persons and of a broader nineteenth-century culture.

This chapter begins with discussion of the law in fiction as viewed from a legal perspective, in particular the criticism leveled by nineteenth-century legal readers at fictional treatments of law and of themselves, which says as much about their expectations of realism as about the nascent field of law and literature. A survey of Victorian novels follows which demonstrates how authors who may otherwise have held antagonistic theories of the novel invoked the will to work out those theories.

A final section focuses on Dickens, specifically on his last complete novel. Unlike *Martin Chuzzlewit* (1844), for example, with its protagonist's tantalizing bequests and dispossessions, *Our Mutual Friend* (1865) does not give us the living testator. I turn to it, however, because it embodies in miniature, and in the Victorian period, the sort of thematic focus on transition that occurs in the shift from the nineteenth to twentieth centuries generally. Although the rhetorical strategy of the realist novel employed the literal, documentary will, thereby suggesting its continued allegiance to materiality and empirical or experiential ways of knowing, *Our Mutual Friend*'s interest in the will is grounded in abstract questions as to the nature of inheritance and to the contours of personal identity that the Edwardians would come to foreground. In these terms, Dickens's novel suggests that epistemological doubt did not always lead to more vigorous assertions of certitude and that by engaging directly with these issues, the Victorians acquitted themselves of naïveté.

Before Wigmore Made his List: Law, Literature, and the Realist Enterprise

Finlay Knight was right to see the romance in law, and even to see an opportunity to increase his earnings by joining other barristers who had tried their hands at fiction, but he was somewhat behind the times in gauging his market.[1] In an 1865 article for *The St. James Magazine*, "J.C.S." affirmed that "notwithstanding the seeming incongruity, there subsists a very strong connection between law and literature" (194). Advocating the familiar image of the lawyer as man of letters, he suggested that literary pursuits, including reading and writing, might actually improve a lawyer's practice (195), and conversely, for those actually "gifted with the poetic faculty," professional study might even "contribute materially to his success as poet or novelist" (198). Two years later, an anonymous essay in the *American Law Review* led with the provocative claim that "The law is, after all, the most romantic of professions" (477). More than any other, the Law (the term is used monolithically) sees human nature at its limits: it deals in the "striking episodes in men's lives"; it "knows and understands the motives, and sees the workings, of the minds of the actors" (477), on which writers of fiction have not been slow to capitalize. Turning its attention to "law in romance"—"which is the shade or [mirror image] of romance in law"—the essay classifies both the types of law in literature and the lawyer's experience of reading them. The author's categorization of legal fiction is a point I will return to in a moment; the more

[1] John Sutherland estimates the number of Victorian novelists at 878 of whom 411were men. Of these, 110 (or one out of every five) were lawyers or failed barristers. See *Victorian Fiction* 162. *The St. James Magazine* explained that in addition to substantive training in law, the nature of legal practice for barristers especially created the ideal conditions for literary pursuits: students of an Inn of Court were not permitted to work and many fully-fledged barristers could find none anyway. Short funds paired with the restless energies of a long vacation, thus led to an employment "so seductive that in many cases its legal votaries are drawn away from their regular studies [...] and adopt literature as a profession" ("J.C.S." 197).

striking aspect of the piece is its sense of fatigue. By the end of the essay, the author wearies of the predictable plots he has just surveyed:

> The falsely accused is restored to the bosom of his family, the perjured witness has fallen in a fit or gone to jail (who cares?); the judge has retired to his venison and port; the jury are discharged; the contestant counsel are jesting and hobnobbing at their inn, and we will close our note-book. (494)

In this passage, it is the parenthetical "who cares?" that's so telling. A not-uncomplicated expression of disdain for the morally corrupt witness, it also passes judgment on an enervated genre. The conclusions of these stories, that is, signal an end for the law in romance, a whole enterprise in which the writer seems to have lost interest. In this context, Finlay Knight might have done better had he written his novel twenty years earlier.

Obviously, authors of fiction continued to turn to the law for many years to come—and have not stopped. In the nineteenth century, periodicals also continued to churn out stories on legal themes or those which used legal incidents to advance their plots, and many of the best examples of realist treatments of the law still lay ahead (for example, *Middlemarch*, the works of Hardy and James).[2] The disdain seems to be focused more on sensation fiction, which, it is true, was especially opportunistic about the tools it used to titillate and excite readers.

But what of the romance in law? Two trends can be seen emerging from the discussion of law and literature. On the one hand, law in romance seemed to be giving way to law in sensation fiction or to more naturalistic treatments of law; in other words, shifts within literature were changing the ways in which law was used and understood there and how it was received by legally-minded readers. (The sheer volume of literature at the end of the century also meant, more basically, that there were many more examples of legal literature to peruse.) On the other hand, the modern legal profession had reached maturity, which meant that the tacit competition between novelists and lawyers to represent human character became explicit, as essayists began to devote more formal attention to law and literature as a recognizable conjunction of terms. John H. Wigmore's "A List of Legal Novels" (first published in 1900 in *The Brief* and twice subsequently in the *Illinois Law Review*) is regularly cited as creating the category of the legal novel and introducing the study of literature in law.[3] Yet well before then, we see titles such as *Law and Lawyers in Literature*, "Novelists' Law," "The Literature

[2] A sample of stories either loosely or truly focused on the will include Ellen Wood's "A Last Will and Testament" in *Bentley's Miscellany*; Sheridan LeFanu's "Squire Toby's Will" that appeared in *Temple Bar*; and "Uncle George's Will," Margaret Majendie's two-part story that appeared in the May and June issues of *Temple Bar* in 1883. Less memorable examples include E.C. Grenville Murray's "Old Joquelin's Bequest: a Tale About Women" (a tale of a fund to set up a chair of gynecology at a French university) in *The Cornhill Magazine*, and Felix Eliot's "Mummy's Bequest" in *Belgravia*.

[3] See Richard H. Weisberg, "Wigmore's Legal Novels Revisited," 17.

of Law," even "Wills in Fiction," and shortly after Wigmore's essay appeared, "The Law as Treated in Fiction," and "Law and Literature." Written primarily from a legal perspective, these essays outline an emerging canon, some of them demonstrating an impressive prescience about the shape of the canon today. What is remarkable about them, however, is their sense that both law and literature have a shared subject in human character—early signs of the humanist argument for law and literature as a field of study—even if as professional practices their purposes and approaches to representing it differ. At the same time, these differences in approach manifest themselves in reading practices as well: what the legal reader expected or wanted to see in his legal fiction was rarely what the novelist thought fiction could or should supply.

Before Wigmore, "Law in Romance" created its own classes of legal fiction: the less interesting, stereotypical type—"where the plot turns on a disputed will, a forged deed, an altered marriage register, or a contested inheritance" (478)—and the better class, which involves an accusation of crime and the ensuing trial. The writer's distinction between the law in its documentary mien and the more narrative processes of a trial suggests a view in which institutional processes afford greater opportunities for character development and comparison of legal and literary forms than does the plot-driven appearance of legal texts. There is some basis for this criticism, but of course those documents are the products of legal processes, which offer as many opportunities for character development, interpretation, evaluation and judgment as the trial does. In either case, however, reading about them doesn't seem to afford the writer much pleasure. Either he finds law "hid, like a snake among the flowers of imagination" where the lawyer has gone to relax, or, in the case of the avid student who turns to literature to learn about his profession, fiction provides only an "unsatisfying morsel" (478). Although the nature of the complaints changes over time, complaint is the consistent refrain when lawyers write about literature.

In the preface to his collection *Law and Lawyers in Literature* (1882), Irving Browne explains the universal antagonism towards clergymen, doctors, and lawyers as class jealousy which dissipates only as the need for professional assistance increases, for example, "to rescue estates, to make wills, to defend against criminal accusation" (iv).[4] Clarifying that his examples will be drawn from a better class of literature—no "vulgar theatricals," "modern light novelists," or serial magazines and papers for him (v)—his chapter on novelists nevertheless consists of a chronological list of their works whose points of law he summarizes and evaluates; few, not surprisingly, fare very well.[5] A review in *The Atlantic Monthly* detected

---

4 "The mass of men do not love men who are able to get a living, and attain honors, without the use of money or muscle" (iii).

5 Trollope comes in for special attack: his fiction is "dull" and "goody-goody," especially when it criticizes barristers for taking on briefs that run against their own opinions or conscience. Better to do that, Browne claims, than try to defend Trollope "for writing such poor, dull stuff that not even his virtue can render tolerable" (118).

more wounded pride than fair criticism in Browne's tone. Although the reviewer grants him "the compiler's qualifications of knowing where to look for good material" (548), Browne was unable, it seems, to find much literature praising law or lawyers and, in its absence, looks for slights, becomes defensive, and resorts to criticism of novelists whose portraits the reviewer seems more inclined to believe. Alfred Bailey, writing for *The Gentleman's Magazine* in 1886, also identified two classes of novelists: those who get the law right, and those who get it wrong (23). Drawing on many of the same examples cited by Bailey, Allan Campbell was more specific in his 1902 Commencement address at Harvard University: "To write fiction without seeking legal advice is highly dangerous. They [novelists] all betray, not misjudgment, but neglect of the law, the usual source of error where the legal question is involved incidentally or has crept in without the writer's seeing it at all" (366).[6] Writing some years later, A.E. Wilkinson makes the by-now inevitable first comment: "The writer of fiction who proposes to deal with the law or courts as incidents in his story, unless himself of the brotherhood, had best secure the services of a competent professional coach" (217). Each of these essays adheres to essentially the same model. Each one surveys legal novels (*Ten Thousand a Year*, *Felix Holt*, and *Orley Farm* appear most frequently) and evaluates them in accordance with the author's understanding of legal procedure. The only point seems to be that novelists typically get their law wrong and ought to take better counsel if they want to claim the realism of their representations.[7] However, Wilkinson concedes that even if writers were to seek professional guidance, there would still be plenty of lawyers to criticize their law: "though he have been coached by the chief justice or the lord chancellor, he shall not escape having his ignorance shown up, even as we demonstrate, from day to day, that of the shallow pretenders who oppose us at the bar" (221). It is litigiousness, then, that draws lawyers to focus on the correctness of law—a result of legal training

---

6 He continues: "Novelists, by exercising freely their absolute control over their facts, should never have any difficulty in choosing safe legal ground. All these things considered, it would seem fair to judge them by the rule that ignorance of the law is no excuse for their misdemeanors" (367). The address also appeared as an essay in *The Green Bag* in 1902.

7 Others focus on law as literature. Ernest Huffcut, Dean of the Cornell University Faculty of Law, noted in 1892—thirty years after J.C.S. had argued for "a strong connection" between them—that "the divorce of law and literature seems in these latter days to be well nigh complete" (32):

> One never hears that a professor of literature in our schools of polite learning refers his students to legal literature for example of elegance or eloquence, yet historically it is probably true that no two branches are more closely united and interwoven. Indeed, it may not be too much to say that the earliest and most characteristic and original literature in all languages is the literature of law.

Wilkinson, too, comments on the state of legal writing, noting that legal practice—in particular the professional compulsion "to fully and accurately qualify every thought expressed" (206)—is anathema to inspirational writing.

under an adversarial system, but also a source of the competition with novelists and an explanation of their resistance to reading fiction about law as fiction.

Taken together, these articles become a way of policing the boundaries of writing about law and protecting professional interests. However, their ubiquity also betrays the way that lawyers were reading literature. In these essays, the accuracy of the law is important because the plausibility of the fictional plot depends on it. This is a realist stance, and in fairness, the lawyers' complaint has some legitimacy.[8] Alfred Bailey, for example, had singled out women writers in his list of authors who got the law wrong, but he acquitted himself of being ungallant "by reflecting that ladies cannot be expected to acquaint themselves with a subject so dry and repulsive as law must be to them in all its branches" ("except," he adds, "that now luxuriant one which is laden with the rights of women") (28). Putting aside his condescension, we might hear George Eliot's own advice to "lady novelists"—and indeed to all writers of fiction—to stick to what their education and experience has led them to know well. Eliot herself consulted Frederic Harrison on the legal points of *Felix Holt* and, one has to assume, would have criticized any author who wrote unintelligently about law. The more surprising example, then, comes from Allan Campbell's criticism of *Middlemarch* in writing which, he surmises, she "abandoned the Felix Holt plan" (365). Referring to Mr. Farebrother's assurance that Mary Garth's failure to destroy Mr. Featherstone's second will would not have revived the first one benefitting Fred, Campbell expresses his disappointment that Eliot should have made such an "unfortunate" mistake as to apply the law as it stood in 1872 when she was writing the novel, instead of the law as it was in the novel's setting of 1832, before passage of the Wills Act. However, Farebrother's comments did not figure in the novel during its serial publication. Eliot added them to the first edition, ironically on the advice of an "affable barrister" who had written to her in June of 1872, "pointing out her error over the legality of Featherstone's wills."[9] Like Bailey and Campbell, A.E. Wilkinson perceived the same general problem of fidelity to the law but framed it differently. Novelists could achieve a reality effect through their use of law, but only for the uninitiated among their readers whose involvement in the world of the novel would not be disrupted as when technical errors recalled the lawyer-reader to his professional life outside the novel (217). Nevertheless, these modes of reading rely on a very narrow understanding of realism and hence of the novelist's purpose.

The missing piece in these legal accounts of literature is an openness to the possibility that getting law "wrong" means getting something else very right. Trollope's narrator in *Dr. Thorne* (1858) shows a remarkable *sang froid* about his lack of legal acumen. Acknowledging recent suggestions that contemporary

---

8 But see also Robert Weisberg's discussion of Judge Posner's reading habits: in reading Kafka, "Posner's error is to confound such different matters as realism, naturalism, topicality, referentiality, and reductionism" (28). More plainly, he "misunderstands literary realism" (29).

9 See David Carroll's notes to the Oxford World Classics edition, 805.

writers of fiction ought in future to have a lawyer on staff, he excuses himself in the interim, particularly in reference to Sir Roger Scatcherd's will:

> I can only plead for mercy if I be wrong in allotting Sir Roger's vast possessions in perpetuity to Miss Thorne, alleging, also, in excuse, that the course of my narrative absolutely demands that she be ultimately recognised as Sir Roger's undoubted heiress [...] If under such a will as that described as having been made by Sir Roger, Mary would not have been the heiress, that will must have been described wrongly. (468)

Trollope's sense of the inconsequentiality of his legal descriptions relative to the demands of the novel's narrative conventions raises a different set of questions: Is the book a novel or a romance? Is realism or idealism at work? Is plot or character driving this narrative? These are not questions that Bailey, for one, tends to ask (although he cites this passage in his essay). Wilkinson again comes somewhat nearer the point when he explains that the feeling or aura of law created in the novel is more important than its actual specifics, but he too articulates the preference for better law in literature.[10]

The problem for these lawyers is precisely that they read literature like law. Realism does not always mean adherence to the "facts"; at least, the degree of fidelity marks the point where realism verges into idealism, or where parody and satire trump serious realism. There is indeed a realism of content—of fidelity to the material world, yes, but also to experience, to feeling, even to practices of interpretation and procedure (so that novelists' substantive law can prove to be wrong yet remain realistic because the argument or process was the focus of depiction)—and there is a realism of form and literary convention. "Novelists' law" might be more fruitfully understood, then, as just enough depiction of things as they are to make possible a larger point about things as they could—and even in some cases—should be.

In a review of Rider Haggard's courtroom adventure *Mr. Meeson's Will* (1888), Nathaniel Newmark posed the broader question,

> Where would the novelist of the period be without the disinheriting will, the manipulated will, the secreted will, and all kinds of wills in every style of obliteration and in every stage of destruction? Why, he would be nearly as bereft of staple stock in trade as if he had lost the lovelorn maiden, the tender-hearted soldier, or the grand old "hall of my ancestors." (467)[11]

---

[10] "It is not commonly the specific law of the novel which is wrong; more frequently it is the atmosphere of the court which we miss from the novelist's pictures. The speeches are not the kind which a lawyer would make; the examination of witnesses are not of a character which would be committed, or even attempted; and the blunders are of a kind which [...] we all learned to avoid in the first year of our practice. We have much in fiction about law and lawyers, and much of it is excellent; but where it is so it is almost invariably by some one so connected with the profession as to give him an inside view of its workings" (Wilkinson 218).

[11] Allan Campbell also cited *Mr. Meeson's Will* in his 1902 speech criticizing novelists' understanding and use of law. The irony of Campbell's argument, however, is

Anticipating L.S. Lewis's similar observation (in the epigraph to this book) that wills had become an especially rich plot device in the latter years of the nineteenth century, Newmark characterized the will as "machinery to help make the story go" ("Wills in Fiction" 467), but he was only half right. In many novels, the will is a source of narrative conflict, an obstacle characters must maneuver around, or, in other examples, that God-like voice from the beyond rewarding the just through the timely spread of wealth and confirmation of pedigree. As fanciful as these outcomes sometimes are in fiction, they are not unheard of in the real world, as the examples of curious wills has shown. Rather, if in fiction wills became a popular mechanism to "help make the story go," it was because they were already so in life.

Writers such as Newmark and Lewis did not always discriminate between the popular and serious literature they discussed, although Newmark does refer in this piece to S. Baring-Gould (who wrote his own essay on "Strange Wills" for *Once a Week*) as an author "of a higher grade" than those writing in the more sensational or popular vein. One has to be mindful, however, that the ubiquity of wills in popular literature means that the idea of the will is circulating in a much wider context in the last third of the century. There is much to be said on this point about the spread of literacy, changes in education, circulating libraries, increased wealth and improved standards of living (including leisure time), but these social changes alone do not explain a cultural interest in wills as the subject of this reading.[12] In his prologue to the review, Newmark also reflected on a new project inspired by that old but "interesting" article "Law in Romance" which attests to the breadth of this interest in wills: "it would be interesting to bridge over a period of nearly a quarter of a century since this review of law in fiction was written, and merely to survey the notable novels in which the story hinges upon the execution or validity of wills" (468). I have said that Newmark was only half right about the will's usefulness as a plot device because the will can be (and often is) more than a tool to generate action; it is also a means of revealing character, both that of the testator and of those heirs or legatees whose lives his will most affected. The difference between action and character, the world as it is and as it ought to be, between the novel and the romance are points rarely discussed in essays such as Newmark's which use the terms "Law in Romance," but they form an important conceptual background about literary conventions and the purpose of what we so loosely call the novel. The point to keep in mind here is the distinction between idealism and realism, not to argue, as proponents of each side in the debate did, that plot or character is categorically more important than the other, so much as to ask why one or the other was preferred at a given cultural moment. Why does the will become such a fetish when it does? Why are all those associations and aspirations mapped onto the will? And what can these tell us about

---

that it demonstrates the lawyer's literal-mindedness and strict adherence to rules, which Haggard spoofed in his novel. For more on Haggard's legal parody, see Frank.

[12] For discussion of reading practices throughout the century, see Richard Altick's classic *The English Common Reader: a Social History of the Mass Reading Public*.

the scope of the novel and its relationship to law? The answer, in brief, is that the will was both a document and a concept that resonated for both realists and idealists at the end of the century, when many of the "law and literature" essays were written, as well as earlier when the novel was gaining its own definition and stature in the world of nineteenth-century literature.

The will and the novel grew together in the nineteenth century. The will became an empirical register of the testator's desire and the law's social control, while the realist novel engaged readers in the creation of minutely imagined literary worlds that cultivated an affective response, be it endorsement or critique, to social realities. Read as a legal text, especially within the context of contemporary debates about free-will and determinism, the documentary will embodies the tensions between a testator's desires and his legal capacity to express and enact them.[13] The novel, notwithstanding the "powers of the omnipotent novelist" to control and will the behavior of his or her characters (David 74), opened such models of legal subjectivity and the world they inhabit to scrutiny by a wider audience.

Readers agreed from the outset to accept a world of interconnectedness, though it may seem fantastic to their fragmented and incomplete experience, because it gave them a vision of bounded wholeness within which to locate themselves. This is not the negatively phrased suspension of disbelief, but a positive engagement with recognizable forms in a symbolic register, which allows readers to participate more fully and self-consciously in shaping the world that, in the factual social register, comes to them in large part ready-made. That is, the novel can examine the fictional or symbolic quality of all social constructs by importing the real into its realm and redefining the boundaries for meaning. In this sense, realism need not be understood as an invocation of reality for its own sake, but as a means of

[13] One of the most useful discussions of philosophies of the self is John Reed's *Victorian Will* that not only gives a fine historical account of developing theories, but reads several Victorian novels for their imbrication with the concept of the metaphysical will. See especially Reed's characterization of the Victorian's "reflective" and "optimistic" concepts of self (9, 13). In contrast to the romantics, nineteenth-century philosophers viewed the human will as capable of action and self-determinism even though they also felt that such action had to be attached to some larger purpose. That purpose might be defined in religious terms, or in the secular terms of science and natural law, but whatever the domain, the point is that individual agency was scrutinized and frequently deemed capable of meaningful action. But if men had the power of self-determination, that will needed, as James Stephen advocated, a strong hand of external "moral and political authority" to guide it (19). And so we see that the best expression of will is self-restraint (402), whether it be the Christian submission to God's will, the fatalists' "stoic endurance," or the self controlled by a sense of higher purpose that the "secular determinists" espoused. If the legal institution is added to Reed's list, the last will and testament becomes an expression of individual intention and an active ordering of one's public material universe in terms of one's (private) sense of volition. But to enter a legal domain is also to submit to its authority and to act within the confines of its higher, public (communal) purpose that does not always match one's own.

evaluating it.[14] So when George Eliot, for example, separates the legal effectiveness of the will from the testator's morality, or from the morality of freedom of bequest generally, she is working in a positivistic mode, defined by Bentham and Austin in the legal sphere, that insists that legal commands must be separated from normative questions of morality in order to create a vantage point from which to critique their utility.[15] In the same way that the nineteenth-century novel places the individual character in a communal context and traces how each evaluates the other, so the novel offers itself to a readership that must endorse the reality depicted there before it can succeed.[16] But the status of the novel and the role of the reader were nothing if not contested throughout the century and nowhere so much as in the question of what function this new genre might have in shaping and reflecting its community of readers.[17]

---

[14] An anonymous contributor to the *Prospective Review* suggested that as society expands and becomes more self-analytical, so too does the novel. It becomes a sounding board or platform for discussing the large questions of the day, the answers to which are tried out in fictional form, "assuming an imaginative expression and embodying themselves in concrete form" (in K. Dolin 17). For Dolin and for the critic, the novel has become a market for the exchange of ideas among authors and readers, while the development of narrative techniques designed to involve the reader or "enlarge the sympathies" indicates the communal dimension of the narrative project. Moreover, its typically serialized form in the papers meant that readers viewed the novel literally alongside questions of the day, so that when the novel's subject was the law, the "imaginary world" of justice was also being grounded within the reader's "everyday life" (19).

[15] See Robin West's discussion of the legal positivists on morality in *Narrative, Authority, and Law*: "To see law solely and exclusively as expressive of political power, as a part of that which is rather than of that which ought to be, [...] is the first and necessary step toward both legal criticism and morally progressive reform" (3–4).

[16] Catherine Belsey in *Critical Practice* objects specifically to the model of the author as mediator between reader and reality and, indeed, to the concept of reader consensus in general. She defines classic realism as "expressive realism:" "the theory that literature reflects the reality of experience as it is perceived by one (especially gifted) individual who expresses it in a discourse which enables other individuals to recognize it as true" (7). The enabling discourse in this case (apart from empiricism) is humanism, to which Belsey objects because it fosters a view of people as "the origin and source of meaning, of action, and of history" that hides what is really their interpolation in a system that deprives them of real autonomy (67). For the most part Belsey exemplifies the post-structuralist position so adverse to realism. Where the consensual position argues that author and reader are jointly responsible for objectifying the world, she retorts that one of the humanism/realism dyad's most treacherous practices is its suppression of the "role of language in the construction of the subject;" the reader cannot freely agree to the author's vision because the author's use of language has created that reader in the first place.

[17] The classic study of realism is of course Ian Watt's *The Rise of the Novel: Studies in DeFoe, Richardson, and Fielding*. For discussion of Victorian realism, see Levine; McGowan; Furst; and Pascal's "Narrative." On the role of the reader, see Ermarth.

Edwin Eigner suggests that in the early part of the era, to speak of a theory of the English novel would be to speak in tongues: foreign tongues, more precisely, since "theory" was associated with a continental mentality (*Victorian Criticism* 1).[18] For the English was reserved a "doctrinaire realism," or one focused on action, objectivity, and description. For Bulwer Lytton, who wanted the novel to take its place as an art form, such a limited focus was neither sufficiently ambitious nor particularly "true" for that matter. In his 1838 essay "On Art in Fiction," Bulwer provided the clearest articulation of the romantic or idealist conception of the novel by proposing that the novel had to incorporate philosophy and attempt "metaphysical analysis" if it were to achieve artistic status (in Eigner 30). As he wanted the novel to have a system, so, too, did he want the novelist to have a "conception" or "preconceived design" that would prevent the action from dictating a story's development (30)—a mistake that impedes author and reader's ability to *use* the story.[19] He does not dismiss the importance of "incident" or careful description, but he is very clear that the novel should really urge the reader to self-study, appeal to his sense of humanity, and cause him to think about the novel's themes. To accomplish this end, the novel had to focus more fully on the way the world should be, rather than how it was (25). Later advocates of this so-called "idealism," such as Henry James (whose 1884 essay "The Art of Fiction" shows just how far Bulwer's hopes for art *in* fiction had been achieved), thus opposed delineation of character or theme to incident or action, preferred exploration of subjectivity to objectivity, and in some schools advocated didacticism instead of pure description.[20]

---

[18] Even more than the theory of realism, the term's history is especially prone to complication. Hardy called it "copyism" ("Science of Fiction" 262), and although literary realism tends to be associated most strongly with the Victorian novel in England, its nearest relative is the *vraisemblance* of Balzac's and Flaubert's French school. In both of these instances, the word denotes fidelity in representation to the material world, its surroundings and experiences, because they are the means by which we discover truths about our existence. But this definition is a direct inversion of its originally philosophical, Aristotelian meaning, a lost distinction George Gissing particularly lamented because it created such confusion about the novel's function (Barnett 179). "Realism" in literature, that is, is much closer to philosophical *idealism* and its notion that the world is ontologically dependent on our perception of it. However, when the material world is felt to become more complex and our senses less able to convey the right ideas, as occurs throughout the nineteenth century, we arrive at a version of literary representation that comes closest to resembling philosophical realism in the sense that the idea is once again prominent and separated from things. This is, as Levine suggests, the "modernist predicament" (9) that reiterates the questions so often asked by the Victorians: what is real and what does literature have to do to help us understand this?

[19] See also Linda Peterson's discussion of "practical hermeneutics" in relation to the development of autobiographical writing in the nineteenth century, 22–8.

[20] In *The Metaphysical Novels*, Eigner delineates a paradox in the relationship of idealist methodology to its message. In an effort to guide the reader to consideration of metaphysical questions, the author of romance retains his controlling presence in the text. Realists, in contrast, opted for an invisible narrator, which allowed the story to develop in

Although George Eliot shared Bulwer's conviction that the novel should appeal to one's sense of humanity or sympathy, she differs in the means through which this appeal could best be made. In "Silly Novels by Lady Novelists" (1856) she deplores the precocity of "lady novelists" who pretended to know more than they did in contrast to those "who have modestly contented themselves with putting their experience into fiction, and have thought it quite a sufficient task to exhibit men and things as they are" (450).[21] For Eliot the proper, or realistic, course of novel-writing is the recording of one's personal experience that in its referentiality and communality is also universally true.

The dichotomy between romantic idealism and novel realism gained such solidity and circulated so widely that David Masson felt compelled to comment in 1859, "The terms Real and Ideal have been so run upon of late, that their repetition begins to nauseate; but they must be kept, for all that till better equivalents are provided" (150).[22] Using Thackeray and Dickens as exemplars of the real and ideal modes respectively, he suggests that literature has room for both and its evaluation must be conducted in the terms of the school a novel can be said to invoke. "The question with the Real artist, with respect to what he conceives, is," he asks,

> 'How would this actually be in nature; in what exact setting of surrounding particulars would it appear?' and, with a view to satisfy himself on this question, he dissects, observes, and recollects all that is in historical relation to his conception. The question with the Ideal artist is, 'What can be made out of this; with what human conclusions, ends, and aspiration can it be imaginatively interwoven, so that the whole, though attached to nature by its origin, shall transcend or overlie nature on the side of the possibly existent—the might, could, or should be, or the might, could, or should have been?' (151)

---

accordance with its own internal consistency, which in turn enabled the reader's knowledge to develop empirically from experience (63). The irony is that readers were more comfortable with the realist mode of writing even though it actually told harsher truths than they were with the typically more optimistic messages the romance authors were so busy making sure the reader would understand (64).

21 Women's main impediment is their limited education (a thought to be echoed and expanded in Woolf's *A Room of One's Own* [1929]), where greater experience than theirs had not enabled even men to answer the great questions. The "woman of true culture," in contrast, is one who "had [sic] absorbed her knowledge instead of being absorbed by it" (Eliot "Silly Novels" 455) and—this is the crucial prerequisite for novel-writing—had consequently developed a greater sense of perspective about herself and her understanding of the world around her. Thus, she comes to provide not just "information," or "the raw material of culture," but culture's core constituent, "sympathy" (455).

22 G.H. Lewes had attempted such a neologism in 1858 when he collapsed the distinction between novel and romance, or realism and idealism, and pitted the new hybrid against "falsism." Here the most authentic representation of life would become possible only when the author is able to select necessary details, rather than merely to record them all, and to deal in the larger questions once reserved to idealism (Eigner 3). Clearly, the alternative was not a success, not least because it made the new "realism" far too broad to be meaningful.

Masson's questions draw attention to the temporal focus of the novel and the romance: realists are present-focused, while idealists use the present as a means of discussing either past or future. Because the written will combines the material and metaphysical interests of both camps, Masson's formulation provides another means of viewing the novel of wills as bridging this literary divide. Because it invokes all three modes—the past of the deceased testator, the present of the testator seeking to order the world that succeeds him, and the future of the beneficiaries who exist in that later world and are influenced by the past—the testamentary novel uses devices and raises questions that complicate our sense of what a "realistic" novel might be.

Debate about the merits of idealism and realism tells us how novelists understood the relationship between fiction and the real. An anonymous reviewer insisted in 1853 that the novelist had a duty to invent an "ideal world in the midst of prosaic realities" (Eigner 85–6), an injunction which can be further specified as the question, what sort of ideal world might the novel fashion out of prosaic legal realities? Masson surveyed the novel and found that "its capabilities have been increasing simultaneously as regards each of the three kinds of intellectual exercise which make up total literature—History, Philosophy, and Poetry" (in Eigner 152). His salubrious view of the novel's progress within "total literature" not only belies charges of simple mimeticism often made against it, but it also provides a template for the novel's participation in other discourses and its project of changing the real into what it "ought to be" (in Eigner 151). In this framework, the novel's incorporation of the will (even to the extent that made its very inclusion seem "prosaic") is a direct statement of literature's reformation of the law.

Literature has engaged with many legal issues and appropriated other legal forms, most notably the trial, but the will surpasses even it in terms of its appearance in the nineteenth-century novel. One reason the will seems especially suited to the purposes of realistic representation is its great "narrative potential" (Green-Lewis 19). As was clear to Finlay Knight, those plot elements that are the mainstay of the Victorian novel have a real-life corollary in the will. It has a cast of characters: orphans and illegitimate children, heiresses and widows, heroes and villains; it deals with alliances and animosities; fortunes are made or broken by a will and conditions set down that alter the life-course of survivors. In addition, the will deals explicitly in tangibles and has real results, even as it raises crucial metaphysical questions of human intention and agency. As a voluntary and apparently unmediated expression of the testator's intention, the will plays havoc with the idea of legal determinism, but the existence of extensive legal forms and a web of attendant laws that predetermine what the testator can do with his own property forcibly illustrate the degree to which his metaphysical ability to conceive and enact are circumscribed by real social institutions. Although the will may have a closural function in the legal world, in the literary, its encoding of the negotiation of self and society generates the sort of conflict that in D.A. Miller's terms makes it an eminently "narratable" subject. If one were looking for a single or one-dimensional model of the novel (and of reading the novel), this mixture would certainly lead to an impasse, and that is perhaps part of what surprises about the post-structural problem with the novel: that it looks for the novel, particularly the capacious Victorian novel, to do one thing only.

More recent studies of the novel that embrace its polyglossia seem more "realistic" because, while they view the genre as constructing a single world, it is a single world of great variety.[23] Just as the novel as a form envelops multiplicity, so does it benefit from, if not demand, reading practices that do the same. Like the novel, the will's own mixture of materialism and metaphysics enables a reading of its dual nature. In novels that combine the literary and the legal, and embrace the will as its focus of investigation, the will can become the fulcrum in a balance between romantic, ideal individualism and real, socially determined selfhood. I say "romantic," "ideal," "real," and "social" purposely to call forth the terms of the nineteenth-century debate over realism and to observe that they are equally instructive of the centrality of the documentary will in Victorian novels which, rather than opposing realism and romance, inextricably entangle them.

A Literary Heritage: Mid-Victorian Testamentary Novels

Although the general public had been reading legal novels long before the genre was given its name, the new interest which lawyers took at the end of the century—to a greater extent in America, it has to be said, than in England—suggests a new sensitivity to the profession's public image as well as a desire to distinguish law and law-writing (real legal acumen) from the amateur lawyering of novelists. Whatever motivated the respective professionals, readers had much to choose from: Wigmore lists five novels by Wilkie Collins, seven by Dickens, only three by George Eliot, but an impressive eleven by Walter Scott, and he

[23] Linda Shires suggests that the only way to read the novel is through a dialectic of "partial views" that can come to provide more insight than any single perspective (63). Similarly, Lillian Furst advocates recognition of the way the novel is at once a "record" and a "texture of verbal signs" (24). John McGowan's model of "representation and revelation" also makes room for two modes of experience as a narrative route to knowledge (for both character and reader) in the novel. Similarly, George Levine has highlighted the "mixed conditions" of the novel, while the oxymoron "metaphysical novel" belongs to Edwin Eigner, who suggests that the generic splits within a single Victorian text are not the results of error, as critics believed, but their authors' intentional engagement with realism for the sake of more idealistic aims (9, 11). Adding to this collection of views, Elizabeth Ermarth argues for a consensual mode of reading through which repeated exposure to a view *per se* establishes an "horizon" of meaning, or sets boundaries for meaning, that permit the viewer to evaluate what falls within them without changing the basic make-up of the things represented (16). Transposing this consensual world to the legal sphere, Kieran Dolin borrows Robert Cover's theory of the *nomos* or "normative universe" that provides a framework for understanding the ways law and literature operate on the basis of agreement.

concedes that the list is incomplete (125).[24] A list of novels that feature or refer to the will would be too great to compile even here, and what I offer is a brief chronology only of some of the more notable examples in order to provide a sense of how use of the will changed over time. However, the prevalence of testamentary documents in the Victorian novel provides circumstantial evidence at least that the will's properties made it appealing to writers as a way of working out their own positions in the debates over the novel and literature's superior modes of representing character.

In *Wuthering Heights* (1847), Brontë works more closely than the realist Eliot, for instance, within the romantic tradition and its focus on the primacy of the internal self in interpreting the material world. Heathcliff's self-perception, for example, does not change with his financial circumstances; he is as vigorous and demanding as a man of wealth as he was as an obscure boy. His sense of Cathy's betrayal (and hence his motive for revenge) lies chiefly in his view of her failure to adhere to her own romantic impulses, her attempt to make her interior match the exterior of Edgar's social standing and its accoutrements. Associating individual subjectivity with the possession of things, she allies herself with Edgar's refined persona instead of Heathcliff's uncouth yet more authentic character (uncouth because natural, unadulterated by social concerns). In this way, her choice between the two men is a choice between her romantic and realist selves, which articulates Brontë's own ideological conflict between an arguably more vibrant and emotive romanticism that could resist social and moral strictures and her sense of the growing primacy of realism and its orderly world of things.[25]

If Cathy lives as a realist in defiance of her other, romantic self, and dies in the process of bringing forth the daughter who symbolizes the union of these contrary forces, one must ask: who is fit to survive in the coming new world? Cathy dies because she lived an unresolved life. Heathcliff's mastery, in contrast, is a strong counterforce to the coming world—one that could use its own terms and tools against it, as he does when he returns from abroad unchanged in all but financial position, or when he wins the Heights from Hindley and trains Hareton to hate his father. Maria Aristodemou argues that Heathcliff embodies a pre-Symbolic principle that places him outside the law yet enables him to adopt its standards and redeploy them against the social world (113). The ease with which he does this suggests, on the one hand, the lawlessness of the Heights (Nelly threatens to inform on Heathcliff

---

[24] He also concedes that his categories and selections invite argument. See John H. Wigmore, "A List of Legal Novels."

[25] Maria Aristodemou provides a similar reading of the novel as Brontë's experiment with romantic and realist principles. While I agree with her general view of literature as an imaginative counter to the law's efforts to maintain the "inevitability" of its constructs, I depart from her sense that realism is the only aesthetic mode that does want to be taken as real, in other words, that mimesis is an end in itself. Accordingly, I share many of her particular claims about *Wuthering Heights*, but do not agree that the novel's merits are directly proportional to its resistance to realism. For a psychoanalytic reading of the novel, see chapter five of her *Law and Literature* (105–31).

for forcing Catherine to marry Linton, "There's law in the land [...] though we be in an out-of-the-way place" [208]). On the other hand, Heathcliff's manipulation suggests that the laws themselves are rhetorical strategies rather than inevitabilities, and that to continue the struggle requires both desire and willingness on his part.

Heathcliff dies only because he concedes the fight, not because he was about to lose it. As he observes to Nelly, Catherine and Hareton's friendship—their ability to thrive in spite of his efforts to "demolish" them—is "an absurd termination to [his] violent exertions" (244). He explains, "I get levers and mattocks to demolish the two houses, and when everything is ready, and in my power, I find the will to lift a slate off either roof has vanished!" (244–5). Heathcliff's power as the vengeful testator is well intact; what lacks is the will. His animosity towards his enemies has been expressed, first, in his acquisition of their "two houses" and, second, in his tyranny over their children, a true visitation of the sins of the father—and mother—on the next generation. In the most striking example, after orchestrating the marriage between Linton and Catherine, Heathcliff shows her his son's will in which he left all his property ("what had been her, moveable property") to his father. Though Zillah provided the details, Nelly interprets the story and recognizes that "the poor creature" Linton "was threatened, or coaxed, into that act" (223) with the result that Catherine "cannot disturb his possession."[26] If ever there were a case of undue influence, a compelling argument could be made for the invalidity of Linton's will. However, even though this particular testament expresses Heathcliff's desire, not Linton's, Brontë allows it to remain a potentially effective legal instrument in the plot. Brontë uses the linguistic tools of realism as the "levers and mattocks" to pave the way towards Heathcliff's revenge by linking exterior structures with internal meaning—the literal houses and their symbolic function as signs of a past wrong (such tools can be creative as well as desctructive). But she also gives him, in contrast, the legal structure of the last will whose internal meaning can be manipulated through coaxing and threats and yet remain intact. Nevertheless, if Heathcliff has gathered those signs of authority and control in order to proclaim the way that his will gives them meaning rather than the other way around, that will must respond to a higher purpose; it must be attached to and actuated by something beyond itself (Reed 19). "But where is the use?" Heathcliff asks, "I have lost the faculty of enjoying their destruction, and am too idle to destroy for nothing" (245).

---

[26] Nelly, ever watchful, is right to wonder about the legality of Heathcliff's claims. She notes that the real estate could not pass under Linton's will because he was still a minor, and so Heathcliff "claimed and kept them in his wife's right, and his also, I suppose, legally" (223). Isabella's elopement precluded the possibility of a marriage settlement for herself or her children, and in this sense Heathcliff might well have claimed all her property. However, Edgar Linton's own will, which he altered after learning of Catherine's marriage, should have prevented even this. In his new will, "Instead of leaving Catherine's fortune at her own disposal, he determined to put it in the hands of trustees, for her use during life, and for her children, if she had any, after her. By that means, it could not fall to Mr. Heathcliff should Linton die" (214).

Where Cathy has exhibited Brontë's stylistic division between romanticism and realism, the intuitive self that sees directly into things versus the self that depends on things to mediate and even to change meaning, in this passage Brontë makes Heathcliff her spokesman. The romantic character he represents might survive in the world and in the novel of things, but he would remain antagonistic to it, determined to destroy the community that was coming to envelop and define the figure of the individual. Already cut off from the one person he actually does love, Heathcliff perceives that to enact his revenge would only remove his reason for living and thus compound the misery of separation; he could destroy this second generation, but reunion with Cathy in a world beyond material concerns has taken on a higher purpose than revenge. His tantalizing visions of Cathy at the novel's end redefine his monomania, and thus he concedes the fight without necessarily losing it.

Through her use of the wills, Brontë reveals the emptiness of material forms that have no informing volition in them, or, worse, the danger of forms whose outward appearance and social sanction disguise either the absence of will or its distortion, its replacement with someone else's desire. Heathcliff's own will remains unwritten, ostensibly because he cannot decide how to leave the property, yet, rejecting both legal and spiritual guidance, his avoidance of the task and his wish that he could "annihilate it [the property] from the face of the earth" (252) suggest more tellingly that in his case the document itself would be a meager formalization of desires he has expressed in action throughout his life, on the one hand, and that finally his desires themselves have changed, on the other. Brontë's own contribution to the novel debates, offered through the formal strategies of *Wuthering Heights*, suggests that she, too, could choose to invoke realist tools to satisfy aesthetic desires that were ultimately more romantic. She defies the linearity of realism, but her convoluted structure departs equally from the idealists' care to lead the reader towards a preconceived point. She provides multiple narrators who could supply the various views that together might form a unified picture so important to realism, but then Heathcliff's experience is so unassimilable to everyone else's that as a hero he cannot be said to represent anyone beyond himself. Arguably, Brontë, like Heathcliff, sees a use in realism, but she also sees it as a temporal, secular corruption of the integrity of a natural, even supernatural, order in which, as Heathcliff puts it, "the entire [material] world is but a collection of memoranda" of Cathy's continued spiritual existence (245). In Brontë's treatment of the wills, she offers an example of the way metaphysics and materiality, romance and realism, co-exist, albeit antagonistically, in her "novel."

Wuthering Heights marks a point in the chronology of nineteenth-century fiction when the aims of idealism and realism were offered as answers to the question of what the novel should represent and how representation should proceed. The novel's focus on property pushes it towards a greater materialism, but the choice of the will offers a way-out, so to speak, of the conundrum. Even in the most realist of novels, the will's presence allows for discussion of the relationship between desire, intention, and its effects. These are key components of character in the novel, as well as in moral and philosophical understandings of subjectivity; yet by highlighting these, the novel did the further work of modifying an increasingly bureaucratic turn in law towards documentation. That is, where the law presented the will as a fantasy of unified selfhood, the novel adopted the document (thereby serving its own interests in cueing readers to a recognizable material milieu) and showed the real, potential disjunction between the legal presentation of an identity in documents and the personality thus reduced and represented.

The quintessential realist novel, Eliot's *Middlemarch* (1872) includes three wills and, although her fastidious and patronizing Casaubon, much less the petulant Featherstone, would hardly seem to have a forerunner in Brontë's Byronic hero, both of them, like Heathcliff, view the control of property as the best means to control other people and thus to satisfy their self-obsessions. Ironically, neither succeeds, or at least not in the ways they expected, but their failures are illustrative of the problems (for the testator, the lawyer, and the novelist alike) of framing intention, securing it through writing, and making it effective in and constitutive of the many communities (familial, municipal, legal, and imagined) to which one belongs. Two questions are posed during the course of Eliot's narrative—the narrator's "who shall tell what may be the effect of a writing?" (386) and Dorothea's own musing, "Was inheritance a question of liking, or responsibility?" (394)—which, when viewed together, unite the characters in the communities of Middlemarch. They also bring together my central concerns with freedom of bequest, the constraint of inheritance, and the literary critique of legal forms which must nonetheless confront the novel's own problems of reconciling formal conventions and desired effects. This problem—the potential mismatch between form, content, and function—becomes especially acute when the basis of literature's critique of law and its use of language goes directly to the foundations of subjectivity and the ordering of communities. How to make an imagined world seem real? How to engage readers in its creation yet maintain control of the narrative? As the narrator acknowledges (contemplating the scrap of paper that alerts John Raffles to Bulstrode's presence and hence the possibilities of blackmail), "a writing" once let loose assumes an independent life in spite of attempts to tether it to intention or frame it by circumstances.

As we have seen in Chapter 1, reverence for the legal form (within the legal community at least) means the will's effectiveness as an expression of testamentary desire will always be assumed, and for this reason testators were urged to have their wills drawn by a professional man: so that he might know his intentions and express them rightly, avoiding language that, albeit effective, would not achieve his desired ends. Testamentary language, after all, can neither be recanted by the deceased nor answered by the living until after it's been uttered. Endorsed by law, this language creates a speaking likeness not just of the testator and his character, but also of the people named and described in it. What endorses Eliot's language, though? What warrants readers' acceptance of the novel's rendition of character and culture, its embodiment through writing of individual wills coexisting and acting in a communal context? What does her literary handling of the last will and testament imply about the uses of language in maintaining community?

As in *Wuthering Heights*, the will's two essential elements of material form and informing volition are broken apart, rearranged, and reconstituted in a variety of ways in *Middlemarch.* Featherstone's wills (he tells Mary Garth he has made two, but Lawyer Standish confirms that he had drawn up three, even apart from the surprise will made by the lawyer from Brassing) are both legally drawn and properly executed documents. They express his intentions at the times they were written and are assumed to speak from the moment of his death, but, as the scene with Mary dramatizes, at the moment of his death, Featherstone's last wishes took no written form, except that of the novel. Still, it is effective, both as a legal instrument and as a catalyst for the plot. The petty tyrant Causabon's will and its infamous codicil are also effective documents, but they also fail to accomplish his actual desire to keep Dorothea from Will Ladislaw and bind her to the completion of his work on the *Key*. Through his will, the law makes good on his threat to disinherit her, but we can only imagine that it is small compensation, not just for the memory of Casaubon that the will creates, but also—in what amounts to the same thing—for the failure of the project that should have been his legacy. The more interesting commonality between these paired wills of Featherstone and Casaubon are the way they house secrets, the keys to each one's cherished plans and jealousies—Featherstone's to surprise and disappoint his relatives (to say nothing of his having a son) and Causabon's to preserve himself in language by binding Dorothea in "painful subjection" (464) to his project. Their effects, however, divide on comic/tragic lines. Reading these wills together shows the will's usefulness as a principle of order in a world created in harmony with the law, on the one hand. On the other hand, it shows the violent potential behind the order created and maintained by strict adherence to legal forms.[27] In the same ways that Dorothea and Will must imagine a new life for themselves and inhabit an alternative world outside of the one projected in Causabon's will, however, so does the novel offer readers a way of seeing in things as they are, things that might be.

Featherstone is nothing if not the exemplum of those mercurial testators who see their will (or wills as the case may be) as an occasion to disappoint and frustrate fortune-hunting relatives and mete out justice for their trivial offenses. For those testators, the will's primary function may not be amusement and diversion, but Featherstone's collateral enjoyment is one of the chief adjuncts of this exercise of power, or what Hazlitt called "a trial of skill between the legacy-hunter and the legacy-maker, which shall fool the other" (118). In the end, and much to her chagrin, it is Mary Garth who fools both, however. Keeping her usual vigil at Featherstone's bedside, Mary hears him "rattling his bunch of keys against the tin

[27] See Robin West's discussion of "interactive communities" whose moral bearing "depends entirely on the quality of [...] affective interaction," for example, the degree to which our being with others supports or represses them ("Communities, Texts, and Law" 146).

box" that lay beneath his bedcovers. Ordering her to come nearer, he opens the box and reveals yet another key which will give Mary access to another chest and another will stored there.[28] Featherstone's directions are coupled with assertions of a sound, disposing mind—"I've got all my faculties"; "I know all my property, and where the money's put out, and everything" (296)—as well as his intention to change his mind, all of which is warranted by the familiar maxim that freedom of bequest enables him to "do as I like at the last." In this case, that means burning one of the wills. When Mary objects, he repeats that he is "in [his] right mind" and invokes, this time as a question, the property-owner's right to "do as I like at the last" (297). When these appeals fail, he offers a bribe, throughout the exchange holding forth the key—"holding the one key erect on the ring" (297); "stretch[ing] out the key towards her"; "his bony hand holding out the key" (298); "dropping his keys" in order to throw his stick at her, but "taking his keys again" so that when he dies, it is "with his right hand clasping the keys" (299)—and repeating the words, "I shall do as I like." Mary's refusal to touch either the key, the money, the chest, or the will is based on her own conviction that to tamper with anything so solemn as the will, especially in the middle of the night and at a sick man's bedside, will put her under suspicion. She was probably correct, just as Featherstone had been that her burning the will in his presence and in accordance with his wishes would have been a valid revocation.[29] In the event, however, the will is not revoked, nor

[28] This scene recalls the hidden wills in *Our Mutual Friend*, their hiddenness a sign of the opacity of legal language and the difficulty of locating intention. See also Theobald Pontifex's "shake of the will" in Butler's *The Way of All Flesh*, begun just one year after the publication of Eliot's novel, as the counterpart to this key-dangling.

[29] Recall, however, Allan Campbell's complaint that although by section 22 of the Wills Act, the mere destruction of a second will could not revive a former one, at the time the novel was written, the law "was just the other way" (365). Section 20, however, explains the steps that will revoke a will. Not only does Featherstone possess the *animus revocandi* so important in judges' decisions, but he also had every intention of watching Mary burn the will. But as Dr. Deane, Queen's Counsel argued in *Cheese v. Lovejoy* (1876), "All the destroying in the world without intention will not revoke a will, nor all the intention in the world without destroying it: there must be the two" (253). See also *Powell v. Powell* (1866) and its application of the doctrine of dependent relative revocation; *Andrew v. Motley* (1862) which held that "mere abandonment" of a will without its destruction in the testator's presence and by his direction would not revoke it; *Giles and Clark v. Warren* (1872) in which the testator destroyed his will on the false assumption that it was invalid; *Brunt v. Brunt* (1873) in which the testator destroyed his will in a fit of delirium tremens. Sir J. Hannen held that "the act done by the testator can in no sense be considered his act, for he was out of his mind; so that there has never been anything at all amounting to a revocation" (38–9). In *Jenner v. Finch* (1879) the President of the Probate Division referred to s. 20 of the Wills Act and determined that "no express words of revocation are necessary" in a duly executed second will since "the authorities now appear to establish that revocation by implication is sufficient" (111). The more surprising aspect of his decision was the admission of external evidence as to Emma Loring's intention regarding her wills since the "instrument," when considered in light of what was known about her, "raised a doubt." But see *Brenchley v.*

is she spared the suspicion of unhappy relatives. Certainly, she is not spared her own crisis of conscience and wavers between the belief that "it was she who had virtually determined the production of this second will" in favor of Joshua Rigg (314) and the consciousness "that fatally, without will of her own" her inaction had disinherited Fred Vincy (319).

But what has been the result of this second will? Standish reads both to the assembled relatives on the assumption that Featherstone, not having destroyed the first one, wanted both to be heard. Featherstone's instructions regarding the funeral and his contemplation of the lawyer's surprise at discovering another will confirm that he wanted his testament to annoy and astonish (304, 314), but not even he imagined publicizing one set of bequests only to take them away. The principal effect of the second will, in any event, is to enlarge the real and personal property designated for Featherstone's son, not for Fred Vincy, with the remainder to go to the establishment of Featherstone Almshouses for old men (317). Although there is dark humor in the idea of his using even charity as a weapon, these results are comic in the sense that they support what we as readers have been positioned to see as a rational, even natural order. Sycophantic relatives have been disappointed; Fred has been saved from the idle life money would have enabled him to continue living, and the illegitimate son has been restored to his patrimony. That there is no actual love lost between the father and his equally scheming son—who hides his plans to sell Stone Court—only completes the circle. Mary's story has given us access, in ways that the will and the lawyer cannot, to a more complete story of intention, and it's tempting to think of it as another example of literature's better ability to constitute and represent subjectivity than the law's. However, in this case, Mary's story exposes Featherstone as the testator who cried wolf, whose indecisive tampering with his will—not Mary's—led to his own disappointment. The poetic justice of this fable aligns Eliot's novel with the law, but it makes both of them subject to a higher order in which the legal justice of Featherstone's will seems more accidental than deliberate.

Like Featherstone, Causabon has his key as well, but the will it leads to is more malign—if not less valid—than either of Featherstone's. Eliot constructs Casaubon as a man defined by words (P. Milton 60) for whom the control of language becomes as much a part of his estate as the things within it and, therefore, an integral part of his personhood. In his lifetime, his sense of self is entirely bound up with the unfinished *Key to All Mythologies*. Sensible of his own failing health, Casaubon explains to Lydgate that where his body may fail, his work may live on to represent him, but this compensation will be possible only if his wife dedicates herself to the book's completion. The more remarkable text, and the one he does complete, however, is the will. Mistrusting her fidelity to him and thus to

---

Still (1850) regarding the execution of Elizabeth Lynn's will in which Herbert Jenner Fust declaimed, "Grievous indeed would be the state of the law if, upon the loose recollection of witnesses as to the order in which the execution took place, the intentions of the testatrix were to be defeated" (176).

his project, Casaubon threatens Dorothea, in essence seeking to control her by the only material means left to him—the distribution of his property. The validity of his will makes it no idle threat, however. Not only does the will establish that she will inherit only on condition that she not marry Ladislaw, but it also articulates his private suspicions which cast a public slur on her character.

Also like Featherstone's, Casaubon's will is legally effective: a testator might put into place conditions to restrain his widow's remarriage. B.B. West explained that "custom" is more generally the reason behind such conditions, but sometimes sheer "malice prepense" guides the testator in his "wife-robbing" mood. "A self-respecting egotist," he muses, "would assume his wife to be so completely his own as to be incapable of union with another" (60), but Casaubon's egotism lies in paranoia. In *Jenner v. Turner* (1880), moreover, Vice-Chancellor Bacon would decide that "there is no reason nor any authority for saying that a testator may not make it a condition that the person [who is] the object of his bounty shall not marry any particular person by name, or any person of a particular nation, or belonging to any specified class" (196). Moreover, the court cannot question such a testator's motives: "if it could properly be said they had been prompted by spite or malevolence the condition would nevertheless be valid; for the law does not prohibit testators from indulging such bad feelings, provided that no principle of public policy is thereby contravened" (196–7).[30] But if the law cannot judge of motives in such cases, the novel can.

Casaubon's will is met with outrage, embarrassment, and a sense of betrayal, but what differentiates these reactions from those of Featherstone's relatives, for example, is our esteem for the opinions of Dorothea's circle and the knowledge that she has not deserved his suspicion (besides which, there is nothing funny about Casaubon). Neither she nor her friends recognize her in the wayward widow implied by his will; one of the problems for Sir James is precisely that the codicil will make everybody who does *not* know Dorothea believe she was in love with Will, and as the narrator's concluding comments show, Middlemarch lore assumes she was not 'a nice woman' (784). In fact, the codicil is "a positive insult" (455) added secretly to a will that originally had been "made at the time of his marriage with the knowledge and reliance of her family" (455), including Dorothea herself who "knew the purport of her husband's will made at the time of their marriage" (458). Presumably an aspect of her marriage settlement, this open and consensual understanding of the will implies a moral contract that extends beyond the distribution of property and

[30] In *Jenner v. Turner* (1880) Bacon allowed that the will's condition prohibiting the devisee's marriage with a domestic servant was valid because it was neither a general restraint on marriage, nor did it infringe on public policy. For cases decided before *Middlemarch*'s publication, see *Lloyd v. Lloyd* (1852) in which restraint of marriage of the testator's widow was held valid while his attempt to restrain that of a single woman was not; and *Davis v. Angel* (1862) for Lord Westbury's decision that a condition precedent in a will (requiring the testator's nephew to marry a particular niece of the testator in order to enter into a trust) was not overturned by the testator's having agreed to the nephew's marriage, during his lifetime, to someone other than the niece.

informs Dorothea's approach to her marriage. As little inclined as she had been to accept the "new yoke" her husband's cryptic request must entail, for example, she was prepared to submit to it, though "Neither law nor the world's opinion compelled her to this—only her husband's nature and her own compassion, only the ideal and not the real yoke of marriage" (452). Resigned to uphold an idea of marriage as it could or ought to be, she nonetheless delays too long in telling her husband and suffers pangs of conscience that he dies not knowing what she intended. However, the "embittering discovery [...] of secrecy and suspicion" (464) contained in his will is at once an assault on her sensibilities and her autonomy that throws her into "a state of convulsive change" (461). By forcing her hand with his dead one, he reveals "hidden thoughts" that though they may have "pervert[ed] everything she said and did" certainly bring home the naïveté of her belief that continued allegiance to Casaubon would preserve at least the ideal of marriage. Freed from her intended promise by his betrayal, Dorothea reaches her own moral judgment of his motives. As damaging as the picture of Dorothea created by his will might be, it is his own testamentary character that suffers more. At last Casaubon is taken as a man of his words: like the codicil, "there never was a meaner, more ungentlemanly" man (355).

As was true of Featherstone's wills, a kind of retributive justice is served in the novel insofar as Casaubon's will precipitates the very thing it sought to avoid by introducing Dorothea to the possibility of a romance with Will (461). In an insightful moment, Mrs. Cadwallader remarks that Casaubon "had prepared all this as beautifully as possible. He made himself disagreeable [...] and then he dared her to contradict him" (767). That she would take the dare is something her husband might have known, but at bottom the will has done exactly what it was set up to do. This is order, but it is one achieved through humiliation, punishment, and a fully legal manipulation of property, which make women choose between fortune and fulfillment (as Chapter 3 will develop more fully) and gives men the power to frame that choice in the first place. Even Mr. Brooke contemplates breaking the entail of Tipton, transferring the property to Celia's baby Arthur, as a way of formally registering a disapproval he doesn't really feel but which will placate Sir James (783).

The strong preference in trials concerning the validity of wills to trust to the sufficiency of the form itself and to measure its faults by how far it deviates from the rules of the statute explains the fervor with which testators were urged to have their wills drawn up by professionals. Commenting on the "shocking" amount of litigation resulting from poorly written wills, Lord St. Leonards added that when viewed as "a simple money transaction, lawyers might well be in despair if every man's will were prepared by a competent person" (133). Joking aside, what we see in the case law is a focus on the presumption that all acts will have been done rightly and regularly (*omnia rite esse acte*). It is in the nature of the trial to work from effects to causes, and in the case of wills to focus on the finished document not just as evidence of intention, but as the embodiment of intention itself. In *Middlemarch*, however, we participate in a process leading up to these wills—what Featherstone attempted and Mary heard, what Casaubon demanded and Dorothea planned to concede—that allows us to evaluate not whether a will was properly or improperly prepared to take legal effect but whether it is morally actionable. Eliot is not criticizing the practical effect of wills in general or arguing against their necessity. (There is no sense at the end of the novel that readers should disapprove the inheritance of Mr. Brooke's estate by Dorothea's son, for example.) Rather, the novel asks readers to consider them as reflections of their writers' characters and to think about them as powerful tools, possessed by some and as readily susceptible of being used against others as of promoting their welfare. The wills in her novel clearly exert a dramatic pressure on the plot; things happen as a direct result of them, but Eliot is even more interested in her characters' experiences of these imperatives, in particular their sense of whether submitting to the world created by the testator and supported by law promotes human flourishing, or, in contrast, whether it stunts and perverts it. *Middlemarch*'s criticism of law and legal language is directed towards the inequitable distribution of power that opens it to abuse, leaving "young and noble impulse" such as Dorothea's to "struggle[e] amidst the conditions of an imperfect social state" (784). This criticism is clear in the novel's attention to the Reform Bill just as it had been in *Felix Holt*, but it is also clear in the novel's depiction of unrestricted testamentary freedom that makes heirs subject to the whims of their fathers but which was especially powerful in its conjunction with coverture.

Casaubon's betrayal of the contract between himself, his wife, and her family serves as Eliot's own comment on the function of the novel to promote sympathy and to link individual with communal experience. By giving free rein to his own interests and suspicions, Casaubon exercises the prerogative of the testator, but by exempting himself from other values and framing his will solely in reference to his personal desire, he also reaches towards Heathcliff's vengeful isolationism that is so out of place in Eliot's realism. Language in *Middlemarch*, as in the Victorian culture it represents, can generate powerful identities when it derives from or appeals to the "tacit desire for communality" (Green-Lewis 30). When Casaubon writes his will, then, he reveals himself as an outsider in a community that is particularly, and perhaps justifiably, wary of the strangers in their midst (Bustrode, Lydgate, Raffles, and Riggs, even Will: theirs are the actions that disrupt the comfortable sameness of Middlemarch life). In these terms, the legal effectiveness of his will (his adherence to a legalistic community) is almost beside the point—but only almost. The desire for that shared language is strong enough that a willing act of moral transgression such as his is perhaps still more difficult to credit than the false representation it produces, hence Sir James's fear that Casaubon's imputations will be taken as true—and the result that they are.

Wuthering Heights explored the will without legal form and legal forms without will as a way of thinking about the function and style of the novel, what its subjects should be and how they could best be represented. *Middlemarch* explores the same issues by turning to wills replete with testamentary intention. Although Featherstone's story shows the rigidity of documented forms, those snapshots of mood, compared to the fluidity of human feeling and intention, Casaubon's will is consistent with his character and in this sense matches the spirit with its material expression. Eliot uses these wills to separate questions of justice from legality, but they also illustrate differences between the novel's linguistic organization and representation of social relations and the law's. *Middlemarch* implies that law and literature do not share the same language and therefore cannot—or do not wish to—create the same kinds of community, but there would be no competition if law and literature were not trying to do similar things. The novel is voracious; it tries to master many languages or discourses whereas the law tries to impose one. These are different tactics put to the use of giving a comprehensible shape to lived experience. Brontë showed she could be a realist if she wanted to and as clearly showed she did not; Eliot invented a subculture in which individualism such as Dorothea's could be acceptable in spite of the legal effectiveness of Casaubon's will. Their sense of the coercive power of legal language, as well as their rejections of it, is surely owing in part to their position as women and women writers, a point taken up in the next chapter.[31]

Although their resistance answers the question of what the novel could do better than the law, neither retreat nor dismissal are answers that Wilkie Collins reaches in his representations of characters' interactions with the law. Collins's novels of the 1860s, especially *The Woman in White* (1860), *No Name* (1862), and *The Moonstone* (1868), emphasize the importance of legal documentation. The latter two particularly show Collins at work on the proper way to write a will (and the roles women assume in this process) as a corollary to the proper way to write novels. His insistence within his plots on submitting all evidence to professional, institutional authorities implies his submission of the literary to the legal. The "stories of experience" that each narrator supplies, as technically innovative (and ethically balanced) as they initially appear to be, are nonetheless arranged in an overall narrative structure that remains indebted to "strong representation" (Welsh 235). Even Collins's interest in the unconscious is simply a new dimension of an otherwise old issue of how to represent "things not seen" (Welsh 235). Unlike Eliot's realism, then, Collins's sensation fiction ratifies officially sanctioned appearances—and methods—at the expense of individual realities. In *No Name*, for example, the Vanstone's marriage, their family identity, and their daughters' rights as heirs appear to be valid—common knowledge accepts the legitimacy of all these—but because they are not legally recognized and embodied in official legal documents, they are also legally non-existent. In this regard, the novel appears to support more than critique the status quo, making it a disciplinary text more than a liberating one that

---

31 Dorothea becomes a kind of conscientious objector to conventional legal values, as well as to the social codes of Lowick parish, in her marriage to Will. In this regard, Eliot seems equally critical of the moral codes on the basis of which she critiques the law as she is of the positive law itself. To the extent that Mary Garth is reassured by Farebrother's explanation, her conscience reveals, in contrast, a morality whose basis remains within law and is therefore less capable of critique. As with so many of Eliot's pairings, the comparison this doubling allows is a practical illustration of how literary criticism of the law could and could not proceed. For discussion of the limitations of the legal positivists' moral critique, see West, *Narrative, Authority, and Law*, 6–7.

works in conjunction with legal discourse to make identity visible, or in Collins's idiom, to create "recognizable realities" (qtd. in Thomas 63).[32]

The difference between the will and other modes of textual registration, however, is that it constitutes a legal promise that personal autonomy does matter. The gap thus created between the rhetorical presentation of the "will" and the requirements of legal "identity" that it serves—in which personality and idiosyncrasy are interpreted by and reframed in legal language—is the place for the novel to enter. In *The Moonstone* as in *No Name*, Collins submits the literary to the legal by staging a series of capitulations to legal authority, generally centered on women, but he submits the legal to literary authority by excerpting Herncastle's will at the beginning of the novel and comparing it to the narratives about it. These points of the novel's intersection with the law offer competing answers to the question of whether Collins worked with or against legal discourse.

Like Cathy before and Dorothea Brooke after her, Rachel Verinder, for example, acts independently. Her insistence on wearing the moonstone in one sense sets off the chain of events that will end in the deaths both of the falsely suspected Rosanna Spearman and the too-trusted Godfrey Ablewhite. However, as "beneficiary" of her uncle's highly effective will, her inheritance of the cursed diamond is, as Franklin Blake rightly surmises, "a legacy of trouble and danger" to her (58). The curse of the specific bequest heightens the sense in which women's relationship to property is always cursed, always a way of acting out other people's dramas. The particular problematic here is that Rachel so readily assumes the prerogatives of ownership. The ideally welcome condition of being a propertied woman becomes in practice a source of distress and, indeed, is already understood (via Betteredge's narrative) as a case of subterfuge. Rachel is only a nominal heir; like the diamond and the will, she is really a new instrument of revenge on Lady Julia. Her act of independence is thus re-contained by being framed as a bonus in this orchestrated event.

Lady Julia's will offers a second, more pointed version of the propertied woman's submission to legal authority, as well as the potential conflict between private desire

---

[32] See Thomas's discussion of the culture of suspicion out of which sensation fiction arises (23, 28). Suspicion extends the identification of criminality to the identification and registration of all people through the "legitimate institutionalization of the textual construction of identity" (60). Thomas's specific interest in forensic science emphasizes the literal embodiment of personhood—people become discernible as physical signs more so than as collections of abstract qualities—who can then be documented in what amounts to a further remove from the kinds of personality and moral autonomy associated with character (66). His analysis suggests compelling similarities between scientific and legal discourse in so far as identities are not written on the body only but are carried through one's possessions. In these terms, the will's documentation of property becomes the law's way of making identity visible, and the Wills Act a specific instance of law's formal movement towards new models of subjectivity in which identity becomes synonymous with identification. See also Richard Sennett on the physical signs of dress and costume, for example, as public indices not only of social position but of character—the "immanence" of character in public that in private would find expression through behavior (161–74).

and legal, institutional dictates, which the writing of the will occasioned. Matthew Bruff, the family solicitor, describes Lady Julia as the best sort of wife because she prudently does what her husband should have done to provide for his survivors.[33] Bruff's admiration of her rests in her willingness to let him "shape her instructions into the proper legal form" (283) and, when codicils are added, to "embody her recent instructions in a second will." The will is an "embodiment" of her desires whose qualities reflect her own character, yet as a legal document it reflects Bruff's desires as well, especially since this second will allows him to revise aspects of the first that "grated sadly on [his] professional sense of the fitness of things." In Bruff's opinion, Lady Julia's almost instantaneous decision to cede responsibility to the right legal agent shows her proper understanding of women's relationship to the law. In this sense, she emphasizes the point introduced through Rachel, whose insistence on wearing her diamond and ignoring advice demonstrates that when women handle property, untold complications, even tragedies, ensue.[34] In contrast, Sir John's apathy about his property and his cession of responsibility are signs, in Bruff's view, of moral failing. (Sir John's is not a disposing mind, as demonstrated through his tardiness in drafting the will at all and his un-nuanced attitude towards the kind of property he leaves.) But here again his behavior justifies the professional viewpoint that everyone (in spite of gender and class) should submit to legal management.[35]

Bruff's view is one among many in this novel and does not, of course, need to be taken as Collins's own. However, it seems to be ratified by the plotline depicting Rachel. The counterpoint to both these examples is the inclusion of Herncastle's will. Here, the legal text is circumscribed by a literary world, and lay people, including other characters in the novel and the novel's own readers, read the two side by side. This juxtaposition marks an explicit competition between the legal and the literary and between identity and character. Reading the will in this case

---

[33] If there is a specific model for Knight's *A Girl with a Temper*, *The Moonstone* might well be it. As do all the narratives, Bruff's bears the imprint of his own preoccupations. As a solicitor, he feels compelled to explain certain features of his profession, including the difference between real and personal property and that Doctors Commons is where Godfrey has gone to prove the will. Similarly, Finlay's Miles Millington, a barrister cum industrialist, is the source of that novel's descriptions of the geography of Somerset House. But where Collins at least uses the lawyer as a mouthpiece for his legal observations, Knight intervenes in his own narrative voice as well. Knight also shows his indebtedness to Collins in the picture of their self-willed heroines, Rachel Verinder being Collins's own version of a "girl with a temper."

[34] Bruff describes the content of Lady Julia's will and explains that both she and Rachel only have a life-interest in the real estate. The theory is that by removing Rachel's ability to administer her own property, "to relieve her of all responsibility," she will be saved from fortune-hunting suitors (285). The rhetoric establishes the idea that women are prevented from controlling their own property and themselves for their own good. *The Woman in White* (1860) developed this point into a worst-case scenario through Sir Percival's diabolical attempts to get Laura to sign over her personal fortune.

[35] See Thomas for a discussion of professionalization as a new instrument of patriarchy that replaces aristocratic authority (69–70).

involves comparing its explicit claims to the probable motivation and intentions of its author, which the will ostensibly makes transparent. Herncastle's assertion that the gift be taken as a sign of his "free forgiveness" is rendered suspicious by his insistence that Julia be both living and present when the diamond is presented. Blake's question, "am I serving his vengeance blindfold, or am I vindicating him in the character of a penitent and Christian man?" (66) highlights the potential split between text and intention. The role of Christian penitent suggested by the will is contrasted for Blake and Betteredge by their prior knowledge of the testator's character. "Character" in the will becomes understood as a legal identity that in this case is separable from the authentic character demonstrated in Herncastle's actions (for example, the theft of the diamond, the opium addiction, the paranoiac seclusion). In other words, although the will is meant to embody intentions and thus to represent identity, the intentions in this will are not to be trusted precisely because they do not reflect character.

Blake's and Betteredge's confusion raises the question of whether the legal emphasis on documentation and identity allows the lawyer to see these distinctions of character. Bruff's professional ethics notwithstanding, the dissociation of identity from character demonstrates that identity as a construct invites less moral judgment than is true of considerations of character. Moreover, the novel suggests that professional interests compete with judgment: whoever prepared Herncastle's will was either tricked by the testator's outward expressions or was not particularly concerned by them (the same is true for Franklin Blake's father who suspects Herncastle but does business with him in any case because he stands to gain by it). George S. Allnut had suggested that lawyers have a "moral duty" to watch for "contemplated injustices" (9), but in this case legal perspicacity is subordinated to the clearer vision of other lay readers, who in turn become narrators and contrast their voices to the voice of Herncastle's testament.[36] Collins's tendency to minimize similarities between his own narrative approach and the synthesizing mode of legal discourse have been excused on the grounds that his novels work to "expose" the power of the new professionals over private citizens (Thomas 61). Even his ambivalence about the last will and testament in particular, however, suggests that the novel was slower to adopt legal reductions to "identity" and continued to depict "characters" with moral agency. The will can be invoked to bridge an aesthetic gap between romance and realism when it expresses metaphysics through material things, but it can serve as well to widen the gap between legal and literary discourse.

Trollope gives us several examples of testators who, for purposes both laudable and suspect, puzzle over the best ways to preserve after death the property that constitutes their identities in life. In many of his novels, notably *Dr. Thorne* (1858), *Ralph the Heir* (1871), *The Way We Live Now* (1875), and *Mr. Scarborough's Family* (1883), Trollope frames his discussion of identity in terms of property and

[36] Writing of Gilmore's advice to Walter Hartwright in *The Woman in White*, Thomas concludes that texts will always speak louder than testimony. But testament comes from *testari*, to be a witness, in this case a witness to one's own words or intentions as expressed through lawyers' words.

volition and investigates, as did Eliot, the ideas of "justice" and "legitimacy" in both their legal sense and in their sense as fitness or eligibility. Trollope's fiction thus offers a counter-narrative to the law's construction of individual and social identity. By inviting the reader to identify with key figures who each represent various positions in a legal debate, Trollope enables his audience to function as a jury. He lets them acquire experience and form their own verdict in a consensual realist mode.[37] The issue he sets them to adjudicate, however, is one that he himself, like Collins, finds difficult to decide: should the law maintain cultural stability at the expense of individual rights and desires, or are individual desires, specifically those relating to testation, so prone to overstep right as to justify strict applications of the law; when should the law adapt itself to an overall change in the value of individuality? Unlike Bulwer's idealist author, Trollope's narrative voice does not intervene or seek to enforce his own sense of how the world should be, yet Trollope's questioning of the world as it is and the opportunity he gives his readers to enter into such "metaphysical analysis" constitute a more accessible literary alternative to a legalistic world view, which few readers have a share in defining.

And of course Dickens's novels are rife with testators.[38] Martin, Sr. and Anthony Chuzzlewit of *Martin Chuzzlewit* (1844) are elderly patriarchs plagued (as was Eliot's Mr. Featherstone) by ingratiating relatives pursuing their fortune. Martin, Sr. is particularly beset because he has disinherited his grandson in a fit of pique and must now decide to whom the property will go. In *Dombey and Son* (1848) the commercial magnate Dombey is driven by the need for a male heir—the "son" of his firm's title, the "Son and Heir" after which he names his ill-fated ship—in order to secure his material and dynastic identity. John Harmon of *Our Mutual Friend* (1865) has not one but three wills, each providing a different, potential plot for the beneficiaries' actions yet all of them contingent on the testator's shifting desires.

The list is easily extended, but perhaps more than any of Dickens's novels, *Our Mutual Friend* lays bare the way the testator's self-actualization through the bequest of property imposes a burden rather than a benefit on those who inherit. The "hiddenness" of Harmon's wills also adds nuance to the overt legal-literary competition found in Collins. Here the testator's mercurial displays of prerogative function as a legal shell game that signals his own continued control of property and ostensibly of his namesake. The novel's manipulation of texts marks, furthermore, the obscurity of legal language and the difficulties of finding authentic testamentary intention in a legally edited document (not to speak of all the "wills" of those propertyless people who have no access to legal aid and no being—because no "having"—

[37] See Ian Watt's classic construction of the realist audience as jury in the introduction to *The Rise of the Novel*.

[38] Note the number of novels in which testaments survive. A short review of Dickens's novels reveals a will at almost every corner, but many of these appear long after the testator's death or not at all, for example, in *Little Dorrit* and *Bleak House*. The novels to depict actual testators or benefactors include those named above as well as Magwitch and Miss Havisham in *Great Expectations*.

that would require it).[39] The multiplication of wills is matched, however, by John Harmon, Jr.'s own shifting identities and attempts to evade his father's will(s). *Our Mutual Friend*'s parallels between texts and "identities" and its continued search for "character" thus provides a critique of legal influence on subjectivity and provides in miniature a model for the transition from a Victorian to modernist literary aesthetic.

"My Unhappy Self-Tormenting Father": *Our Mutual Friend* and the Willing of a Self

In his postscript to the novel, Dickens mentions more than once his plan for the story that he "devised" long before its last installment was published. Bulwer himself could not have been more pleased by Dickens's assertion that he not only created the "leading incident" for purposes of "turning it to a pleasant and useful account at last" (798), than by his similar claim that the revelation of Harmon's identity, albeit "for a long time unsuspected," was "always working itself out." That is, Dickens shows his idealist side by insisting that he began *Our Mutual Friend* with a clear conception, or knowledge *before* the fact, that dictated his telling of the story and which extended to anticipation of objections by "a class of readers and commentators who would suppose that I was at great pains to conceal precisely what I was at great pains to suggest." Dickens seems willing, in the spirit of idealist authors, to lead his clever readers; less skillful readers must be left to work it out on their own if they refuse to trust "an artist [...] to know what he is about in his vocation" (798).

If Dickens knew what he was about in writing the novel, his choice of a postscript "in lieu of a preface" must also have been decisive, though it illustrates, in contrast, a realist side. Edwin Eigner characterizes the realist position as one which "requires a starting point in ignorance" and "operates only in the absence of metaphysical speculation" (*The Metaphysical Novel* 63). By framing his comments in a postscript rather than a preface, Dickens expresses his wisdom after the narration of experience, or the point when the audience will have come to its own conclusions. He sympathizes with his readers' partial ignorance and attributes it to the exigencies of serialization, confirming that it is, indeed, difficult to "perceive the relations of [the story's] finer threads to the whole pattern" before "they have it before them complete." Yet by using the postscript to admit that closure is essential for the reader's understanding even when it is clear to the author, he reveals that he *could have* given a preface. We are faced with a contradiction. If Dickens was idealist enough to formulate a story that would have a "useful" end, here he seems realist enough to appear not to do so.[40]

---

[39] Thomas classes the mechanisms of "defining personal identity" as the "implicit" control of documents and the "explicit" debates between men of different professions (69–70).

[40] Eigner resolves this conflict through his category of the metaphysical novel. Metaphysical novelists combined the romance and novel, he claims, in an attempt "to expose materialism and its consequences, so that their metaphysics, which the positivists had banned from philosophy, might be restored as a legitimate province for human inquiry" (7). Eigner's

However, to seem to deceive the reader would be a transgression of the consensual model of realism. His postscript implicitly addresses this charge as well when he remarks "there is sometimes an odd disposition in this country to dispute as improbable in fiction, what are the commonest experiences in fact." Seeking to ward off any such objections, he stresses that

> there are hundreds of Wills Cases (as they are called), far more remarkable than that fancied in this book; and that the stores of the Prerogative Office teem with instances of testators who have made, changed, contradicted, hidden, forgotten, left cancelled, and left uncancelled, each many more wills than were ever made by the elder Mr. Harmon of Harmony Jail. (798–9)

Dickens situates his fictional will as a rather tame exemplum of a much wider and fantastic genre that is nonetheless real and available for perusal to anyone who cares, like Rokesmith and Wegg, to lay down their shilling. The attention shown here to the "reality" of his plot device certainly speaks to a mimetic impulse. More important, however, is that the reader feels involved in the novel's development. Dickens does not resort to the will for the sole purpose of making his novel seem true to life, but as a mechanism for testing to what extent the individual is able to enact his own design or is constrained by social forms, thus combining the phenomenal and metaphysical.

Matthew Arnold described the nineteenth-century social world that Dickens criticizes as one bounded by institutions:

> Modern times [...] find themselves with an immense system of institutions [...], which have come to them from times not modern. In this system their life has to be carried forward; yet they have a sense that this system is not of their own creation, that it by no means corresponds exactly with the wants of the actual life, that, for them, it is customary, not rational. (7–8)[41]

The legal system and the last will must be included among Arnold's institutions. Nineteenth-century legal reform brought the law into greater conformity with new utilitarian and positivist principles, but the streamlining of legal practice only made its regulatory function more efficient. In this context, the will does exactly what it ought by restraining individual subjectivity in the interests of an ostensibly objective legal and cultural system, interested here in the maintenance of property.

---

sense that materialism could be invoked in the service of more abstract considerations parallels the hybridization that I argue the documentary will itself rhetorically embodies, and for that reason materialism is not just a stepping stone for the literary writer. It may well be the tool the novelist requires in order to generate the audience's recognition and their consent to his fictional world (and the ideas circulating there), but when that tool itself performs a dialectical movement between self and society, empiricism and metaphysics, it does not need to pass through the "pattern of conversion by contradiction" Eigner describes in order to achieve a multi-dimensional reality.

[41] Arnold's essay on Heinrich Heine originally appeared in 1863 in the *Cornhill Magazine*. Solomon cites this passage in his essay (37–8).

The literary counterpart of this sensed constraint and the desire for individual agency lie in the distinction between realism and naturalism, or between a style of writing that admits negotiation between the individual and social will and another that denies human agency altogether.[42] When the legal will is used in the novel it becomes a form that is open to interrogation. Indeed, it enacts the same dialectic as that attributed here to the "realist" novel and offers a doubling of thematic and rhetorical concerns. J. Fisher Solomon introduces the terms to make the case that *Our Mutual Friend* alternates between these two literary genres in order to offer an allegorical "way of escape" from the world Arnold describes (39). Like past institutions in the creation of which the modern individual has had no part, the will descends upon living generations and presents them with a challenge: it "can either be surrendered to with a naturalistic shrug or ignored on behalf of more subjective values. The novel's characters, in other words, have a choice in the face of the Will" (40). Although Solomon carefully brings us to this important point where discussion of both the generic qualities of the novel and of the properties of the will that make it especially useful in the novel's project could begin, he examines instead the novel's "failed" detective scheme as a means of exploring this dialectic.[43]

By attending to the will's own dual identity and Dickens's pointed rhetorical exploitation of it, however, we do not have to expect a detective story about Harmon's murder and feel defrauded by the early revelation that he lives. Dickens reveals Harmon's disguises specifically to cue the reader that Old Harmon's will and his son's responses to it will be the novel's subject. As Solomon observes, the only way moral lessons can translate into action is if the text's "rhetoric of persuasion" is convincing. In his view, *Our Mutual Friend* does not succeed because it "fails to 'keep contract' with its readers in the development of the Harmon mystery plot" (45).

---

[42] Solomon's view of realism relies on developments in novel criticism that post-date my discussion of the romance-realism divide. Paraphrasing Georg Lukac's view of the two modes, he writes, "Where the realistic novel presents a dialectical relationship between subjective free will and the will of the social group, the naturalistic novel represents the breakdown of subjective freedom itself as all subjects come to be determinately constrained by their objective environments" (38). The interests he attributes to realism are ones associated with romance in my discussion. Here, naturalism represents an extreme version of realism and goes some way towards explaining why writers who would seem to represent idealist interests, like Henry James, were, at the end of the century, known as realists instead.

[43] The novel's detectives (Charley Hexam and Silas Wegg) fail because of their unswervable focus on signs as the indicators of truth and dictators of action (Solomon 41). They are perforce led by clues, but they can't be very good detectives if they don't question their evidence. If like Harmon, we, in contrast, are supposed to resist the imperiousness of the objective sign, then the detective element is bound to fail, not by accident but for the sake of consistency. Through Harmon, Dickens champions the individual. He gives him agency and in the process demonstrates the limited (because changeable) power of the sign in a way that anticipates the Edwardians' investigation of the imperative, desiring will and the self-consciousness of their novels.

The failure to "keep contract" can be read as a breach of consensus on which the success of the novel's worldview depends. However, if we isolate the material will as Dickens's medium, look at the way he explicitly links it to individual desire with its potential to rearrange signs and thus create more apt meanings and identities, then the revelation of the Harmon mystery can be read as a deliberate attempt on Dickens's part to involve his audience and gain their consensus.

In the first of Old Harmon's three wills, he names his employee Noddy Boffin as sole executor and gives to him a portion of the estate, the remains of which are designated for young John. But as Mortimer Lightwood explains, all his possessions will to go to Boffin if John fails to satisfy his father's conditions, most significantly the stipulation of marriage to Bella Wilfer.[44] The first will dominates the first half of the novel, but, as Venus rightly suggests, since "the old gentleman was generally cutting off some near relation, or blocking out some natural affection […] he most likely made a good many wills and codicils" (299). The presence of a second will, discovered in the pump at Harmony Jail, not only gives Wegg the means to blackmail Boffin, but it further splits the already divided novel by emphasizing Harmon, Sr.'s increasingly vindictive mood. The third will comes to light some 30 pages shy of the novel's end when John, newly revealed as the living John Harmon, married to Bella and thus within the bounds of the first will and heir to the estate, has the pleasure of disappointing Wegg. "That will [in the Dutch bottle]," explains John, "gives absolutely everything to my noble benefactor and yours, Mr. Boffin" (767). Furthermore, it is "the latest will of the many wills made by my unhappy self-tormenting father" and so invalidates both the original under which John could benefit and the second under which Wegg hoped to prosper. Most interesting in John's narration is his characterization of his father. The mercurial parent is now a benevolent employer and a "self-tormenting" father; the three separate wills embody three different identities for its writer.

John's comment reveals an unexpected sentiment in one whom we could rightly suppose to resent his father. If old Harmon's various wills reveal different aspects of his own character, they certainly reflect on the son in as many different lights, creating for him a series of roles that he must assume or reject. Like Mr. Scarborough in Trollope's novel or Featherstone in Eliot's, Harmon, Sr. assumes that the rights of property confer on him the right to act as he pleases, but where in Scarborough's case the interest is in preserving property even at the expense of the name, here there is no such ennobling interest. Property is immaterial; it is dust, but it is the foundation of a willed imperative to create an identity for testator and heir alike. In other words,

---

[44] This is the first instance in which John is treated in much the same way as a woman. Harmon's parental tyranny extends equally to son and daughter alike; if he cannot choose his daughter's spouse, he will name his son's. John is also aligned with Bella as the other actor in his father's drama, but where the daughter dies, and Bella appears to forfeit all volition except towards satisfying her husband's, John is given several opportunities throughout the course of the novel to redeem his own identity. These chances, although finally unsuccessful, place John in the trajectory of Catherine Earnshaw's and Dorothea Causabon's rejections of the will.

property and Harmon's use of its cachet may cast the father as a miserly curmudgeon, but it also names the child as an undutiful son and constrains his agency.

Young John's various disguises would seem to belie the last. He does, after all, let it be believed that "John Harmon" has been murdered.[45] By adopting his first alias, Julius Handford, he rejects, or at least suspends acceptance of, the identity molded for him by the first will.[46] His manipulation of signs marks the fluidity of institutional identity (homicide, secretary, sailor), but through his search for character—a more constant sense of self and agency within—he returns to the very identity he first repudiated. The question is just how far his return extends: is it to the man his father designed him to be in the first will? Or is it to a new sense of self, which, though in form it enacts his father's intentions, does so in a world so altered by his experiences of it that in spirit young Harmon can be said to

---

[45] It is worth noting that Julius Handford is the chief suspect in the investigation and that this identity is one Harmon quickly discards in favor of John Rokesmith. Harmon's metaphorical murder is really a suicide. By distancing himself from the perpetrator of the first, "Handford," he can become the quiet and efficient Rokesmith. Yet when "Rokesmith" disguises himself as "George Radfoot," the schism in the former identity widens to the extent that Harmon must acknowledge that he can never return as "Harmon." Harmon's real identity is an untenable position. As Robert Kiely notes, "To exist only as a character in someone else's plot is, certainly in Harmon's case [...] to suffer some form of abuse and violence" (273). Because his father has plotted his life, Harmon cannot occupy that position without doing violence to his personal sense of subjectivity. Kiely suggests that "assuming authorship is necessary for survival," yet Harmon fares little better in his schizophrenic search for another character, and must finally return to the one authored after all by his father.

[46] Much has been written about the efficacy of John's attempts to escape his father's will and fashion his own life through the central metaphors of authorship and narration. Robert Kiely maintains that Harmon's disguises are functional illusions or tools the need for which arises from the characters' "dread of having no story at all" (272). "If individuals do not provide their own versions of things," he writes, "they risk being left out of the design altogether or being the pawns in other people's plots." Similarly, Patricia Marks suggests, "the act of storytelling is a way of regenerating life" (29). Though some stories may be escapist or used to deceive, the successful raconteurs "defend their identities by [...] encompass[ing] the variety of human experience through open-ended fictions [ones that seek relationships with others] that redeem not only those around them from lack of pattern or from ill-chosen pattern but also from themselves." Richard Gaughan counters this view, suggesting that although the characters are "forced to live stories they did not write," neither can they rewrite them or engage in positive action at all (231). For Gaughan, the disguises are a type of passivity, a "suspension of Harmon's will" that are young John's only means of redefining himself in terms of social relationships rather than the social roles, such as legatee or disowned son, set forth in his father's will (232). Passivity is also the principal mode of response in Deirdre David's analysis. She denies the effectiveness of Harmon's pseudonyms, claiming that he "can never be anything other than John Harmon, son of the man who made the mounds" (112). He is entirely constrained by "the destiny, which has been prescribed by his father and by society" (113). Rather than fighting against it himself, he "must remain passive in order to be released from debilitating social reality and remain firmly in touch with that reality in order to be taken into the fabulous world of shiny, rehabilitated money" (58).

have satisfied his own terms? In other words, whose willed imperatives are being fulfilled and what are their relation to the various documented wills?

Harmon's return to himself is two-fold. He is both unlike his father and like him; the will he satisfies is certainly his own, but most interesting here is that it is also his father's will (as expressed at least in one phase of his life). Harmon, Jr. is never vindictive, but if he is innocent of that charge, he is not free of his father's will to control. As a living man, he obviously has to resort to some other means than the documentary will to work changes he hopes to see in his own lifetime; he simply uses disguises, permutations of his identity that parallel his father's various testamentary personae, as the more practicable vehicle to reach his end, particularly regarding Bella. However, when Harmon recounts his drowning, we begin to see him less as a victim than as the potential heir to his father's character, so that "the issue of paternal legacy and the predestined design of the son's life contained in it broadens to the point where it embraces genetic as well as financial and legal consequences" (Kiely 275). To put on the disguises is Harmon's attempt to invent or rediscover himself, but there is great potential, as John knows, that "he may trace a design that reveals him as the mirror image of the dreaded 'venerable parent'" (Kiely 275). The view that his period of disguise is a time for him to test and choose his options seems correct, but the choice he makes does matter. Identity does not trump character in this novel: to return to his former self signals more than mere *acceptance* of his father's will; to marry Bella and to have a share in the fortune is *to want* precisely what his father wanted.[47]

As readers we accept John's disguises because we know they are part of negotiating the written testament. By allowing that empirical document (the actual document as well as its function as a utilitarian marker of identity) to be questioned and potentially transformed, Dickens's novel involves its audience in a process through which its own agency in respect to social codes can be explored. Enacted on a thematic level, this negotiation is duplicated by virtue of its appearance in the symbolic form of the novel itself and, in particular, in Dickens's blending of the romantic and realist traditions. Harmon's disguises are a symbolic response to his father's will that work because, unlike Bradley Headstone, Harmon is always aware that they are only symbolic, temporary devices rather than new realities (Gaughan 233); they are models for interpreting the world (237). Similarly, the novel itself has a dual or suspended identity: as a "closed and ordered mimetic

---

47 The most blatant instance of John's similarity to his father comes in his treatment of Bella. Though initially John appears to be as much controlled by his father's will as is Bella, their development throughout the novel places them on completely unequal footing at its end. The once defiant Bella becomes entirely submissive to her husband, whoever he might be, and wants only what he wants. Her wishes are not so much subordinated to his as made identical to them so that Bella is to John as John has become to his father. If we accept this transformation on her part because the novel tells us that she and John want the right things (fairness, happiness, family, and fortune), in other words that the end justified the means, we are also called upon to endorse Harmon's will because it is another means of bringing them together. For more on Bella and John's use of love as oppression, see Syd Thomas.

system," on the one hand, and an "open-ended system of multiplicity," on the other, the novel is another tool through which assertions about the world can be made that might fundamentally change it.[48] In other words, the knowledge that we are reading a fiction and our temporary consent to its worldview will allow us to draw conclusions that could alter our understanding of the world we do live in as long as we *do not* accept that world to be real, as Headstone does. To accept the fiction as reality is to reinstall it within the empirical world, to refuse our agency, and so to obscure the possibility of altering it. Thus, realism in Dickens, rather than striving after a perfect mimeticism, actually requires that we recognize the real world only so we may bring it closer to its ideal state. Of course, one might well ask whether the world John Harmon occupies at the end of *Our Mutual Friend* is significantly different or better than the one in which he begins it. By having John become only a marginally revised version of his father, Dickens suggests that the strength of the testator's will is stronger than the heir's ability to resist it. The power of disguise is merely a paltry response to that of the socially sanctioned legal document. Nevertheless, if Dickens falls back on the force of the social and empirical, he has shown it to be assailable by giving John Harmon the scope to consider self-consciously who he is and how he relates to that other "self-tormented" figure, his father.

The Victorian novels surveyed here invoke a series of oppositions between literature and law, between romance and realism within literature, between direct and indirect ways of knowing within law, and between character and identity as advocated within each discourse. In the broadest terms, the novel's conflict between romance and realism is essentially a matter of emphasis. Even the study of "things as they are" was not designed to preclude discussion of things as they ought to be, but to bring readers together in a recognizable world where it was yet possible to imagine new models of social organization and relationships between people and, indeed, to see the fictiveness of the "real" world. The incorporation of other discourses (even realism's assumption that ideally language means "one thing understood by all") becomes a way of making those languages available for readers' consumption in contrast to their professional applications in which language is used to control and identify.

Like John Harmon, the novel tries on different personae in order to find its true self and, like Harmon, it seems always to return to the will. The novelist

[48] Gaughan argues that the novel is not like the social world because it is about "not only what it can assert directly and explicitly about its world and about itself, but also about the effects of all assertions on what the world can mean and, therefore, on how the world is. The world the novel represents, then, is not some truer and more fully developed world that has been buried or submerged by society and can be excavated. It is the world that has been obscured by certainty but that is always being revealed through the conflict among the characters' various attempts to define and live in it" (243–4). Gaughan's point anticipates Aristodemou's interest in the law's "inevitability" and the novel's potential to think beyond such certitude towards imagining other possibilities.

often sees too much of the loquacious lawyer in himself,[49] but the lawyer and the novelist have their written texts, too. Indeed, the novel's preoccupation with the will suggests that understanding its own authentic character depends on its writer's autonomy (even the autonomy of art) but nevertheless requires the law to make this contrast clear. The will's combination of interiority with materialism offered the novel a way of resolving its internal conflicts, but it also became a means of pointing out the divergence between law and literature. Thus, the novel's fixation on the will signals a competition between the legal and literary to frame the real world and to claim what literature could do better than the law.

H.B. Finlay Knight's *A Romance of the Wills Act* is neither a story of justice nor any other high legal concept; it is a story about a statute, in particular a statute that transforms subjectivity into text, people into possessions, and character into identity in order to maintain social order. That Knight makes the un-ironic assumption that this statute could be the centerpiece of a romance speaks less to legal idealism than a sense that by 1892 the will had become a recognizable source of conflict within narratives, especially conflicts *about* the legal discourse's reduction of character to textual identity that contrasted to the novel's amplification of the individual. This focus on materialism marks the belatedness of Knight's techniques at a time when the novel was already invoking the will specifically to move away from its material emphasis towards more abstract ideas and representations of interiority. Knight's choice of the will is not entirely misguided, however. Written one year before the final nineteenth-century amendment to the Married Women's Property laws (that would enable a woman's will to encompass all the property she owned at the time of her death), Knight's novel reminds readers that women's wills prompted a special sort of conflict in the nineteenth century and that a girl had to renounce her temper if she were ever to become a wife.

---

[49] See Richard H. Weisberg's *The Failure of the Word* for discussion of Continental writers (4, 6) and *Poethics* for Anglo-American depictions of lawyers, especially 51–7.

PART 2
Proving the Will

Chapter 3
Victorian Daughters and the Burden of Inheritance

The *Westminster Review* published two articles in 1856 that called for reform of legal fictions about women and literary fictions by them. In July, it printed the Law Amendment Society's report on the "Laws Relating to the Property of Married Women," and in October, George Eliot's "Silly Novels by Lady Novelists" appeared. Not only were their authors personally connected, but together these essays drew readers' attention to the relationship between women's property, women's writing, and fiction's potential to affect social reform. Most importantly, both expressed deep skepticism about the different uses to which fiction was being put in legal and literary venues, that is, about the procedural application of "fictions" that erase women's legal identity on marriage and about the goals (and responsibility) of the novel to represent women's experience.

The origins of the Law Amendment Society's report highlight these connections. In 1854 John Chapman, for whom Eliot had worked at the *Westminster Review*, published Barbara Leigh Smith Bodichon's *A Brief Summary, in Plain Language, of the Most Important Laws Concerning Women*. The success of the *Summary* led to a second printing in 1856 when Bodichon was put into contact with the LAS. Encouraged by their support, she drafted a petition to Parliament, which her good friend Eliot signed. Forwarding the petition in a letter to Sara Hennell, Eliot expressed the long-term view that "with proper provisos and safeguards, the proposed law would help to raise the position and character of women. It is one round [...] of a long ladder stretching far beyond our lives" (qtd. in P. Hirsch 93). The petition, signed by 26,000 supporters—3,000 of whom came from London alone and included such names as Elizabeth Barrett Browning, Mrs. Gaskell, Mrs. Carlyle, and Harriet Martineau (P. Hirsch 92)—was printed in the LAS report of 1856. Seeking to lay before Parliament the "manifold evils" of coverture, Bodichon pointed out in it that "since married women of education are entering on every side the fields of literature and art in order to increase the family income by such exertions," the "injustices" that might once have applied only theoretically to middle- and upper-class women, were fast becoming practical concerns (LAS 336).[1]

Bodichon's mention of writing as a growing profession for women is a strategic appeal to the petition's literary supporters, but, although Eliot could endorse the cause of more equitable property laws for women, she was less sanguine about the

---

[1] The LAS report reprints Bodichon's petition from which these lines are drawn. The "Brief Summary" is widely available in electronic form and is included as an appendix in T. Dolin 123–33. Subsequent page references are to the appendix.

artistic and social contribution "women of education" generally were making to literature. "Silly Novels by Lady Novelists" explored the woman novelist's failure either to adhere to her own experience or, when relying on it, to assimilate private knowledge in such a way as to make it culturally representative. An example of the nineteenth-century debates about the scope and function of the novel, Eliot's essay deemed the "representation of men and things as they are" that realism took for its object "quite a sufficient task" for the serious writer to pursue (450).

Bodichon's petition and its LAS support made it plain that in 1856 "things as they are" included increasing agitation for reform of the country's property laws for married women, which like many other laws, operated according to certain "legal fictions" which, the LAS observed, "have no foundation in fact, but are mere convenient modes of speech, invented by lawyers and used for particular purposes" (339). Current laws were a throwback to "semi-barbarism" when law was needed to restrain a "brutalized" population (331), but such prohibitive measures should long since have been replaced by laws to promote human rights, the group claimed. Citing the "true principle of social law" (335) as the defense of the rights to "personal security," "personal liberty," and "private property" (echoes of Blackstone's *Commentaries*), the Society argued that where one of these rights was infringed upon, all others followed (333). Thus, married women, who by common law were denied the right to private property, were similarly deprived of their human right to liberty and security as well.

Eliot's connection to the LAS report, as well as her own authorship, make her an especially interesting figure in these debates. Where the LAS raises the question of what "particular purpose" such legal fictions were meant to satisfy, Eliot allows us to ask what sort of answer the novel could give. Indeed, this chapter will discuss *Felix Holt* (1866) as a novel that has been viewed as problematic but whose problems, I will suggest, illustrate tensions between the form of the novel, its relationship to the law, and the relationship of both to women's subjectivity. By making Esther willingly renounce her fortune on the one hand, yet using her conflict to interrupt the apparently inevitable progression towards dispossession on the other, *Felix Holt* extends the implications of the narrative erasures of women's wills performed by traditional literary and legal fictions.

When personal subjectivity and public identity are made conditional on property, the law against ownership deprives women of one of the most recognizable and conventional modes of signification and action in the nineteenth century. The law may have rationalized its position by asking how someone who does not exist could own property, but for women the question is inverted: how can someone who does not own property really exist? With nothing to bequeath, how can a social cipher perpetuate herself? Notwithstanding the considerable attention that has been paid to the novel's relationship to women's property rights, those aspects pertaining to women's testamentary capacity specifically have been neglected as an inevitable consequence of the law's fundamental assumptions. Like the novels themselves that end in marriage, scholarship has not interested itself particularly in what happens afterwards, least of all in what could not happen afterwards, such as the bequest of property.[2]

Nor do the novels I discuss here—*Little Dorrit* (1857), *Felix Holt* (1866), and *The Woman in White* (1860)—exemplify women's wills that conform to the testamentary models available to propertied male characters. Instead, the propertied single woman is shown to exercise her will before marriage and to plot her own alternative fictions through story-telling. By looking at the way women are figured in three novels about the last will and testament, this chapter asks whether the Victorian novel really shuts the book on single women or whether there are instances in which unmarried status seems preferable to wedlock, thus critiquing the legal ramifications of marriage. Moreover, by importing real concerns with women and property law into the novels, these authors make visible the law's fictional status, the way its fictions work to order the world, and the novel's potential to revise them.

"One Person in Law": Victorian Marriage and the "Legislated" Woman

Writing in 1765 of the legal consequences of marriage, William Blackstone observed that "the very being or legal existence of the woman is suspended during the marriage, or at least incorporated and consolidated into that of the husband: under whose wing, protection, and cover she performs every thing" (*Commentaries* I.5 431). Almost a century later, the LAS wryly noted the oddity of effecting a union "by suspending the legal existence of one of its members" (339), and observed that this alteration has no basis in the "original law of nature."[3] When "the will remains as strong, the reason as clear as before" and, indeed, when "individual needs are as separate as ever, [and] individual health suffers, or vice versa, without the participation of the other party," then, they argued, the suspension of a woman's identity must be a legal fiction.[4] Here, a cultural law invents means of ordering and

2 The notable exceptions here are Jeff Nunokawa, *The Afterlife of Property*; Tim Dolin, *Mistress of the House*; and Hilary M. Schor, *Dickens and the Daughter of the House*, who with varying emphases have discussed many of the issues I raise.

3 The LAS had argued earlier that when people can monitor themselves, they don't need the law to do it for them. In fact, the law should now operate to protect "rights," themselves cultural fictions that essentially return to the well-behaved citizen the same things he demanded before civil law intervened between him and his neighbor. Now the LAS is saying that natural law should be privileged as the more authentic and therefore more accurate barometer of justice: because human nature or individual personalities do not really change, then there must be some sort of truth in their constancy, and the law must be measured by nature's "foundations," rather than nature being altered by law. If the law insists on inventing fictions, then at the very least it has to take better account of what people are likely to feel as true, representative of themselves and in their interests—in other words, it needs consensus to work.

4 In its rather sarcastic tone, the LAS draws on the legal fiction as a mechanism which enables the court to establish jurisdiction, to circumvent old and (more) complicated

controlling societies in the hopes that the individual's baser nature will become conditioned to a civilized, communal life. The problem with the current law, however, is that it propagates a theory about individual nature that in practice does not stand up. At bottom we are all separate beings, goes the argument. Man and *woman* experience no "mental change" simply because they become man and *wife* (note the rhetorical shift from biological sex to cultural role applied to women alone), and, as the LAS says, the legal system that propagates such a theory does so for a reason.

Long before the nineteenth century, the nature of those reasons was largely pragmatic, even when glossed by the spiritually compelling, sacramental nature of the union (Holcombe 18). Feudal rationales that linked ownership of property with services rendered suggested that husbands were better able to fulfill such duties; however, the very concept of marriage itself had historically been the real culprit (Morris and Nott 24). That the law deprived married women of the freedom enjoyed even by divorcées and widows implies not that women were naturally dependent on men but that the marriage contract (the division of labor, the sexual relationship, child-care) made wives dependent on husbands. Although the law was willing to grant a man certain rights by virtue of his sex, the implication is that it was far more interested in women's status (Morris and Nott 12). This emphasis on social position, as opposed to the rights of the individual, meant that married women continued dependent long after the ostensible, practical justification for their subordination ceased to exist. When land could be owned outright rather than in exchange for service, and even when commodities or portable, personal property became more common throughout the eighteenth and nineteenth centuries, the law continued to place control of a wife's property with her husband. "By depriving married women of property," moreover, "the law deprived them of legal existence, of the rights and responsibilities of other citizens, and thus of self-respect" (Holcombe 35).

The loss of personal rights attending this change of marital status might certainly have made marriage less attractive than the thought of remaining single. As Frances Power Cobbe made powerfully clear in "Criminals, Idiots, Women and Minors" (1869), otherwise civically responsible, fully rational, adult women who married—on the grounds of justice, expediency, and sentiment and, thus, in full accordance with cultural norms—were immediately classed with social deviants, mental incompetents, and children. In spite of such detrimental comparisons,

procedures, and to broaden the application of particular "remedies" without requiring or resulting in any substantive change to the law as would occur under new legislation (Stone 128). Bentham famously criticized this practice, notably in reference to its application in cases involving property, and argued that instead of developing still more complex (and deceptive) procedures to apply old laws, new legislation ought to be passed. The legal fiction is especially interesting then as a tool for maintaining legal culture and its traditions, as Dieter Polloczek calls it, the "vehicle of conservative transformation of common law" (136). To the extent that literary fiction has been a means of opening culture to critique, its goals and the goals of the legal fiction are necessarily opposed.

however, for many single women marriage was a necessary component of their overall security. Even though single women held a technical advantage over their married counterparts, like them they had essentially no direct access to the political and judicial spheres of influence and thus "no say in shaping the legal regime that governed her" (Morris and Nott 35). This advantage, moreover, was confined to women with private means. For all others, marriage was the principal source of security.

Part of the reason for this disparity lay in the fact that although the law provided single women with as much latitude in respect to their property as men, it still operated on the assumption that women at some point would have a husband to provide for them; it made allowances for a situation it assumed would rarely exist (Morris and Nott 35). A similar logic informed patterns of inheritance. Charles Dickens, for example, left his daughter Mary an additional annuity of 300 pounds during her life "if she shall so long continue unmarried," a sum she would no longer be entitled to if she had a husband to provide for her. Wilkie Collins established a trust for his daughters for their lives and for any children of theirs up to the age of majority, or—in the case of daughters—until they married, whichever came first. When male heirs reached majority, they could manage their own property, and so could the single, adult woman, but this standard phrase in wills of the period—"as being sons or a son shall attain the age of twenty one years or being daughters or a daughter shall attain that age or marry"—linked women's marriage with perpetual infancy. Indeed, the expectation that daughters would receive a settlement upon marriage was considered to justify the general preference for male heirs, but this exchange obviously offered slim consolation to daughters who did not marry. Nor did it assist poorer classes of women whose limited assets made marriage a necessity, thus rounding a vicious legal circle.

The overriding message behind these laws, and thus behind the objections of those men and women seeking their reform, was that if women could not own certain kinds of property and could not fully control that which they were allowed to possess (because, for example, settlements and other trusts would be administered by third parties, not by the beneficiaries themselves), then women who could not act on their own behalf in the public sphere would be similarly disabled in the private.[5] It was an absolute tenet of the married women's property reforms that "a woman had to be able to possess her own property before she could effectively counterpoise her own will to that of her husband" (Shanley 13).

Legal resistance to the proposed reforms focused on just this idea of separate wills and forecast disastrous consequences for marriage and the family if women were made independent and able to exercise their will. When Eve proposes a division of labor, Adam applauds her, "for nothing lovelier can be found/ In woman, than to study household good," he says, but he also warns that to oppose his wishes and venture alone into a dangerous world (to leave his "wing, protection,

[5] For a discussion of trusts, especially a trustee's relationship with beneficiaries, see Chantal Stebbings.

and cover" in Blackstone's terms) is to invite trouble (Milton 9.232–3, 265–9). The end of that story needs no new accounting, but the legacy of Eve's willfulness and Adam's moral failure to assert his own can be traced in the history of married women's property reform.

In 1857 The Divorce and Matrimonial Causes Act was passed, while the first Married Women's Property Bill went before Parliament. Lord Brougham introduced it to the House of Lords in a rousing speech that compared the proposed reform to common law rules governing women's property to the great and long-fought cause of slavery's abolition. Referring to Bodichon's petition, he noted the signatures of working women who supported themselves, "not a few even by their genius in letters and in the arts," but he focused specifically on working-class women in the industrial towns who no sooner received their weekly wages, than their husbands tore it from their hands.[6] In spite of these and other vivid examples, objections were raised in both Houses precisely to the negative effects women's independent legal status could have on the marital union and the management of the home. Some compassionated as they condescended to the weak or ignorant women who might inadvertently decimate the family savings, while others questioned reform of property law on the grounds of its centrality to English law and custom generally. Mr. Massey opined that if left unrevised, some of the bill's provisions "might disturb the whole of the relations of married life, and revolutionize all the principles which applied to the rights of property in this country" (c. 1518).[7] Nearly 10 years later in July of 1869, Lord Penzance introduced the bill for a second reading in the Lords and doubted whether women would really desire a change "in an order of Providence which was the source of the highest pleasures which either men or women could enjoy" (c. 982). "Unless the old idea of the husband being paramount and the wife subordinate was an effete and worn-out theory," he mooted, "the law obviously ought to follow in the same track, and hence the actual state of the common law." "Was it desirable," he asked, when the Lords sat again the next summer, "to set up in a household two holders of the purse, two powers, co-equal at first and likely to become adverse in the end?" (c. 606). The Earl of Shaftesbury felt that "the provisions of the Bill went far beyond what was necessary, and struck at the root

[6] Anticipating objections to the law's effect on the marriage tie, he referred to the evidence of "those who have witnessed the struggles that so often take place in the immediate neighbourhood of the Lancashire pay-tables, [who] affirm that there is little fear, indeed, of more discord being engendered by the law that should protect the honest industry of the woman from the combined fraud and violence of the idle or dissolute husband" (c. 609).

[7] Sir John Buller in the Commons suggested "that there were very few mothers of families, having the control of property which they ought to devote to the benefit of the whole of their children alike, who would have nerve and composure enough to refuse to grant pecuniary aid to any one of their children—say their firstborn—who might stand in need of such assistance." Worse, even the best-intentioned women, by investing money without their husband's knowledge, might leave him to discover that "the whole of that property, to which he had looked, perhaps, for the maintenance of himself during his lifetime, and for the benefit of his children afterwards, had been swept away" (c. 1515).

of domestic happiness, introducing insubordination, equality, and something more" (c. 610), but Lord Penzance had answered his own question: "if the law were so altered that a man in taking a wife took a partner with separate interests, entitled to trade separately, and to spend her property how she chose, it was doubtful how far there would remain an inducement to the male portion of the community to enter into such a contract" (c. 606), thus implying that there was no reason other than financial control and domestic mastery to make marriage an appealing exchange for men.

Dissatisfied with the failure of the 1857 bill as well as the limited success of the 1870 Act, the Married Women's Property Committee continued over the next several years to campaign and to study legal and political developments with an eye towards any changes that might affect married women. Parliament showed itself willing to amend laws pertaining to the poor, to infant custody, and suffrage, for example, but it was pointedly disinclined to grant women equal property status with men due to its perceived "threat to marital hierarchy and to political order" (Shanley 104). With the return of the Liberal government in 1880, however, and Lord Selborne's installation as Chancellor, the interests of equity—including a woman's right to own property and dispose of it by will—were given precedence over common law.[8]

With the passage of the 1882 Act, hailed as the "Magna Carta for women" by the *Women's Suffrage Journal* (Shanley 122), married women enjoyed nearly the same property rights as the *feme sole*, and with these material benefits came a psychological boon as well. One contemporary commentator, for example, suggested that the law promoted an "increase in individuality," while another linked the protection of property with "a more pronounced individuality of character and position" (qtd. in Holcombe 218), much as Eliot had prophesied when she signed the first married women's property petition of 1856. Undoubtedly, the various married women's property acts had instituted significant improvements in married women's control of their property and the rights that property holding entailed, but they extended rather than altered married women's "special status" (Shanley 125). "Special status" is neither rhetorically the same as equality of rights (because it implies a difference, an exception, unnecessary for those possessing normal rights so to speak), nor substantively the same as rights attaching to *feme sole* status. In addition to distinguishing between married and single women's contractual ability and their liability for debt, for example, the law persisted in viewing marital status as a determining factor of her freedom of testation; women's right to *have* constituted a new way to *be*, but the law continued to discourage the association of women's property rights with the enhancement of women's will.

---

8 Selborne was more or less fresh from his work in the Court of Equity and on the famous Judicature Act of 1873. Most of the legal disabilities under which married women labored came from common law. The Courts of Equity, in contrast, had been more supportive historically in its treatment of married women. (Equity, after all, was the branch of law through which the separate estate could be established.) With the passage of the Judicature Act, however, preference would be given to Equity's ruling whenever it conflicted with Common Law's (Morris and Nott 30), and thus over time judicial decisions favoring equity would come to replace common law rules (Holcombe 195).

In her *Brief Summary* (1854), Barbara Bodichon maintained that "Women, more than any other members of the community, suffer from over-legislation" (129), and as her report bears out, married women were especially burdened. Of the "Legal Condition of Unmarried Women or Spinsters," she notes, "A single woman has the same rights to property, to protection from the law, and has to pay the same taxes to the State as a man" (123). Notably, a single woman's right *to* property brings with it protection *from* the law, and so by extension, the married woman's almost non-existent right to property makes her vulnerable to untold legal incursions.[9] Bodichon, however, enumerates those invasions, and in her list of the laws for married women, cites the rule that "By the particular permission of her husband [the married woman] can make a will of her personal property, for by such a permission he gives up his right" (126), unless of course he changes his mind sometime before probate. *Maas v. Sheffield* (1845) illustrated differing opinions on this point. Jens Wolff not only witnessed his wife's will, but gave her daughter (now Mrs. Maas) a memorandum declaring that "I have not since that period done anything to revoke it, that it continues to have my sanction, and that I now in every respect adopt it," yet shortly before his own death, he attempted to have his wife declared an intestate (364). Sir Herbert Jenner Fust relied on the circumstances of the memorandum to say that he did not wish "to create a precedent" allowing a husband to revoke his consent. Although it was admitted that the authorities contradicted one another, it was the "very formal and continuous assent"—the existence of the husband's own writing—that validated Susan Wolff's will.

The 1870 Married Women's Property Act changed none of this. *Carson's Real Property Statutes* (1902) explains that the Act of 1882 did declare a married woman "capable of acquiring, holding, and disposing by will or otherwise, of any real or personal property as her separate property, in the same manner as if she were a *feme sole*, without the intervention of any trustee" (Carson 313). However, the rule applied only to property acquired after 1882. In other words, the property a married woman held before 1882 was still subject to the unreformed law and still required a husband's consent to draft a will regarding it. Moreover, the new law that confused married women with single women said nothing about widows. The seemingly unlimited right applied in fact "only to what is done by the married woman during coverture in relation to property of which during coverture she is possessed" (Carson 342). In this way, any will a woman wrote while still married could encompass only the property she had available to her

[9] Bodichon articulates here the "doctrine of absolute possession" or the "liberal conviction that private property defines, produces, and protects freedom" (Nunokawa 77). Absolute possession creates boundaries between the public and private world. Possession thus creates a "freedom *from* rule that defines the boundaries of liberal possession" at the same time it creates "freedom *to* rule within those boundaries" (78). Within these terms the caveat that married women could at least control their domestic environments in exchange for their limited engagement with the public world is undercut by the fact that their legal disability to own even their "own" property actually gave their husbands control of the home as well.

at that time. If she acquired anything at the death of her husband, her will was revoked and a new one had to be written. Not until 1893 could a woman's will "speak" from the time of her death, in other words, be considered to include all the property at her disposal when she died, as opposed to what she had at the time she wrote her will.[10]

Testamentary law thus reflected the same attitude towards woman's desire as that suggested in Blackstone's characterization of marriage. The suspension on marriage of a woman's "legal personality" (T. Dolin 3) implied that under the law she had (or was allowed) no personal will separate from her husband's, and thus she could logically write no legal will that her husband did not endorse. The requirement that any will she did have before marriage must be revoked perfectly reflects this dictum: both her metaphysical and her legal will must necessarily change with her altered legal identity or marital status. The same was true of the widow's status. No longer covered by a husband, she resumed her separate identity; she was a new person who needed a new will. The legal system thus worked against the idea that a woman is an individual in that word's sense as a discrete personality, one that is whole and constant, even when (as the LAS argued) her status changes. Relegated to the private sphere though she may be, the married woman appears to have no private identity or at least one that is not at some point contingent on her public, social status.[11]

In terms of the relationship between the private will, property, and the legal will, this double bind means that as far as the legal world is concerned, women have no separate identities. They have no personal will. If they do not exist in this way, then it is ludicrous for them to own property in their own right and unnecessary that they should have full testamentary capacity. There is no negotiation between the woman and the law in the way there is between the male testator and the rules of inheritance. Unlike him, she is fully disciplined, or in Bodichon's terms "legislated," in a way that establishes her conditions for being from the outside in. Men are obviously not immune to these interventions, but they do have greater

[10] J.F.C. Bennett in *The Practitioners Guide to the Duties of Executors and Administrators* (1899) explains: section 3 of the Married Women's Property Act, 1893 enacted that "sec. 24 of the Wills Act, 1837, shall apply to the will of a married woman made during coverture, whether she is or is not possessed of or entitled to any separate property at the time of making it, and such Will shall not require to be re-executed or re-published after the death of her husband" (6).

[11] In his study of the relationship between commodity culture and the domestic sphere, Jeff Nunokawa notes that the value of the commodity, and hence its desirability as a possession, lies in its comparison to other commodities circulating within the marketplace (8). An object's value lies then not in its separation from the market, its security within the domestic sphere, but in its potential loss. In this context, the idea that the married woman, the woman who has left the marriage market and entered the home, is a possession is problematic precisely because it makes her vendible (7). Her value continues to be dictated by a world outside the private sphere and by property laws, which because they prohibit ownership, also prevent her from entering the public sphere as an agent on her own behalf.

scope for their actions, most importantly, in the freedom to acquire and dispose of property in a way that allows them not only to create a social identity in relation to their possessions, but also to perpetuate one. To deprive women of the ability to express their personal volition (or at the very least to make that ability contingent on their husband's desires) is to deprive them not only of the means of self-definition during their lifetimes but of the means of self-perpetuation as well.

Fortune or Fulfillment: Re-Plotting the Novel of Inheritance

As a single woman, the Victorian daughter enjoyed the same property rights as men, but the Victorian novel rarely let single girls remain unwed if the ending were to be at all happy. The female protagonist's progress in the novel could only be validated by marriage, her absorption into a romanticized union with a husband in which the couple became one under God but also "one person in law"—and that person the husband (Blackstone 431). Marriage was not merely a frequent subject of the nineteenth-century novel, however; it was also its "structuring principle": "tradition dictated that the dominant narrative desire of female characters be romance, and that the achievement of marriage signify their ultimate fulfillment" (J. Miller 4). Her good graces and general merit thus rewarded with a husband, a woman's success was made coterminous with the very event that would deprive her of that personality. In the language of the LAS report, marriage brought with it "no less a penalty than the loss of all personal identity" (358) and, oddly, "of all civil rights, which in most countries is considered as the punishment of felony" (339). Far from a story of progress and happy endings, the single woman's movement towards marriage would be a journey towards loss of legal control over her property and thus of her independence and self-determinism: she could be single, in control of her fortune—a failure; or married, legally non-existent—a success. Narrative closure, like legal coverture, in this context comes to connote both finality—the end of the story—and a literal closing off of options for women.

The linear narrative structure of the nineteenth-century novel makes "the end" of the novel both its stopping point and its goal. It is the place where the story achieves its object and ostensibly makes sense of all that has led up to it, but these endings are frequently artificial; less than a confident accession to order, they signal a desire for closure notwithstanding the likelihood that the novel will have created more than its conclusion can account for (D. Miller xiv). Closure in these terms is an arbitrary imposition of order that makes experience intelligible and at the same time makes fiction the means of satisfying a desire that the open-ended nature of lived experience cannot fulfill. This desire for closure in the real world becomes the basis of the readers' consensus to the novel, their engagement in a symbolic register with those aspects of lived experience that could be so inscrutable and over which the average person had little control.

The standard marriage plot suggests, however, that the mid-century novel envisioned scant alternatives for women that would make "things as they are" any more like things as they should be. As in life, fiction depicts women in a process of owning to becoming property, or of experiencing independence as a state of its own imminent loss. The preference for the marriage plot of most novels featuring, or even written by, women during the period of Married Women's Property reform betrays the way that women's independence within the novel as well as the novel's own narrative choices are consistently hemmed in by external "institutional determinants," in particular by legal coverture. The novel's insistence on marrying off its single women thus signals a paradox within the narrative: the progress towards marriage offers "a double sign of the heroine's triumphant accession to a newly apotheosized middle-class domestic realm, and her ritual preparation for legal absorption and dispossession" (T. Dolin 3).

These choices also reflect a paradox outside the novel in terms of literature's relationship to law: if, following arguments that the narrative form of the realist novel is already indebted to legal structures, turning to the law for its content, too, would seem to accomplish nothing more but a further submission of literary to legal ways of knowing and of representing subjectivity.[12] It would certainly limit the novel's ability to get outside those structures to critique law.[13] The challenge for the novel at this period, then, is to find alternatives to the "constricted narrative structures" of the law as well as to fiction's own conventional traditions, in other words to separate the novel from its history of borrowed narrative conventions and offer a new means of constituting women that could say something about modern subjectivity broadly conceived and about the novel's resistance to the limitations of legal narrative.

Literary fiction's self-consciousness about its own narrative conventions and about closure as mechanisms of social organization reflects also on the law's fictions, not only on legal fictions such as coverture, but also, more particularly, on law's tendency to assume the inevitability of its own structures. As an imaginative genre, the novel itself disrupts social closure in the real world by inviting readers to participate in the activities of an alternative world in which legal norms can be seen as propositions rather than as certainties. That is, the novel creates closure in order to show, ironically, how the purportedly authentic or real conclusions put into place by legal structures are not fixed but can change when talk about them changes. Put differently still, the novel's fictions can uncover the law's.

The presumption of stability is particularly true of women's status. As Hilary Schor puts it in her illuminating analysis of Dickens, the daughter's story, imbedded as it has been within patriarchy and within the novel, "calls out for plot" to release it from suspension (5). Her story, like property in general and like her own person in the marriage market, must circulate in order to have value. The particular value of the daughter's story lies in the way she becomes a site of narrative authority that can expose the fictions that initially contained her as being such a site: her

---

[12] See note 10 to Chapter 1 above.

[13] See Robin West on "the critical dilemma" in her introduction to *Narrative, Authority, and Law*.

stories literally impede the novel's progress towards conventional endings (Schor notes of *Little Dorrit* that the novel "continually stops for women to tell their stories" [134]), and in the process, they counter legal narratives by revising them. The daughter's role as revisionist story-teller—a means within the novel of plotting against the legal understanding of subjectivity (Schor 7, 15)—thereby functions as a synecdoche of the novel's role as cultural revisionist.

In light of this new role, the question then becomes what kind of story the daughter tells or, more importantly, how she tells it. Tim Dolin has argued that novels written during the period of Married Women's Property reform registered the social debate less in their content than in their "formal responses to the conventional plot of courtship and marriage" (9). However, in order to complete this story, the plot of inheritance has to be added. *Little Dorrit* (1857), *Felix Holt* (1866), and *The Woman in White* (1860) certainly respond to the limitations of the marriage plot, but, as Henry James would have put it, they are equally about what a woman of fortune can—and cannot—do with herself. Faced with a dilemma, "the novel of the woman of property must either find a way to express its heroine's relinquishment of property as personal fulfillment, or find a way for her to love outside the terms and conditions of coverture without seeing that as unfulfilling, and without collapsing the narrative" (T. Dolin 10). Dolin's sense of the challenge presented to the novel becomes still more compelling when we read the "relinquishment of property" quite literally as the decision to give up an inheritance. Precisely because in most cases women did lose control of their property on marriage, the sorts of formal disavowals that occur *before marriage* in *Little Dorrit* and *Felix Holt* call attention to themselves by their very gratuitousness and raise the question as to why the novelist should make any heroine want to do that which by law she is compelled to do.

The necessity of separating fulfillment from fortune leads the novel towards what Hilary Schor has described as the daughter's own "willed female dispossession" (126) in a way that troubles assertions of the novel's critical role in challenging and expanding the purely legal possibilities for selfhood. To make the daughter willingly renounce her fortune, especially by claiming that she thereby gains the more satisfying rewards of love or agency, may function as the novel's "vicious recuperation of the daughter" (Schor 146) that would seem to place it in the service of maintaining social-legal norms. Because the married woman is "absent" from—in fact ejected from—one set of legal narratives of subjectivity (the *feme sole*) into others in which her identity is suspended (the *feme couvert*), she has to create other ways to be that are contingent neither on property-owning nor on marital status. She has to become an author and tell her own story or, in Marian Halcombe's case, to bear witness to stories the law would not tell. To construct a desire for discipline suggests a conservative apologetics, but to show this desire as a conscious decision highlights the character's internal debate, her assumption that other possibilities and choices exist, or, failing that, can be created, and that the moral standing of these alternatives must also be tested, too. It is the consideration of these other choices, figured in these novels as the heroines' creation of alternative stories, which disrupts the master narrative of legal coverture.

To make a woman's rejection of her fortune the content of a novel also works to highlight the contingency not just of narrative closure but also of ownership. When value depends on circulation, there is always a risk or a gamble that the means of creating wealth (or defining character, or framing a social order) will not lead to the closure that can make these new conditions or entities (re)cognizable.[14] But this inherent opposition between means and ends might also make us think about the possibility that the single woman's decision to give up property is an expression of ownership, just as her ability to revise other people's stories is a way of telling her own. Giving up her fortune marks the realization, or "making real," of the power of ownership that lies in the power to dispose of one's goods. It is also the "realization," or understanding, that ownership will lose its potency once discarded. In this sense, the woman's will *not* to be encumbered by possessions undercuts the importance of ownership to her sense of subjectivity and personal fulfillment. It is her alternative ending within a realist narrative that has also to end, whose horizon of meaning has to be closed off if the alternative world it offers is to be any more intelligible than the world it represents. But neither the final disposition of property nor the end of the story can be understood as more than a formal contingency. The psychic work of both extends beyond these boundaries, and this narrative abundance is perhaps the reason that the single woman's expression of metaphysical will offers a compelling alternative to the legal will married women were debarred from exercising.

At least three sorts of fictions circulate in *Little Dorrit* (1857)—those about marriage and inheritance specifically and those about social identity generally—and all are intimately connected to property. In the novel, Dickens models a consensual view of realism by showing readers how fictions are made, as well as about the purposes they serve. The novel's secondary plots revolve around characters who act as authors and readers themselves and negotiate the relationship between fact and fiction. In some instances, as in William Dorrit's case, the contrast between felt experience and its representation is too great to sustain the fiction. In others, Mrs. Merdle and Fanny's especially, the actors are shown to enter into tacit agreements as to how they will relate to and understand one another. In this respect, the novel trains readers in the ways of creating and—equally as important—of recognizing fictions. This kind of self-exposure can signal authorial anxiety (a question of

---

[14] D.A. Miller discusses the limitations of closure. Tim Dolin focuses on the "tenuousness" of a single woman's financial independence (3). Jeff Nunokawa argues that "possession, like narrative, is prologue to its demise" (89). The doubled and contradictory conclusion of the marriage plot is matched by the paradox of ownership: "the alienation of property is an irreversible act, at once the realization and termination of ownership's potence" (85). And Hilary Schor adds that the daughter is a transmitter of value responsible for the secure legal passage of property and the narrative passage of story, but whose entrance into both the market and narrative economies necessarily opens the transfer to failure or diversion (4).

whether the author's own fictions will gain consent),[15] but it also asserts a more direct or open relationship between author and reader than obtainable in the reader's engagement with non-fictional discourses, or with textual communities to which they have no access, or from which they have been excluded.

In *Little Dorrit*, Dickens brings these general ideas of fiction and representation together with fictions of property (specifically marriage and inheritance) in a critique of legal representations of subjectivity. Hilary Schor has argued compellingly that the law, like the novel, has it own "plots of property" that determine how individuality is constructed and how it is socially, publicly recognized (5), but the clarity of Dickens's own fictional constructs offsets the obscurity of the law's, or its tendency to reduce character in favor of managing identity. He thus suggests that the novel is the better, more expansive form of creating character and representing subjectivity. Between Dutch bottles in mounds and missing tins full of documents, for example, legal texts, especially wills, are nearly always absent or hidden in Dickens's novels. Representing the opacity of law, their hiddenness usually requires characters who do not formally, professionally represent law to bring their meaning to light. The direction of the inheritance plot, therefore, is not merely towards a traditional restoration of property to its rightful owner, but also towards uncovering the character and intention of the testator who no longer speaks for himself but is spoken for by the law. The inheritance plot's trajectory of uncovering character thus becomes the novel's formal critique of the (legal and literary) marriage plot's "covering" of its female characters.

Inheritance and marriage come together in Amy Dorrit. Indeed, in one sense Amy herself is "a kind of narrative last will and testament" in that she as daughter represents a principle and a vehicle of transmission, but like other daughters in Dickens, she is absent from the transactions themselves (Schor 129). Like the hiddenness of other legal texts, Amy-as-text is a way of marking out legal processes of obfuscation, both in the will and in the suppression of women's legal personality on marriage. But Amy-as-character does not in fact uncover Clennam's will, and by marrying Arthur, she herself becomes covered. Even though Amy suppresses the Clennam will, suppresses her fortune, and suppresses herself in her proposal to Arthur, for the readers, her story has become the means of exposing the way the law suppresses character in its move towards a form of subjectivity dependant on property and its institutional registration. She does not so much duplicate the father's story as revise it by keeping one will hidden in order to assert her own. She suppresses the law, burns the will in fact, in order to let her character show through and to let her will dictate the closure of the marriage plot.[16] In Amy, then,

---

[15] See Schor's discussion of Dickens as an author and as "the author" whose work represents "what it means to write, to own, and to publish" (7).

[16] As Schor puts it throughout *Dickens and the Daughter of the House*, revision is the better form of authorship. Re-writing implies the ability to look over all that has been written and the authority to reshape it (15); "It is the daughter's job to embody and recompose the past" (60).

we find a daughter who does not accept her own father's fiction, who does not accept the Clennam will, and does not accept Arthur's fiction that he is not in love with her. Although she may be just the sort of compassionate woman who could be "come over" (Schor 126) and persuaded to part with her money, in the final scenes of the novel, she does all the overcoming. She also provides importantly a final example of the way characters create their own fictions to live by.

Amy-as-text and her parallel to the will constitute one form of doubling in a novel full of twins and mirror images. But multiplying nothing by something still results in nothing. Hilary Schor links the daughter, the law, and the novel so: "In the same ways that the daughter's relationship to the law was precisely to stand for relationship, and her work for Dickens is to represent a powerful dispossession before the law, so the daughter's story-telling is vexed by the problem of absence" (15). Following the analogy, we arrive at story-telling without the story and the questions of how to represent relationship without recourse to the things related; how to explain becoming a subject as ceasing to be; how to make dispossession palpable; and how to signify story-telling through the daughter without directly telling her story. In short, the problem the novel tries to solve through its experiments with representation is the nature of authenticity, or subjectivity, and how to make something out of nothing. The novel uses its various doubles to comment on mimeticism and the problems of knowing what is original and what copy—questions that are equally important to discussions of the will—but also to invoke the process of constructing fictions as a mode of revision, a re-envisioning of the "authentic" or real world that admits its made-up-ness and makes this realization a condition of consensus.

Dickens gives us two sets of twins in *Little Dorrit*: the Meagles girls and Jeremiah and Ephraim Flintwinch, to model the way in which the novel doubles the real world and its documents like the will. When Clennam first sees the painting of Minnie and Lillie Meagles, Pet enters the room and asks if he can differentiate between them, to which he responds, "I cannot even now say which is not your portrait" (195). At the same moment, he sees Tattycoram's reflection in a mirror that hangs next to the painting. The varied modes of representation and shifting gazes here—the twice-doubled Pet (repeated through her twin and through the painting itself), the lack of contrast between the real girl and the image, the simulacral reflection of Tattycoram—position Clennam as a reader and the novel's women as texts. Even the presence of the authentic Pet is no aid as he looks for the portrait that is *not* her, her negative, her absent self. Afferey Flintwinch in contrast is confronted by too much presence. Her first vision of "Double" causes her to doubt her senses, but she is finally able to differentiate between the "original," the "waking," and the "sleeping" Flintwinch "just as she might have distinguished between a tangible object and its reflection in a glass," notwithstanding that her head goes "round and round" (54). Afferey's confusion, however, becomes the reader's own clarity. Like her at this early stage of the novel, readers must first be confused in order to see more clearly later. They have to be shown the ways in which fiction presents an inverted image of the real world for comparison and scrutiny.[17] And they have to become good readers.

By thus showing the reader the principle that informs realism, Dickens lays the groundwork for demonstrating how fictions are constructed. Jeremiah and Afferey Flintwinch model the negative relationship between author and reader. The vision of her husband's twin (58), the overheard conversation between "the two clever ones" about Arthur's father (188), the sounds emanating from the house, the meeting between Blandois, Mrs. Clennam, and Arthur (527)—all these realities, she is told, are nothing but "dreams," and she is too frightened by her visions to accept them as real. Nevertheless, as her fear that it is more dangerous *not* to trust her senses strengthens, Afferey finally withdraws her consent, first by exposing and then by rejecting her husband's fiction, so that, like the Clennam house, it crumbles. The Flintwinches thus exhibit the way that fictions fail. He misunderstands the way the author—and the law—must work: not, as he does, by aggressively imposing his own vision on a doubting audience but by enlisting his audience's agreement. She in her turn fails initially to trust her senses, which is clearly a problem in an empirical world where experience matters. If real world fictions that deny their artificiality can be exposed as such by clever readers, then they too might be dismantled.

Afferey becomes a much better reader as the novel progresses, but the novel also provides already canny practitioners, almost all of whom are women. Mrs. Gowan objects to her son's proposed marriage to Pet Meagles on the feigned basis of her superior social station (in spite of her own straitened circumstances) and approaches Mrs. Merdle for "Society's" opinion. Here the narrator outlines the framework for their discussion: "Knowing, however, what was expected of her, and perceiving the exact nature of the fiction to be nursed, she [Mrs. Merdle] took it delicately in her arms, and put her required contribution of gloss upon it" (381–2). Perfectly aware of Mrs. Gowan's "real" situation in spite of her representation of it, Mrs. Merdle adheres to social convention and allows her friend the consolation of sustaining her well-bred veneer, however flawed the financial situation such a "gloss" disguises (reminder of Dickens's other glossy couple, the Veneerings, in *Our Mutual Friend*). But as the narrator makes clear, Mrs. Gowan does not deceive herself either; she "saw through her own threadbare blind perfectly" and "came out of this form, notwithstanding, as she had gone into it, with immense complacency and gravity" (382). The "form" is a fiction that for all its known falsity is nonetheless accepted as true for a particular purpose, in this

---

[17] Schor writes of Bella Wilfer, "The heroine, like the reader, must be confused in order to be saved; the reader must be dazzled by fraud [...]" (192). The fraud on Afferey Flintwinch suggests more than anything else that fictions are only fraudulent when they are not presented as such. In other words, Dickens's insistence on teaching readers to see the elaborate construction of his own fictions makes the novel truer, if not more real, than the fiction by which the everyday world is organized.

case a denial of the mercenary aspects of marriage and of the failing potency of the upper classes which require the professional man's fortune to sustain them.

The Dickens narrator here explains that fiction works through tacit agreement, which Dickens presents to his own readers as a model for their engagement with his text. He also provides an opportunity for readers to enter into the process of fictional representation by showing characters not just entering into pre-existing fictions but themselves transforming and creating new fictional worlds in which to move, in other words, revising them. Mrs. Merdle and Fanny, for example, recount the history of their relationship as a narrative transaction in which each woman uses Amy as the audience of their co-authored tale: Mrs. Merdle pointing out that Sparkler would be disinherited if he married Fanny "merely as a fact which is part of the narrative" (240), and Fanny asserting that if Mrs. Merdle wants to have her version of the story credited, then she must "pay for it" (241). The narrative is revised, however, when they meet again in Italy. Fanny and Amy are positioned outside the inn as the focal point of a "grand pictorial composition," the center of another representational form, and it is Mrs. Merdle who first treats them as wealthy strangers (446). As readily as she sees through Mrs. Merdle's "deception" and "pretence," Fanny consents to Mrs. Merdle's story—"She shall find me go her way. She took it, and I'll follow it"—because by acting her part, she can avenge her hurt pride. Both she and Mrs. Merdle model the way that fictions are constructed and the basis of exchange (through which both gain) on which they can be accepted. These are the sorts of "narrative tricks" (Schor 12–13) that the women storytellers play in order to understand themselves and to gain control of the way they will be represented to those around them. They also serve to make the point that readers must become more self-conscious about the tangled relationship between the world of fiction in the novel and the fictions by which the "real" world is already organized because it is only through this awareness that the novelist's fictions can be viewed as more authentic than the law's and that the novelist can save himself from doubling rather than inverting its reductive construction of subjectivity.

The particular focus of these fictions revolves around the marriage market and heightens their importance as keys to understanding Amy Dorrit's rejection of her inheritance and the nature of the fictions in which she is willing to act. Little Dorrit is the most unwilling heiress of all the novels canvassed here, for whom penury is less burdensome than her family's recovered wealth. Content as the "Child of the Marshalsea" to nurture her father and provide for her frivolous siblings, she is hurt less by their ingratitude than by the pose of wealth and gentility they universally maintain. Mr. Dorrit's delusions especially are second only to his determination that the entire family actively promotes them, a fiction into which Amy cannot enter and which earns her family's disapproval. In Italy, she is meant to behave as "Miss Amy Dorrit," to appear at ease in "painted rooms" (448), in a city whose "crowning unreality" is its streets "paved with water" (450), and, worst of all, to cease to minister to her father. Accused by him of purposefully hurting him through reference to their past life, Amy admits that she has not yet accustomed herself to the "novelty of the position" nor to the "novelty of [her] life" (457, 458). The pun is surely intentional, for Amy is moving in a world of fiction. Mrs. General, "that eminent varnisher" is enlisted to help Amy "in the formation of a surface" (459), rather like Mrs. Merdle's "gloss." But the result is that Amy comes to see the whole of English society abroad as another form of imprisonment, a "superior sort of Marshalsea" (491). Her resistance, however, is based in her ability to see all these fictions around her, including the "unreality of her own inner life" (448). Her dissent from her father's narrative thus signals the suspension of his control of her sense of subjectivity (Schor 4) and her turn away from the story that leads to his own collapse.[18] But if this fiction fails, what will become of the novel? How can it continue? Amy has to create her own narrative, her own novel about her life, so that the revision of Mr. Dorrit's inheritance plot in which she was a passive, or at most a resistant, reader functions also as Amy's active management of her own marriage plot.

Although Amy cannot embrace this fiction of moneyed gentility, there are others of her own design, which allow her to pursue the life with Clennam she really wants. Her position with him reversed, she takes upon herself the role he should have assumed before the Dorrit inheritance was claimed. After weeks spent visiting him in her old room at the Marshalsea, she begs him to "make me of all the world the happiest, by saying Yes!" (725), to give her "the joy of knowing that I have been serviceable to you" (726). She insists she has neither use nor wish for money except as a means of paying her own debts of "affection and gratitude" along with his financial ones. Clennam's rejection of this marriage proposal follows a long passage in which he admits having misunderstood his own feelings for her and laments "the opportunity there is no recalling." But Amy's offer does recall that opportunity—and will again—and moreover inverts it. Her letters can convince Arthur that his old saw about being past love was just a fiction; her money can help him out of the prison; her service can redeem him. The only obstacle to this new narrative in which Amy takes the active role, is the persistence of Clennam's power of refusal.

Clennam is certainly not one of the society swains whom Mrs. Merdle observes—in an echo of Lord Penzance's comment to Parliament—must "gain by marriage," else "Society does not see [...] what he has to do with marriage" (378). However, Amy's identity for him continues to be defined by the amount of her fortune, just as their relationship is determined by his insistence that he must *not* gain. Amy's fortune thus continues to pose a threat to her happiness that must be eliminated, as it is when she makes the pact with Mrs. Clennam and

[18] William Dorrit suffers from the same problem that plagues Bradley Headstone in *Our Mutual Friend*. Having entered into a fictional world, quite clearly marked off here as another country, Dorrit does more than fail to differentiate between it and his past life; he actively tries to submerge the old reality. This is not the proper course of realistic fiction, which can only help readers understand their own world so long as they allow the real and the symbolic to coexist. For Dorrit, the denial of reality results in a sort of psychic collapse.

when (via Tattycoram) she regains the tin box containing Flintwinch's documents. Not only has she been relieved of one inheritance by the same financial collapse that ruins Merdle, her family, and even Clennam, but she also declines the reparation Mrs. Clennam would make her for having suppressed the codicil and kept her in poverty. Amy thus covers herself, disguises and protects herself, through her fiction of impoverished status without which Arthur will not marry her. On the day they do marry, she takes "an odd fancy" to have a fire, and asks Arthur to burn a "folded slip of paper" (784). As the "charm" burns, Arthur asks if any word should be spoken, to which Amy responds, "You can say ... I love you" (785). Amy's own will is achieved as the legal will burns.

These pacts between women, and their exchange and suppression of narrative documents, allow them to control the story.[19] Particularly by suppressing the will, however, Amy seems to double the sorts of dispossession that would occur on marriage to Arthur (even with an advisor to draw up a separate estate, Amy is just the person who would want to cede all her property to her husband). The only way this renunciation makes sense is if Amy does not base her sense of subjectivity in the property itself but in the power to refuse it, in her own will. She is the final recipient of the novel's most important documents. By disrupting the transfer of multiple legacies, Amy's will marks a pause in the novel's plots of inheritance and marriage and her opportunity to rewrite them in accordance with her ethic of service and love (Schor 136).[20] Without property, without reason or recourse to write a will, she can most fully exercise her desire to be with Clennam. In this way, her rejection of a fortune and her participation in selected fictions become the means through which she makes her own "real" world with Clennam possible.[21] By using the will plot to uncover Amy's will for the reader, moreover, the novel performs its own editorial function and re-writes legal narratives that link subjectivity to the acquisition of property.

Felix Holt's (1866) split structure is a more overt form of doubling than that found in *Little Dorrit*, but as was true in that novel, its inheritance plot works to "uncover" its heroine's identity and to create a set of choices for her (between husbands, yes, but also between fortune and fulfillment), which she imagines as stories she can step into or re-write. Set in 1832 and focused on radicals of various stamps, *Felix Holt* calls attention to its politics in a way which critics of the novel

---

19 See Schor on women's stories in *Little Dorrit* (131–42).

20 Schor also notes that it is especially difficult to think of Amy's renunciation as "anything other than a disguised wish for something in another form" (145). Since material property can be stolen, lost, or otherwise coerced from its owner, Amy's "romantic and spiritual" fortune is a more secure legacy (142).

21 See also Schor's analysis of the novel's final scene (124–6). The re-ordering of the parish registers (in which marriage becomes the third volume and follows death) suggests that marriage in this novel no longer leads to the wife's legal death but that death is a prelude to new forms of spiritual union, which is suggested by Amy's devotion to service. The more obvious point is that by signing a third volume, Amy in effect signs off on the novel, linking her creation of fictions with the marriage it effected.

have felt compelled to address at the expense of focused attention to the legal plot.[22] However, the political and legal plots emphasize the divergence between the state of legal reform for men and for women. In this way, the dual plots of Eliot's novel emphatically counter those narrative forms that delimit women's stories. Moreover, Eliot's choice of setting situates readers, not in the contemporary debates about women's relationship to property, to suffrage, or even to the Second Reform Bill, but to the days of the First Reform Bill. Without overtly taking up the terms of the married women's property reform movement, her displacement nonetheless allows her to comment on the slowness and obstacles to reform of women's legal position and rights in contrast to that of men's and in this way to use her fiction to make what Bodichon considered "her best contribution [...] to the Cause" (P. Hirsch 70).

The novel unites its apparently disparate contexts (its focus on radical politics, the Reform Bill of 1832, and the laws of inheritance relating to the Transome estate) by their shared investment in property: the possession of property that renders some men eligible to vote (with emphasis on "some" and "men"), and the legal possession and transmission of property. Both plots are further united by the play of individual desire, but this free will is closely linked to and contingent on property. That is, the democratic will to elect one's political representative, although extended by the Reform Bill, nevertheless remains restricted to those with a specified income, while the will to bequeath or even retain one's property is similarly limited by complex legal constructs such as entail or "base fees." Although Esther's sex bars her from taking an active share in the course of suffrage reform, she is at the center of the legal plot. To learn about the scope of women's ability to frame and act upon their wishes, then, we have to pay attention to the legal plot and the options it opens for Esther's choice. Moreover, we have to attend to the ways that she herself thinks of those options as opposing stories *about* personal volition and the differing life narratives she can expect to pursue on the basis of her decision.

Esther's "utopian" dreams of wealth and a better station never accounted for the route towards their fulfillment (360). After her true identity as the Bycliffe heiress is revealed (a position she is placed in unexpectedly and through no action of her own), she struggles with a sense of freedom and the burden of responsibility it entails, not only for herself, but also for those around her.[23] This new identity

[22] Commenting on reviews of the novel, David Carroll observes that literary critics of the 1860s demanded an "Aristotelian unity of action" (Carroll 26), so that "between the divided structure of *Felix Holt* on the one hand and the incredibly complicated legal plot on the other, [critics] did not find the unity they were looking for" (Carroll 25). This was especially true of the legal plot, which in spite of its faithfulness to Frederick Harrison's legal tutelage, struck one writer for the *London Quarterly* as a "mystery" that was "degrading" to a "serious work of fiction" (Carroll 26).

[23] Esther's identity does not long remain a mystery. Like Dickens's revelation of John Harmon's identity or Trollope's of Mary Thorne, Eliot's depiction of Esther Lyon constantly points out the "irreconcilableness between the objects of her taste and the conditions of her

confirms that her former one as Rev. Lyon's daughter has been a kind of fiction and that it is now up to Esther to determine what course her life-story will take. This sense of her own life as a story she can tell invokes once again the idea of woman as author. The novel's emphasis on her "day dreams" (360) and "imagination" (382), even though they conjure up traditional narratives of social advancement, provide her with the basics of authorship. Indeed, while staying at Transome Court, she "found it impossible to read in these days; her life was a book which she seemed herself to be constructing—trying to make character clear before her, and looking into the ways of destiny" (383). Compelled by destiny on the one hand, on the other, Esther assumes authorial agency and becomes a character in her self-authored and more interesting tale.

Esther has to compose a life-narrative, which means she has to account, as she never has before, for the means of reaching the closure of her daydreams; she has to develop a story for her plot. The simplest available is the marriage plot, and she has two suitors ready-made to people it. She tells Felix early on that a woman is "dependent on what happens to her. She must take meaner things, because only meaner things are within her reach" (263, 407), but when Esther is made the center of the legal plot, she suddenly finds that the things "within her reach" will require a choice after all. That is, the marriage plot that traditionally forms the boundary of a woman's power to choose is complicated in *Felix Holt* by the necessity to choose between fortune and fulfillment as well, between Harold and Felix.

The choice between good and bad suitors is clearly no innovation. The point that differentiates her choice is that she eliminates a third possibility, which becomes Eliot's means of pulling in the political plot. At no time does Esther entertain the idea of accepting her inheritance and assuming her place, without marrying, as grand dame of Transome Court (Mrs. Transome is example enough of the limitations of this sort of existence). Instead, Esther confronts the completely prosaic conundrum of whom to marry. In this light, *Felix Holt* appears as a novel of reform only for men that contrasts the public world's increasing democratization with the absence of reform in the private world and the limited potential for women to exercise their own will there and elsewhere. Esther can choose either to be the source of income for one man or the source of inspiration for another, but she cannot be single, and in each case the question of her money is a central element. As was true of *Little Dorrit*, the potential for fulfillment rests on the rejection of an inheritance rather than its acquisition. Eliot thus injects the novel's political

---

lot" (76), so that her "native tendencies" and demeanor always strike those who see her as out of place in the Minister's household. We are meant to expect, as Denner does, who "thought the law might have something to do with it" (374), that Esther's rightful place is at Transome Court. But that same "pretty instep," the "cambric handkerchiefs," and "wax candles" that cue everyone else, incite in Felix the desire to "see if she could be made ashamed of herself" (74). Thus early on, Esther is both positioned as an object of speculation and resentment, the subject of other people's stories about her, and as a woman who will have to choose between these competing views or fashion some new identity for herself.

concerns into the marriage plot by raising the question of whom Esther will elect for her husband and therefore which ending she will write for her marriage plot.

Although much of Esther's ruminations rest on which man she can least afford to disappoint, rather than which one will make her happiest, in the end she chooses Felix precisely because she has come to share his vision about what is important. By having Esther give up her claim to the Transome estate, Eliot reverses traditional expectations that a woman's fortune will conduce to marriage. (What would Mrs. Bennett not have given, after all, to have her girls as well provided for as Esther stood to be?) If Felix had not already insisted that money distracts from nobler pursuits, Eliot's move here would be completely unnecessary; much of Esther's fortune (certainly the personal property, if not the land) would legally have come under Felix's control. But the radical potential of what Eliot does do rests in her emphasis on the importance for women (and men) of finding alternative means than property by which to define themselves. Moral, not monetary, superiority is the motivating force for both Esther Lyon and, later, for Dorothea Brooke, not in the sense that they become self-righteous, but in their felt need for a moral purpose distinct from the idealized roles of wife and mother. They reject great fortunes because they see more wealth in a life of purpose that will benefit the community and, in this pseudo-altruistic way, themselves. In one sense, they entirely aspire to the role of helpmate to their husbands, but it is their husbands' own sense of forwarding a cause that directs their wives' subordination of personal interest, changing their objectives from maintenance of a domestic haven to the creation of a political staging ground. Wives continue to be a source of inspiration and aid: this is what Felix tells Esther the ideal woman would do; it is what Dorothea thinks she can be to Casaubon. But in another sense, to assist in such a cause is to broaden the scope of women's action. Dorothea wants more of life than to lounge about Sir James's estate. Esther worries that Harold's ambitions are insufficiently lofty to inspire her to better ways of being and thinking. Neither marries for the purely practical or acquisitive reasons that propel Gwendolen Harleth towards Grandcourt.

And here we come to a set of double binds. Eliot's critique of marriage implies that there should be better ambitions for women to have and better ways of accomplishing them. (Marriage is fine for good-natured if rather vacuous couples like Celia and James Chettam, ill-advised for Rosamund and Lydgate, and disastrous for Gwendolen and Grandcourt—the important element seems to be compatibility of temperament and purpose, and yet in these novels, at least, good examples seem scarce.) Yet the existing options for women are such that in her novels it is only through judicious marriage that women find both emotional and intellectual fulfillment as well as the ability to act. Dorothea clearly mistakes Casaubon's character and the self-absorbing fastidiousness of his project, but her intentions, we know, have been admirable. Esther may inspire Felix, but she develops this ability only because Felix has first inspired her and, importantly, subdued her baser ambitions. His approach is more straightforward than John Harmon's duplicitous treatment of Bella Wilfer in *Our Mutual Friend*, but like Bella, Esther becomes a willing pupil, and all her wishes become subsumed by and identical with his. His is a noble purpose, and Esther's renunciation of even a small part of her inheritance symbolizes the match between his, now their, theory and practice. (Esther notably retains the right to work, but instead of spending her wages on fine gloves and other frippery, as she was wont to do, she puts it towards supporting their aging parents [474].) One is tempted to ask, "Why this need to identify their purpose with their husbands?" Why don't they have ambitions that originate within themselves? The point is that Eliot's women in these novels do want to do something important, but there is no readier conduit for directing that desire than through marriage with already focused and determined men. This is "things as they are."

In *Little Dorrit* and *Felix Holt*, a version of marriage, however revised, continues to dictate the shape of the novel and to demand a woman's relinquishment of her financial and social independence. Wilkie Collins's heiresses embody the ideal center of the marriage plot in the sense that they make very attractive wives, but their privileged social positions also make them vulnerable to unscrupulous suitors. His novels thus offer a contrast to the models suggested here by Dickens and Eliot because his heroines often are trying to retain or regain an inheritance, rather than choosing to relinquish one, and trying to evade a wrong husband even more than find a right one. Although all single heroines require protection from erasure in the marriage plot,[24] Collins's in particular model the antagonism between single and married status, rather than the transformation of the single woman into the married one. The doubling of characters and documents in Dickens, the doubling of plots in Eliot, and the emphasis on writing in each, become a doubling of heroines in Collins.

In *The Woman in White* (1860), the single woman becomes interesting as a single woman and as a writer, rather than a potential bride. Collins keeps the marriage plot, beginning rather than ending with it in order to represent the literal suppression of Laura's identity, and he maintains the inheritance plot as well (and here, again, there are two: Sir Percival's fraudulent inheritance and the restored inheritance to Laura's son), but writing—even more than story-telling—acquires a different trajectory. The whole course of the narrative, the "detection," is an uncovering of Laura's identity (where "detect" means "to take the roof off").[25]

---

[24] Where there is a woman of fortune in Collins, a lawyer cannot be far away. Gilmore is at great pains in *The Woman in White* (1860) to protect Laura from Sir Percival by establishing a suitable settlement. His example is a reminder that women of property had protections through the Courts of Equity before the passage of the Married Women's Property Acts and that having money can offer protection from the law (in this case common law). A second point is that Collins is interested in various forms of legal erasure and ways of preventing them. The settlement that circumvents coverture's suppression of female identity is one. The issue of illegitimacy is another. *No Name* (1862) is a particularly insistent example of legal dispossession following from the Vanstones' failure to complete their marriage and their wills that highlights how one legal disability impinges on others.

[25] Much of course has been written about Collins as founder of the detection genre. By far the best recent work linking detection narratives with other Victorian discourses of subjectivity is Ronald R. Thomas's *Detective Fiction and the Rise of Forensic Science*.

Marian's detective story uncovers both of Laura's deaths (her "legal death" in marriage as well as her fraudulent one in the asylum), but if Marian's story has been focused on Laura, her story-telling has been a means of drawing attention to herself and, in Fosco's terms, to her "resolution." Her power to resolve or end Laura's story refocuses attention onto herself and makes Collins's novel an exploration of what it means to be uncovered in the world. Through her, Collins anticipates and in some ways even outlasts later efforts to reform the single woman's potential in the novel.

Laura Fairlie is the quintessential victim of a husband's attempt to steal her fortune and an example of the married woman's legal death. In *The Woman in White* the suppression of her identity on marriage is ironically forecast through doublings. Laura is linked with Anne Catherick even before she marries Sir Percival, but the comparison strengthens after her marriage when her new status and the status of the lunatic, united in the rhetoric of the legal system, become synonymous in the novel too. Laura Fairlie "dies" when she becomes Lady Glyde. She dies again when Fosco forges the death certificate and commits her to the asylum in Anne's place. In each case, institutional identities, both legal and medical, are literally registered in documents.

As the central single woman of the novel, Marian becomes the agent who resurrects her sister from legal death through the new document of her diary. Among the novel's many official texts, Marian's diary offers an important distinction. It is her private journal, begun before Walter's narrative required its evidence, and therefore differs from the novel's other commissioned narratives. Furthermore, as a text imbued with her own feelings, surmises, and plans, it emphasizes character (Marian's as well as those of the people she writes about) as opposed to the forms of identification (death certificates, marriage registers) the lawyer Kyrle demands. Marian's writing thus retains the understanding of subjectivity as character in contrast to the bureaucratic registration of identity that even Walter's narrative exploits. Through her journal, the novel maintains a supplementary relationship to the law, providing fuller representations of subjectivity than the legal emphasis on manageable identities can allow.[26] Although Marian brings Laura back to life only to facilitate a new marriage with Hartright, the contrast she herself presents to her sister's married status allows her to realign a much-derailed marriage plot without herself having to marry. Laura becomes the sweet but enfeebled angel of the house, while Marian remains, in Walter's terms, "the good angel of our lives" who, as she dandles her godson, is given the last words and the right to "end our Story" (622). Through the restitution of narrative

---

I do not, however, focus on detection in its colloquial and generic senses. This particular emphasis on the etymology of the term "detection"—a literal translation of the German *Entdeckung*—comes from Ian Ousby (via Allison Millbank and quoted in Hilary Schor [5]) and offers a way of understanding how Collins's narrative structure extends the way Dickens's and Eliot's dual plots counteracted or uncovered the traditional marriage plots.

[26] See Thomas's discussion of the way the novel "exposes" the power of the new professional classes over private citizens (61).

authority to Marian, the novel isolates the single woman, whose own uncovered personality allows her to go where she will, as the figure best equipped to expose the limitations of Walter's official narrative.

Marian ends the story by informing Walter that his son is the "Heir of Limmeridge." In this way, Collins makes Marian the instrument of the desired marital closure and of an inheritance regained as well.[27] He provides the conventional ending through the efforts of the unconventional single woman who, in Tim Dolin's phrase, finds love "outside the terms and conditions of coverture without seeing that as unfulfilling and without collapsing the narrative" (10). Instead, Marian shares in the material and emotional fulfillment of a story that she has helped to author—her sister's life-story—and completes the narrative. Her authority to end the story, albeit ceded to her by Walter, marks yet again the way women's narratives are structured as transferals of property (Marian giving her narratives to Walter, but Walter giving back narrative authority). Ronald Thomas has suggested that this authority lies in fact with the law (59–60). Without Kyrle's endorsement of Walter's many documents, Laura's identity might not be informally recognized at Limmeridge but certainly would not be formally, legally recognized beyond it. However, Marian's narrative extends past the imperfect closure of Walter's plotting. She has to finish his, as well as Laura's, story because he abjures interest in the inheritance plot and its necessary legal relationship to Laura's restored identity and, finally, to her own. By telling Laura's story and ending it with reference to her nephew's inheritance, Marian's own story can continue, first, precisely because she is not married and, second, because she becomes a new kind of testator. Her story becomes a narrative tangent in the sense that it branches from the main marital line, but, importantly, it gets to continue without end.

Without the typical physical and financial assets, Marian is unlikely to marry, but their absence expands her ability to act. Unlike the negligent Frederick Fairlie, Marian is the actual head of household both at Limmeridge and in London. She has been "mother and sister both" (150) to Laura, yet she often functions as a father-figure with the paternal power, as she tells Hartright, even to influence her marriage (116). It is appropriate then that the news of young Walter's inheritance should come from the property-less Marian who, like the father who protects his own interests by protecting the fortune he transfers through his daughter, secures

---

[27] The restoration of Limmeridge House (that was always entailed on the male heir) to young Walter Hartwright marks the completion of the inheritance plot as well as the end of Laura's story as a transmitter of property. Laura's departure from her father's house marks the dangers of transferal, the potential for property to go missing or be damaged in transit, developed in Hilary Schor's analysis of Dickens. Marian's and Walter's disclaimers aside, however, their efforts to restore Laura's identity amount to a restoration of property to the right heir—not Laura, but Laura's (and Walter's) son. Although they claim as their object the public acknowledgment that Laura Fairlie lives, that is, the novel ends with Laura Hartwright; she is still covered. Married women do not fare well in this novel, and they don't even tell their own stories. Instead, where Laura's story ends, Marian's, the single woman's, continues.

her own position. In this way Collins adopts the most vulnerable figure—the single, penniless woman—and imbues her with much of the strengths of the masculine testator. At the very least, he makes Marian's apparent liabilities assets of a different kind.

As a determined *feme sole*, Marian has both the freedom to act like a man as well as the right as Laura's sister to act for her. Hartwright laments that he has no legal foundation for protecting Laura even though she is most in need of the protection or "cover" the right husband could provide (555, 557). Marian, in contrast, seems not to require the same protection. One has to ask why Marian's future should seem any clearer than Laura's, or why it should not depend on a spouse's intervention. Further, why should the legality of Hartright's relationship with Laura be a factor in his ability to help her when it has no bearing on his position towards Marian? Laura's problems were created by marriage and must be solved by a different marriage; in her case, neither wealth nor poverty changes the need for a woman to be "covered" by a husband's protection. Yet there is no less reason to sense impropriety in Hartright's relationship with Marian than there is with her (both of whom share his "assumed name" and "assumed relationship" in their London household [412]) except in so far as he is not called upon to act on Marian's behalf.[28] The traditional marriage plot is thus implemented through Laura's character in a way that makes it a novelistic default position in which she seems to have little agency or will. But by splitting the heroines, Collins exempts Marian from the exigencies that determine Laura's outcome.[29] Laura's plot tracks the covering of the single woman, while Marian's tracks the uncovering that only a single woman can perform.

Marian offers readers the alternative Laura might have enjoyed had she not been forced to marry Glyde: the woman who remains independent. Yet when their positions are equalized, when Laura shares with Marian the social anonymity of impoverishment, it is Marian who acts on both of their behalves. Just as poverty freed the trio from recourse to a legal system that, as Kyrle tells them, could do nothing

[28] One of the most curious facets of this novel about identity is Walter's slim aside (immediately following his resolution to conceal Sir Percival's "character" by preserving his secret) that all the names in the story are assumed (540). On the one hand, the novel presents "character" as unreliable, an "impersonation over time" (Thomas 60), while on the other, it asserts that names are only labels. This story of Laura's identity can take place under any name because her character, her authentic subjectivity, has been constant.

[29] It is also important to look at the ways poverty seems to have worked to their advantage because it made them look for alternative solutions than those the legal system could have provided. As Hartright asks, "If we had been rich enough to find legal help, what would have been the result?" (616). Collins focuses on the two factors which could make a woman most vulnerable, lack of male protection and presence of financial resources, and made Marian's lack of both the conditions of a successful recuperation of her sister's identity and status. See Dieter Polloczek's analysis of Bentham, Mill, and Arnold (in his chapter on *Bleak House*) for discussion of mid-Victorian desires for more access to the law, including greater clarity as to its mechanisms (126–7).

for them, Marian's status as a single woman oddly frees her from the advances and impositions of men like Glyde (Fosco's interest in her notwithstanding, Marian is not subject to the same sort of scheming that surrounds Laura). She can care for Laura and act on her behalf in ways that, as Walter points out, he is unable to because of social opinion.[30] (Hierarchical gender relationships suggest that his help will always risk being construed as a form of coverture, a form of protection but also a reminder of the sexual implications of becoming one person.) She takes control of her own interests by caring for Laura's, and she obviously benefits from Laura's marriage to Hartright and their return to Limmeridge. However, the family tableau at novel's end is interesting precisely because it centers on the single woman. It is Marian who holds the baby, Marian who introduces the son to the father, Marian who ends the story. Collins situates the single woman at the center of the household and of the family. He has not discarded the domestic model of fulfillment, but he has displaced it. Marian has been the instrument of establishing this picture-perfect family, but she retains the independence that made it possible in the first place. In this sense she offers an image of things to come to parallel her own advice to Hartright. Rather than looking to the past to understand their altered circumstances, "We can be just as explicit and much more interesting," she says, "by referring to the future" (622).

If we look to Collins's alternative world for a view of marriage and the single life for women, we get a pretty clear indication that the legal system of equity, try as it may to protect a woman's assets, is no guarantee against the long-established common law rules that make a wife's property her husband's. As he would do in *No Name* for illegitimacy, Collins gives in *The Woman in White* a sensational example of the sorts of stories of abuse and coercion to which married women could be subject.[31] Marian does not possess the property so important to the Victorian sense of identity, and her financial situation makes her a less-attractive bride, but her single status is not constructed so as to appear limiting. Part of the reason lies in Collins's formalization of multiple narrative voices, from which Laura's is noticeably absent as a teller of her own tale, and Marian's authority as author.

[30] To the extent that they both want to take care of Laura, they treat the married woman, or the potential bride, as a child (like the lunatic, another analogy to be found in the legal rhetoric and used to justify the idea of protecting the woman). This language casts them both as parents, but it also works to masculinize Marian in the sense that it becomes unclear whether at the end of the novel she is a surrogate bride to Hartright or a surrogate husband to Laura who introduces her "godson" to his father.

[31] The Law Amendment Society's report cites numerous horror stories in which women are deprived of their incomes by unprincipled husbands who nonetheless have the law in their favor, for example, the woman who established a successful business after her husband lost his job only to have her entire fortune bequeathed in her husband's will to his illegitimate children (343). The report provides this and similar examples to illustrate even the judges' regrets that the legal codes require them to support such flagrant moral abuses precisely because they are not at all legal abuses.

If like Marian we look to the future, to future representations of single women, then, we have to look for changes in the form of the novel.[32]

In the latter decades of the nineteenth century, the shape of fiction about women specifically changed to accommodate new stories about them. From the naturalism of Gissing and George Moore, to the New Woman novel, and Hardy's working women, the novel moved away from representations of single women whose narratives would end comfortably and without controversy in marriage. In some Edwardian examples, the growing concern with the male protagonist's own need for a new narrative form pushes women once again to the margins, yet even there they continue to exert pressure on conventional modes of defining women's identities. For example, the relatively new figure of the woman-as-testatrix uses her will differently than the Victorian male testator. Butler's spinster Alethea Pontifex in *The Way of All Flesh* (1903) is the means of saving her nephew from his overbearing father, and her will, rather than dictating the terms of his identity, makes the inheritance a reward for his own successful growth. Bennett's *Clayhanger Family* (1925) is peopled by several non-traditional women: from the unmarried Maggie Clayhanger and Janet Orgreave, to Hilda, to Auntie Hamps. Auntie Hamps, the matriarchal widow introduced in *Clayhanger* (1910), survives into its sequels *Hilda Lessways* (1911)—itself the back-story of Edwin Clayhanger's unconventional wife—and *These Twain* (1915). Always more interested in "person and individuality" than in "environment" (Bennett *These Twain* 410), she lives a nearly ascetic life and defines herself by her principles rather than her possessions. Without her family's knowledge, she drafts her own testament, and Bennett gives her the scope to write "a wise if rather a ruthless will" whose "provisions, like the manner of making it, were absolutely characteristic of the testatrix" (473). Here a woman's will is allowed both to express her desire and to correspond to her persona in ways traditionally available chiefly to men. And Ruth Wilcox's will presides over *Howards End* (1910) despite her only brief appearance in the novel. It is left to her spiritual heir, Margaret Schlegel, to bring to fruition the desire expressed in Mrs. Wilcox's simple document that the men in her family ignore. In this instance especially, the will acknowledges and rewards the beneficiary's character, rather than molding it into a specific image of the testator.

What bears emphasizing here, however, is that the Edwardian sons are preoccupied with questions Victorian daughters had entertained decades before them. Burdened by an inherited legal system that deprived them of the most conventional modes of identity formation available to men through the ownership of property, Victorian daughters had to find other ways of identifying themselves. As *Little Dorrit* and *Felix Holt* show, that alternative might be a wholesale rejection

---

[32] Jane Miller operates on the assumption that "form makes meaning, and that challenges to social and political forms cannot be expressed within traditional narrative forms without some degree of disruption, subversion, or contradiction" (5). In this light, the critical objection to the double plots of *Felix Holt* certainly registers the extent to which Eliot contradicted traditional narrative forms, creating a new one to support her radical meaning.

of inheritance, a decision for women protagonists to define themselves through narratives of their own creation that emphasize the importance of fulfillment over fortune. Although this sort of idealistic enterprise could lead to happy endings in the fictional world, the practical importance of reform in the real, legal world cannot be overemphasized. On the one hand, it is tempting to welcome the female protagonist's accession to a role from which in effect she had been debarred. On the other hand, the new emphasis on the beneficiary and the necessary relegation of the testator and his will to the past make the woman testator a novelistic latecomer. (This is perhaps why their wills remain in the shadows of the text, already established and known to the reader, but hidden from the beneficiary's knowledge, yet to be fulfilled.) Even if objections to the overly idealistic conclusions of *Little Dorrit* and *Felix Holt*, for example, are justified, one attribute of these fictional worlds is that in them women do not capitulate to the inherited stories about them. Especially for Esther Lyon, the rejection of the "legal plot" suggests the possibility that other legal fictions, like the nineteenth-century property laws then under reform, could also be rejected and re-plotted. In this sense, Victorian daughters begin the process that their Edwardian brothers take up in the twentieth century as they respond to their own burden of inheritance.

Chapter 4
Edwardian Sons and the Burden of Inheritance Redux

Virginia Woolf's 1925 essay "Modern Fiction" pursues the much discussed debate between her and Arnold Bennett as to the merits of each one's literary practices and of the modernist and Edwardian schools of writers they respectively came to stand in for. Referring by name to three of the best-known authors of the early twentieth century, Woolf remarks:

> Mr. Bennett, Mr. Wells, and Mr. Galsworthy have excited so many hopes and disappointed them so persistently that our gratitude largely takes the form of thanking them for having shown us what they might have done but have not done; what we certainly could not do, but as certainly, perhaps, do not wish to do. (151)

Labeling them "materialists," she narrows their fault primarily to an "enormous" and "misplaced labor" put to the task of "making the trivial and the transitory appear the true and enduring" (153). "Is life like this?" she asks. "Must novels be like this?" (154).

Woolf is a natural starting point for any discussion of this new age of fiction because she so clearly articulates the perceived division between the modernist and the Edwardian novel.[1] Her answer to these rhetorical questions is, unsurprisingly, no: life is not to be understood as "a series of gig-lamps symmetrically arranged," nor must the novel confine itself to the dictates of tradition, convention, or any other literal, social structures when attempting to represent it (154). Rather, the novel should convey the *spirit* of life in a form that enters "the dark places of psychology" (156). For Woolf, the modern emphasis should be on "something hitherto ignored; at once a different outline of form becomes necessary, difficult for us to grasp, incomprehensible to our predecessors" (156–7). Although the essay as a whole is clearly meant to provoke (to urge other writers to experiment, yes, but also to twit Bennett), this particular contention seems to have its share of blinkered willfulness. Woolf's accusation seeks to obscure, or at the very least ignores, the degree to which the modernists and the Edwardians shared a sense of purpose about the novel and its project. Certainly, the

---

[1] Robert Squillace casually states in an aside that Woolf "invented" modernism (16), and Douglas Hewitt observes that Woolf is in fact one of very few novelists to write what could be usefully considered a modernist manifesto. The poets wrote about poetry, and other novelists, such as Lawrence, focused on single authors. Woolf alone seems to write about techniques of the novel in the broader context of her social climate so that the methods she advocates appear "inevitable" for, or at least generally applicable to, contemporaneous writers (129).

Edwardians were as interested in individual psychology as Conrad and James had been, and, indeed, Hardy before them, and as the last chapter has shown, women writers among Woolf's predecessors were already experimenting with new forms that would accommodate narratives of their experience and their psyche outside of the conventional marriage plot. Woolf herself would survey some of these writers in *A Room of One's Own* (1931), but many Edwardian authors were already heeding their example. Although they pursued Victorian themes, they too did so through new, more abstract forms. While their forays into formal innovation admittedly never reached towards the experimental limits of a *Ulysses*, they nonetheless work against Woolf's contention that the Edwardians neither felt a need for change, nor could understand it when it arrived.

Samuel Hynes has suggested that the debate between Woolf and Bennett was essentially a personal one, more than a generational squabble between the Georgians and the Edwardians (*Edwardian Occasions* 37), but the same cannot be said of the transition from the Victorian to the Edwardian era and its novels. Critical discussions of those years between Victoria's death and the onslaught of war routinely talk of the Edwardians as a new generation, one that alternately labored under its Victorian inheritance or longed nostalgically for a return of its certainties, but one which, either way, was clearly obsessed with writing about it.[2] "Inheritance" is a grand term: no piddling legacy, it conjures vistas of property and value bigger than any specific object, and although it comes from the past, it ostensibly widens one's opportunities in the present and can even create prospects for the future. But talk of "generations" assumes a vertical pattern: it might mean evolution, but it might as easily mean decline. It might mean building on or squandering one's inheritance, and so Edwardian writers would have to consider which cultural and aesthetic values, which legal structures and literary forms would best reflect their own sense of themselves and their new time. Inheritance in its material form, its abstract significance, and its aesthetic potential is the subject of all the novels I discuss in this chapter where what is at stake, though certainly "transitory," is not at all "trivial" in the way Woolf describes it. Rather, the Edwardians' adaptation

2 To attempt to date an Edwardian Age is in some respects to make arbitrary decisions, not because such an era does not exist, but because there are so many possible brackets for a period that is at best "muzzy at the edges" (Batchelor 2). One could begin quite specifically like the modernists with Victoria's death, which provided the symbolic "historical rupture" they needed in order to view themselves as a new generation (Dickson 23). Equally plausible are the Boer War or the Wilde trial, which signaled for imperialism and aesthetics respectively an irreparable loss of stability (Batchelor 2). The end of the era is no more easily pinpointed than its advent. The death of Edward VII in 1910 coincides with the post-impressionist exhibition and Virginia Woolf's famous bit of history that declared "on or about December 1910, human character changed" (Hynes, *Edwardian Turn of Mind* 325), but WWI is as cogent a point of demarcation, as was the appearance in the same year of the literary magazine *Blast* and its new theory for the arts (Batchelor 2). For discussions of the period more generally, see D. Paul Farr, Geoffrey Harpham, Robert Squillace, Douglas Hewitt, and Jerome Thale.

of the Victorian testamentary novel reinvigorates questions of how the individual defines himself in relation to his predecessors and his culture, how this translates for the writer into a negotiation of the means of representation, and ultimately how the cultural inheritance of realism can be understood.

The Edwardian son and heir, like the Victorian daughter, is constrained by the father's will (in some cases even he must choose, as she did, between fortune and fulfillment). However, the important difference between these children of the Victorian father and the novels about them is that Edwardian sons, though burdened by their inheritance, are freer on the whole to resist its impositions. Samuel Butler's *The Way of All Flesh* (1903) literally bridges the nineteenth and twentieth centuries. John Galsworthy's *The Forsyte Saga* (1922) similarly casts its eye on past generations, which, given its publication history, include the Victorians and the Edwardians; and Arnold Bennett's *Clayhanger* (1910) recounts one son's struggle to overcome his Victorian father and the price of his victory. These literary sons might well be said to labor under a Bloomsian "anxiety of influence," to feel compelled to address and surpass their literary fathers' achievement on the way to becoming stronger writers, but while "influence" and tradition provide a starting point for new works of art, the past's monumental status can also impede originality. That is, when trying to reach an aesthetic ideal, all writers must engage their forbears' work, hence the "anxiety" that they will be overcome by more masterful writers and fail to create new art. While "weak" writers deny influence, unconsciously replicate their inheritance and become lesser versions of previous writers, the "strong" artists can (and will choose to) invoke this past. The Oedipal parricide prevalent in Bloom's theory certainly resonates in the Edwardian writers' relationship to the Victorians. How, indeed, does tradition plot a sort of destiny for these new writers, and what creative agency can they exert to reshape it? What space for themselves can they carve out of a crowded literary pantheon? How, as T.S. Eliot writes in "Tradition and the Individual Talent" (1919), can the mature poet abandon himself to his medium and yet actively alter both the present and the past?

These are questions Bloom sets himself to answer. However, for the same reason that I resist psycho-biographical readings of authors' wills in Chapter 1, I do not invoke Bloom's theories or, for that matter, Lacanian readings of language as the Law of the Father. I am less interested in psychological theories of consciousness formation than in culturally specific, aesthetic developments and their increasing divergence from legal discourse. Taking Eliot's example, then, this chapter charts how the novel becomes different rather than better, or the way it participates in a "development which abandons nothing en route," and "is not from the point of view of the artist, any improvement." And as Eliot continues, "perhaps not even an improvement from the point of view of the psychologist [...]" (para. 6). The questions addressed here through recourse to the novels are: what was the Edwardian sense of subjectivity? How does the novel answer this question? How does the novel situate itself in relation to changes in legal discourse and, integral to this, how did the Edwardian authors use and revise realism in a way that both presages the modernist cult of originality and marks a growing split from law?

Edwardian Dialectic

The Edwardian period offers a kind of dialectical crucible in which the self and society, the will and the novel, Victorian and modernist are recast. In all this talk of "eras" and the term's connotations of temporal, linear boundaries, there is a tendency to forget what is often tacitly understood as shifts in schools of thought, here schools of aesthetic theory. Put differently, a strictly developmental model can obscure the way that trends circulate simultaneously and thus can minimize the complexity of any theory's formative stages. However, if one considers that the winners of this struggle for theoretical ascendancy are often retrospectively determined, then the notion of abrupt breaks must be complicated. Given the confusion over dates, it is more useful to think about the era's characteristics because here the prevailing outlooks are limited to two: one typifies the period as a golden age: socially stable, wealthy, innovative; the other focuses on signs of decay, on an unraveling of the Victorian fabric that finally rends in 1914.

To look at the literature of the period is to see these conflicting viewpoints repeated. Literary periods, like history, are inevitably shaped by subsequent generations whose categories reveal the needs of the present perhaps more strongly than they give insight into the past. Carola Kaplan and Anne B. Simpson explain that for the Georgians at least, to denounce the not-quite-past was a crucial and deliberate part of their own self-fashioning. From 1901 to the outbreak of war, the Edwardian writers had been "highly respected and widely read as artists, critics, and reviewers" (viii), and were only afterwards "grouped together, their differences and disagreements forgotten, as fervent agitators who had tried to rouse the complacent English from their slumber." They become in the minds of the modernists, "pedestrian craftsmen who had spoken with a single, too-strident voice in an earnest-minded literature protesting the smugness of the Edwardian age." To think of the Edwardian era as one of transition rather than break, however, tempers the largely negative effect such views have on our conception of the Victorian novel and the practices of realism, but they should not therefore preclude an appreciation of the Edwardian writers' uniqueness. A better way of understanding them might share William James's theory on time and memory. Arguing against strict boundaries for either, James suggests that the present bears within it aspects both of past and future (Kern 25), and this "stream of consciousness" can provide a model for thinking of the Edwardian era, as well as of the literary techniques emerging then.

In contrast, the modernists' totalizing views are marred by their tendency to exempt themselves from this very pattern and to ignore just how much the Edwardian authors were conscious of their writing as art and of their understanding of what that art should do (Kaplan and Simpson x). In its best sense, "Edwardian" should connote experimentation as much as "modernist" does, in so far as one of its chief attributes is "the ability to hold in tension competing philosophical positions on contemporary culture" (x), and to adapt the novel's form to accommodate these rival claims. Rather than divorcing their literary representations of subjectivity from the social, as the modernist proclivity for an apolitical aesthetics would do (Anderson 4), the Edwardians combined psychological realism with social concerns. "Society" may have been in disarray or at least fragmented, but individual subjectivity could not exist independently of this new human condition. Even in their sense of the history of the novel—indeed because of their sense of it—the Edwardians juggled two competing forms. Responsible in part for the "invention of tradition," they also sought to resist placement in that tradition, to resist the past and formulate a new image of themselves (Trodd 4).[3] In broad terms, then, a consideration of Edwardian literature needs to address three factors: the writers' sense of the relationship between subjectivity and society (especially legal society), their sense of the novel's function in relation to these, and the means through which they implemented their theory.

In a climate of failing First Principles, the idea of ordering systems external to the self and capable of putting the individual in relation with the world around him suffered during the Edwardian years.[4] However, this climate offered the novel an opportunity to reflect on its own development and to re-trench. As influenced by legal models of representation as the novel had been, one of its chief points of contrast to law was its ability to represent the individual more fully, in part by allowing more evidence, so to speak, in its development of subjectivity than the models of the trial and even of the will afforded or allowed. Characters in the novel literally had "character." However, while the novel continued to espouse this understanding of subjectivity, changes in the political make-up of the State and in the discourses, such as law, that supported it pushed towards more utilitarian models of identity.[5] The Edwardian novel by continuing to emphasize subjectivity as character—specifically *as* consciousness and as a character's purposeful response to the institutional frameworks of the previous generation—renewed cultural emphasis on individual experience, on the self and its "becoming" rather than its "being."[6]

---

[3] Anthea Trodd reminds us that many of the major literary anthologies appeared during the Edwardian years: *The Cambridge History of English Literature*, 1907–16; the *Oxford Book of English Verse*, 1900; the Oxford World Classics series, 1905; and Dent's Everyman's Library, 1906; along with the inception of the *Times Literary Supplement* in 1902 (1–2).

[4] See Michael Levenson for discussion of the way these changes prompted a focus on the individual as a "refuge for threatened values" (*A Geneology of Modernism* 61). See also Linda Anderson's discussion of individualism—"the quest for more subjective ways of understanding the self and its relation to the external world" (8)—as a new guiding principle.

[5] See earlier discussions of this difference in the introduction and in Thomas (11, 31). Thomas takes his ideas of the State from Benedict Anderson's *Imagined Communities: Reflections on the Origin and Spread of Nationalism.*

[6] The distinction between being and becoming is one that William H. Marshall makes in his discussion of Edward Overton, narrator of Butler's *The Way of All Flesh*. "Being" implies a sense of "absolutism" and the inability to question received opinion (585), while the "relativism" associated with "becoming" connotes experimentation and compromise (588). Overton's preference for relativism and the idea of a mobile rather than fixed identity is an appropriate description of the Edwardian project of self-definition.

Its candid engagement with the novelistic past meant, moreover, that changes in literary style nonetheless confirmed and strengthened literature's difference from law.

Galsworthy, for example, attends to the primacy of the self but makes certain that the process of self-definition does not occur in a vacuum. Beginning with the question: "What sort of Forsyte am I?" his protagonists move on to consider "Who am I in relation to society?" and further to "Who am I?" Because the novels of the *Saga* are written in different literary periods and are critical of different social periods, the angle of the question is tweaked, revealing both the way individual novels espouse material and spiritual principles of subjectivity as well as the way Galsworthy's emphasis changes over time. *The Man of Property* (first in the series), for example, parodies the Victorian equation of personhood with property so that the novel, because it is written at a distance from that era, reveals a shifting foundation for one's sense of self. In the sequel *In Chancery*, this sense eventually becomes ownership of oneself. Bennett is similarly invested in this development of individual character. Though he may have believed that "the stuff of one self is rather like that of another" (Squillace 97), that essential substance is "utterly plastic" and allows individual people to differ radically according to their experiences. One of his chief complaints against the "more individualistic novels of English literature" is that in them "you will find a domestic organism described as though it existed in a vacuum [...] as though it reacted on nothing and was reacted on by nothing; and as though it could be adequately rendered without reference to anything exterior to itself" (*Author's Craft* 11). "How," he asks, "can such novels satisfy a reader who has acquired or wants to acquire the faculty of seeing life?" (11). And if for the moment we take Conrad as the quintessential border figure (typically taken as a modernist writer for his style, although his major works were all published before 1911), then his sense that human consciousness "provides permanence, pattern, and significance" in contrast to the "evanescent flux of the phenomenal world" (Levenson 2), pushes us towards a view that human consciousness is in some sense unitary without ruling out individual perception or its role in ordering experience.

In these examples, the relationship between the material world and subjectivity varies. It becomes a point of departure for introspection, or a strident, defining force, or a collection of details to which the individual gives shape and meaning in a process that is equally self-definitive. The question of where one places emphasis is important for the novel because the emphasis pushes us in different directions along, or allows for different combinations within, the spectrum of representation: objective worlds are the stuff of realism, malleable worlds of idealism; the individual in community realist, the isolated psychology romantic and increasingly modern, and these permutations help to explain how realism survived Victoria's death and was reincarnated in the hybrid novel of the Edwardian age.

Coming of Age in the Passing of an Age

Edmund Gosse describes his relationship with his father as a "struggle between two temperaments [and] two consciences" (35). With Philip firmly entrenched in the Victorian era and quite literally charged with the "trust" of raising Edmund alone, the autobiography (or biography, depending on which part of the title *Father and Son* [1907] one emphasizes) depicts Edmund's individual efforts "to fashion his inner life for himself" (237) as the much broader conflict between "two epochs" to do the same (35). Just as the young Gosse, newly independent and established in London, was barraged by letters that he describes as a "burden which could hardly be borne" (236), so was the new age confronted with "exquisitely penned" (237) missives from its literary past. Gosse will be the subject of the next chapter, but the three novels discussed here engage the sense of transition he describes by isolating the beneficiary, the son, whose conscious response to his father's textual will signals a *thematic* interest in the metaphysical will even as it offers a *stylistic* counter to the realism of the nineteenth century.

This new generation of artists did not have far to look for a model of their concerns. In "Mr. Bennett and Mrs. Brown" (1924), Woolf identifies Samuel Butler's *The Way of All Flesh* (1903) as one of "the first signs" of the change in character that occurred in 1910 (*Captain's Deathbed* 96). Similarly, a reviewer for the *Times Literary Supplement* noted in 1919 that, although the book's early sales had been slow, "in 1910, the flames caught" ("The Way of All Flesh" 347). At the time the review was printed, the second edition had gone through 11 impressions, and the contributor notes, "The novels that have been fertilized by *The Way of All Flesh* must by this time constitute a large library, with well-known names upon their backs." Indeed, Galsworthy, who read the novel at Edward Garnett's suggestion and "heaped over-lavish praise" on it (Frechét 17), may have learned the technique of interior monologue from Butler (160), while Bennett admired Butler's "ruthless book" for its use of satire and irony (LaFourcade 124).

Butler's posthumous novel (written in 1873 but published 30 years later) enjoyed such popularity partly because his was "a voice from deep within Victorianism mocking the sanctity of the family" along with other traditional institutions (Trodd 54), and, indeed, the novel does illustrate generational conflict and the demise of paternal authority. However, the rationale of this critical reception is more striking than the book's popularity insofar as Butler's admirers cite him as an authority even though Victorian authority is precisely that which they otherwise abhorred. If the point was that even one of their own could criticize the Victorians, then, while it may confirm the opinion of later generations, it paradoxically carries with it the sanction of tradition from which the modernists most strongly wanted to separate themselves. One would expect this sort of ambivalence from the Edwardians, but the modernists' adoption of Butler shows just how selective their break from history was.

When the novel appeared, however, public opinion was more circumspect. An unsigned review from May 1903 comments that "it has for average readers neither the piquancy and importance of the present nor the curiosity of the fairly remote past" ("A Bitter Legacy" 158). Rejecting the suggestion that the book is a "practical illustration of the theory of heredity embodied in *Life and Habit*," he says simply, "we are reminded that we are largely the creatures of our ancestry and that is about all."[7] More important is Butler's purpose "to denounce evil systems of training, false ideas of respectability, and what he believed to be bad conventions generally, and to illustrate the benefits which may be got by defying them." Arguably, the book succeeded in the end precisely because those systems and conventions became associated with a Victorian ancestry, the denial of which formed an important, because conscious, first step in creating the new personal, cultural, and literary identity of the Edwardians.

Edward Overton, narrator of *The Way of All Flesh*, asks a question whose implications hover over the novel as a whole:

> Why should the generations overlap one another at all? Why cannot we be buried as eggs in neat little cells with ten or twenty thousand pounds each wrapped round us in Bank of England notes, and wake up, as the sphex wasp does, to find that its papa and mamma have not only left ample provision at its elbow, but have been eaten by sparrows some weeks before it began to live consciously on its own account? (85–6)

Raised as Overton describes George's death (the second in this story of five Pontifex generations), the question links parental authority with financial control. At the same time, it implies that financial dependence is the chief motivation behind filial observances and suggests that until the child has an "account" of his own, his consciousness will always be in conflict with the father's ability to manipulate it, right along with the purse strings.[8] Although Butler's ironic tone

[7] *Life and Habit* (1878) recounts Butler's theory of evolution in which Lamarck is favored over Darwin (Rubinstein 240). For Butler, natural selection was an unsatisfactory evolutionary model because it depended on "chance and struggle" instead of "the ability of the organism consciously and unconsciously to adapt to its needs." Under the latter theory, the conscious "repetition of an act under differing circumstances" acts on one's memory of past performances to the point where the act becomes unconscious, "perfectly assimilated knowledge," which then "modifies the instincts of successive generations." If the novel is read as an application of Butler's theory, then through George and Theobald Pontifex we see the accretion of the instinct that so troubles Ernest and in whom, in turn, we see the development of consciousness that runs counter to these instincts. "Progress," writes Jill Rubinstein, "demands occasional conscious, intellectual moral decisions, but too much consciousness bars our access to the assimilated knowledge of past generations, the 'continuous evolutionary personality.'" This conflict may explain some of Ernest's haphazardness as an imbalance between instinct and choice. This imbalance eventually becomes a break with the Pontifex personality, which signals Butler's negative application of his own theory as a positive triumph for the individual.

[8] Jill Rubinstein recounts an episode from Butler's life in which his father, disappointed in his son's career choice, similarly threatened to cut him off. Butler left England to take up sheep-farming in New Zealand and, though remarkably successful there, invested his

indicates his own sympathy for the child who miscalculates his father's will (in both senses of the term), he nonetheless maintains that "No one can deny that the testator had strict right on his side," and that George "had a full right to do what he liked with his own money" (86). But "right" is not the same as "just," nor, certainly, "merciful," in Butler.

The chief vehicle for animating this principle is "will-dangling" or "will-shaking" (28), which illustrates both the Victorian primacy of the testator and the restraints placed by his will—the father's intention and his document absolutely equated here—on the beneficiary. George is particularly liberal in his use of the device: "when not quite well he would have [his sons] in for the fun of shaking his will at them" (28), and when they act against his wishes (as when Theo and Christina are engaged), his admonitory letters always include "the more or less obvious shake of the will near the end" (54). Theo is essentially powerless to resist his father whose authority extends so far that Theo, if outwardly different, becomes essentially like him. When his expectations for his own son Ernest are rudely disappointed by his sister Alethea's apparent bequest of her fortune to Overton (instead of to Ernest), Theo writes a preposterous letter to his son in which he questions the legality of his own father's bequest to his grandson and contemplates deducting the costs of Ernest's education and upbringing from it. For Overton, it was all "the same old will-shaking game" (170).

Because Butler believes that money is the foundation of all forms of independence, both material and metaphysical, he is categorically critical of any "abuse" of its "power": from his perspective, it is perfectly sensible that the acquisition and possession of property should influence a person's sense of self, but his autonomy on that account may not be used to deprive another of the right to develop himself simply because he owns nothing. Describing the shake of the will as an "engine of torture" too often employed, he in fact contemplates a new law:

> I would pass a law, if I could, to incapacitate any man from making a will for three months from the date of each offence [...] and let the bench of magistrates or judge before whom he has been convicted, dispose of his property as they shall think right and reasonable if he dies during the time that his will-making power is suspended. (28)

A harsh sentence, this dispossession inflicts on the guilty testator the same inability to define and perpetuate himself that he has visited on his heirs (and that had been visited on married Victorian women as well).

The above examples correlate the legal document with the individual's subjective sense of agency. Free exercise of the latter is an essential component

---

profits badly when he returned home. In need of income, he proposed to borrow money on the strength of some property his grandfather had bequeathed him. But Butler's father, who controlled the property, would not change his own will so that Samuel could take immediate possession. Instead, he offered him an allowance contingent on Samuel's submitting a record of his expenditure. As Rubinstein suggests, this sort of control must have grated strongly on Butler's autonomy who was then 41 years old (238).

of character, but the financial dependence of sons leaves no object on which to exercise this will, and in fact no agency to exercise in the first place when its material foundation requires property. In this sense, Butler's rhetorical strategies show his Victorian side and even augment the criticism Dickens leveled at John Harmon just eight years earlier in *Our Mutual Friend.* However, Butler's novel differs from the usual Victorian emphasis on the testator in two important ways. The first is the contrast Alethea Pontifex's trust offers to these examples of the male testator and their negative use of the will.[9] In possession of some £20,000 (nearly all accruing interest), the unmarried and childless Alethea has her fortune to thank for releasing her from dependence either on her brother or on a husband, as well as from both her father and brother's sense of wealth's punitive potential. In want of "someone to leave her money to" (150), she views the will as a tool to be used "genially and sensibly" and to make people "happy."[10] The second and chief difference between her will and theirs, however, is her feeling that the actual money is separate from her sense of self. This distinction is at once a privilege reserved for the single, propertied woman whom Butler allows to remain single; it is also women's compensatory response to being otherwise cut off from the forms of subject formation reserved for property-holding men in the Victorian legal and literary worlds.

In Butler, money certainly encourages autonomy and enables one to fulfill desires, but it does not necessarily alter those desires or the character that derives them. Commenting on Ernest's "impulsiveness and sanguine trustfulness" (160), Alethea observes that money would only make her protégé a more obvious target for deception (what we might think of as a male Laura Fairlie). An outright gift would certainly make him a target of his father. Her task is to make a loving will and to extend her spiritual guardianship, which she does by establishing an unofficial trust, one which she knows will be "unpleasant and invidious" to carry out, and which Overton, as trustee, does experience "keenly" as a burden he's been "saddled" with (165). This trust places the burden on Overton precisely so

9 Alethea's position as a single woman with "absolute control" (145) of her property recalls the discussion of property law as it impinged on women's ability to be self-determining. Alethea assumes sponsorship of Ernest in 1849 (146). Overton remarks that she had been living in London for 12 years (149) since the time of her father's death (145). So she came into her money in 1837 in the same year the Wills Act was enacted.

10 Overton notes that although Alethea avoids her other siblings, she remains interested in Theobald because "they two were the hares of the family, the rest being all hounds" (145). Theo, in whom "the power to oppose was so completely lost for want of exercise that hardly did the wish remain" (33), reacts to this "hounding" by doing as his father wishes and eventually becoming like him. It is hard to know why Alethea should apparently escape. She may just be a more perceptive, more self-assured person. Or it may be that as a single woman, she is in fact burdened with fewer roles than Ernest is expected to fulfill. For lack of information to the contrary, this last would seem to be true of at least George's expectations of her; of her siblings, Overton writes that they had "made her life a burden to her until the death of her father had made her her own mistress" (164).

that Ernest will not have to experience it. And because it is negotiated outside of law (Overton appearing publicly as heir but privately agreeing to invest the money until he deems Ernest ready to manage it), it makes the sanctions and potential censures purely moral instead of legal.[11]

Ernest certainly lives up to his Aunt's perceptive expectations. Deceived by religious quacks, jailed for assault, unwittingly married to the bigamous servant Ellen with whom he has two illegitimate children, Ernest learns his lessons. When he comes into his fortune (by now £70,000) after not having communicated with his parents for years, he is largely independent, both in spirit and in terms of his career and associates. He even intends not to tell his father about the money because "it would be too cruel; it would be like Isaac offering up Abraham and no thicket with a ram in it at hand" (387). These reservations notwithstanding, however, Ernest does tell his father in a scene that marks the transformation money can affect as well as Butler's second point of departure from the Victorian emphasis on the testator. Shortly after he comes into the money, he receives a sanctimonious letter from Theobald telling him his mother is dying and offering to pay for a suit of clothes for the funeral. When Ernest arrives at Battersby, his father deflects questions about Christina and insists on learning if Alethea's trust has been "open and above board" (391).

Ernest's return to Battersby for his mother's funeral brings with it past associations, but though "the surroundings were the old familiar ones [...] the surrounded were changed almost beyond power of recognition." As one of those "surrounded," Ernest is the only one really to have altered. He turns on his father "in a moment" and delivers a few "effectual" words that instantly change Theobald's sense of their relationship so that he "never again spoke to his son in such a way as to make it necessary for him to repeat what he had said on this occasion" (392). Having lost the power to shake his will at Ernest (in fact, it is agreed later that Theo can divide all his money between Ernest's siblings only), Theo is forced to abandon his right to dictate to his son. "What he had said" is never told, but Butler orchestrates this conversion in the context of a passing generation and an inheritance. Two questions are posed—Ernest's about his mother and Theo's about money—but for the reader they remain incomplete communications. This reticence might be understood as narrative decency, an effort to spare both Ernest and Theo's private exchange from the prying reader in the same way that Ernest originally intends to spare his father's humiliation. But those crossed questions also demonstrate the difficulty of communication across generations that Edwardian authors could appreciate so well and which they thematically adopted in their novels—that the reluctant Ernest does finally muster the decisive word would be further reason for praise.

This mixture of reticence and self-assertion is an important dimension of Butler's position as the anti-Victorian Victorian. It recalls D.H. Lawrence's

---

[11] See Chantal Stebbings's excellent study *The Private Trustee in Victorian England*, especially her discussion in Chapter 2 of the special relationship between the testator—or, in the terms of trust law, the settlor—and the person chosen to act as trustee.

complaint against Galsworthy: whether one is materialist or anti-materialist, one's outlook is nonetheless bound to some consideration of the material and therefore makes a "social being" rather than a human one ("John Galsworthy" 211, 219). To the extent that Ernest is passive, willing to enjoy his new mental and material position without flaunting it before his father, he achieves a moral (anti-material) victory in this generational struggle by refusing to fight. However, he responds when provoked with the (material) weapons that are no less familiar to him than they are to the quintessential Victorian who has used them against him, that is, a will backed by money. Butler, by allowing the son to conquer the father, clears the field for the Edwardian struggle for consciousness, much as Edmund Gosse will do in *Father and Son* (1907). However, by maintaining the material and legal terms of this contest (and allowing these to become more important components of interiority than the false religious spirituality the novel famously exposes), he also lays the foundation for their literary confrontation with the Victorians.[12]

Similar to that of *The Way of All Flesh*, the publishing history of John Galsworthy's *The Forsyte Saga* (1922) is itself emblematic of shifting generations. Originally written as three separate novels, the saga began in 1906 with the publication of *The Man of Property*, which, set in 1886–87, offers an Edwardian view of the Victorian period. The second installment, *In Chancery*, did not appear until 1920, but concluding as it does with the deaths of Queen Victoria and James Forsyte and, as Geoffrey Harvey observes, with the birth of a third generation (viii), it foretells a coming Edwardian age from the perspective of one writing in modernism's heyday.[13]

The novels' thematics of inheritance, perhaps more strongly than their style, registers Galsworthy's sense of transition. This distinction is especially true of *The Man of Property* where the focus is fairly evenly split between the aging personae's stance towards the up-and-coming generation and that generation's

---

[12] Butler's novel, along with Gosse's biography and Anthony Trollope's *The Warden* (1855) form an interesting subset of works. In all three, religion is the primary institutional framework associated with the father's, or in Trollope's case, with the testator's charitable will. Yet in all three, the critique of the religious institution or the characters who represent it is conducted in legal terms of inheritance, money, and the will. The religious and social debates about free will and determinism are thus carried out in legal terms and comments on the relative social significance of each institution. For more on Butler specifically and his satiric inversion of biblical teaching, see J.L. Wisenthal.

[13] Alec Frechét speculates about the reasons for the *Saga*'s instant success: "Following publication of Lytton Strachey's biographies," he writes, "*The Forstye Saga* provided the most comprehensive, powerful and monumental expression of the anti-Victorian climate of the post-war period" (2). Nevertheless, this past provided ballast for shaken sensibilities looking to reassert themselves. If the Victorian age was "an object of mockery," on the one hand, on the other, "it was also regarded with curiosity and a peculiar pride": "satire and nostalgia were, or appeared to be, blended in just the right proportions to nurture self-esteem and sensitivity" in such a way that readers and the nation itself could "regain its self-confidence, reassert its identity, understand itself better."

response to it. In this sense, the saga's first installment is very much like the Victorian novel in its focus on the testator, the contingency of his social identity and sense of self on material property, and his use of the last will as a mechanism to control his own and his children's identity; they become his agents in a parallel of the political transformation of nation to state and of character to its agent. *In Chancery* shifts this attention more fully to the new, mature generation and its reactionary efforts to "possess oneself." This relocation of subjectivity from the outside world of things to the internal one of consciousness maintains the theme of inheritance, but even here the kind of inheritance is divided. If young Jolyon and some of his cousins seem to have loosened the bindings of their Victorian Forsyte heritage (choosing fulfillment over fortune like Amy Dorrit or Esther Lyon), Soames represents the persistence of the past. As a eulogy on the Edwardian age, *In Chancery* thematically depicts its dual character as a time of loss and an opportunity for change, but as the indirect discourse of James's ruminations over Victoria's funeral illustrate, the novel pushes towards stylistically modernist treatments of interiority.

The overwhelming sense in *The Man of Property* of Victorian clutter, of being surrounded by things, is an essential component of revealing the Forsyte character, and yet the novel is too obsessively concerned with the "law of possession" (71) and its ethos that everything—art, real estate, cash, and people—is quantifiable to be taken as an endorsement of this Victorian ideology. Young Jolyon defines a "Forsyte" as "a man who is decidedly more than less a slave of property," one whose "grip on property—it doesn't matter whether it be wives, houses, money, or reputation—is his hallmark" (194). Theirs is an obtuse mentality that can disparage Swithin's obesity (47), yet fail to see its analogy to the family's own identification with massive wealth. With doubly layered irony, Galsworthy has young Jo describe his father's generation as a distinct type. Despite the forward vision implied by their name, the Forsytes are "hereditarily disposed to myopia" (194), he tells Bosinney, capable of recognizing "only the persons and habitats of his own species." By having Jolyon speak of what must be his own heritage, yet allowing him greater vision than possessed by his predecessors, Galsworthy establishes a difference between the old Victorians and this son. Although the Forsytes are presented as a type that transcends time, it is clear that for Galsworthy this type reached its mature form in the nineteenth century. Infusing *The Man of Property* with images of the deaths of these Victorian founders, Galsworthy creates a Victorian setting and focuses on the transmission of their material property (along with the sense of group identity it represents), yet he shows their ethos in decline. Like young Jolyon, he assumes the critical distance that enables him essentially to parody the Victorian novel's use of the documentary will and, through his portraits of Soames and young Jolyon, to express the antagonistic Edwardian values of adherence to tradition and separation from it.

Like the Victorian novel, *The Man of Property* deals explicitly with a legal will and its power to transmit feeling, personality, and desire via material possessions. After Old Jolyon renews his relationship with his estranged son, he visits his brother James (who along with Soames acts as the family solicitor) to view his will. James is immediately intrigued: "Perhaps nothing in this life was more stimulating to him than a will; it was the supreme deal with property, the final inventory of a man's belongings, the last word on what he was worth" (245), and, one can add, the last word on "who" he was, how true a Forsyte.[14]

Jolyon is well satisfied with the will as a piece of legal work and smugly anticipates the "majestic effect of that little paragraph in the morning papers accorded to Forsytes who die with a hundred thousand pounds" (246)—a reminder of the weekly Wills and Bequests columns George Sala joked about and *The Spectator* mined for its examples of "degenerate" wills. The paragraph of bewilderingly dense legal language that follows (sample of the further "seven folios of brief and simple phraseology" Galsworthy with tongue-in-cheek calls it) reveals a comparatively modest bequest to his son with the residue of the property designated for June.[15] Old Jolyon reverses this arrangement, but mixed with this pleasure of having recompensed his son is the satisfaction of revenge—"against Time, sorrow, and interference"—and of self-assertion. The altered legal document "presented itself as the one possible way of asserting once more the domination of his will; of forcing James, and Soames, and the family, and all those hidden masses of Forsytes [...] to recognize once and for all that he would be master" (247). With one stroke, old Jolyon uses his legal will as a means of establishing the paramountcy of his desiring will and of himself as "master." Even more interesting, however, is his sense that the power to define oneself which property conveys is not quite satisfactory. As a man for whom the acquisition and possession of property has been central to his sense of self, the aged Jolyon wonders, "What pleasure was there left but to give?" (248). Though this legacy does not seem much of a burden for young Jolyon to bear (for whom, echoing Hazlitt, the news revealed "vistas of property [...] in his brain" [249]) part of the reason lies in his father's acknowledgment of his son's already self-designed life. Old Jolyon signaled his disapproval of his son by withdrawing his legacy in the same way he now shows acceptance by restoring it.

In some respects, Old Jolyon's "pure Forsytism" is alloyed by such examples of eccentricity (349). He is the first not to be buried in the family vault at Highgate, and he raises the collective Forsyte eyebrow by being the first to leave money

---

14 Frechét observes that Galsworthy "will provide any information on a will, the value of a stolen object, the price of a house, only if the understanding of a character requires it" (122). These examples of Jolyon's will work to convey his sense of mastery and control, and ultimately these are offered as the reasons one acquires and maintains property, and Galsworthy's alternate focus on his characters' interiority suggests that "he uses the theme of property in such a way as to transcend it" (124).

15 Galsworthy read law at Oxford and after graduation continued his studies in London until finally coming to the Bar in 1890 (Sternlicht 14). He worked only very briefly for his father's firm, but one of his jobs was to construct "his own family tree, in order to sort out a particularly thorny legal issue" (Frechét 12). Apart from the similarity to the prodigious Forsyte family tree that fronts the *Saga*, he seems to have used his legal knowledge, as Frechét suggests, for satiric purposes (14).

outside the family. His perceived oddities mark the beginning of a shift in attitude encapsulated in an observation, made by one of the younger generation on her aunt's cremation, that "people have a right to their own bodies, even when they're dead" (350). However, as the remaining older generation of siblings observes: "[H]er remark did undoubtedly show expansion of the principle of liberty, decentralization and shift in the central point of possession from others to oneself" (350). Her father also testily comments "there was no denying the revolt among the younger Forsytes against being owned by others" (351). Written about the emergent Edwardian age from the perspective of 1920, these comments convey the "shift," "revolt," or response of a new generation asserting its own self-possession, its psychic will, against the dictates of that older branch that lumps children with Consols. Indeed, this younger generation reaps further disapproval for their failure to reproduce as ostentatiously as their parents: "Sooner in fact than own children, they preferred to concentrate on the ownership of themselves, conforming to the growing tendency—*fin de siècle*, as it was called" (352).

Like his provocative cousin, young Jolyon senses that "the very hub of possession is to possess oneself" (540), but his attitude has always been less doggedly literal than that other cousin's, Soames. Soames, some 30 years after old Jolyon came to the same realization, finds the accumulation of money insufficient unto itself because he has no children, "no real object for going on with his religion" (354). Described as always having had a "philoprogenitive side" (354), Soames is fixated by the idea of having a son, the possession of whom would signal further self-possession for him. But where Old Jolyon's self-assertiveness is mitigated by a real desire to make amends, Soames's is purely selfish, an extension of the belief that real "Forsytism" is not merely the creation of wealth but its transmission. "To have an heir, some continuance of self, who would begin where he left off," he muses, would "ensure, in fact, that he would not leave off" (354). The consolidation of property is rendered synonymous with complete self-hood, and just as Soames's particular genealogy will pass away if he has no children "to leave himself to" (438), so will the property be diffused if he has to leave it to others. Even contemplation of the "Forsyte Bequest" (559) is more satisfying than the reputation his nephew Val is making in the Boer War: Forsyte lineage notwithstanding, Val's name is only Dartie, and his successes or failures cannot thus reflect on the Forsytes (558). These equations of children with property transforms them from characters with independent wills into agents of their parents' wills, individual identities whose energies are dedicated to furthering someone else's aims in a post-industrial society. They demonstrate the way that Galsworthy makes Soames representative of the Edwardian compulsion to protect the past and ensure continuance of its mentality and values in the face of such radical change as reflected in his cousins' attitudes.

That Soames is a solicitor also reveals the way that law works to maintain this social order and its conception of subjectivity (the importance of will-making heightened by having children but also, as here, having children precisely to satisfy the strong desires of will-making). Incorporated into the novel, however, his viewpoint offsets the novel's ability to develop its own critical distance not only from history, but also from such institutional projections of identity in favor of internalized models of subjectivity grounded in consciousness. Galsworthy locates these paired representational and historic changes most clearly in the other paired passings of the Queen and of James, Soames's father. In the chapter "The Passing of an Age" Soames and his new bride attend Victoria's funeral. As the cortège makes it way through the city, Soames grasps his wife more tightly and worries over Edward's accession, "Things would never be as safe again as under good old Viccy" (568). In response appear Irene and Jolyon: "rebels to [her] ideal," and reminders of the fragility of Victorian principles in a modern world. Galsworthy marks the oscillation between these two views of Victorianism again when that "vision of the past" Irene recedes just as Victoria comes again into focus. As the "coffin of an Age" nears, Soames hears the spontaneous last gasp that is the "tribute of an Age to its own death" (569). His father, watching from home, asks his wife if she's heard the noise coming from the crowd, and this time the reader is assured it is "the groaning in his own heart at sight of his Age passing" (571). Soames's view of the funeral parallels his father's. They offer two separate but simultaneous views of an object available to both. That their views coincide makes Victoria's death an "horizon of meaning," to borrow Elizabeth Ermarths's phrase, for this scene—Galsworthy's nod to the consensual techniques of realism—as well as an horizon of meaning for the era his novel reflects upon.

Soames and James's shared sense of the passage of time and of cultural identities nevertheless provokes different reactions. James can resign himself to his own imminent death because he has Soames to secure the future, but Soames, who has already gripped the present, must look to the future. On the night his father dies, for example, he goes to James with news of his own long-awaited child. Like Dombey revisited, Soames is disappointed that he has a daughter (because, like Val, she cannot always remain a "Forsyte"), but when he returns home and sees the baby for the first time, paternal pride asserts itself as a sense of "renewed possession" (593).

In Chancery ends with Soames's triumph. His individual identity is secured through the extension of his family, as much of his forlornness as he sits at Highgate at the end of *To Let* is attributable to his having just married off Fleur and buried Timothy, last of the old Forsytes. This link between the foundation of the self and things outside it led D.H. Lawrence to posit a split between one's "subjective and objective consciousness" ("John Galsworthy" 212): when a human being "becomes too much aware of objective reality, and his own isolation in the face of a universe of objective reality," he writes, "the core of his identity splits [...] and he becomes only a subjective-objective reality, a divided thing hinged together but not strictly individual." Galsworthy asserts that Soames has too much "primeval wisdom" (850) in him to be beaten by the changes multiplying around him. This provision should satisfy Lawrence's requirement of "naïve assurance" and "natural innocent pride" for the maintenance of coherent humanity (213), yet Lawrence's criticism of Galsworthy's typological treatment of his characters is one that other critics felt the need to address even before Lawrence's essay.

When *The Man of Property* first appeared, the presentation of a type from its own viewpoint, itself an oxymoron of sorts, was a technique to be admired. One reviewer for the *Times Literary Supplement* noted that reading the novel was like "watching a procession": "you sit still and see things and people go by; but you see them through others' eyes, and the progress of the story is the progress of your comprehension of those others' point of view" ("The Man of Property" 116). (In light of James's vigil at his own window in *In Chancery*, written long after this review, the extended metaphor is predictive: "you sit with the other members of the family and watch—affected but not changed—from your dignified post at a first-floor window" [116].) There is no objection to this "Forsyte point of view" because it is accepted as the author's lesson for his audience. Another reviewer in 1922 was rather more willing to quibble with him. He quotes Galsworthy's comment that his decision to call the trilogy a "saga" might draw questions because of its association with mythic or imagined times and because "'it connotes the heroic and there is little of heroism in the pages'" ("The Forsyte Aga" 411). The reviewer agrees; he does in fact object because for him "Galsworthy's people exist and move on the same plane as ourselves." Yet the novel's greatest virtue lies in its "real, recognizable characters" and its ability to make the reader identify with them: "indeed, while we are in the book, it *is* our own family, we ourselves are Forsytes." The interest in the book is very much the result of the reader's sense (that Hardy cited as a principal criterion of a novel's worth) that its characters are real, not heroes, but people presented in such a way that readers are convinced of their genuineness without the novel's being "merely a transcript of reality."

Though the reviewer does not attempt to define this method, Alec Frechét suggests that Galsworthy's characters acquire their individuality by "contradicting the type they represent" (128).[16] He defines group characteristics and insists that individuals must be members of some forum beyond themselves, yet he exposes the limitations of any institution to define character or subjectivity entirely (129). Galsworthy thus enables readers to view his characters in their social context (indeed, the discussion of types indicates that social context is an "identity"—the Forsyte), but he also pushes them to view his characters' internalized responses to this outward identification and to the shifting terms of Forsytism. Property can function as a kind of social millstone, weighting character to material foundations and legal mechanisms, or it can afford Galsworthy's characters the luxury of self-possession. Caricatured in *The Man of Property* as the older generation's emphasis on the possession of things, the younger generation's self-possession becomes the focus of *In Chancery*. In the same way, that text offers the opposing movements of Jolyon's and Soames's understanding of self-possession and provides a further set of oppositions between the acquisitive past (because focused on possessing things outside the self) and the

---

[16] One can certainly ask in what sense Soames is not fully a Forsyte. The statement seems to apply better to young Jolyon, and, of course, it matters whether this lack of integration is a case of failure or of choice. It seems more important to emphasize this idea of opposing movements and their complementarity.

more generous future (because focused almost exclusively on possessing only the self). Written 21 years after Victoria's death yet taking her passing as its central (and centrally located) emblem, *The Forsyte Saga* emphasizes the individual's conscious response to his inheritance. If Galsworthy is guilty of typologizing his characters, then in the *Saga* they typify their own era's opposing movements towards the past and future.

Arnold Bennett criticized Galsworthy's brand of realism, saying that the lines were too harshly drawn to be beautiful, which is to say that what he gained in thematic clarity, he lost in artistic subtlety. Early reviews of *Clayhanger*, however, attest to Bennett's own realist heritage. T.M. Young said in *The Manchester Guardian* that the novel "rivals in dimensions the world of […] the middle Victorians" and praised its "large view of human life" (rpt. in Hepburn 255).[17] An unsigned review in the *TLS* likened *Clayhanger* to the French naturalist novels that seek "not to exalt, or essentialize, or satirize, but to present, life," and called it a "triumphant epic of the commonplace" (244–5). James Douglas, writing for the *Star*, modified the basis of Bennett's realism and found the novel "a masterpiece of emotional verisimilitude with just the physical verity that is necessary to make you feel like an eye-witness" of its episodes (248). As was suggested of Galsworthy, Bennett's success lay in his character development, which the use of material details was meant to evoke without overshadowing. The method succeeded for Douglas, who maintained "there are few novels that take you so absolutely into the inner consciousness of a human being" (247), thereby marking out the novel's newly reinvigorated domain. Claiming at one point that "every generation has its own view of its own life," he asks later "is there any novel which depicts quite so sincerely the terrible gulf between a father and his son?" (247).

One could certainly answer with Gosse's *Father and Son* or Butler's *The Way of All Flesh*. Like these, Arnold Bennett's *Clayhanger* (1910) chronicles the relationship between another father and son, the eponymous Darius and Edwin, whose conflicts evoke the Edwardians' view of their own generation, as Douglas's comments imply. On a thematic level, Edwin's maturation naturally signals a decline in Darius's authority and his eventual death. The overlap of the generations they represent, reminiscent of Overton's analogy of the wasp in *The Way of All Flesh* and of Galsworthy's multiple Forsytes, depicts this transition as a process of consciousness rather than the result of a mechanistic or legal shift. In this sense, the execution or probate of Darius's will becomes essentially a formality in light of the transfer of authority that occurs before his death. However, it is a formality that has to be observed in Bennett's stylistic association of the past and past literary methods with external detail and the present with interiority or consciousness.[18]

---

[17] The following reviews are reprinted in Hepburn, *Arnold Bennett: The Critical Heritage*. Page references are to that volume.

[18] Anthea Trodd argues that Bennett's materialism is a consciously deployed facet of his style, a means of reinforcing the "sheer weight of the material inheritance with which

Readers are given glimpses into Darius's own consciousness early in the novel. He is infuriated by Edwin's desire to become an architect instead of taking control of his father's printing business. Through the novel's quick narrative shift to interior monologue, we hear Darius assure himself, "He meant to save his business, to put his business before anything. And he would have his own way. He would impose his will" (147). The printing business is the principal outward expression of Darius's individuality and social mobility, the result of his will to raise himself from the degradations suffered in his youth at the Bastille workhouse. In the conversation that ensues, however, he asks his son, "What's this business o' mine for, if it isna for you?" (148). The question is not entirely disingenuous because Darius's sense of his own success is informed by the better position in which it places his son, but he looks for Edwin simply to occupy the place he has created, to maintain this monument to his father's achievement, rather than to continue the process of evolution in accordance with his own individual desires.[19] Edwin pleads with his Aunt that "a son could not be expected to be exactly like his father" (149), but this is essentially what Darius, like Soames Forsyte, wants because it would mean the perpetuation of his ambitions and of himself.

Edwin Clayhanger suffers continually under a sense of his father's tyranny and waits for the time when, in an echo of his father's own words, he "would have his own way," and "would impose his will" against his father's (147). Book III entitled "His Freedom" reveals that Darius has two years to live and balances his physical decline with Edwin's assumption of responsibility for both the business and his own life.[20] At first, Edwin experiences a sort of psychic unraveling, "as if his own egoism

---

his young protagonist has to contend" (48). In this way, the story of Darius's childhood, as an instance of Victorianism, must be presented as and in a realistic episode (50). Robert Squillace likewise suggests that Bennett's "great theme" is the "inadequacy of observation of material facts" to complete knowledge (33). Rather than create "new languages of fiction" that would make the point more obvious, Bennett uses the time-worn and unsuspected language, the revelation of whose complicity makes the point more powerfully (35). This, incidentally, is the reason Woolf objects to Bennett. For Squillace, she simply misreads him, mistaking his use of the form for his endorsement of it (28). Squillace's is a persuasive reading, but I am uncomfortable with his implication that nineteenth-century realists never questioned the adequacy of material observation or that their use of language was devoid of twentieth-century skepticism. If Bennett did not adopt an overall realist philosophy, neither do his novels amount to its wholesale rejection.

[19] For a full discussion of the influence of Herbert Spencer's theory of social evolution on Bennett's fiction, see Lincoln. Squillace picks up this discussion and argues that Bennett departs from Spencer's theory to the extent that he won't wait for evolution; he advocates "deliberate human action" as the hallmark of self-determination (88).

[20] Squillace points out that at the time of Darius's collapse, Gladstone had introduced the Home Rule Bill for Ireland, which was still on the table when Bennett was writing the novel in 1910. For Squillace, Bennett's use of social, political markers is part of his evolutionary theory that shows the way human and social development parallel one another. The introduction of this bill for political independence, then, should be read as Edwin's similar bid for autonomy.

was lying about in scattered pieces" (327). This fragmented self suits the idea of an alienated identity, one that is separate from its own internalized foundations and dependent on the organizing agency of the literal patriarch. In this sense, Darius's decline erodes that external foundation so that Edwin must "reconstruct" these pieces of his identity in order to "resume possession of himself" (327). This cutting loose of the individual from its social, objective foundation is offered both as a traumatic experience and as an opportunity. It clears the way for new subjectivities, but it also leaves the question of how the new character will emerge—whether from within and, if so, whether it will be reunited with something external to the self. Lisa Rodensky has suggested that modernist narratives typically reject such efforts to reintegrate character through a "coherent narrative of one's past" (215). Edwin thinks of "resuming" self-possession, but up to this point in the novel, this "self" and his personal history have been more fully his father's to define than his. His maturation will require the recognition of this distinction and the movement away from his father's story into his own, hence the section's title "His Freedom." The novel depicts this coming into the self as a gradual liberation, the resumption of a process predicated on the history of the first two books. It marks the overlap and slow separation of one generation from another, one era from its predecessor (rather than the abrupt break claimed by the modernists) in a narrative of one's future rather than the past.[21]

Symbolic episodes highlight this complex transposition of father and son roles. On the night Darius falls ill, for example, Edwin sits in his father's easy chair. The chair, which had once "meant that the father's presence obsessed the room" (63), has "silently, and without permission" been moved to Edwin's room. Although Edwin is comfortable with such subtle instances of self-assertion, he recoils from more direct confrontations, such as inquiring into the status of Darius's will, or

---

[21] Rodensky focuses on *Tess of the D'Urbervilles* as a "critique of the idea of a coherent, continuous personality that may be held accountable for its actions" (215). The novel's separation of the body that acts from the internalized will signals a fragmentation in literary conceptions of the relationship between intention and action, and therefore of character, in contrast to their persistent equation in law (214). This legal equation carries over to the legal document in the sense that the testament, like the body, is a conduit of intention. I concur with Rodensky's argument in the sense that the novel is more skeptical about the sufficiency of the external, in this case the documentary will, to represent intention. This is why the Edwardian novel emphasizes a movement away from literal testaments and realist methods towards a thematic of inheritance and explorations of character from the inside. However, if the new literary model of "character" implies that the individual can no longer be held accountable for its criminal actions (because acts were performed under different states of self-consciousness and therefore of being), then neither can purposive efforts to define oneself be credited. I see the movement towards modernism as an attempt to return identity to its roots in consciousness, but I do not share Rodensky's implicit view that by making the individual the arbiter of identity, the novel necessarily divorced intention from the idea of "coherent personality." But see Martin Wiener on criminal character in a deterministic worldview in *Reconstructing the Criminal Character*.

asking for the keys and financial responsibility for the shop. Indeed, when Darius and Edwin do make arrangements for the administration of the business, Edwin is surprised by his father's apparently instantaneous submission. The passage that describes this shift blends Darius's thoughts and mood with Edwin's, revealing through the son's interpretation of his father the presence of Darius's consciousness in Edwin's own:

> It meant that always in the future he would have the upper hand. Probably nobody realized as profoundly as Darius himself his real and yet mysterious inability to assert his will against the will of another. The force of his individuality was gone. He who had meant to govern tyrannically to his final hour, to die with a powerful and grim gesture of command, had to accept the ignominy of submission. (340)

And, we learn, Edwin "had merely announced his will." More than any external sign, the internal will is the defining feature of individuality. The keys and checks are important solely as emblems of Darius's strength of will. Passing them on to his son marks a more symbolic bequest than the testament can do at his death because it is hardly his own volition that rules the house any longer.

The transition is at once uncomfortable and exciting. Edwin regrets what he deems acts of "humiliation" by which he assumes his father's control for himself, the worst being when the invalid Darius, weeping, can barely articulate his wish that Edwin should have his watch with its "massive Albert chain" (378). His father's sense of gratitude is humiliating for him, but ennobling for Edwin. Darius dies on the same night as the Tories win the election with a 439-vote majority. Edwin, a Liberal, is disgusted, and vows to become a better Radical. This vow confirms a sense of freedom, "The chain was at last broken that had bound together those two beings so dissimilar, so antagonistic, and ill-matched—Edwin Clayhanger and his father" (378).

The great Albert chain of Darius' *memento mori*, at this moment of his death, fails in its purpose against Edwin's stronger will to assert himself. Against the many such physical tokens of inheritance, Bennett juxtaposes a constant stream of individual consciousness working to redefine itself in opposition to the previous generation's bequests. Anthea Trodd has suggested that this rejection of the stylistic past is incomplete because Bennett maintains an authorial voice that directs the reader's attribution of value to particular scenes (51), but the oscillation between this narrative perspective and the novel's more subjective modes, along with Edwin's thematic fate, suggest that the novel, like its protagonist and like the era in which it is written, is in an ongoing process of transition. "Things" still have rhetorical value, and Edwin's Joycean epiphanies, like John Harmon's disguises in *Our Mutual Friend*, are always concerned with his conscious awareness of their symbolic function. The depiction of his consciousness of the relationship between external and internal and the primacy finally given to Edwin's will mark Bennett's revision of the Victorian documentary will.

A New Generation: Law and Literature in the Edwardian Era

Theories of the novel emerging at the end of the nineteenth century participate in a doubled transition. They accentuate the new position in which literature stood to law as parallel, competing discourses, and they provide an immediate context for the stylistic changes implemented over time by the new generation of Edwardian writers. The configuration of reality in both law and literature is indexed to individual subjectivity: legal conceptions of the individual placed him ever more in the service of social structures, reducing individual complexity in the interests of legalistic ways of framing reality and maintaining social order. The realist novel's incorporation of recognizable structures into its alternate worlds established a further basis of comparison between law and literature, particularly between the will and the novel, yet the novel's amplification of details excluded in law, especially those pertaining to the individual as private character versus public identity, provided the novel's critique of law as the most naturally authoritative way of understanding people and the world. This reinsertion, and reassertion, of the facts left out by law gave the novel its own supplementary and reformist character.

At the end of the nineteenth century, the question of how literature defined reality and subjectivity, how much of the social was present in the individual and therefore should be in its representation, began to be answered differently, however, as the above has shown. Nor was law static; rather, the tendencies of each discourse show how they diverged from one another and weakened the basis of comparison between them. Alexander Welsh in particular characterizes the late-century novel as one in which direct "testimony" (in contrast to the managed evidence of "strong representations") became the primary mode of representation through which individual points of view and the "experience of knowing" (or indeed of not knowing) became the primary purpose of narrative (200–201).[22] Realism's interest in empirical epistemologies thus resurfaced, but with a new emphasis on its limitations and a return to the individual character and metaphysical thought that had defined idealism earlier in the century. In this sense, the novel at century's end developed in an inverse relationship to the law, becoming further entrenched in an understanding of subjectivity as an internalized state of consciousness that defines reality—including the "reality" of inherited assumptions, social structures, and representational strategies—in reference to the self.

Realism in the 1890s was associated with the new French naturalism; however, the latter's status as a particularly aggressive literary mode freed "realism" from its material associations and contributed to a renewed application of its philosophical

[22] Lisa Rodensky and Ronald Thomas share an interest in the novel's representation of character, its relationship to intention and overt acts (Rodensky 7) and the "legibility" of identity assumed by forensic science (Thomas 17). However, Rodensky pushes back the point at which these changes occur. Where Thomas argues that the 1850s and 1860s mark a "fundamental shift in the conception of persons" (61) towards identities rather than characters, Rodensky argues that as late as Hardy's *Tess* (1891), the law remains "an institution that holds on to the very notion of character that the novel has set aside" (214).

origins. More specifically, under the older school of realism as idealism, the novel's value lay in its "reconciling influence" that could promote a sense of individual interiority grounded in experience yet overlay it with a spiritual fellowship with others (Anderson 6–7). The new realism as naturalism, however, dispensed with this need to reintegrate the individual into the containing structures of social reality and so marked a first step towards inverting the primacy of social referents to subjectivity. Moreover, the revised realist viewpoint saw in the earlier form's ability to order human relations the possibility that art could become an arbiter of reality; reality would be judged as it accorded with fiction rather than fiction being held to account by its duplication of reality. Paired with naturalism's dedication to showing society its ills in spite of their protests, this rejection became the enabling condition of art's eventual separation from society, which made aesthetics take precedence over reality, made the artist's subjectivity more important than his representativeness, and made the craftsman care more for his works' organicism than public opinion.[23] These shifting values for realism and art, specifically for realism understood as fidelity to something beyond the material world, also explains why lawyers reading in a literal-minded legal culture withdrawn from aesthetics criticized fictional representations of law: they were still reading for the old realism, imperfectly understood.[24]

Both Henry James and Thomas Hardy, the two most prominent critics of the novel during this period, subscribed to the idea that the novel could (and should) so order its author's experience that his interpretation of life became "more true, so to put it, than history or nature can be" (Hardy "The Profitable Reading of Fiction" 144), yet which the good reader will be able to feel as true. In this view, realism comes to connote verisimilitude more than mimeticism. Indeed, Hardy's view of the material detail of realism as "life's garniture" only (145) suggests that "realism" was reductively and indiscriminately targeted for modernist rejection. Writing against the backdrop of contested theories rather than a uniform inheritance, the Edwardians could either reject its premises or adapt them in their own debates about what the novel could do.

Bennett and Woolf are the best-known opponents in the debates about the novel, but before their squabble began in 1923, James and Wells were engaged in one of their own—James criticizing Wells in "The Younger Generation" (1914) and Wells spoofing James in his 1915 novel *Boon*.[25] And Lawrence would follow, first, in the 1913 letter to Edward Garnett where he dismissed the "rather bony, bloodless drama" of the "rule and measure mathematical men" (*Letters* 509), and again in 1927, when he singled out Galsworthy's books as "fake" because "the

---

[23] See Linda Anderson's introduction to *Bennett, Wells, and Conrad* for discussion of this "narrative transition." Although naturalism and aestheticism would seem to be divergent principles, Anderson describes them as "complementary aspects of the same transitionary phase" (14), which formed the Edwardians' "most immediate literary inheritance" (38).

[24] See discussion of late nineteenth-century assessments of law and literature in Chapter 2.

[25] See Harry Blamires's discussion of Wells's response to James in *Twentieth-Century English Literature*, 22.

characters have no blood and bone [and] the emotions are faked, faked, faked" ("John Galsworthy" 221). As Lawrence's point of attack suggests, much of the substance of these debates revolved around issues of characterization versus material representation. And of course one of the greatest ironies of the conflict between the Edwardian writers and the modernists is that both stressed the importance of character development to the representation of "Life": "They appear to me to be interested more in details than in the full creation of their individual characters," wrote one figure in the debates. But which one? This comment would certainly represent the modernist critique, but in fact it is Bennett's statement in "Is the Novel Decaying" (1923), that inadvertently sparked the contest with Woolf (*Author's Craft* 88). The point is that, while they could agree about the centrality of character and thus shared a sense that the novel in the twentieth century had to tackle subjectivity, they differed about how the individual was shaped and consequently what shape the novel had to take.

Raymond Williams has commented that between 1895 and 1914 the main question preoccupying the novel was just this relationship between "psychological" fiction and a competing emphasis on the "sociological" (119–20). The dates form a gap between what can comfortably be considered Victorian and modernist, but they also highlight the available "choices" or artistic models the novel could pursue during this period. Further, they highlight the testamentary novel's mixture of the individual and the social as a teasing out of new possibilities for character formation inside and outside the novel. While James, Conrad, and Forster are named in their own right, Williams represents the Edwardians as a whole by "that composite figure H.G.A.J. Wells-Bennett-Galsworthy" (120). Two points bear making: first, the idea of "choice" is important to keep in mind when considering the Edwardians because it indicates that they were conscious of themselves as having options and being in a position to give new direction to the novel, rather than being bound by "the inherited shaping form of the novel" (126), to accept which was tantamount to accepting the "consciousness" that informed it (this is the same reason their Victorian sisters had to reject the marriage plot). Second, the hybridization of these authors offers a comment on, more than an endorsement of, the fact that these three usually are lumped together, but it is doubtful that they viewed themselves simply as a literary parcel.[26]

[26] Contemporary critics of the Edwardians have certainly gone to great lengths to individuate them. Sanford Sternlicht states categorically that at the time of Galsworthy's death, he was "*the* English writer" whose *The Forsyte Saga* "was the first and only great English three-generation family epic" (1), and Alec Frechét unabashedly declares "he equals and even surpasses George Eliot in the art of literary portrait, and shows greater skill than either Wells or Bennett" (156). In Bennett's corner, we have Georges LaFourcade who names *Clayhanger* as "pretty near to being the masterpiece of English realistic fiction" (123). These accounts are interesting primarily because of each critic's apparent need to raise each writer to prominence and place him somehow above the common perception of the Edwardians, especially since the measure of their greatness (in spite of LaFourcade's claims specifically for the early sections of *Clayhanger*) lies so strongly in the degree to which they outdistance the Victorians and thus approach modernist complexity. I am not at all interested in judging who

Writing in his diary on Christmas day 1910, Galsworthy contemplated his image as reflected by his current work on *The Patrician* (1911). Seeing in it "an impressionist working with a realistic or naturalistic technique," he compared his method to that of his contemporaries; unlike him, "Wells is a realist with an impressionist technique, Bennett a realist with a realist technique, Conrad an impressionist with a semi-impressionistic, semi-naturalistic technique, and Forster an impressionist with a realistically impressionistic technique" (qtd. in Frechét 173).[27]

Galsworthy's effort to fix each author in a literary mode, although clearly ironic, is interesting just the same as a history of the narrative modes—realism, impressionism, and naturalism—circulating not just at the time but also within each writer's work. All of nineteenth-century origin, these aesthetic ideologies constitute a literary inheritance, but in the sense that they are also artistic "techniques," they lose some of their ideological force and become for the writer tools to use in whatever new combination suits. If Galsworthy himself took account of "traditional methods while making them evolve" (Frechét 156), then the same might be said of the other Edwardians without reducing the differences between them.

In contrast to Galsworthy, for example, Arnold Bennett almost certainly would have taken issue with his realist label. Writing in his journal near the time of the publication of his first Potteries novel, *Anna of the Five Towns* (1902), he declared:

> The day of my enthusiasm for 'realism,' 'naturalism,' has passed. I can perceive that a modern work of fiction dealing with modern life may ignore realism and yet be great [...]. My desire is to depict the deeper beauty while abiding by the envelope of facts. At the worst, the facts should not be ignored. (*Journals* 1:84)[28]

In 1908 he remained convinced that realism was not a mode that could produce beauty. Commenting on Galsworthy's *The Man of Property* and *The Country House*, he writes, "They both lack a sense of beauty" and are "as hard and hostile, and as harsh in colour, as a portrait by Sargent. They are also almost entirely deficient in characterization, being crowded with types, not with persons" (*Author's Craft* 203). Identifying Galsworthy's method with that of the premier portraitist, Bennett seems to prefer the impressionism that in literature is most associated with Conrad. Like Conrad's protagonists, who look within for the source of order in the outside world, Arnold Bennett maintained, "when the real intimate work of creation has to be done [...] the novelist can only look within for effective aid. Almost solely by arranging and modifying what he has felt and seen, and scarcely at all by inventing, can he accomplish this end"(*Author's Craft* 24). Without this appeal to "his own individuality [in which] there is something of everybody" (25),

---

was the better writer, but in finding out how they handled their Victorian inheritance so that the question of how one gets a modernist out of a Victorian becomes less difficult to answer.

27 The original passage Fréchet cites is a diary entry for December 25, 1910, collected in H.V. Marrot, *The Life and Letters of John Galsworthy*.

28 The passage is cited in Squillace (20), who uses the three-volume English edition, *The Journals of Arnold Bennett*.

the novel would be nothing but a stale and lifeless idea. Bennett's essay, written in 1913, is interesting because its claims for novelistic realism rest neither with reproducing the material world (this the novelist should "arrange" and "modify"), nor with ignoring it in favor of an imagined one. Rather, it locates reality (called here as in Woolf's essay "Life") with individual perception so that one observer's reality is made to be recognizable to others. In this way, he works towards the consensus that characterized realism, while at the same time focusing on the single consciousness that would typify modernism.

D.H. Lawrence remarked in a letter to Edward Garnett in 1913, "we have to hate our immediate predecessors, to get free from their authority," (*Letters* 509), but if the modernists hated the Edwardians, then what did the Edwardians themselves hate? In one sense, Lawrence's question implies that the Edwardians in fact did not hate the Victorians, at least not enough to have moved beyond them in any meaningful way. In contrast, however, Anthea Trodd's use of the comment to describe the Edwardian novel's thematic and stylistic thrust as "parricidal" (47) suggests that the Edwardians shared with their contemporaries an aggressive need to get free of their literary fathers. Even though fathers do have a convenient way of dying in *The Forsyte Saga* and *Clayhanger*, their sons' responses are never unequivocal, nor is their authors' attitude to their own forbears. Both Galsworthy and Bennett take up the Victorian model of the last will and testament with all its associations: the equation of interiority with external sign, or of selfhood with property; the ability to control identity through control of property; the potential conflict between one's metaphysical will and the social, legal will that binds subjectivity to its jurisdiction rather than allowing the separation of public and private selves.[29] However, rather than focus on the figure of the testator or on his documented will, they only begin with it in order to highlight the beneficiary's response, his own attempts to enact his private will, and they do so in a mode of representation which, because it focuses on the abstract, desiring will, is itself more prone to abstraction, fragmentation, or to a blending of methods that combines tradition with innovation in the same way that familial generations overlap in the stories.

If Virginia Woolf was looking for novels that trace consciousness from moment to moment and espouse the belief that life is located in even the smallest things (Hewitt 129), then *Clayhanger* should have earned praise for Bennett, rather than critical disdain. But modernism is famous for "suppressing its origins" (Levenson x) or "expunging [its] immediate predecessors" (Squillace 19). Raymond Williams points out that the "assault" on both the novel's form and "the idea of literature itself" was already underway at the turn of the century (126), and Samuel Hynes suggests that the modernist movement began before the war. "When it did flower, after the war," he writes, "it was different—more cynical, less assertive about points of morality, and most of all, determined to reject anything that could be identified

[29] This separation of the public and private directly opposes their synonymity in Trollope's mid-Victorian novel *The Warden* (1855) where the conflict between Mr. Harding's private consciousness and his public role and reputation cause him to retreat entirely from the institutional identity.

with pre-war England" (*Edwardian Occasions* 11). Even its pose of newness was in fact no new idea at all, but one that placed them in a trajectory, which began as early as the Renaissance and extended through Romantic originality to their own belated position (Kaplan xiii).[30]

Even if the modernists' claims are approached with skepticism, however, their tremendous determination to be new, as well as the innovation of their methods certainly must be acknowledged. The irony, though, is that their new methods should share so much with the past they repudiate. Even their focus on consciousness and the interior monologue is powerful precisely because of these methods' real-seeming.[31] Woolf's way of talking about her novels in "Modern Fiction" exemplifies her own realist yearnings. She says, again, that the "older" Edwardian generation provided a model of what the rising one "certainly could not do, but as certainly, perhaps, do not wish to do." "As certainly, perhaps": an interesting comment, it suggests indecision at the very moment certitude is proclaimed. Her chief objection to their method is that "Life escapes," but dissatisfied with the term "Life," she concedes:

> We scarcely better the matter by speaking, as critics are prone to do, of reality [...] whether we call it life or spirit, truth or reality, this, the essential thing, has moved off, or on, and refuses to be contained any longer in such ill-fitting vestments as we provide. Nevertheless, we go on perseveringly. (153)

What begins as a critique of her opponents ends, with this "we," by implicating herself in the same failure to convey what the novel sets out to represent. And here we come to the heart of the matter for literary representation: to pose the question of just how one gets a modernist out of a Victorian (in other words, how we may account for the terrific leap from, for instance, Trollope to Lawrence, Joyce, or Woolf), requires for answer that we go through the Edwardians and think about the ways in which they bridge the two larger eras, and the way to understand this bridge is through the sense that each group had of what they were trying to represent in their novels.

---

[30] In arguing that the Edwardians' representation of subjective consciousness is the immediate forerunner of modernist methodology, I have also sought to suggest that it follows from Victorian idealism and the romance genre and thus provides a point of continuity between these otherwise disparate literary schools. The history could be extended back to the Romantic expression of individuality and its poet-heroes. Hewitt suggests that the modernists' "unhistorical yearning for a supposed past golden age" and their "tendency to grasp at extreme and apocalyptic interpretations and creeds" might reasonably be viewed "as a survival of that strain in Romanticism which exalts the individual vision after its libertarian drive has perished" (131).

[31] As Douglas Hewitt so nicely explains it, "just as novelists had increasingly made their characters talk differently from one another, so they now set to work to make them think and perceive differently. The stream of consciousness novel is, in this sense at least, a natural continuation of realism" (Hewitt 112). "Indeed," he continues, "despite her repudiation of Bennett's kind of realism, Virginia Woolf's way of talking about her novels and her practice within them clearly starts from certain realistic premises."

Woolf describes this Life as a "semi-transparent envelope surrounding us from the beginning of consciousness to the end" (154). She asks, "Is it not the task of the novelist to convey this varying, this unknown and uncircumscribed spirit, whatever aberration or complexity it may display, with as little mixture of the alien and external as possible?" In this image of an envelope, encasing yet separate from us, we find the same belief in an external essence that preoccupied the Victorians and that Bennett dubbed the "envelope of facts." True, Woolf allows that this essence is variable and through this concession expresses the "fragmentation, discontinuity, and introversion" of the modernist ethic and its responsiveness to what Douglas Hewitt has identified as "general breakdown in agreement about continuity and order in society" (130). Breakdown is perhaps the clearest expression of the way modernism challenges realism and its devotion to consensus. Here that agreement is gone. At best, one might find consensus about the method of presenting what is otherwise differentiated experience, but as far as purporting to offer a view of reality, the tacit agreement that words (their limitations notwithstanding) stand for something universally tangible or knowable has been revoked, and the reader, like language, is set adrift, much as the author who seeks new ways to convey his or her impressions.

Nevertheless, the sense that people are together in this experience, that we all have individual responses to what is otherwise the same experience ("spirit," "truth," "reality"; perhaps the aesthetic experience) is made clearer through the Edwardians. Their inherited sense that the empirical, utilitarian, and legalistic ordering of the individual and the amorphous world, albeit attractive in its neatness, bound them to a view of the self and their own agency that was significantly limited, prompts their focus on the will as a metaphysical imperative. In other words, they adopted a mode of representation that, while engaging the same issues as their Victorian fathers, took greater account of the way their own desires and consciousness could create a subjectivity that was separate from the "alien and external" facts of social rules, in this case, the laws of inheritance. Their sense that they could refashion themselves, release themselves from the burdensome imposition of their fathers' literary identity, is expressed in a refashioning of the novel that narrows the gap between both themselves, their benefactors, and their modernist beneficiaries.

PART 3
Contesting the Will

Chapter 5
Broken Trusts: *Cy Près*, Fiction, and the Limits of Intention

One of the most common forms of testamentary bequest, the trust reinforces the ideas of a social contract or pact between free individuals and the institutions that make up civil society. A legal form that, like the will, takes its name from the moral imperative it encodes, the trust depends on the writer's faith in the people on whom he settles his estate, and on the more basic confidence that the law will oversee the administration of his will and disposal of his property in accordance with his own stated intentions. That there may be a discrepancy between what the testator states and what he intends, or between his intention and how the law interprets it, or between the ability of his trustees really to know his mind becomes the central point of contention in Anthony Trollope's *The Warden* (1855).

The dilemma created in the novel is, on the one hand, that the will can be a perfectly legal form and still be administered in such a way as to make its effects seem to thwart the document's informing intention (thus doing and amounting to an injustice), or, in contrast, that it can be properly and effectively administered only by ignoring its writer's stated purpose in order to privilege what he really "means" but which his words could not represent. Trollope's novel suggests that, contrary to longstanding doctrine, empirical evidence of intention such as the will provides can nevertheless produce flawed conclusions as to what it means, ones that undermine the trust established through the will between the individual and his society as it is represented by those chosen friends or by the rise of professional trustees in the nineteenth century.[1] Yet an alternative understanding that assumes the will has no determinate meaning undermines its legal function in the cultural imagination: one can almost hear the Victorian testator querulously asking what may be the point of the much touted freedom of bequest if the testament itself transfers no meaning, or at least not the testator's? In this sense, the will takes on the quality of fiction, and it becomes very much like the novel in terms of its availability to rhetorical analysis and the interpretation of its social function under the Court's application of *cy près*. Through *The Warden*, the operations of the law are critiqued, and though the case against Septimus Harding never comes to court, law's meaning remains contested in a way that challenges even the posture of certitude in the empirical epistemologies of mid-Victorianism.

---

[1] See Stebbings on the increasing complexity of trust law throughout the nineteenth century and the emergence of the trustee as civil servant.

Over half a century later, Edmund Gosse's *Father and Son* (1907) would raise similar questions about inherited systems of meaning and about the relationship between an author's intentions and the work that embodies them. In the process, he returns the meaning of "trust" to its moral groundings as an imagined bond. As a non-fictional genre, biography's appeal lies in its pretension to tell the truth about its subject, but Gosse was disappointed in biographies of the period precisely because they broke trust through "'their deliberate attempt in the interests of what was Nice and Proper […] to conceal what any conventional person might think not quite becoming'" (qtd. in Abbs 12).[2] He suggests that both the author and the audience tacitly agree to keep the private, private and to make public acts of heroism the measure of its subject (180), but these are half truths that, by attending only to actions in the world (let alone only heroic ones), keep concealed the workings of mind and spirit that inform them. In writing *Father and Son,* Gosse promises a more truthful account of his father's life, but in the process writes a book in which his own search for meaning, and by extension for his own sense of self, remains an interpretive act. Like biography a notoriously and purposefully selective genre, Victorian autobiography especially loads its selections with symbolic weight in a continuation of traditions of spiritual autobiography (the forms of personal exegesis borrowed from a tradition of biblical hermeneutics), but its appeal for readers is precisely its truth-status as a narrative of personal facts. Still, as a literary form it raises more questions about the reliability of intention (and more broadly the value of empirical forms) in the process of constituting individual and cultural consciousness.

There are two different forms of trust, then, that this chapter will discuss: the legal instrument, and the moral faith and obligation informing it and other bonds between people. And there are three different genres of writing: the legal or non-fictional, the literary fiction, and the literary non-fiction or, to put it less diagnostically, the will, the novel, and the (auto)biography. These are disparate forms, certainly, each of which has its own conventions, but all of them are in an important sense forms of life-writing. The will and the autobiography are acts of self-creation initiated by the subject of each text. Biography and the novel are acts of self-interpretation, not necessarily of the author interpreting his or her own life (although this interpretation would be explicit in autobiography and potential in any novel) but of arranging, evaluating, and commenting on the lives of the people and characters created in his text. But, to return to those conventions, neither these acts of creation nor of interpretation are free-standing. They occur within institutional frameworks that determine what constitutes a life, how it should be ordered, and how it will (or did) function in the real or imagined social world.

When taken together, these forms of trust mark a distinction between the will's legal and social functions, or how it may be understood within a legal context and how it participates in social order, as against what it represents for the testator.

2 The passage Abbs cites comes from Gosse's *Some Diversions of a Man of Letters* (London: Heinemann, 1919), 321.

The legal professional may be comfortable with this distinction between what the will claims to be and the lengths law must sometimes go to make it so, but the image projected for public consumption masks that process. The laws themselves may be so complex that they require professional mediation—Bentham's critique of the "justice shop"—but the will itself could not have a simpler *métier*. As a statement of desire and intention, it invites literal-mindedness. It is meant to formalize the individual's control of property and thereby acknowledge the self-determinism implied by concepts of "character." However, it also draws the individual into that mechanism of political and social organization whereby the law transforms character into "identity," which in a capitalist state means making property the condition of subjectivity and social identity.

Literature's ability to access characters' minds and represent intention offers a more complete representation of subjectivity that emphasizes the individual over the institution. Literature of course is its own institution, profession even, with its own conventions, but in the nineteenth century, the novel's social realism allowed it to take up the law and create social worlds in which the individual had greater play. The points of comparison between law and literature were closer in the early part of the century, but, as this chapter will show, the law's movement towards more regimented conceptions of identity gave literature itself something against which to define its own project. These shifts over time between a character-centered and identity-centered model of law are paralleled, in other words, by the movement from social to psychological realism and towards modernist means of representation. The law moved to social markers, while literature moved inside the mind, and the trusts discussed here mark this transition.

"As Nearly as Possible": *Cy près* and Interpreting the Legal Will; Or, the Limits of Intention

The legal system distinguishes private trusts from charitable ones. Where the former are subject to the Rule Against Perpetuities—the law established to regulate any one testator's undue control of property, for example through endless entails, by setting a time limit on his stipulations—charitable trusts are in contrast maintained through applying the doctrine of *cy près*. The term *cy près* itself is derived from the Old French phrase *cy près comme possible*, meaning as near as possible (Bogert 95) and means that where a trust demonstrates the testator's "general charitable intention," but the mode of the trust is in jeopardy of failure, the court reserves the right to determine a new mode of enacting that purpose that is *as near as possible* to the originally stipulated intention. Its basic assumptions lie in the distinction between the so-called general charitable intent and the mode of its application, the rationale being that where a trust is established with a general charitable intent, it is charity in the abstract that is to benefit, and it cannot be allowed to fail simply because changed circumstances prohibit its application in the manner originally dictated (any named beneficiary, for example, is held to be merely a mode of enacting that intent).

The trust, by its very name, signals a particular bond of reliance and moral obligation between the settlor and his trustees who were chosen most likely because of their special understanding of the testator's character and wishes.[3] Although their affective relationship increased their insight into the testator, it did not, however, improve the trustee's ability to understand and navigate a body of property laws that had grown both larger and more complex in parallel with the sheer increased quantity of commodities and their own more intricate nature. Unlike private trusts that would end, however, the charitable trust outlived that original relationship and those original models and values of property. It survived precisely because the Court assumed the trustee's function, but, far removed from the testator and his world, the Court's ability to put itself into the mind of the testator depended on reading the will.

Though its origins cannot be exactly pinpointed, *cy près* is a doctrine of long standing that derives from the Ecclesiastical Courts of the twelfth or thirteenth century. Magna Charta granted the Courts jurisdiction over wills and intestates. When a will left the distribution of any property undesignated or when a man died intestate, his estate was divided into three parts: one each for his wife and children and another for himself. This third part was then administered by the Courts for "pious and charitable works" (Tudor 142). It is certainly likely that clerical judges exercised a personal bias in reserving funds for religious institutions, but as George Bogert suggests, their spiritual logic placed the benefit with the deceased whose sins would be ameliorated by a gift to charity (98). The general charitable intention, far from originating in altruistic principles, then, comes from the court's assumption that "the donor's object was to benefit his own soul by charitable works" (Tudor 142).

The modern application of *cy près* was established early in the nineteenth century by Lord Eldon in *Moggridge v. Thackwell* (1802) and *Mills v. Farmer* (1815), the "*loci classici* for the law relating to charities" (Tudor 143).[4] *Moggridge v. Thackwell* came before the courts first in 1792 because the beneficiary charged with distributing "charities" had predeceased the testatrix, thus making the will impossible to execute. Accordingly, Lord Thurlow ruled that because the beneficiary was "merely a trustee," his death could not affect the testatrix's standing intention: to "give all the rest and residue of my personal estate to James Vaston [...] desiring him to dispose of the same in such charities as he shall think fit, recommending poor clergymen with large families and good characters" (465). Instead, Thurlow declared that a

---

3 See Stebbings's discussion of the relationship between settlor and trustee and trustee and beneficiary in chapters 2 and 3 of *The Private Trustee in Victorian England*. Her focus on the trustee parallels mine on the testator and the heir in many respects, but the trustee is interesting as their intermediary and as a figure whose interests are necessarily divided: he represents the testator's interests and control of property—in what Stebbings calls a "quasi-parental relationship" to the beneficiaries (63)—but, like them, he is burdened by an inherited responsibility of fulfilling the testator's vision of his property, literally to be his posthumous representative.

4 Tudor reads these cases in his discussion of *cy près*, but unless otherwise noted, my citations are to the trial reports.

new trustee should be appointed. In 1802 the case came before the court again, and this time Lord Rosslyn suggested that the earlier decision tended more towards "making, not construing, a will" and called for a rehearing. In other words, Rosslyn suggested that to apply *cy près* in this manner was to create a different gift, and thus a different will, than the one written in consultation with the deceased. Upon further appeal, Lord Eldon nevertheless upheld the original decision.

In his 1815 decision regarding *Mills v. Farmer*, Eldon referred to the earlier case, describing it as "'a case that, bound by precedent, I decided as much against my inclination as any act of my judicial life'" (qtd. in Tudor 125). However, those same precedents led him to decide *Mills v. Farmer* as well in favor of the testator's general charitable intention. In this case, the testator bequeathed "The rest and residue of all my effects [...] for promoting the Gospel in foreign parts and in England for bringing up ministers in different seminaries, and other charitable purposes as I do intend to name hereafter, after all my worldly property is disposed to the best advantage" (56). Reluctantly reversing a decision that the gift failed because a subsequent codicil neither referred to nor specified the charitable purpose, Lord Eldon argued that the will taken as a whole indicated an intention to give all the residue to charity and, thus, that the Court was bound to decide the mode by which this was to be accomplished.

These two cases represent, as Eldon himself recognizes, the way that interpreting intent can be legal and yet potentially run counter to the testator's intentions, insofar as one act of law runs counter to or subverts another. In cases of general charitable intent, "if that intention is declared absolutely, and nothing is left uncertain but the mode in which it is to be carried into effect, the intention will be carried into execution by this Court, which will then supply the mode which alone was left deficient" (95). Eldon is critical of the court's decision to arrogate to itself a right to distinguish between the formal or stated intent and an inferred one because to set aside the testator's explicit instructions is tantamount to a rejection of the principles of the word of the will as the best indicator of the will of the testator.[5] Chief Justice Wilmot in *Attorney General v. Downing* (1767) stated the potential hazards of this practice more plainly:

> The right of the heir at law seems to arise as naturally in this case as in any other; but instead of favoring him as in all other cases, the testator is made to disinherit him for a charity he never thought of; perhaps a charity repugnant to the testator's intentions, and which directly opposes and encounters the charity he meant to establish. But this doctrine is now so firmly settled, that it cannot be departed from. (qtd. in Bogert 98)

[5] Eldon also expresses great concern that in differing from the opinion of the Master of the Rolls, his own decision "will not hereafter possess all the authority which might otherwise attach to it" (94). But see Richard Weisberg's *Poethics* for the argument that form and meaning are inseparable. When the form is bad, the meaning must suffer (10).

Wilmot's decision, like Eldon's, demonstrates more than a reluctance to depart from the testator's stated intentions despite judges' ability to do so; it adds a suspicion of injustice. Along these lines, late eighteenth-century jurists who, according to Tudor, were skeptical of the degree to which charitable intention could be manipulated, decided that *cy près* could be exercised only in relation to gifts exhibiting the general intent, whereas those with a specifically named charitable purpose would be allowed to fail without application of *cy près*.

As Tudor points out, however, the decision as to which sorts of gifts would be deemed specific and which general was left entirely to the court's discretion (144), which begs the question as to how intention shall be determined. The above cases were decided, in the first instance, because the gift had become impossible to implement as directed and, in the second, because no specific beneficiary beyond a type of charity was indicated. But it is often the case that apparently specific instructions are overruled (Tudor 143) as, for example, when Lord Eldon in *Mills v. Farmer* describes a gift to found a synagogue, which the Court transferred to a Foundling Hospital (101).[6] Commenting on his decision there, Eldon made the point that what is at issue is "not so much what *was* the intention, as what, in the contemplation of the law, must be *presumed* to have been the intention" (80). In examples such as this, the absence of clear rules for deciding the nature of intention has been widely remarked. On this basis, Tudor observes, "no rules can be discovered as to what will be held sufficient indicia of such an intention, and the reported cases show surprising instances of both liberal and conservative views upon it" (145). Seconding Tudor's observation, Bogert actually refers to the "fictional character of the general charitable intent" as one of the main arguments against the application of *cy près*. When, as he states, "different courts sometimes come to diametrically opposite conclusions on quite similar sets of facts" (157), the conclusion can be drawn that if intention is no longer vested in the testator's document, then the gap between a will and a novel is virtually eliminated (except in terms of their popular, political significance). Another way of saying this is that if "quite similar sets of facts," themselves unchanging, can produce different meanings, then the empirical reliance on the letter of the law is undercut in the same way realism's reliance on shared language and perceptions is undone when it cannot establish consensus. The will fails in the same way the novel must.

If *Moggridge v. Thackwell* and *Mills v. Farmer* are foundational cases for understanding the doctrine of *cy près*, the 1850s saw several cases come before the Courts which gave Trollope the conceptual foundation for his plot in *The Warden*. Although it has long been known that he based many of his details on the scandal at St. Cross and on similar events in Rochester, the long-running case of the Earl of Beauchamp's will and St. George's Hospital in Middlesex provides a further parallel (if not precedent) for the questions of interpretation Trollope develops in

6 If a testator's particular bequest is counter to public policy and therefore not legally enforceable, the court will apply the gift *cy près*. However, the equivalence of religious services and orphanages is not readily apparent and opens such decisions to Wilmot's criticism.

the novel.[7] In his will of 1847, Reginald John Pindar, Earl Beauchamp made two separate bequests. He devised eight acres to one of his executors, and in a separate bequest gave £60,000 to his executors to be used to build an Almshouse "for the residence of twelve or some larger number of poor men and women, members of the Church of England, who shall have been employed in agriculture and have been reduced by sickness, misfortune, or infirmity" on the conditions, first, that a suitable piece of land would have to be provided for the site, and, second, that his executors had to approve of both the "scheme" of the charity as well as the proposed rules for governing it. In the event that no land was given, or that there was an objection to the scheme or to the rules, then the money would go to the trustees of St. George's Hospital. Following Beauchamp's death in 1853, Charles Scott, who had been left the eight acres, conveyed the land to the other trustees to use as the site for the Almshouse, and the Rev. Philpott brought a bill against St. George's to clarify the rights of all the parties. It is unnecessary to go into the details of that case other than to point out the Master of the Rolls John Romilly's decision that the initial gift of money failed because it violated another law and, since that was not a condition the testator had contemplated among those that would allow the money to go to St. George's Hospital, that bequest failed, too.[8]

In a series of appeals concluded in 1859, Romilly's decision was finally reversed in the House of Lords, which supported the charitable bequest and directed that "a proper scheme for the management of the charity be settled and approved by the Judge of this Court." (*Philpott v. St. George's Hospital* [1859] 107).[9] The Attorney-General accordingly drew up a plan for The Beauchamp Almshouses, but in doing so he proposed that the main building should have a center for offices and two wings: one for the almshouse and the other for a hospital for "persons labouring under some permanent or chronic disease" (110). Philpott and the trustees objected to this plan as a variation of the scheme and so as a departure from the testator's stated intentions (111); attorneys for the Attorney-General argued that his version "would be more beneficial to the objects of the charity" and that the Court, in any event, "had full jurisdiction to sanction it" (110).

The case came again before the Master of the Rolls, John Romilly, whose comments bring us back to the difficulties of interpreting intention under *cy près* as well as to the potential for the Court in its application of the doctrine

---

7 See *Philpott v. St. George's Hospital* (1855). Although *The Warden* was not published until 1855, Trollope began the novel in 1851 and finished it sometime between Autumn 1853 and Autumn 1854 (Gilmour viii).

8 Romilly assumed that the case would be appealed but wanted his view of it to be clear: "the original gift fails, by reason of its being contrary to the Statute of Mortmain, and that the gift over fails, by reason of the events, on which that gift over is directed to take effect, not having arisen" (142). That event could not arise because although "the land has been given and the rules approved," the law "interposes and prevents it."

9 See also *Philpott v. St. George's Hospital* (1857).

to overstep its charge, or to overcompensate for the difficulties of effecting a particular mode of charity by redefining it altogether. His comments are worth quoting at some length:

> It has, I think, of late, been sometimes considered that whenever the Court had to direct a scheme to be framed for the establishment of a charity, it had power to deal with the property as it pleased, and in point of fact to do anything, which, within certain limits, it thought expedient to be done with the property. A more erroneous opinion, and one less in accordance with the decision of this Court in matters of charity, can hardly be conceived. (111)

Romilly explained the error as confusion between cases in which the charitable intention is specific and those in which it is more general, between those in which *cy près* actually may not be applied and those in which it may. In the first case—and provided (in a reminder of his earlier decision) that the directions don't transgress another law—the Court is "not at liberty" to evaluate the quality of the gift or to act on what it thinks the testator ought to have willed. "Accordingly," he concedes, "instances of charities of the most useless description have come before the Court, but which it has considered itself bound to effect" (112). The only occasions for applying "what is called the doctrine of *cy près*" are those already outlined in the discussion of the earlier cases and, what is especially relevant for Trollope's question in *The Warden*, where there are "accretions to a charity" that the will itself does not account for.

If the general charitable intent is really little more than a judicial convention or a procedural mechanism, then one could ask why or how the will can claim to represent the testator's intention. In what sense isn't the will as fictitious in this regard as a novel? Romilly's ruling seeks to avoid just this sort of construction by distinguishing evaluation from interpretation and then limiting recourse to the latter. Taken together, the above cases outline the broadest considerations and consequences of the court's decisions as to authorial intention and the application of *cy près*, which is itself part of a still broader legal discourse of "construction." In an earlier case involving interpretation of a testator's will, *Abbott v. Middleton* (1855), Romilly held that "whenever the context [of a specific clause] requires it, words may be supplied, changed, and transposed" (816), even though the Wills Act does not permit the testator to alter the document after it has been executed precisely because to do otherwise would damage its integrity.[10] Although *Abbott* was not a case involving charity, it accentuates the difficulty of framing and preserving intention through the will, especially when the Court's attitudes veer between the sanctity of the black letter and the necessity of supervening it in order to make the will do what it claims to be—to effect the will of the testator.

---

10 See also *Walker v. Tipping* (1852) in which Vice Chancellor Turner held that "no addition to or transposition of the words of any clause in a will can be made if a reasonable construction can be put on the clause as it stands" (742) and the Wills Act s. 21.

These problems of intention and interpretation are the same that trouble Septimus Harding whose resignation from the wardenship in spite of the case's being dropped signals his disappointed conviction that legality can sometimes have very little concourse with justice. But in fact the case never goes to trial, and even legality ceases to be an issue in the novel. When pointedly asked if the warden is "legally and distinctly entitled to the proceeds of the property, after the due maintenance of the twelve bedesmen" (*Warden* 152), Haphazard "couldn't exactly say in so many words" that he was.[11]

The doctrine of *cy près* thus illustrates two points of contention within law and between law and literature: the relationship between intention and action, and the use of fiction as a tool for representing this relationship.[12] Lisa Rodensky's study of criminal responsibility—in which she focuses on the complexities of the otherwise straightforward legal maxim that an act cannot be considered criminal unless the intention informing it is also criminal (*mens rea*)—is a useful model in this regard. The issue for *mens rea* is whether to locate intention in the mind or in the act itself, and, when the former, how to access the mind of the accused in order thus to establish criminal intent and link it to a specific act. This problem in criminal law sets off the way testamentary law confronted similar challenges, albeit with very different effects.

The last will and testament is interesting in this context precisely because of its claims to document intention and will. It serves as a legal mechanism of causation that determines the disposal of property and for that reason would seem to avoid the problems posed by *mens rea*, not least because intention in this case is neither criminal, nor is it introduced in defense of an already executed act. Rather, the will begins with intention and looks forward to an act, a future disposal of property. The doctrine of *cy près*, however, demonstrates the limitations of even such a clear-cut

---

11 The law regarding surplus suggests that he in fact was not. When property, or the income resulting from property, is devised with the general charitable intention of benefiting, in this instance "scholars or almsmen," then once that gift takes effect, any surplus of what is needed for maintenance of the charity falls under the court's jurisdiction to apply *cy près*.

12 For twentieth-century theories of intention and interpretation see Wendell Harris, *Literary Meaning: Reclaiming the Study of Literature*; Donald Keesey, ed. *Contexts for Criticism*; E.D. Hirsch, "Objective Interpretation" and "Meaning and Significance Reinterpreted"; Stanley Fish "What Makes an Interpretation Acceptable?" and *Doing What Comes Naturally*. For analysis of Hirsch, see Michael Leddy, "Validity and Reinterpretation." For linguistic analysis of Hirsch, see Lutz Dannenberg and Hans-Harald Mueller, "On Justifying the Choice of Interpretive Theories." For linguistic accounts of intention generally, see Stein Haugom Olsen, "Authorial Intention." Olsen responds to Wimsatt and Beardsley's seminal piece, "The Intentional Fallacy." Alfred R. Meale and Paisley Livingston approach Fish's arguments from within philosophy in "Intentions and Interpretations." For more on Fish, see Steven Knapp and Walter Benn Michaels, "Against Theory"; John Searle's "Literary Theory and Its Discontents," and Knapp and Michaels's response in the same issue "Reply to John Searle." For a good variety of readings, see Gary Iseminger's collection, *Intention and Interpretation*.

statement of intention as embodied by the will. We know that an instrument cannot be testamentary without a disposing mind (or with the executory acts that confirm it), but is testamentary intention also linked in a phenomenological sense to specific objects? Must a will fail if its objects are no longer applicable? Or is intention a more general state of mind, the will a more general disposition to give, that can be enacted through other means and on other objects?

The necessity of entering a state of mind in order to determine intention—as well as its conceptual neighbors "voluntariness" and "causation" (29–30)—posed problems for theorists of criminal law, which Rodensky argues even the provision of defense counsel could not circumvent as well as the omniscient narrator of a realist novel (24).[13] Two points bear elaboration here. First, the 1836 Prisoner's Counsel Act allowed an accused felon's intentions to be represented in court and illustrated the growing importance of interiority—mental states as well as character—in the analysis of criminal acts. This interest in interiority was renewed in the passage of the Wills Act in the next year and its broadened understanding of testamentary intention. In law, therefore, the representation of intention was taking center stage in the late 1830s. Second, these new legal mechanisms notwithstanding, the novelist's ability to override practical limitations through the omniscient narrator, and thereby to imagine and bring forth his characters' minds, marked the way that mid-Victorian fiction in general shared the law's preoccupation with intention and its connection to (possibly foundation in) character but offered a more effective alternative to its legal representation.[14] For novels about the last will and testament specifically, "intention" comes to represent the foundations of the legal text and of individual subjectivity, as well as the creative ability of the novelist. That is, characters step forward out of institutional frameworks—in *The Warden* the institutions of law and religion collude—that define them in order to define themselves. In this sense, the novel is able to provide an important supplement to contemporary understandings of the individual's relationship to social structures and of the novel's role in reshaping them.

In his comments on the application of *cy près*, Sir Romilly implied the timeliness of his opinion since it was decisions "of late" that suggested to him the Court's imperfect understanding of when it was appropriate for them to formulate the charitable scheme, but charities and wills together had been attracting a great deal of attention throughout the 1850s, and in other forums as well. Wherever they appeared, though, the institutions of the Church and the Court that framed them suffered. Writing about his plans for *The Warden*, Trollope explains that he was "struck by

[13] See Rodensky's analysis of Alexander Welsh and, most notably, Jan-Melissa Schramm in the Introduction to *The Crime in Mind*.

[14] With the important caveat that fictional representation could also create dangerous sympathies, Rodensky makes the point that the novel itself is not at all sure about the effects of its penetration and representation of the private self. By making intention palpable and activating readers' imaginative sympathy, the novel can make intention itself seem like an act (11, 29).

two opposite evils [and] thought that I might be able to expose them, or rather to describe them, both in one and the same tale (*Autobiography* 64). The first evil was "an egregious malversation of charitable purposes" that had been brought to light and made much of in the press, particularly in *The Times*.[15] *Household Words* also skirmished over the subject of wills. Its "I Give and Bequeath" contrasted worthy gifts to charity with those by "vain and stupid testators" who squandered their estates on the "foolish and miserable" ends of vanity (24).[16] Exhorting testators to think of the "claims of Justice," the anonymous author recasts these as the moral obligation to family. In his final sentence, he exhorts his readers: "Think of this will-makers! I may 'give and bequeath' my soul to everlasting sorrow and remorse, if I neglect those paramount claims, for any consideration" (24). The passage recalls the origins of *cy près* in the Ecclesiastical presumption that one-third of an intestate's property would go to charity precisely for the benefit of his soul, but in this final appeal, the soul itself is framed as the testator's most important possession and one which he can save by performing the moral duty of using his legal will to satisfy the claims of family.[17] Although the essay canvasses wills dating back to 1603, it seems safe to assume that its attention to charitable wills made good copy in 1853 because of its relevance to contemporary happenings in the legal sphere and to the growing secularization of otherwise religious concerns.

Three years earlier, *Household Words*, under the editorship of W.H. Wills, had run an exposé of church registries in a series of letters (co-authored by Dickens and Wills) called "The Doom of English Wills" (Longley 26) in which the whole system of ecclesiastical oversight of wills was excoriated. The lead article in the issue of

---

[15] He continues: "The first evil was the possession by the Church of certain funds and endowments which had been intended for charitable purposes but which had been allowed to become incomes for idle Church dignitaries," and (the second evil) "the undeserved severity of the newspapers towards the recipients of such incomes" (*Autobiography* 64). Robert Martin gives a very full rendition of the circumstances surrounding the scandal at St. Cross Hospital in which the Earl of Guildford was involved and to which *The Warden* makes reference "some nine times" (*Enter Rumour* 183). For more on the historical precedents for *The Warden*, see G.F.A. Best, as well as Robin Gilmour's introduction to the Penguin English Library Edition (vii–xxvi).

[16] The full passage reads as a warning: "There is something very magnificent about Bamborough Castle [...], and something very good about Lord Crewe, Bishop of Durham, who turned it into a seaman's hospital; but, in the long list of bequests that lie buried in Parliamentary blue books, it is easy to find many—we are afraid to say a majority—in which vanity has guided the testator's hand [...]. [A]ll such persons will do well to remember before they gratify, not to say Vanity, but even what would be commonly (often erroneously) called Charity, whether they are neglecting claims of Justice" (24).

[17] The contractual dimension of "consideration" also bears pointing out here. Consideration is the action or token that signals agreement between the parties of a contract. In this case, the testator who allows other considerations to influence his distribution of property (including those which are in some way conditional, for example, that such and such beneficiary under the will say an annual prayer for the testator's soul or will keep the path to his grave swept clean) in effect breaks the moral contract with his family.

September 28, 1850, emphasized the importance of wills to individual families and to the whole nation in order to put into relief both the horrible physical state of the records themselves and the criminal negligence of the Registrar and his proctors. In the visit to "Cathedral No. One," the investigator is first denied access, then charged two guineas per day to see indexes that are searchable only by the alphabetical listing of first names, and is finally only reluctantly admitted to enter a storage area in which a charter of William the Conqueror and part of the Great Seal are discovered "by chance in a lime-basket" along with "several pardons of King John" (Dickens and Wills 3): two guineas instead of the two shillings Rokesmith and Wegg are charged in *Our Mutual Friend*; indexes so corrupt that they prolong the work and the profit for Church officers, just like the obscurity of legal procedures ensured money for law's professionals in Bentham's view. The immediate point of the essay, like *The Times*'s attacks on other Church officers, is reform of church sinecures which pay out, in the case of the Registrar, an annual salary of £7,000 and yet cost families the unnecessary expense of litigation over wills.

My point in discussing it here, along with all those examples focusing on the legal aspects of charity, is to think about the way charity and the charitable trust embodied a conflict between law and religion—or, more precisely, between secular and spiritual jurisdictions over and interpretations of the will—which nevertheless were similar in their tendency as institutions to diminish the sense of the testator's character at the heart of the will and of the charity in the first place. The law wins this conflict later in the decade with the establishment of a new Court of Probate and a new national registry.[18] Lord St. Leonards, at the conclusion of his letters on testamentary law, extols the new Court which "provides not only for the custody of your will after your death," he tells readers, "but directs that convenient depositories shall be provided [...] for all such wills of living persons as shall be deposited there for safe custody" (158). And indeed the new act turned the "documentary chaos" chronicled by *Household Words* in 1850 into the "system of arrangement" L.S. Lewis called "absolutely perfect" in *The Strand Magazine* in 1897.

New legislation like the above is, as Henry Maine would point out in *Ancient Law*, the most sophisticated and most immediate means of effecting legal reform (24). As mechanisms to simplify complicated legal procedures and to extend the application of desirable solutions, legal fictions were in contrast the most simplistic. They also offered the most gradual means of changing legal practice, so gradual in some cases as to seem to maintain existing legal culture and the power of its professionals instead of improving it. The application of *cy près* proposed in *The Warden* demonstrates the convergence of these legal fictions with a literary one and its own potential to influence social reform or, in this case, to retard the process by which private character was being diminished in public institutions of law and religion.

---

[18] See the Court of Probate Act of 1857. In this context, the Matrimonial Causes Act passed in the same year is also germane.

The Warden: Interpreting the Private Will

As was true in many of Dickens's novels, in *The Warden* the will is concealed from readers, but here the problem is less one of a missing or hidden document than a document to which only interested and professional interpreters have access. The religious and legal communities in the novel each create fictions to explain and leverage a will that the reader (save for one sentence) never sees. As the foundational document of the novel's legal dispute, the missing will gives legal discourse a simulacral quality.[19] The court's discussion of precedent in the application of *cy près* illustrates this point. The process of analogy through which ruling by precedent works operates like a paper chase with no originary decision; one judges based on other judgments that were themselves grounded in still further removed judgments *ad infinitum*. Without Hiram, one has to rely on his will; without his will, one has to rely on the representations (including legal decisions) of interested parties whose manipulation suggests that no legal document can represent its testator's intentions as well as the novel can its characters'.

The law reduces character to identity because the latter is more manageable, which implies, further, that willingness is directed away from one's own desires or intentions and into paths determined by institutional forces. On this view, the conceptual category "identity" contravenes the voluntary principle at the heart of intention and of free will; at the very least, it conditions what the individual *can* want or do. In these terms, the will represents the deceased's intentions or desires in a formal sense, but it does this only in so far as those desires were enabled and modified by law. By insisting on mediating the reader's access to the will at its very center, *The Warden* duplicates the epistemological problem within law of accessing the inner life in order to determine intention. To offset this problem, however, the novel can and does provide direct access to Septimus Harding's intentions and his refusal of the identity created for him through law's recourse to fictions. Trollope uses Septimus Harding to expose the way individuals can get lost amidst the struggles of institutions, as well as the simulacral quality of subjectivity itself as defined in legal discourse and, increasingly for this novel, in religious institutions as well. Put differently, the missing will at the heart of the novel becomes the missing sense of intention and character at the heart of subjectivity. By representing Harding's character and intention, however, and by allowing him to renounce these legal and religious discourses and their potential abuse of fictions (a renunciation similar to the Victorian daughter's rejection of fortune), the novel privileges the individual over the institution.[20]

---

19 This is Bentham's critique of judicial authority in which legal fictions "instead of providing the security [of expectations] desired, create but an arbitrary simulacrum of equity. In Bentham's opinion, they turn the maxim of strict adherence to established rules into obscure manipulations of precedents beyond the reach of public censure" (Polloczek 111).

20 His renunciation, like theirs, is a rejection of both fortune and legal fictions and, more prominently, of the fictions created by *The Jupiter*. And although Harding does insist on maintaining his own artistic and spiritual role as precentor, his creative energies are not

To return briefly to Trollope's characterization of his project for the novel, we see that he shifts from a plan "to expose" evil to the more neutral one "to describe" it. Unwilling to pass judgment on those evils, he nevertheless expresses disappointment with the result: "I was altogether wrong in supposing," he says, "that the two things could be combined. Any writer in advocating a cause must do so after the fashion of an advocate,—or his writing will be ineffective" (64–5). By his own estimation, the gaps in the novel might well result from this desire for neutrality in a world that demands conviction—he should have been an "advocate," or more like a lawyer. Still, Trollope's claims should be taken with the proverbial grain of salt. He has indeed been criticized for the timidity of his moral judgment in this first of the Barsetshire novels.[21] However, the novel is adamant about the intrusions of institutional interests into private lives, or the manipulation of the individual by institutional forces, that has to be resisted.

Septimus Harding differs from the novel's other characters because he will not pretend "as if there were a divorce between his public role and his private life" (Gilmour xxii), as when John Bold factitiously insists that he can attack the wardenship without impugning Harding's reputation. The assumption that public and private selves, what amount to identity and character, should complement one another does not mean in Trollope that the public should dictate the private. Rather, one's intentions should determine how one acts and, importantly, how one's actions are received. This is to say that the character of the individual influences his intentions and thence the kinds of actions that become the indices of his public self. The episodes with *The Jupiter*, however, accentuate the inverse influence of public opinion upon behavior, its ability to create identities irrespective of the characters involved, as well as (in this case) the self-serving interests of such fictions. Harding's intentions are made to count for nothing because his actions are deemed selfish (indeed, they may be problematic in the sense that although he gives the bedesmen exemplary care, his failure to give them more money is a form of negligence). Still, the actual legality of Harding's position becomes irrelevant in this revised question of right; as Harding muses, he "was not so anxious to prove himself right, as to be so" (24).

The novel's primary conflict is an internalized one, one character's resolution of a personal moral dilemma, and although this sort of conflict might indeed make legality seem beside the point, it does not therefore follow that the Law is as well. Like the Church and the Press, it is one of the institutional forces—and its legal fictions one of the contemporary topics (Stone 134)—that Trollope draws

put towards writing fiction or telling stories, but towards music. In a sense his retreat to the non-verbal altogether suggests an even more complete rejection of the conflicts between law and literature because it abandons their linguistic basis of comparison.

21 Ross Murfin argues that Trollope actually sidesteps answering the question of injustice by having Harding resign without advocating the redistribution of funds. According to Murfin, Harding should either defend or repudiate the Church's position; little retribution is accomplished (as the contest in *Barchester Towers* demonstrates) if the wardenship remains intact (27).

on and which gives *The Warden* its means of combating the cultural shift towards public, institutional identities. Harding is unable to separate *The Jupiter*'s fictions about him from what he knows to have been his intentions—that the reforming newspaper actually succeeds in effecting real introspection and reform in the very person it accuses of having no conscience is one of the novel's ironies—but his feeling that the legality of his position *is* separate from the justice of the case and therefore from his own dilemma opens the way for a critique of legal fictions.

Bentham's famous invectives made the legal fiction a controversial Victorian topic, one taken up by Sir Henry Maine in *Ancient Law* (1861) where, for all his caution against Bentham's excesses, he agreed that legal fictions would have to be "prune[d] away" if English law aspired "to assume an orderly distribution" (27). Albert Venn Dicey also returned to Bentham in his lecture "The Period of Benthamism or Individualism," the sixth of his *Lectures on the Relation between Law and Public Opinion during the 19th Century* (1905). Using testamentary freedom as a test case of utilitarianism's happiness principle, Dicey also compared Lord Mansfield's limited success in reforming the law through the accumulation of precedent and application of legal fiction against Bentham's rejection of the "fraud" in favor of more straightforward legislative reform (22). Marjorie Stone suggests that up to the mid-century, and thanks in fact to novels like *The Warden*, the legal fiction took its place in the public, as well as the legal, imagination where it was viewed either as "nonsense or chicanery" (Stone 135).[22] Harding's similar sense of justice cannot be satisfied by "an error as to some legal form" or the workings of "some legal fiction" (Trollope 80); he cannot remain in his position as warden without better grounds than a "quibble" (Trollope 114), the same "quibble" that irks the lawyer when the "unprofessional man" uses it against him (Trollope 160). The emphasis here on the legal fiction as a procedural device (in this case, one that distinguishes who the defendants in the case should have been) separates the operations of the law from the questions of justice Harding believes they should serve. Moreover, the point that legal fictions as procedures were designed to permit the application of sound and desirable laws, the "spirit" of the law, in the face of changed circumstances further highlights the degree to which the substance of the case has been obscured not only by the passage of time but also by the legal process. "Equity" is the legal term for conscience (Polloczek 14), but this is precisely what Harding finds lacking in all the institutions that seek to distract him from the main question of his own conscience: whether he actually has a right to earn so much money.

The legal fiction invoked in *The Warden* develops through the application of *cy près*. The novel does not name it as such, but Trollope's focus on the problems of interpreting the will and the necessity of determining whether Harding is a "paid servant" (69) or a trustee of the charity point to the limits of the law's ability, first, to adequately represent intention through the will and, second, the limits of

---

[22] I am grateful to Marjorie Stone's reference to Dicey's *Lectures on Law in the Nineteenth Century* (1914). The edition used here is from a 1917 reprint of Macmillan's 1914 second edition, digitized by The Online Library of Liberty.

its ability to interpret it. The "before and after" of the legal document is so fraught that the novel makes a compelling argument that the promise of the will itself to insure the disposal of property is simply a legal fiction. In fact, Trollope goes to extraordinary lengths to preclude legal resolution of Mr. Harding's questions. Early descriptions of Hiram's will identify *for whose* benefit the property was left but not *to whom* (2). Changes are made in the amount of the bedesmen's stipend that confuse the issue of who actually administers the charity. Distinctions are drawn between the prosperity of the estate and the charity, and doubts cast as to what sums "became [the warden's] due" (3). These are all questions for the law to answer before it can decide whether a charity may continue and how best to make it do so. They are equitable questions that demonstrate the legal conscience at work to acknowledge the particularities of a case and thus to supplement the common law. In spite of these allowances, however, the novel's refusal to resolve this question on legal grounds creates a point of contrast to fiction's ability to do just that. In other words, the novel does not have to "quibble" over technicalities as the lawyers do and thereby fail to confront the principal issues of the case.

The Warden's care to distinguish the means of winning a case from the issues of justice it should decide, its abandonment in fact of the formal legal conflict, is the chief part of the novel's many criticisms of the law. One can see Bentham's ghost return to point its finger at Finney, Messrs. Cox & Cummins, and Haphazard, Q.C. as their costs and legal counsel mount in tandem, but by far the most significant example of this disconnection is Harding's trip to London and his interview with Haphazard. This meeting of the country cleric and the "machine with a mind" (Trollope 150) marks the confrontation between the individual and the institution and the final point of separation between the novel and the will, literature and law.[23] Harding confronts the attorney with his specific fears that "the affairs of the hospital are not arranged according to the will of the founder" (Trollope 152), and Haphazard freely admits, "None of such institutions are, Mr. Harding, nor can they be; the altered circumstances in which we live do not admit of it." Harding's question goes directly to the issue of determining authorial intent, while Haphazard's answer blithely contends that testamentary intention is a legal fiction to be construed and applied as context will allow. Put to the question then of whether the warden is "legally and distinctly entitled" to his stipend, however, Haphazard dissembles and ultimately diverts discussion to the point's irrelevance now that the case has been withdrawn. The point of testamentary law is to provide a statement of the testator's desires and his intention to bequeath property.

[23] Robin Gilmour deems this trip the novel's climax (xxvi) and Harding's glimpse of the Lincoln's Inn chapel as a sign of "the healing of Mr. Harding's spirit, the restoration of harmony between private being and public role" (xxvi). Certainly, the warden's meeting has helped him finalize his decision and gives him a clear sense of direction, but it has to be said that whatever his feelings for the Bishop, his son-in-law, and his music, Mr. Harding finds this peace of mind by resigning his official position. The Church can be as much a coercive institution in this novel as the Law, and Mr. Harding's sight of the chapel indicates his separation from his most public role within the church as well as from the lawsuit.

The new Wills Act of 1837 marked the way this branch of civil law could avoid the problems of accessing interiority which in contrast confronted criminal law by making that intention visible from the outset and using the document to effect the disposal of property. However, Haphazard is not only nonchalant about the limits of the testament to convey intention at the outset, he is unable to interpret it in retrospect, after probate, and therefore unable to answer Harding's question. The law in both these branches cannot represent the individual as well as the novel.

The novel's fictions allow it to determine justice where the law cannot because they allow the novel to enter and represent its character's mind. The individual and his intentions are emphasized so as to privilege the novel over the legal institution and its interpretations of the will. However, the problem of interpreting intention in a document meant to preclude interpretation can have its parallels for the novelist as well. Trollope's comments in the *Autobiography* say as much when he describes the inefficacy of his attempt to "expose" the evils of professional misconduct and journalistic libel. His retrospective assertion that advocacy must be one-sided to be "powerful" conveys to the reader his own desire to have been less neutral. "There should be no scruples of conscience," he writes; "such scruples make a man impotent for such work" (65). Ironically, he makes this comment about a novel about conscience, equity under the law, and the ability of fictions both legal and literary to represent the characters who feel it. If Trollope was less decisive than he later wished to have been, his fiction, nonetheless, left Harding and his own readers free to judge.

As an examination of what Stanley Fish has called "presently recognized interpretive strategies" ("Interpretation" 352), *The Warden* is critical of contemporary ways of using fiction to make meaning. The further irony of the novel, then, is that Harding is so literal-minded; his distrust of the legal fiction if logically extended must imply a preference for the literal (hence his very direct question to Haphazard), and this preference raises the question of just how far a critique of fiction can extend when it is presented through a fiction itself. Given the choice between the Law, the Press, the Church, and the novel, for the conservative Trollope the only place imagination is allowable is in the latter where it has no "real" effect.

Fiction is a tool whose function changes depending on who wields it. If Trollope implies that fiction writing were better left to novelists than to lawyers because it can represent the inner life of the individual, Gosse suggests in *Father and Son* that fiction can be the means of creating and sustaining subjectivity in the first place, of enabling him, as he writes in his conclusion, "to fashion his inner life for himself" (251). In Gosse, fiction does have real effects on its readers, but similarly to the generic inversion found in *The Warden*, this conclusion as to the salutary effects of fiction and the imagination is developed through the non-fictional form of the biography and its "interpretive strategy" of equating life-writing with story-writing; Gosse must tell the story of his father's life and consequently of his own.[24]

---

[24] See Linda Peterson's chapter on Gosse and scientific autobiography in *Victorian Autobiography*. For a brief reading of *Father and Son* in the context of mid-Victorian autobiography, see Jerome Buckley.

Father and Son and the Imagined Self

Critical response to *Father and Son* (1907) typically discusses its place on the borderline between ideas and attitudes, practices and forms: is it biography or autobiography, Victorian or Edwardian, spiritual or scientific, the literal or the imaginative?[25] In the broader context of this study, is *Father and Son* realist or modernist; how does it frame the individual differently than or in relation to institutions such as religion or law, and in this case science? As non-fiction, biography and autobiography are collections of objective data—people, dates, pivotal events and actions—brought together as the material evidence of a life. As life-writing, it aspires to and cultivates the appeal of empiricism that in the nineteenth century runs through natural science, philosophical and legal positivism, and even through that part of realism that emphasizes plot. Like the will and its list of possessions, the biography's generic form gave credence to its contents.

But what were these facts meant to tell readers? Although it selected and collected details and moments, its mode of inquiry was deeply introspective. Borrowing its methods from the traditions of biblical hermeneutics and typology that ran through the spiritual autobiographies of the eighteenth century, biographical writing in the nineteenth century changed under the pressure of "problems of construal and meaning" and assumed a critical approach to its subjects rather than a practical application of their lives (Peterson 25). Left with the generic form of the spiritual autobiography, Victorian autobiographers confronted the paradox, as Linda Peterson so usefully explains it, of filling that form with narratives and "systems of interpretation" taken from science and literature (27, 161). To the extent, then, that the biography or autobiography is a literary form, it also raises questions about the reliability of its stated intentions, its interpretations, and its meaning for the identity it constructs.[26] For example, Gosse begins a "document," "record," and "study" (33)

---

[25] In "Edmund Gosse and His Modern Readers," Roger Allen says *Father and Son* "feels like a historical document but reads like a novel" because Gosse "interprets his life in terms of variations on a number of traditional literary forms" (495). Among these are tales of "spiritual discovery," of the child-victim, and of the parable (492). Roger Porter focuses on the ambivalence that prevents Gosse from either fully accommodating or rejecting his father's way of thinking. The reason, he argues, is because the book's struggle is "both within Edmund and between Philip and Edmund" (175). Linda Peterson focuses on the distinction between the biblical hermeneutics informing Gosse's parents' world-view and his response through scientific and literary methods as a breakdown in the genre of scientific autobiography (158, 170). And working from Harold Nicolson's claim that the book defies traditional categories, Peter Abbs suggests it be read as both history and autobiography, where the Preface and the Epilogue function as primers for reading the respective father and son halves (31).

[26] In *Fictional Techniques and Factual Works* William Siebenschuh argues that art and fact needn't work against one another; rather, the art actually allows the writer to judge and interpret what he calls "interpretive factual statement" (4), or "self-interpretive statement" (32). In other words, by attracting attention to itself, the use of specifically

of his father's life—and in this regard speaks to the empirical demands of the genre—but it becomes a manifesto of "the struggle between two temperaments, two consciences, and almost two epochs" (35). Although this statement certainly describes the struggle between Philip and Edmund, it also represents a duality in Edmund himself (Porter 175). Edmund cannot tell his father's story without implicating himself, but his methods can convey the sense of difference between both men, their eras, and their ideologies.[27]

Gosse's autobiography clearly shows its debt to religious models for interpreting oneself, and Linda Peterson is helpful again in understanding Gosse's response as a series of experiments with, or "localized" applications of, alternative strategies found in science and literature (170). By the time Gosse was writing, however, law had come to provide an equally compelling and complicated framework for self-presentation and for self-interpretation insofar as it replaced explicitly religious models of interpretation with secular ones, or at least substituted secular for spiritual content (for example, free will as freedom of bequest, the moral imperative "to will" as a legal document "the will," character expressed as the accumulation and preservation of property). To the extent that law and religion collude in the autobiography as they did in Trollope's novel, we can situate Gosse's generational struggle in the discourse of inheritance as it was framed by social, as well as natural, science. We can then begin to see how Gosse's application of literary strategies satisfies a need for imagination and wonder stifled not only by his parents' fundamentalism but also by the literalism of law and, consequently, how the encounter with literature becomes necessary to the self or subject he writes into being in the autobiography.

Like other early twentieth-century writers, Gosse takes up the Victorian interest in a formal, textual will and abstracts it, changing it from a literal document bearing his parents' imprint into a trope for his own, the beneficiary's, "privilege to fashion his inner life for himself" (251). As is true in *The Warden*, the trust is the specific form of testament, but where the will or trust is forward looking, life-writing looks backwards and in the process can evaluate effects. *Father and Son* is predicated on these two opposing movements: the character Edmund must move forward and can only do so through the author's retrospective. If Harding's renunciation of his position was like the Victorian daughter's rejection of fortune for fulfillment, Gosse's biography of his father shares in her revisionary powers put to the rewriting of his story as her own. Victorian ideology must give way, but it must be relived in order to be revised in the narrative. The question then is how Gosse's biography in both its choice of legal metaphors and in its narrative form performs this double duty.

---

literary techniques makes the statements so made stand out as examples wherein Gosse is deliberately analyzing as opposed to merely presenting himself. Peterson, in contrast, works very hard to distinguish autobiography from the novel on the grounds that too many critics of the former misunderstand the secondary importance of presentation to interpretation (4–6).

[27] Or, following the logic of natural science, Edmund cannot tell his story without beginning with a story of his origins. See Peterson's discussion of Herbert Spencer and Samuel Butler (165–7).

In this move away from Victorian ideology, the conceptual basis of subjectivity shifts from property in the external, literal sense to the more abstract one of consciousness. But *Father and Son*'s dialogic form reveals that, like the legal will's control of property, its primary concern is still the issue of ownership and control of that consciousness.[28] First by positioning the debate specifically between the vertically related parent and child, Gosse develops his own and his father's identities in terms of inheritance. Thus, the book's "struggle between two temperaments" (35) becomes the much broader debate between "two epochs" and the merits of their respective modes of representing subjectivity. Second, through the course of the biography, Gosse defines his emergent subjectivity through constant reference to literature so that reading itself, the response to a text, becomes a conversion experience.[29] Where the "father" half is filled with the literal language of the trust, the imaginative "son" half charts a private form of resistance through fiction. In this way, *Father and Son* emphasizes fiction's ability to counter or supplement the limits of legal concepts of identity and its representation. More specifically, its treatment of the will offers a way of thinking about the abstraction of principle from the text—of trust from the trust instrument, of intention from the will—as a spiral process: less a forward or evolutionary movement, it offers a return to the moral foundation of the text but expresses it in a new form. In its departure from realist methods of representation, it suggests that this gap between law and literature widens in the movement towards modernist methodologies.

In the epilogue to *Father and Son*, Gosse quotes at length from one of his father's letters. Phillip explains to Edmund that his wife "*left you* as a solemn charge to me" and that he has therefore through all manner of matters great and small "sought to act for you" (249).[30] The passage exemplifies both the way Phillip's words are left to speak for themselves (Edmund's method of emphasizing his father's empirical ideology by himself using empirical evidence to demonstrate it), and the way that Edmund's identity is held in trust: his childish self is held in reserve for his adult self, and he has little overt say in how he will be directed or disposed of. Indeed, Gosse refers earlier to this trust as the "Great Scheme" that "had been the aspiration of my Mother [which] at her death she had *bequeathed* [...] to my Father" (212).

[28] In an argument similar to Roger Porter's, Cynthia Northcutt Malone suggests that the dialogue in *Father and Son* renders it in Bakhtinian terms a "'polemically colored autobiography'" (16). Focusing as much on the characters' internal divisions as on those between parent and child, she argues that Edmund is able to be an actor in and a spectator of his own development (22). The text mimics this split in such a way that Edmund is able to depict his own forward movement towards an enlightened position from which he can recognize and describe his father's regression (27).

[29] Peterson describes the turn to texts and away from supernatural events as the rational turn in autobiography (16–17). Gosse's turn to literature in my reading returns some of the spirituality to his rational, empirical, non-fictional form of representation.

[30] He continues: "That responsibility I have sought constantly to keep before me [...] in my choice of a school for you, in my choice of a residence for you, and in multitudes of lesser things—I have sought to act for you" (249).

Though Gosse makes use of no legal will (choosing other documents instead, like his father's letters above, or his mother's diary), he zeros in nonetheless on imperative will. (One might object to the absence of an actual will, but as statutory changes that narrowed the Church's jurisdiction over wills shows, Gosse was living in a world where covenants had long since become contracts and the trust a legal instrument; that is, law is there even where it doesn't appear to be.) Using the rhetoric of a nineteenth-century focus on property, he highlights the way his (spiritual) identity is controlled by his father "behind [whom] stood the ethereal memory of my Mother's will, guiding him, pressing him, holding him, to the unswerving purpose which she had formed and defined" (42) in that "little locked volume" (40), her "secret journal" (68).[31]

If the later discovery of this secret trust provided a key for the adult Edmund (the clue that revising her text would be a way of reclaiming his self-determination), his description of his mother's deathbed dedication recalls the binding nature of religion but also of law. Emily's confidence that Edmund's spiritual future is secure comes from her own "emphasis of will" and her belief in a "covenant God" (77). Her life has been dedicated to fulfilling her side of that contract and securing her own salvation, but she needs Phillip to continue that work for their son. Her repeated imperatives, "Take our Lamb and walk with me" (81) are not immediately understood by him (and certainly aren't comprehended by the child Edmund), but in this scene of triangulation Phillip becomes her mediator and trustee as he presents Edmund to his mother whose hand "sealed with the most solemn, the most poignant and irresistible insistence" the dedication which her diary has only later revealed to the adult Gosse.

Throughout the text, this association of his parents' plans for him with the binding nature of the will is countered by his own references to his private will that struggles under its burden. Gosse describes himself first as "a mere part of them, without individual existence [...] swept on, a satellite in their atmosphere" (53). His mother's wishes are "a weight, intolerable as the burden of Atlas, to lay on the shoulders of a fragile little child" (81). He is "imprisoned," "caught," "helpless," forced towards an "intellectual surrender" (168), but against this terrific burden, he claims to have "clung to a hard nut of individuality." This "innate and persistent self," he writes, "was something I never resigned." As was true for Septimus Harding, Gosse experiences a split between his outward identity and his internal sense of subjectivity. His description of the obstacles ranged against the emergence of his character raises the question as to *how* he managed to overcome them.

---

31 Peterson's reading of this scene emphasizes the diary's function as a "pre-interpretation" of Edmund's life the discovery of which—its opening with a key—provides a key to his own life so that the autobiography responds even more to her writing than to his father's presence (172–3). Considering that her will drives Phillip, it makes sense to think of her writing as the documents which formalize her will, changing what was a contract or promise during her life into a testament at her death. See also Charles Fried's discussion of contract as a promise that creates expectations (8).

Early in the book he describes the critical moment when he discovered "a companion and a confidant in [him]self," a "sympathizer in [his] own breast" (58). Though his external self succumbs to the impositions on it, his internal, abstract self knows that there is more to his identity than his role as conduit for his parents' designs. This life of the mind is sustained by exercise of the imagination (which Gosse declares his father lacks) and by fiction's role in this process. Gosse's many literary allusions, which at first seem an odd method of substantiating his claims about events and people in this "scrupulously true" (33) account of his life, can thus be read as a move away from the literalism of his parents' thinking. Furthermore, the presence of fiction both accentuates the book's literary form and locates the origin of meaning within the reader's own imagination.

Gosse emphasizes this difference first by establishing his parents' lack of imagination. Their outright fear of fiction makes them almost Benthamite parodies, just as Edmund will appear as a young Jeremy in his first encounter with fictions.[32] Their religious faith, though it might be supposed to invoke some imaginative faculty, in fact develops into an "iconoclastic literalness" that depends on the absence of any "sympathetic imagination" (78). Indeed, his father's "very absence of imagination" is a leading cause of his scientific success (113). Furthermore, in an effort to encourage their son's "truthfulness," his parents are said to have "exclud[ed] the imaginary from [his] outlook on facts" (50) by prohibiting his exposure to any kind of fiction. Indeed, Emily believed that "to compose fictitious narrative of any kind was a sin" (48).

Against this framework of injunctions, Edmund (in the role of rebellious child) peppers the story of his life with allusions to a variety of literary forms. He becomes a new Caliban, obsessed with words as "instruments of expression" and "busy providing [him]self with words before [he] had any ideas to express with them" (220). For example, he challenges the implication that his mother's philanthropic work interfered with her care of him by claiming she was no Mrs. Jellyby, then jumps to the garrett, that "fairy" place and its trunk lined with sensation fiction (58–9). Anxious to get out of London and into the country, specifically to experience landscapes first found in Donne's poetry, he compares himself to the "dying Falstaff [who] babbled of green fields" (62). Again, he likens himself to the trapped heroine of a medieval romance whose release from isolation by a prince signals for Edmund the same salvation the discovery of his inner self brings to him (55–6). He will later embarrass himself by reading Marlowe aloud to his

32 In C.K. Ogden's collection of Bentham's writing on fiction, he includes Bentham's account of his own early experiences with fiction. On confronting his grandmother's sampler of Adam and Eve, the work's techniques for emphasizing the apple call forth a response at once precocious and alarmingly naïve: "What to make of it [the apple], at a time when my mind was unable to distinguish fictions from realities I knew not" (qtd. in Ogden xi). Bentham reiterates the lamentable difficulty, indeed the almost moral failure, of differentiating fiction from reality when he encounters the devil. Of his appearance in both *The Pilgrim's Progress* and the picture "Sowing Tares," Bentham asks, "How was I to know it was not a copy from the life?" (xiv).

stepmother (228) and then turn to the romantics (230). Gosse's use of this material is a patent rejection of his parents' ideas. As an adult he can call attention to the instrumental view of language and to the emptiness of forms without meaning, words without ideas.[33] The text of *Father and Son* shows that his parents' language of religion and will was itself a form without meaning for him. It is this conflict that made living under their system such a burden. His book's reliance on fiction in particular, however, signals the way the inner life or consciousness—his personal meaning—is a function of the imagination which literature can fuel in contrast to the reductive identities preferred by social institutions.

The link between fiction and subjectivity is made explicit in his encounter with *Tom Cringle's Log*, which Gosse includes almost immediately after assuring readers of this persistent sense of self. Although instructed to "'skip' the pages which gave imaginary adventures" (170), the adult Edmund recalls, the child Edmund's enforced separation from fiction has made him ignorant of the concept of "literary invention." He therefore takes the story to be true, and from the characters' adventures and internal struggles learns to hope for escape from the "narrowness" of his home life (171). As narrator, Gosse is careful not to ascribe too much sophistication to his childish mind, but he does declare that this novel was the chief source of "fortitude" for his "individuality." This emphasis on fiction as the formal catalyst of imagination links it to subjectivity, while the narrator's reconstruction of his origins also suggests that identity itself is in some way fictional. Gosse anticipates this possibility as an objection in the preface, "At the present hour, when fiction takes forms so ingenious and specious, it is perhaps necessary to say that the following narrative, in all its parts, and so far as the punctilious attention of the writer has been able to keep it so, is scrupulously true" (33). Gosse denies that his own book might be one of those "ingenious" forms of fiction, which for skeptical readers of course immediately raises the flag of warning. Gosse maintains the veracity of his narrative, but is there a way for this statement to be true? Can Gosse privilege the imagination and still fulfill his intention of telling a true narrative?

Part of the dilemma presented by *Father and Son* is the apparent contradiction between the literary form and the non-fictional content, but these need not be opposed. The use of literary techniques can function as a symbolic or affective shorthand that positions readers to respond in particular ways to the events or characters described in the narrative, thereby enabling the author to pass judgment

---

[33] His example of Caliban, as Peterson points out, also shows his incomplete, early reading and his later strategic inattention to the parallel of Caliban's use of language to curse his master and Gosse's own use of it to reject his parents' teaching (188). See her discussion of Gosse's use of parody (176–82) and her conclusion that the use of literature does not "complement a biblical scheme" but works against it (187). These scenes of reading in which content is separated from form are also a reminder of *Wuthering Heights* and its lesson of the dangers of misrepresentation and misreading into which an uncritical respect for forms can lull the reader.

on them (Siebenschuh 32).[34] In terms of content, then, Gosse's allusions provide examples of literature's function for his own imaginative self-development. For readers, these allusions prompt their own imagination and experience with fiction, so that the recollection of particular affects influences their response, in this case to the character of Edmund. These emotional responses are then heightened by the awareness that the story being read is "true" (Siebenschuh 34). If the reader responds imaginatively to the text's construction of identity, where realization of that identity is effectively the narrative climax, then so might the text's meaning be a product of the reader's imagination.[35] Burton Pike suggests this possibility through his observation that autobiography is in effect "a novel written in the present, with one's past life as its subject" (qtd. in Siebenschuh 51). Arguing that the past is never "retrieved" but "reinvented," Pike's suggestion allows us to see that any searching after truth or intention is a necessarily flawed undertaking because of the differing contexts of writer and reader (much like Haphazard's explanation to Harding). Thus, Gosse's use of fiction in a non-fictional form to sustain his own identity counters his parents' project in two ways. First, it shows the way the abstract, imperative will centered in the son replaces the rhetoric of the concrete documents associated with his parents (the letters, texts, and diary). Second, it exposes the insufficiency of empirical assumptions and methodology simply to locate a discrete meaning by redefining meaning as a transactional or interpretive process.

Literary and legal representation both are concerned with giving shape to past but also to present experience and both require reinvention—in literature the imagined world and in law the translation of experience into a legal language and framework—but much has been written to suggest that more gets lost in the translation from life to law than from life to fiction.[36] The legal text's inability to convey intention even in such intentional documents as the will is the more particular problem since it provides a point of departure and contrast for the development of the realist novel's omniscient narrator. What the lawyer could not do, the novelist could accomplish (albeit not without complications of its own). Literature could become a supplement to the law. Literature's legal fictions could become a way of ensuring attention to particulars, of including the voice of the individual and his or her stories, of modeling processes and of emphasizing character over identity, in

---

34 Siebenschuh focuses primarily on the dramatic elements in Gosse's text, stressing highly visual character development and "symbolic episodes" (38). He does not, however, deal explicitly with the book's extensive allusiveness and inter-textuality.

35 Siebenschuh uses Burton Pike's work on autobiography to highlight the degree to which the nineteenth-century conception of identity was formulated along linear lines. In the tradition of Victorian biography within which Pike locates Gosse, "an autobiographer's search for or revelation of self *meant* telling a story" (30).

36 See Maria Aristodemou's argument (paralleling Robert A. Ferguson's account of American law and letters) on law's rejection of its imaginative, mythic past for the sake of positivism in *From Her to Eternity*. Although I find her argument generally compelling, I don't share her view that realism is the one mode of literature as lacking in this regard as law. See also James Boyd White's *Justice as Translation*.

short of providing an equitable balance to the law's modes of representation that surpassed the law's own use of fiction or, in the Benthamite view, provided the necessary corrective to self-serving legal professionalization. Fiction in this sense is only as good as the author who wields it, however.

The uses of fiction are a concern in both *The Warden* and *Father and Son* where imagination is central to deciding each text's particular question of justice, but the comparison breaks down here and raises the question of why fiction is abjured in Trollope but applauded in Gosse. Notwithstanding Septimus Harding's literal-mindedness and distrust of legal fictions, the literary fiction that tells his story shows itself better able to access and to represent individual intention than the legal, religious, or even journalistic forces ranged against its central character. The potential caveat to this basic argument is that literalness in the law would cause the good intentions of Hiram's charity to fail; the use of legal fictions, however suspect in nature the technique may have been deemed, stood to do justice to a character who at the very worst was unintentionally remiss. If Trollope advances a critique of law by showing it in the service of the powerful, nevertheless he backs out of it as carefully as Mr. Harding and John Bold retreat from their conundrum. Their capitulation shares the feeling that Mr. Harding's private character does not match the public identity that emerges from the lawsuit. And together they raise a set of questions about the relationship between subjectivity and social institutions, as well as the kinds of texts that sustain both.

These are the same questions Gosse tackles in *Father and Son*. Gosse's pact with his readers performs the equitable function of legal fictions insofar as it promises to present a truer biography by supplementing the history of great (public) deeds with personal, even unflattering (private) details about his subject. And in the reverse of Trollope's importation of the legal into his novel, Gosse's act of supplementation works literally by importing fiction into the "real" or "true" biographical text. Fiction bolsters the child's imagination in contrast to his parents' "iconoclastic literalness" (78). Their lack of "poetic character" is clearly associated in the book with their religious fundamentalism, but Gosse draws on legal metaphors as well in a way that places his biography within the novelistic conflict with law. This conflation of religious and legal institutions makes a generalized statement about Victorian realism, empiricism, and literalness that is put to the task of separating son from father. However, the conflation of biography and the novel at the end "forgets" this first implicit critique of realist methods in order to mark the greater creative scope and liberating potential of the literary overall.

These two directions of opposition—the parallel of generic opposition and the perpendicular of temporal opposition—emphasize the continuation into the Edwardian era of a literary approach to subjectivity that, although less categorical than the more easily managed identities that define the legal approach to personhood, for that very reason gave Victorian literature one of its most powerful claims to represent things, and people, as they are. But Gosse's own generic innovations suggest that the move towards further internalization of character and increasingly abstract modes to represent it erodes the basis of comparison of legal and literary discourse.

The will, the novel, and the autobiography discussed here are about self-creation and self-interpretation both within legal terms and outside of them. To say that Gosse in particular abstracts the law or that legal tropes appear in his autobiography is not to say that these texts have ceased to be about law.[37] Rather, it is to think of their approach to law as a critique of what law is *not*, or what law is failing to do in some way and in a particular context, instead of what law is or is doing. Put another way, being "about law" does not require a faithful representation of rules or procedures, nor does it mean, as law and literature's critics at century's end would have had it, that novelist's law is bad law when it deviates from rules. The subjectivity created and expressed in writing the autobiography is radically unlike the one created in the will, and yet both assume that individuals have the right to determine their lives. But as Gosse showed, the right "to fashion one's inner life for himself" is as much about the mode of fashioning as it is about the inner life.

The Warden's depiction of the conflict between the legality of Hiram's will and the justice of its administration highlights the struggle between intention and interpretation as the foundation of objective and personal meaning in the nineteenth century. In the same way that Dickens in his will had to "use the form of words" his lawyer said was necessary for the purpose, Gosse had to engage with the forms of spiritual and scientific biography—as well as legal forms of contract and trust—en route to his own design. His life held in trust and dominated by his parents' will, Gosse gains control of his consciousness through the freedom of imagination. As he says in the epigraph from Schopenhauer: "Der Glaube ist wie die Liebe; er lässt sich nicht erzwingen." If belief, like love, cannot be compelled, neither, his book demonstrates, can the private life of consciousness. He resists the prior generation's will and the systems of interpretation in which such empirical strategies are valued, thereby opening the way to replace them with others that more properly reflect his emergent cultural values. In effect, his use of fiction to fashion his inner life embodies a return to the principles that had been emptied out of Victorian religious and legal forms—the trust in trust, the will in will, the character in identity—and their reshaping in a realism faithful to human consciousness.

---

37 See Richard Posner's argument that when law appears in literature it is not law but a metaphor for something else in *Law and Literature: A Misunderstood Relation*. His critics have been vocal, too. See Robert Weisberg's account in "The Law-Literature Enterprise."

Chapter 6
Fictions of Justice: Testamentary Intention and the Illegitimate Heir

Propertied men throughout the century embraced the theory laid out by J.S. Mill in *Principles of Political Economy* (1848) that as long as private property exists, ownership must encompass the ability to alienate property—either "bestowing it, at death or during life, at the owner's pleasure" (33)—or it is not ownership. Turning logic into sentiment, testators everywhere, even in literature, claimed their freedom of bequest as a sacred tenet of Englishness.

As Trollope's Mr. Scarborough of *Mr. Scarborough's Family* (1883) asserts, "If a man has a property he should be able to leave it as he pleases; or—else he doesn't have it" (389). Yet as Blackstone had pointed out as far back as the *Commentaries* in 1766, as Lord St. Leonards would point out again in *A Handy Book on Property Law* (1858), and as numbers of essays in the periodical press and legal manuals reminded readers, to speak of absolute freedom of bequest was to overstate the right. By restricting the type of people who might write wills, the type who might benefit under them, the type of bequest that might be made—in short, everything that goes into a will and might be said to constitute freedom of testation—the law made the will of the testator and the "pleasure of the deceased" (Blackstone II.12) seem a rhetorical act indeed.

As previous chapters have shown, testators often mistook their right to make a will for their ability to make one without legal assistance; what could a lawyer know about his client's desires that he was not competent of articulating on his own? But the Courts routinely had to deal with poorly executed or witnessed wills, with wills that contravened a rule of the statute, with wills whose meaning was not at all clear, or was clearly not to be allowed. For as long as legal subjectivity remained grounded in property, social identity could be defined by the written will; however, under those terms, the process of writing that will would have to exclude those other aspects of private subjectivity that were either incompatible with or extraneous to it. And so, just as the papers and magazines plied readers with examples of eccentric testators and their outrageous fortunes, the novel imported this conflict between the legal professional and the man of property and created a space where an alternative view of the legal reality could be developed: where, for example, the will was as much about self-determination and moral autonomy as about the transfer of goods, where testators had property *and* character, but also where they used this power to control their heirs; where women learned how to tell stories and fashion narratives that did not end in dispossession, or where sons took a lesson from their Victorian sisters and looked for ways to reframe property as self-possession. In the imagined world of the novel, all those aspects of character not necessary for social identity, or those ways of thinking and being that were ruled out by legal procedure, could be explored—and contested.

Chapter 5's discussion of *The Warden* (1855) and *Father and Son* (1907), for example, illustrated the law's commitment to honor testamentary intention in cases of charitable trust, but it also showed the limitations of any document, even the black letter of the will, to frame and convey something as abstract as intention. Moreover, it showed that the expulsion of the moral and spiritual dimensions of subjectivity from this area of civil law deprived it of its ability to constitute and represent human character as fully as literature could. Looked at together, these two literary texts show the limits of the will's effectiveness and hence of testamentary control. In this chapter, however, I turn to two of Trollope's novels, *Ralph the Heir* (1871) and *Mr. Scarborough's Family* (1883), and E.M. Forster's *Howards End* (1910) for examples of the opposite problem—of testamentary intention that, albeit clearly expressed, cannot be enacted. As Victorian and Edwardian revisions of the negotiation between the individual and the law, these novels illustrate the shifting value of empirical forms within literature, as well as the widening gap between literary and legal models of subjectivity.

The more specific legal problem posed by these novels, however, lies in the particular terms of this conflict. By introducing the figure of the illegitimate child, both Trollope and Forster present two opposed, potential heirs whose legitimacy or eligibility as heirs is better determined by their attitude towards property than by legalities surrounding the circumstances of their birth. In *Ralph the Heir*, the novel's focus oscillates between Squire Gregory's attempts to draft his will and the responses of the heirs (identically named cousins: one legitimate by birth, the other not). *Mr. Scarborough's Family* further tests the distinction between legal principles and legality by showing how law can be manipulated and its realities undermined, how one person can have two identities, or none. In the spirit of realism, Trollope gives equal attention to the will as a written document and as an expression of personal subjectivity. By contrast, in *Howards End* the textual will is no more than a penciled scrawl; still, Ruth Wilcox's desire, her will, presides over the entire book. Margaret Schlegel's spiritual connection with the first Mrs. Wilcox and her understanding of the house's symbolic significance make her the proper heir in contrast to the Wilcox clan. Margaret's nephew is the only legally illegitimate heir, but like his aunt, he is Mrs. Wilcox's spiritual successor. Forster's trope of the will and legitimacy is just that, a metaphor that revises realist methodologies through a more modernist interpretation of the legitimate means of representation.

Sins of the Father: "Bastardy" and the Right to No Name

From *Wuthering Heights*'s (1847) Heathcliff to Esther Summerson of *Bleak House* (1853), and from the Vanstone sisters of Collins's *No Name* (1862) to *Ralph the Heir*'s (1871) Ralph Newton, the Victorian novel is often peopled by illegitimate children, whose un-locatability within the social structure makes them frequently pitiable and sometimes threatening figures.[1] The novel's recurrent preoccupation with them expresses a cultural anxiety over the un-nameable calmed ironically by giving these children without patronym the dubious appellation of "bastard." By fixing the socially fluid individual, the empiricist mindset laid the groundwork for knowing and controlling it.

The impulse to regulate and the mechanism through which such control became possible both lie in the development of the legal category of illegitimacy. Describing the rights of illegitimate children under Roman law, as compared to the "much superior" reason of the English system, William Blackstone refers to the folly of allowing any number of children born before their parents' marriage to be legitimated at any time by a subsequent union and, thus, to "be admitted to all the privileges of legitimate children" (*Commentaries* 1.443). "This is plainly a great discouragement to the matrimonial state," he observes, "to which one main inducement is usually not only the desire of having children, but the desire of procreating lawful heirs." Blackstone's alarm at the possibility that children born out of wedlock might have the same rights as "lawful heirs" is more nearly a fear that proper, familial inheritance patterns would be disrupted. As the preceding chapters have argued, the materialism of the nineteenth century and the statutory changes that made the will a written document aligned the transmission of goods with one's legal or social identity. The ability to pass on one's possessions, to control them even after death, became synonymous with shaping one's individual identity and conferring it to posterity. The preservation of property was thus tantamount to a preservation of the self that would be doubly confirmed by the procreation of lawful heirs of the body.

And yet Henry Maine, in his more thorough study of Roman law, declared that if early societies had relied on bloodlines as a criterion for inheritance, civilization could not have been achieved. Explaining the "legal fiction" as a highly useful if primitive method of effecting legal reform, he turned to adoption—"which permits the family tie to be artificially created" (26)—as one of the tool's best illustrations without which, he wrote, "it is difficult to understand how society would ever have escaped from its swaddling clothes." Although in Maine as in Blackstone, these categories are directed towards defining the family, they create and perpetuate two distinctly different models of the legal subject: one that depends on status and one on contract, each of which in turn is associated with a specific type of property and mode of ownership. The status associated with the landed estate, for example, emphasized continuity and implied a more conservative approach to ownership, one intended quite literally to conserve the estate, which positions the owner as steward. In contrast, the money and commodities comprising personal property allowed for and even encouraged a more mobile and fluid model of ownership

---

[1] Hilary Schor's observation of the banality of the will plot is repeated here in Jenny Bourne Taylor's description of illegitimacy as "both an excessive and predictable, even banal, plot device" in the nineteenth-century novel ("Nobody's Secret" 569).

that complemented the contracting individual for whom choice and promise, not inherited forms, were the key components of his relationships. This is the liberal subject of civil society, and the contest over inheritance and legitimacy that emerges in the Courts and in the legal categories themselves is the contest between two models of social organization.

For the illegitimate person, however, the equation of selfhood with ownership creates a more immediate and circular problem. Anny Sadrin's formulation that "one must have in order to be" helped to explain how women who lost their property rights on marriage also lost their legal personality and were absorbed into their husband's. However, the formula finds its reverse here: one must first be in order to have, and to be illegitimate by birth, to be the *filius nullius* or "nobody's child" Blackstone describes, is to be disqualified from inheriting the very (real) property that carries with it one's social identity (1.447). In novels of Blackstone's time, such as that story of bastardy and adoption *Tom Jones* (1749), the illegitimate child became the picaresque wanderer, the modern individual *par excellence* in search of a place and a stable sense of self. The journey continues in the nineteenth century in novels about figures, who, although situated in the center of the home, are nonetheless dispossessed by the circumstances of their births and the laws of "bastardy."

England's so-called bastardy laws were notoriously strict and remained so far into the twentieth century.[2] During the nineteenth century, the law was guided primarily by the Bastardy Act of 1845. As "An Act for the Further Amendment of the Laws Relating to the Poor," it sought mainly to assist the mother, who was primarily responsible for the child, to gain support for its maintenance from the alleged father.[3] Less a matter of moral than fiscal concern, at least in the eyes of common law, the object was to defray the costs to the parish that arose when the child or *filius populii* was born within its precincts and eligible for its aid.[4]

For fathers anxious to secure lawful heirs to their property, the act could be particularly detrimental. If brought up by the mother in bastardy proceedings and confirmed by the court as the natural father, he became liable for care until the child reached the age of 13. Failure to do so resulted in the "distress and sale of [his] goods and chattels" to recuperate the sum and, where these proved insufficient,

---

2 The 1953 edition of *Halsbury's Laws of England* retains a chapter on "Bastardy," and it was not until the 1970s that the statutes abandoned the pejorative title in favor of the less inflammatory "illegitimate person."

3 For a comprehensive social history of illegitimacy, see Iva Pinchbeck and Margaret Hewitt; Jenny Teichman, and Jenny Bourne Taylor.

4 Taylor explains the difference between the common and canon law's attitude towards the illegitimate child. Common law is secular, governed by statute, and based on a view of the family as "an economic and social network for the maintenance and consolidation of property." Canon law, in contrast, took a more ideal, if no less strict, stance towards bastardy (seeing the child as the innocent victim of its parents' lapsed morality) at the same time that it debarred the child from privileged offices and other rights. Nevertheless, it was through the Church courts that the Poor Laws developed and out of them a communal, Christian responsibility for the child of God's family ("Nobody's Secret" 571–2).

imprisonment for up to three months. Subsequent amendments to the act, notably the Bastardy Laws Amendment Acts of 1872 and 1873, extended both the time frame during which a woman could make an order for proceedings and the variety of expenses for which the father could be made responsible, inclusive of court costs and reimbursement to the parish. The existence of an illegitimate child could severely undermine the integrity of its parents' assets and their own characters, their public reputation, which is to say nothing of the damage done to the child's rights in a society so contingent upon the possession of property.[5]

The child born out of wedlock lacks a name but inherits a social stigma that literally prevents him from inheriting property. Halsbury records that "the rule that a bastard is *nullius filius* applies only to the case of inheritance and cases analogous thereto" (*The Laws of England* 438). The statutes show, in other words, that although his rights as an English citizen are the same as any legitimate person's (inclusive of the right to acquire property and to leave it to his children), his relationship to his own parents actively debars him, as well as his children through him, from inheriting by descent (439). Though he may have a name "by reputation," he has no "surname by inheritance."

This focus on the parent-child or "natural relationship" was justified in one sense by laws that prohibit marriage within certain degrees of relationship, laws that after 1908 could subject the parties to the Punishment of Incest Act. However, the bulk of the law concentrates not on blood-lines, since the bastard is a "stranger in blood" (440), but precisely on the issue of patrilineal inheritance. Even where a child was subsequently legitimized, for example, he was not entitled to inherit by descent from his father, and the restrictive nature of married women's property laws frequently left the mother no property to bequeath.[6] So apart from preventing

---

[5] These provisions notwithstanding, the law's attitude towards paternal responsibility is lenient to say the least and places greatest responsibility on the mother. In *Seaborne v. Maddy* (1840), for example, the court determined that the father is "under no obligation to provide for the child, in the absence of any affiliation order [outlined above]." And in the 1861 case of *R. v. Brighton (Inhabitants)*, it was determined that "the father of an illegitimate child is not recognized by the law of England for civil purposes" (Halsbury *The Laws of England* 441). The existence of measures to exhort paternal care for the child seem, then, to beg the question as to the frequency of an affiliation being granted. In terms of *Ralph the Heir*, knowledge of the law reveals just how vigilant Squire Gregory's efforts on his son's behalf are in comparison to what was actually required of him, his moral rectitude challenging the legal justice of the times.

[6] For women of the lower socio-economic classes, the issue of how to provide for their children during their lives was more pressing than what they were unable to bequeath at their own deaths. Taylor points out that with the passage of the New Poor Law in 1834 (a law so harsh that reforms followed as soon as 1838) mothers themselves were no longer able to sue the putative fathers so that the child became her sole responsibility, thus affirming the symbolic and material link between mother and child ("Representing Illegitimacy" 133). Ironically, the economic straits to which unwed mothers were subject often led to a physical separation from their children. Because mothers could not afford

certain marriages, the rules of bastardy were drawn primarily with a view towards the preservation of property for both the testator and his legal heirs, which in turn solidified the patriarchal and material basis of social identity: no name equals no property equals no identity, save what one can cobble together for oneself.

The question Trollope raises in *Ralph the Heir* regarding such laws is whether they are even practical, let alone just, in respect to both the testator and his potential beneficiaries. The early bastardy laws paint a picture of wayward fathers, the "dead-beat dads" of the early nineteenth century who might well land in jail for failure or inability to maintain their children. But case law shows fathers who wanted to provide for their children, and under certain conditions might, yet were legally unable to give them a name. *Hill and Simmonds v. Crook* (1871), for example, established that where a gift of property was made *inter vivos* (between living persons) or by will to children, the gift "prima facie includes only the legitimate children" (282), although Lord Cairns noted the possibility of a different interpretation ("where it appears on a proper construction of the will that 'children' was intended to include illegitimate children" as well). But, according to Vice Chancellor Hall, in *Atkinson v. Anderson* (1882), "however close the natural relationship between [the illegitimate child] and the donor may be, he is yet in law only a stranger in blood" (104).[7] Inheritance proceeded on the assumption of legitimacy. "Child" or "children" (even "issue") automatically meant legitimate children; neither term was allowed to encompass illegitimate children with them, so even in cases where some legatees were legitimate and others not, the court had to pretend that the latter didn't exist—which by law they did not.

Moreover, it had to assume that these children were not even within the contemplation of the testator. Mary Overhill's legacy to the six children of Mary Bentley, for example, was denied on the argument that Bentley had no "lawful issue." Although she was 49 years old when Overhill died (and therefore unlikely to bear any more children), she already had six living. Admittedly, Overhill assumed they were legitimate, but because her will left the money to "children," it was also assumed she couldn't have meant the six legal non-entities in whom otherwise she took such a great interest. It was argued on behalf of the children that the testatrix had used "the best description in her power" to include those children she meant to benefit, but the Vice-Chancellor John Stuart reluctantly decided against their title to the money, claiming that the "rule of law [was] established on authority too great to be shaken by [him]" (*In re Overhill's Trusts* 366). Rules were followed;

---

to support them, children were often sent either to the workhouse or to so-called baby farms. "Commissioners [of the Poor Law]," according to Teichman, "seemed to believe that the best […] way to reduce illegitimacy was to subject the unmarried mother to the 'providential' operation of economic forces […]. At all events, they were concerned to remove from the statute books those regulations which tended to ameliorate the economic plight of the unmarried mother, while adding new regulations that imposed the duty of support upon her" (66). For more on the 1834 Poor Law, see Irene Tucker.

[7] Both of these cases are discussed in vol. 3 of *Halsbury's Laws of England* (Symonds, ed.).

the authority of precedents and tradition was honored, but the testator's wishes, which even the Vice-Chancellor believed were meant to benefit Bentley's children, were denied. And the illegitimate child's worth, already complicated from a moral standpoint, was further degraded in the material, social sense.

As these cases show, illegitimacy was a legal category and a rhetorical strategy—a "legal fiction," according to Jenny Bourne Taylor, that responded to a fundamental anxiety surrounding fatherhood by creating legal paternity and using it to perpetuate patriarchy ("Nobody's Secret" 570, 571). The law's definition of the bastard as "one born out of lawful wedlock" (Halsbury 426)[8] draws attention both to the anxiety as well as to illegitimacy's status as a legal category: Trollope raises no question in *Ralph the Heir* that Ralph Newton is the *biological* descendent of his grandfather Ralph, or that he would inherit his estate, if only his parents had been *lawfully* joined. Although Taylor uses the term legal fiction to signal these symbolic and performative dimensions of bastardy (as distinct from its material effects) even within law, it will be useful to pause for a moment to consider the implications of thinking about bastardy as a procedural device because, unlike legal fictions that seek to promote reform, the fiction of illegal birth would seem to retard it.

It seems doubtful, considering the rulings above, that the fiction of illegitimacy was promoting gradual reform in the make-up of the family, still less so in the body of inheritance law. A case might be made that by being prevented from inheriting, the illegitimate child grew into the contracting adult. Where the heir to an entail, for example, might be led by the security of his expectations into an idle and dissipated life, younger sons who could not expect as great a share would be compelled to submit their "success in the world" to market forces and the "fair use of their talents," as the economist J.R. McCulloch (enamored of "Dr. Smith") conjectured in *The Edinburgh Review* ("Disposal of Property by Will" 363). Without the promise of money, or more particularly of status or cultural capital, the bastard individual would be similarly motivated to become "the architect of his own fortune" (363) and of his own relationships, by basing them in choice, rather than inheritance. However, even if bastardy were a legal fiction that gradually promoted the sphere of contract—by creating individuals who had no choice but to follow its model—the legal fiction is not at all the route Bentham (who, along with the other utilitarians, promoted the idea of individualism that was associated with freedom of contract and laissez-faire economics) would have advocated.[9] The legislation that was passed in 1845 and again in the 1870s, moreover, had less to do with the status of the child itself than with bringing the father financially (and symbolically) back into the picture of mother and child created by the Poor Law. Rather, the connection between illegitimacy and fiction is more oblique and suggests, as the

---

8 Reference is to the 1908 edition of Halsbury, *The Laws of England*, as opposed to later editions of *Halsbury's Laws* and *Halsbury's Statutes*.

9 Albert Venn Dicey's discussion of Benthamite individualism leads to the "extension of the sphere of contract" as an outgrowth of the basic principles of legislative utilitarianism (legislation as science, utility, and *laissez-faire* economics) (14).

distinction between freedom of bequest and its restriction through other laws does, that invoking illegitimacy in the areas of family and inheritance law preserved a traditional model of legal subjectivity based in the family and in land that was being countered with the expansion of testamentary freedom, and redefined in the area of contract.

As an over-determined symbol, bastardy represented many different social, moral, legal, and economic concerns, and illegitimacy became a site for working out new models of subjectivity. If in legal terms the bastard was no fiction at all, but a legal category meant to perpetuate specific models of property and inheritance, elsewhere he became a figure of "modernity and mobility" (Taylor 572).[10] When Henry Maine described legal fictions as being useful "at a particular stage of social progress" (25), he was referring to younger, less developed societies, not the England of the 1860s. However, fiction can become useful at any time when improvement is needed but change is feared—this in law. Literature, by assembling possibilities and projecting outcomes, gave readers the psychic space as well as the time to cultivate their own subjectivity and to grapple with the relationship between their real experiences and the made-up-ness of any social world.

By bringing together the two figures of the testator and the illegitimate child, both Trollope and Forster in the novels discussed here confront the problem of subjectivity and autonomy as it relates to changing economic models. Both authors are attracted to ideas of cultural tradition and continuity, but their novels critique the creation of illegitimacy to safeguard it in the legal and social arenas. In *Mr. Scarborough's Family* Trollope does this by satirizing the inconsistencies of legal identity and in *Ralph the Heir* by creating two contrasting Ralphs; Forster creates two families. Where they differ is in the respective weight each gives to the testator and to the illegitimate heir—a contradiction in common law terms, to be sure, but one that these novels highlight, since illegitimacy does not make sense outside of the terms of inheritance.[11] By drawing the parallel between the testator's freedom of bequest and the illegitimate person's freedom of contract—

---

[10] Taylor distinguishes elsewhere between illegitimacy and bastardy: illegitimacy relies on the binary notion of oppositions, whereas bastardy "suggests an identity constructed as an aporia—the indeterminate space in which an opposition breaks down and difference collapses into sameness—and as a simulacrum [...] in which that strangeness becomes strange" ("Representing Illegitimacy" 121). Her definition is a much more sophisticated way of saying that bastardy has a cultural and symbolic valence beyond its technical usages, which is the same point I make in respect of the differences between subjectivity and identity encoded in the last will and testament.

[11] Taylor parses the verse from Exodus 20:5 that "The sins of the fathers shall be visited on the children" and explains how it was used at different points in the historical discourse of illegitimacy (sometimes to call attention to the father, sometimes to the plight of the child). As "shorthand for the transference of stigma itself," however, it makes the point that I make in terms of subjectivity and the will, that is, that "inheritance is always shaped through social fictions of identity and through specific concepts of transmission" ("Nobody's Secret" 574).

both rights that emphasize individualism respecting the accumulation and control of property—these novels show how the laws of bastardy severed the link between parent and child and in its absence, if not promoted, at least created the possibility of an atomized society of mobile individuals. As will become clearer, Trollope, while more resistant to law's intrusion into private affairs is yet unwilling to forego its stabilizing influence whereas Forster, in contrast, sees more potential in these changes as a way of revitalizing without abandoning tradition.

As obsessed as the Victorian novel was with the testator and his freedom of bequest, it rarely condoned abuses or countenanced the exercise of will outside of a larger set of beliefs or containing structures (for example, religion, metaphysics, science, economics, law). The novel could explore those connections, weigh the value of one system against another, and posit new relationships based on different foundations, but it was wary of aggressive individualism and, at the very least, explained abuses as a failure to understand that the sources of autonomy were also mechanisms for their control. Here we can recall the solicitors' litany that freedom of bequest was meant to privilege the testator only because he knew better how to benefit and thereby fulfill his duty to his family; there was never a notion that the freedom should be used to their detriment, although many testators seemed to have missed that point. Thrust outside of the containing narrative of family origins, the illegitimate child had to look to other models for defining himself and crafting new relationships. This dispossession could be a disadvantage or an opportunity; the illegitimate child could be an object of compassion, or, as has already been suggested, its *sui generis* authority could be perceived as a threat to the very order illegitimacy was meant to protect.

Once again, Heathcliff provides an example of the dangers of individuality. Heathcliff managed to make his way in the world, clearly, but his world hardly seems an argument in favor of such free-floating ideas of property as associated with the contracting individual. His abuse of the power conferred on him by ownership may be a revenge on the legal system that deprived him of legal status, but his adult behavior at the Heights actually demonstrates his alienation from that system as well as the failure of adoption—his tombstone bears only one name, Heathcliff—to make up for his illegitimacy. Mr. Earnshaw's informal adoption of Heathcliff (itself the impulse of a contracting individual) succeeds initially in nurturing the orphan but, as Hindley's reaction shows, the illegitimate child cannot be allowed to displace the natural, rightful heir and expect to be—or to feel—fully integrated into the family.

From the standpoint of retributive law, it would be hard to blame Heathcliff for his response to the years of humiliation under Hindley, or even for his anger at Cathy's defection. It seems too much to expect, let alone require, that under these circumstances he should remember and preserve Mr. Earnshaw's kindness. Nevertheless, the adoption seems incomplete. He lacks a name, but he also lacks the affective connection that binds the family, which is precisely what allows him to use property as a tool for destruction. The moments we glimpse of affection towards Hareton, while they seem drawn from that initial, temporary phase of belonging, still, by their irregularity, demonstrate its stunted growth. And the return of the Heights to Catherine and Hareton at novel's end, especially when paired with the affirmation of Heathcliff's singularity and outsider status as marked on his tombstone, reaffirms the natural order of the legitimate family. Some 20 years later, Trollope's novels continue to wrestle with status-bound models of subjectivity based in traditional, landed property and the newer figure of the contracting individual. Ralph Newton's affective bond or sympathy with the environment of Newton Peele derives from natural affiliation, but Trollope will not allow nature to supersede the social order, and, as Ralph the heir demonstrates, "natural" ties are no guarantee of shared ideas in any case.

"What's in a Name:" Patronyms and Patrimony in Trollope

Ralph the Heir (1871) is a complicated familial and legal drama. It tells the story of a testator's attempt to circumvent one law through recourse to another and ultimately questions what constitutes justice and whether strict adherence to the law always produces it. Specifically, it recounts the story of Squire Gregory and his illegitimate son, Ralph. Ralph is a model child and would make a model squire of Newton Peele were the estate not entailed upon his younger, imprudent—but legitimate—cousin Ralph whose legal eligibility to inherit and run the estate has no reference to actual fitness. The social order created by these property laws is out of sync with the lived reality of the local community, but law's commands make it possible, as Coral Lansbury puts it, "to impose this fictitious version of reality upon people" (85). In reality, the illegitimate Ralph should be "Ralph the heir." In reality, the Squire rightly perceives that the estate would be better maintained in his son's hands rather than his nephew's, but the legal reality dictates otherwise: Squire Gregory's will is not his own since the entail ties his hands in terms of how he may manage his property.[12] As Mrs. Mountjoy succinctly puts it in *Mr. Scarborough's Family*, "when a property was entailed the present owner had nothing to do with its future disposition" (24). Thus hampered by the imposition of his own father's will, Squire Gregory concocts a plan to buy out his nephew's interest.

[12] R.D. McMaster explains what he calls the conservative and liberal tendencies of bequeathing real property. The conservative approach, which derives from the original owner's desire to "keep the property intact and in the family" (13), informed the fee tail's restriction of descent to "a person and the heirs of his body." The liberal tendency is held most often by the heir who feels he "ought to be able to do what he likes with what he possesses." Thus, *Ralph the Heir* illustrates the way that the old Squire follows laws of primogeniture even where there is no entail, but then makes one to punish Gregory for his illegitimate son and to "preserve the English way" (13). The importance of primogeniture as a facet of English law and national identity continued until 1925. Repeating Dicey's comparison, in 1905, of England's constitutional democracy to its aristocratic land laws, McMaster notes the paradox and observes that "despite various attacks and schemes for revising land law in the period, its general features prevailed until 1925" (15).

The laws of bastardy held that although the illegitimate child could not inherit by descent, he may "always do so by purchase" (*Halsbury's Laws* 105). If the Squire could possess Newton Priory outright, he could memorialize himself by his own good works and rest confidently in the knowledge that these would be perpetuated by his son, rather than squandered by his ne'er-do-well nephew. Even Sir Thomas, the Squire's attorney and guardian to Ralph the heir, admits that if Gregory's son were somehow to inherit instead of his ward "the estate [would] go to a better fellow, though out of the proper line" (17). However, just when it seems that the heavily indebted Ralph the heir will sell his interest, the Squire is killed before being legally entitled to draft a new will. The Squire's projected will fails. Ralph the heir remains the heir; Newton Priory goes to him.

Trollope's decision to outline the Newtons' legal conundrum, develop a loophole, and then close it in favor of the status quo entertains the possibility that what the law decrees from a distance may, upon closer examination, prove the less judicious course. Yet the novel also questions whether defiance or manipulation of the law would result in still greater losses. While Squire Gregory deserves attention as both an heir and a testator, the majority of the novel focuses on the two Ralphs. By giving them the same name, Trollope deliberately closes the gap between their titular identities in order to shift attention to their character or "ideological legitimacy" (Teichman 132). In effect he asks the question "what's in a name?" which, applied here to the legal categories of illegitimacy and inheritance rights, serves as a critique of the law's preoccupation with potentially superficial markers of identity—the literal patronym versus the consciousness of belonging—that may ultimately damage the integrity of the property such laws are meant to protect. In this way he operates on the basis of a more equitable ethic, as opposed to the edicts of a pre-ordained (common) law, that considers the evidence of personal accountability and the reader's response to it as the final arbiter of justice.[13]

Trollope's play with naming in the novel illustrates this point. The senior Ralph Newton had two sons: Squire Gregory and Ralph, the Parson of Newton Priory. Squire Gregory is father to the illegitimate Ralph. The now deceased Parson is father to his own namesake, Ralph the heir, and to the current Parson Gregory. This proliferation of names makes it difficult to distinguish between characters and generations, but sharing a name is the extent of the similarity between them, as the two living Ralphs and the two Gregories exhibit such divergent attitudes.

---

13 Lansbury argues that in terms "of language and of structure," Trollope was indebted to the law's forms and to the methods of legal reasoning. However, he "allowed [his fiction] to be governed by an ethic wholly different from that which the law was assumed to defend. His was a vision of a social order in which individuals knew success or failure as a result of free decisions reached in circumstances unaffected by external contingencies" (Lansbury 24, 20). "External contingencies" strike me as one of the central components of this new ethic insofar as the characters' responses to them form the basis of the reader's evaluation. If, as Lansbury also affirms, reason is "the arbiter of his fiction in the persona of the reader" (20), then the reader needs to have some understanding of the significance of what's at stake in their behavior. In this lies the novel's symbolic value.

In a move that further accentuates the centrality of a name to the novel, Trollope hones in on their attitudes about the family name and concomitantly the role that legitimacy plays in the correct distribution of property.

Just as he had done in *The Warden* with Harding's confrontation of both his legal and clerical identities, Trollope uses law to provide a framework for exploring "the tensions between public behavior and private scruple" (McMaster 155). Informed by justice but expressed through law and administered by professionals, the legal system is a hierarchy at the bottom of which lies the citizenry who may reasonably feel the weight of such tradition (McMaster 155). By creating a narrative voice for the individual experience of the law, however, the novel reverses this hierarchy. Trollope suggests that a better rule for gauging the two Ralphs' eligibility as heirs lies in their attitudes toward legal principles and practices than in the law itself. If in theory he favors the illegitimate Ralph, however, he does so in large part because of that man's sensitivity to English tradition and his own intuitive understanding that he is not the right man for the job. In this context, the fact that Ralph the heir is actuated by his shifting financial circumstances becomes a major point of contrast to his cousin's more constant sense of the order of things.

Pushed to extremities by expensive habits, Ralph the heir waffles between his long-term desire to keep his interest in the lucrative Newton estate and his immediate need for cash. Nearly dissuaded by his own brother's arguments that "Almost anything would be better than abandoning the property" (215), Ralph nevertheless decides to sell. Lamenting his imminent loss, he vows never to visit the Priory again: "Nothing on earth could induce him to go there, now that it under no circumstances could be his own. It would still belong to a Newton, and he would try to take comfort in that" (322). Ralph's attitude to his cousin's inclusion in the Newton family, though likely to garner agreement and sympathy from twenty-first-century audiences, is neither entirely applauded nor supported by the novel. His negligent attitude towards the property, and in this instance towards the law, discourages the reader from accepting his judgment.

Indeed, neither his brother nor the illegitimate Ralph himself views the issue of the name in the same light. Parson Gregory, who could be generous when the sale was only contemplated, is shocked by his brother's decision: "though he must have known that Ralph the base-born was in all respects a better man than his own brother, more of a man than the legitimate heir,—still to his feelings that legitimacy was everything" (339). Gregory even makes the astounding proposition that it would be best if "neither he nor his brother should have a child" so that the "proper line" of the Newtons should die out. In the context of the bastardy and inheritance laws, extinction is preferable to the ongoing injustice that would exist if "real" Newtons were to live dispossessed of their patrimony. Extreme as the younger Gregory's sentiments are, the reader is positioned to favor his opinion by virtue of his loyalty to the traditional English system of land tenure.

The base-born Ralph's feelings confirm this attitude. Even before the lawyers are consulted, Ralph squirms under his father's proposal: "Let what might be done in regard to the property, nothing could make him, who was illegitimate, capable of holding the position in the country which of right belonged to Newton of Newton" (217–18). By reputation only is Ralph a Newton, and, while this social concession may sustain a pleasant life-style within the family and the community, it cannot eradicate the fact that at law he has no name. His grandfather's will, not his father's, was "more consistent with the English order of things" (29).

This order recalls England's feudal organization and in this sense is a facet of traditional attitudes towards a squire's relationship to his tenants. When the "richest and most intelligent" of the Newton tenantry congratulates this Ralph on his new position, he reminds the new heir that "there will be a feeling" (347). And Ralph acknowledges, "After all, such a property as Newton does not in England belong altogether to the owner of it." Rather, he has a "part property" with those who "make it what it is, and will not make it what it should be, unless in their hearts they are proud of it." Unlike his cousin, the illegitimate Ralph is a visible and active figure on the landscape, attuned to the mentality of the people with whom he lives. In contrast, Ralph the heir does not consider the land's social significance and views it as another personal possession. Significant here is what this clash of values means for Trollope's view of the justice of legal dictates and their impact on personal and national identity.

Trollope's fictional community and his readers can only regret the ultimate failure of Squire Gregory's will and Ralph's projected inheritance if it is clear that Ralph himself believes in his own ineligibility. That he has this conservative attitude places him in a traditional camp that values real property or the landed estate in its capacity as "a symbol of order and continuity" (Harvey 420). As such, Ralph's theoretical position, like Roger Carbury's in *The Way We Live Now* (1875), further endorses the law's symbolic power as the engine that sustains familial and national identity. The closest Ralph comes to criticizing his institutional identity derives not from his inability simply to inherit what others have made, but from the possibility that it will impede him from making a life for himself. The possibility for human agency in the Trollopian world, as Carol Lansbury explains it and as I have shown in my discussion of *The Warden*, is constituted by the relationship between one's private sense of self or subjectivity and the identity conferred by public institutions and systems of organization onto the self. And in Ralph's case his grandfather's formal will, embodied in the entail, has created a situation that forces a competition between other imperatives: first, between the entail and his own father's failed plans, and now between the private wishes of his cousin, of the tenantry, and himself. Having become engaged to Mary Bonner on the assumption that this new inheritance will alleviate the stigma of his birth, the dissolution of that prospect likewise blurs his marital outlook. Although in the end Ralph does marry, the fact that his personal sense of subjectivity suffers at the hands of the same law without prompting his own willful rejection of its values—a rejection made possible by his father's efforts—solidifies his traditionalism.

Ralph the heir's attitude, in contrast, tends towards a more liberal interpretation of the individual's personal rights, a modern sense of property as personal, not communal, wealth (Galsworthy's "Forsytism") and of the latitude to create one's own public identity through testamentary acts. The irony here is that, although otherwise opposed to one another, Ralph the heir and Squire Gregory share this willingness to subvert tradition for the sake of personal interests in contrast to Parson Gregory and the illegitimate Ralph, whose love for one another cannot efface their shared sense that the latter should not inherit. Their close relationship in general and their unity on this point mend the rupture between their fathers and indicates that adherence to the law maintains familial order. And Trollope's decision to support the status quo "in proper conformity with English habits and English feelings" (85) suggests, moreover, that the law lies at the heart of English identity. However, his painstaking efforts to create sympathy and respect for the illegitimate Ralph and for his father's efforts on his behalf reveal a troubled stance towards the law's equation of familial with cultural identity and consequently its right to define family.

Mr. Scarborough's Family (1883) in contrast is a study in Trollopian irony taken to the point of cynicism about the family and the law. Although the novel's title may conjure images of the domestic ideal at the heart of so many Victorian novels, familial order is precisely what Mr. Scarborough disrupts when he trifles with the law and through it with his wife's memory and his children's sense of their place in the world. In this way, the novel offers a partial revision of Trollope's conservative conclusion in *Ralph the Heir* and opens the way for the further interrogation of the laws and aims of inheritance in *Howards End*. Squire Gregory's moral will fails, even though his intended bequest is more just than what the law will allow him to make, because he doesn't respect the law's social significance, its world-creating and world-ordering functions.[14] His son, however, supports the law because he does understand its role in the preservation of familial and national identity. As in Trollope's previous novel, *Mr. Scarborough's Family* also questions the law's practical relationship to justice and dissects the testator's ability to define himself through the paired tropes of inheritance and illegitimacy. It also evaluates the testator's formal will through reference to his heir's attitude. One of the key attitudes Mr. Scarborough expresses, for example, is the belief that with property one has no need of a legal name, since in his opinion the real stigma of illegitimacy is its capacity to disqualify one from ownership. Mountjoy, in contrast, is sensitive to the symbolic significance of the name to his public identity and is unable to forgive his father's attempted un-naming of him. However, if his father's attitude towards the law itself marks a radical shift from Trollope's handling of it in *Ralph the Heir*, Mr. Scarborough's justification for his behavior still rests in the relationship between the control of property, personal autonomy, and private subjectivity.

Mr. Scarborough's Family is a problem text focused on problematic wills. Its protagonist's attitude suggests the conservatism of *Ralph the Heir* and even of *Howards End* in the sense that property or, more exactly, one's control of it is an outward expression of private subjectivity, a way of shaping personal character through drawing the will but also of preserving the corporate identity of the estate

---

[14] These are Robert Cover's terms in "Nomos and Narrative" collected in *Narrative, Violence, and the Law*, 95–173.

for rightful heirs. Like Squire Gregory, Mr. Scarborough believes in his right to maintain the integrity of his estate, primarily by determining who that rightful heir will be, and feels thwarted by legalities surrounding something as superficial as a name. As little swayed by the legal enormity of illegitimacy as either the Squire or Margaret Schlegel, he focuses on the prospective heir's symbolic suitability instead. Yet in its outright manipulation of the law, *Mr. Scarborough's Family* is totally unlike either novel. Squire Gregory may have seen clearly "how to supersede the law, and to make the harshness of men's enactments of no avail" (*RH* 70), but no other character actually abuses the law as Mr. Scarborough does.

Trollope's containment of this radical plot device within a conclusion that, like *Ralph the Heir*'s, sustains the legal status quo, however, raises questions about his purpose, the novel's relationship to changing standards of realism, and of broader cultural values relating to models of individuality and property. By going through two marriage ceremonies, one before his oldest son's birth and one afterwards, Scarborough plots to defeat the laws of primogeniture and leave his estate equally to his sons. He delegitimizes Mountjoy in order to defraud the creditors, but then reinstates him when he finds his other son unworthy of inheriting. Legitimacy in this novel is strictly a rhetorical tactic: used by Scarborough to save the property and as an exercise of his "power over the estate [for] as long as the estate should still be his" (192), but used by Trollope as a worst-case scenario of what happens when the private will is freed from legal constraint and of the inefficiency of the law that could be so manipulated.

Trollope's main revision of *Ralph the Heir*, more specifically, lies in his new attention to the legitimacy of the testator's actions (instead of to the heirs' legal status, although its very changeability comments on its difference from Mountjoy's more constant consciousness of self) as if to show what might happen when property passes to unsuitable, albeit legal, inheritors like Ralph the heir and even Mr. Scarborough himself. The novel's Victorian character comes through, then, both in the fact that the estate never does leave the family—the plot point that links it more solidly with *Ralph the Heir* than with *Howards End*—and in the outrage Mr. Scarborough's legal maneuvering excites. But its emphasis on the liberal view of private property (as a private right, not a communal duty) and on the testator's moral imperative shows the way Trollope's skepticism (about the testator's latitude, the law, and the effect of both on the heir) anticipates the Edwardian themes without abandoning his nineteenth-century foundations.

Mr. Scarborough's Family begins with a brief history of events central to the development of the story. Mr. Scarborough, the ailing and widowed owner of a sizable estate, declares that his oldest son and heir is in fact illegitimate. Although he married Mountjoy's mother after his birth and prior to the arrival of his younger brother Augustus, according to the laws of inheritance (those pertaining both to illegitimacy and to entail), the spendthrift Mountjoy is disqualified from inheriting the property that is now destined for Augustus, the legally eldest son and heir. Mr. Scarborough makes no secret of the fact that he was prompted, after many years of silence, to reveal the facts of his marriage by the prospect that the entire estate would be consumed by Mountjoy's creditors if he were to inherit. And as proof of this declaration, he produces his foreign marriage certificate (having been married and the children having been born abroad) and convinces his attorney Mr. Grey that a new will must be drawn.

Initially repelled by his client's daring "to act so directly in opposition to the laws of his country" (4), Mr. Grey finally concedes to act on the dying man's behalf. He knows, as do all familiar with Mr. Scarborough, that "of all things he hated most the entail [of Tretton Park]" (2), and suspects him of trying to circumvent it, as ultimately proves to be the case. And yet in spite of Scarborough's revelation, "in no sense had he broken the law":

> though he had wished his eldest son to inherit the property wrongfully he had only wished it; and that he had now simply put his wishes into unison with the law, and had undone the evil which he had hitherto only contemplated. (12)

In fact, the narrator's conclusion is a tongue-in-cheek assessment of the circumstances. Mr. Scarborough's wishes are in line with no one's but his own. Indeed, "He had lived through his life with the one strong resolution of setting the law at defiance in reference to the distribution of his property; but chiefly because he thought the law to be unjust" (74). Scarborough arrogates to himself the right to determine what is and is not just as it concerns his property, his family, and his own behavior. His life's-goal had been "To run counter to the law [...] To arrange everything so that it should be seen that he had set all laws at defiance" (366), but to entangle Mountjoy in his scheme is to impose on him an identity that is as unjust as the law his father seeks to undermine and which in the end incriminates Scarborough even more than it does his son. In the process of creating an identity for himself, that is, as one who had "struggled to free [himself] from conventionalities" (175), he simultaneously and irreparably defames his son.

As the narrator explains, "it did not occur to [Scarborough] that, in making such a revelation as to his son's mother, he would inflict any great grief on his son's heart. To be illegitimate would be, he thought, nothing unless illegitimacy carried with it loss of property" (6). Illegitimacy, in this case, is deployed as "a kind of protest against primogeniture," rather than a safeguard of it, and to secure the property for both children (561). Mountjoy's reaction defies expectation, however, and is reminiscent of Ralph Newton's. Conscious of his own recklessness, he resents nonetheless his family's perceived plot against him. He is still more distressed, however, by the "nameless position" (381) in which his father places him and by his status as "nobody" (33). When Mr. Grey tells him of his father's intention to leave him all the personal property of the estate, "all those loose belongings which gave its charms to Tretton"—and amount to about £30,000 (374)—his response is that "[The creditors] could not have robbed me of my name":

> Let them have done what they could with the bonds, I should at any rate have been Scarborough of Tretton. My belief is that I need not blush for my mother. He has made it seem that I should do so. I cannot forgive him because he gives me the chairs and tables. (383)

For him, the inheritance of property is only as important as the name that goes with it. Even when his father reveals a second marriage certificate, the one that proves Mountjoy's legitimacy by proving his parents had married before his birth after all, his father's reputation as "the wickedest man the world ever produced" (157) only fuels suspicion of what might be just another fraud. Mr. Grey declares that "the father has been a great knave. He has set the laws of his country at defiance, and should be punished most severely" (187); in this case, the sins of the father are visited on the son.

Mr. Scarborough's Family wreaks havoc on one of the most significant triads in Victorian fiction and culture: subjectivity, property, and the law. Scarborough himself is the testator run amok who gleefully ignores the effect on his heirs and on the social contract of his efforts to prove his own superiority to the law. He engages with the law only to reveal its susceptibility to manipulation. Property, the principal (because empirical) foundation of one's social identity, becomes the prize in this ideological struggle between the testator and the law, and illegitimacy the vehicle for, rather than the bar against, attaining it. While he may be right to see that legal forms are too readily manipulated and that there must be something more to one's self concept than just the legal category, still Trollope's satire suggests that Mr. Scarborough is wrong to assume that the law is a toy and naïve in his belief that its authority is purely rhetorical and not moral as well. In *Ralph the Heir* one's response to the duties and obligations of ownership translated into an understanding of the law's social significance for an individual identity and a communal English culture. But Mr. Scarborough focuses on property less because of its meaning for his own sense of self than as an opportunity to challenge the law on one of its most important battlefields: to exploit the rights of private property, to get the better of the law, and by these means to create the image of himself that really matters as someone who beat the law at its own game. By raising the specter of illegitimacy and then containing it, Trollope uses Mountjoy's maligned identity to refocus on the father, whose un-naming of his son creates for himself a deviant social identity that is the real analog to illegitimacy.

Howards End and the Ends of Property

Written in 1910, Forster's *Howards End* continues Trollope's investigation of a testator's right to determine the shape of his (or in this case "her") will in opposition to legal constraints upon it. However, where Trollope's realism demanded that a legally authorized, explicit will take center stage, only the idea of one haunts the perimeters of this Edwardian novel. In fact, official legal artifacts are noticeably absent and have been replaced by the ghost of Ruth Wilcox's desiring will. As a twentieth-century foray into the will's impact, *Howards End* revisits the conceptual issues of subjectivity and inheritance, property and legitimacy, intention and outcome, and law and justice examined in Victorian novels, but by focusing on the consciousness of its donors and inheritors more than on their documents, it revises the method through which these issues are understood. As was true of Trollope's novels, the conflict between testamentary volition and its established legal expression centers on illegitimacy and its bearing on the preservation of familial and cultural identity. Forster's preference at novel's end for Helen and Leonard's baby thus serves as a coda to Mrs. Wilcox's search throughout the novel for the most eligible "spiritual heir" to herself, to her home, and to England. While neither the base-born Ralph could win the estate, nor Squire Gregory legitimize his family, Margaret and her nephew and, most importantly, Mrs. Wilcox can.

Forster presents the ethereal Mrs. Wilcox as a conceptual problem in the modernizing age, someone whose identity other characters need to sense. An heir to the past, she is unattuned to modern trappings: "Clever talk," for example, "alarmed her, and withered her delicate imaginings; it was the social counterpart of the motorcar, all jerks, and she was a wisp of hay, a flower" (57). Only the Schlegel sisters "discerned that Mrs. Wilcox had only one passion in life—her house—and that the moment was solemn when she invited a friend to share this passion with her" (66). This house, which the Wilcoxes find so poky, belongs entirely to her and provides the substance of her two wills. Contemplating her unexpected death, the family thinks little of her plans for Howards End. Her original will, for instance, presented no mystery: "There were no legacies, no annuities, none of the posthumous bustle with which some of the dead prolong their activities" (73). Mrs. Wilcox's desire "not to vex people" has made her a passive figure within her family, which bowls ahead with their plans for improvements and fancy weddings with little regard for their matriarch's character. Content to view her as a sensible if somewhat backwards woman, they are indignant at the perceived deception her second will represents to them.

Assembled after her funeral, the family read her simple but provocative pronouncement: "To my husband: I should like Miss Schlegel (Margaret) to have Howards End" (75). Henry tells his daughter-in-law that of course the will is not legal (although not because it's written in pencil): "Legally, I should be justified in tearing it up and throwing it into the fire," he says, but not before considering it "item by item" in typical board-room fashion. Henry and Charles view the will as the isolated act of an invalid, someone diminished and therefore irrational, and the narrator agrees—up to a point. Mrs. Wilcox's appeal was indeed "too flimsy" for them to act upon because they see it chiefly in material terms. Because they have always been alienated from Ruth Wilcox, they fail to see the consonance between her character, her sense of Howards End as a "spirit," and the will that would pass it to Margaret. In one sense, then, the narrator is sympathetic to the family; they could not be expected to accept a will that essentially rejects their age of suburbs and motorcars, and by extension them. Indeed, the narrator wonders: "Is it credible that the possessions of the spirit can be bequeathed at all? A wych-elm tree, a vine, a wisp of hay with dew on it—can passion for such things be transmitted when there is no bond of blood?" (77).

Bonds of blood themselves are shown to be unreliable affiliates, however, when Ruth Wilcox's own family can controvert them. As the narrator points out: "one hard fact remains. They did neglect a personal appeal. The woman who had died did say to them: 'Do this,' and they answered: 'We will not.'" Moreover, by ignoring Ruth Wilcox's wishes, they relegate her memory to the same fire in which they burn the will: no longer "true," or "dear," she becomes "treacherous to the family, to the laws of property, to her own written word" (78). For them the will itself is illegitimate because it disrupts their sense of order. It redefines family and property, most importantly, and creates a spectral version of Mrs. Wilcox that survives the funeral and discomfits the narrow Wilcox empiricism. As the narrator chides, however, "A funeral is not death any more than baptism is birth or marriage union. All three are the clumsy devices, coming now too late, now too early, by which Society would register the quick motions of man" (80). Ultimately, one has to agree. A legal will, even a socially ratified one, cannot be the full measure of its writer, yet that is precisely why it has to be viewed as a rhetorical device, something invested with the power to express the ephemeral, which the novel was becoming increasingly more invested in exploring outside of the context of empirical forms. Mrs. Wilcox's connection with Margaret and the survival of her desiring will despite attempts to squelch it form the novel's hopeful, but perforce uncertain, grip on this spirit, while Forster's modernist style dispenses with bonds of blood and the documented will as less critical counterparts of the more significant imperative to connect the past with the present and to preserve those "wisp[s] of hay."

The question of who should inherit depends here, as in Trollope's novels, on the sense of property. In contrast to the literal-minded Wilcox view, the Schlegel outlook on both property and inheritance is more idealized. With the contents of Wickham Place reduced to the appearance of a rummage sale, the narrator voices Margaret's concern for the future of the modern, mobile world. Preferring feudal "dignity," Margaret muses that "historians of the future will note how the middle classes accreted possessions without taking root in the earth and may find in this the secret of their imaginative poverty" (118). In this rising trend towards "cosmopolitanism," Margaret fears that the things that once counted, the "trees, and meadows, and mountains," which once bound people to their country and to one another, "will be only spectacle," something else to survey without nearing, as the Wilcoxes fail to connect to their Shropshire estate. Their inability to perceive the collaborative relationship between people and their things and places—a relationship that changes possessions into historical companions—also prevents them from connecting to their past. What the Wilcoxes know under the generic "property," which makes cars and houses and rubber companies all the same, the Schlegels and their ilk know by name: Howards End, Wickham Place. For example, during Margaret and Helen's night at Howards End, Helen's argument against the Wilcox type takes form, granting themselves a metaphysical and aesthetic knowledge far superior to the others' prosaic, practical mode of understanding. She claims for the type that Margaret and she herself embody a right to the house and all it signifies: "We know this is our house, because it feels ours. Oh, they may take the title-deeds and the doorkeys, but for this one night we are at home" (238).

Henry, in contrast, asserts his legal right to dispose of Howards End as if it were his alone and not his wife's, not Miss Avery's, not part of Hertfordshire history.

He reassures Charles that the house will be his, regardless of his own distaste for the place, and does so from the conviction that to give in to Margaret's wish to overnight there is to contravene his own fundamental principle. His insistence that property confers "rights" and not, for instance, duties, recalls Ralph the heir's stance towards Newton Peele. Like Ralph, Henry perceives the house as a material value. If his attitude towards it extends Ralph the heir's already more modern interpretation, his promise to leave it to Charles belongs in contrast to that older pattern of inheritance in which the only legitimate heir is the "real" family.

The Schlegel view of the relationship between the land and the spirit is also inverted. Privileging the feudal connectedness between manor and community, they nonetheless disregard historical, social rules for distribution and look for heirs whose eligibility is not determined first and foremost by their name. Their sense of the duties that ownership confers is exemplified by their conversation with Henry on the Chelsea Embankment. After a night at their Debate club, the sisters rehash the subject of their discussion. The topic "How ought I to dispose of my money?" is especially significant from the testator's standpoint whose intentions and their ramifications are carefully mapped and used to justify the contemplated gifts. In this case, the decision of how to use one's money revolves around the testator's sense of the "right" thing to do, versus Henry's view that a testator's proprietary "rights" automatically confer legitimacy on his decisions.

Margaret shares Mrs. Wilcox's sense of stewardship and historic and communal responsibility. Just as Mrs. Wilcox searches for a spiritual heir, Margaret seeks to enlarge her understanding of and connect to the world around her. Ironically, the debate club's various charitable enterprises converge on Leonard Bast who figures prominently in their discussion. When he takes umbrage at the sisters' intervention in his business life, Margaret upbraids him because she views his reaction as a selling-out of sorts: "Haven't we all to struggle against life's daily greyness [...]? I struggle by remembering my friends; others I have known by remembering some place—some beloved place or tree—we thought you one of these" (112). Her references to Mrs. Wilcox (Howards End the "place," the wych-elm the "tree") and Leonard's inclusion in their spiritual circle plainly suggest that if he is yet unable fully to embrace their way of thinking, then his illegitimate child, who inherits that potential and is nurtured by Helen, will be the rightful heir to Mrs. Wilcox's vision.

On the night Helen's pregnancy is discovered, she and Margaret stay at Howards End. Their conversation, in addition to confirming their sense of "at-home-ness," further uncovers Leonard's membership in the Howards End circle. As she sits under the wych-elm, Margaret muses "how incomprehensible that Leonard Bast should have won her this night of peace. Was he also part of Mrs. Wilcox's mind?" (249). Although Margaret little knows at this point that she, with her furniture uncannily arranged throughout the house, will be the legal heir to it, her night there establishes her, and through her Leonard's child, as the new rulers of Mrs. Wilcox's spiritual kingdom in contrast to the earthly Wilcox empire.

The link between these otherwise opposed views of the ancient kingdom and the modern empire is Margaret herself, and by positioning her this way, Forster recalls Trollope's investigation of the laws of bastardy as well as Maine's comments on adoption. As a feudal legal invention meant to preserve property, illegitimacy excluded "natural" children from sharing in a familial identity. Trollope's criticism of that law lay in his sense that what it decrees for the sake of solidifying a geographical identity through the family is not always just or even guaranteed to work because it takes no account of the character or attitude of the legal heirs. This same dynamic is at work in *Howards End*, in which Forster's own concern with the shallowness of modern materialism and its meaning for England's future is framed in terms, first, of the contest between the abstract, desiring will and its documentation in the written will. Part of the difficulty of this modern age is that it is so focused on the concrete and observable (a nineteenth-century bequest) that its intuition has deteriorated, hence the Wilcox obtuseness.

The transmission of property, the practical purpose of the legal document, introduces the second point of contention. Forster is concerned not only with the transmission of movables (though the Schlegels' attachment to their parents' furniture invests even these with personal, historical significance), but with the transmission of a cultural identity. How one responds to ownership and the things owned indicates his or her suitability as heir to this cultural heritage. If Howards End itself serves as a symbol of England, the selection of its heir serves, too, to indicate the future of the nation.[15] What is needed, then, is the right heir, and Forster's choice of Margaret and her illegitimate nephew affirms Mrs. Wilcox's view that the legitimate heir is not necessarily a member of the titular family.

Margaret's guardianship begins when she first visits Hertfordshire to make arrangements about her furniture. As she tours the house, she comes to the hall door hiding the staircase. Recalling Helen's characterization of her engagement as a giving up of something, she in contrast approaches the hidden passage as an opportunity to "double her kingdom" (158). Several strands converge here. First,

---

[15] Pat Hoy maintains that in *Howards End* "the mind and its byproduct, the ideal, are paramount," so that the house itself becomes Forster's "own ideal," an "English symbol" (221). Similarly focused on the novel's metaphors, R.N. Parkinson describes Margaret's unused single to Howards End as one of many "prophetic, symbolic touches which suggest the power of the house to choose worthy heirs and owners to and for itself. These people alone go to Howards End without needing or wanting the return half of the ticket" (55). Parkinson's observation is important because it adds dimension to the house. It may be a symbol, but it is a symbol that can't be possessed or owned without participating in its own occupation. Here, the absence of any "direct line of familial descent" that defies "the symmetry [...] of the genealogical table or the Victorian novelist" (60) is one that makes way for ideological symmetry. In this way, Ruth Wilcox and Margaret do not possess Howards End, but form links in a long chain of stewardship. And if the house stands in for England, then they are also ministers of culture, whose suitability for the task depends on their understanding of both the house's historical significance and their own temporary relationship to it.

Margaret's right to occupy and explore the house, to walk about it as Mrs. Wilcox did, confirms the rightness of Mrs. Wilcox's bequest and marks Margaret's entrance into the house as the entrance into her own kingdom. Second, Margaret is surveying the house as if it were precisely that, a kingdom, which calls to mind the narrator's commendation of feudal life and connectedness to a past rooted in the land. Third, by again linking it to Helen's comments on her engagement, Margaret views her marriage to Henry, the connection of her poetry with his "gritty" prose, as another mode of doubling her kingdom. Fourth, the passage gestures towards imperial expansion of which, indeed, Margaret thinks, too, as she contemplates her husband's business and her own parental inheritance of the "two supreme nations," Germany and England.

Against this backdrop, Henry's unfitness as heir is dramatic. His characterization of the back to the land movement (and of Margaret's interest in Leonard) as unprofitable "philanthropic bunkum" contrasts sharply with her suitability as Mrs. Wilcox's heir; the desiring will is winning out regardless of legal sanction, which in Forster's novel is but a vestige of the materialist past over whose future the Wilcox brood reigns. Forster's new method here, his interest in the abstracted will, is about revising, not just about rejecting, an old mode of privileging the empirical will. Mrs. Wilcox's desire as expressed in her textual will succeeds despite its informality. And the inherent idea of transmission is doubled and intensified by reframing it as connection among disparate elements of the present, rather than a simple replacement over time of one thing for another.

In the final scene in which Henry leaves the house to Margaret, Dolly inconveniently refers to the family's first meeting about Ruth's will and comments on the irony that Margaret should after all get the house: "Margaret did not answer. There was something uncanny in her triumph. She, who had never expected to conquer anyone, had charged straight through these Wilcoxes and broken up their lives" (270). When Henry explains the circumstances to her, still characterizing Ruth Wilcox has an invalid prone to fancies, Margaret is again silent: "something shook her life in its inmost recesses, and she shivered" (271). Assuring Henry that "nothing had been done wrong," she is corroborated by the sudden appearance of Helen and her child proclaiming the harvest of the hay, that other emblem of Ruth herself. Margaret's own plans for the house echo the Chelsea embankment debate by leaving it to her nephew, the child of her sister and Leonard Bast for whom either too little or too much had been done. This is a scene of connection: one that Margaret intuitively and here symbolically understands, one that Henry even yet cannot fully grasp, but one that brings Margaret face to face with the spirit of connection that is so often an intangible quantity or force. What she knows intuitively has taken physical shape, confirming the force of the desiring will by forever linking her and her kind to the house.

Howards End revisits and revises in the twentieth century the nineteenth-century understanding of the relationships between testamentary intention and the law, specifically the importance of the legal concept of legitimacy to the rights to property, and between property, law, and culture. Reframing legitimacy as eligibility and relinquishing identity from its strictly empirical grounding, Forster ratifies the importance of the abstract will in ways Trollope anticipated but ultimately could not commit to. Like him, Forster wants to preserve the continuity of the spirit, the idea of history and culture, but he values the freedom of the contracting individual to overturn outmoded or ineffective forms, hence Mrs. Wilcox's "adoption" of Margaret and Margaret's own creation in her nephew of the illegitimate heir.

Michael Levenson describes Forster as writing between the Edwardian authors and the modernists. Like the modernists, he has "a sense of an irrevocable historical transformation that necessarily alters the methods of art, but [like the Edwardians] he could never muster the conviction for a programmatic assault on traditional forms" ("Liberalism and Symbolism in *Howards End*" 295–6). However, Levenson describes what I take to be the Edwardian position itself. Viewed in this way, Forster does offer in *Howards End* just that "assault" on form that links him with the modernists, while maintaining the Victorians' conceptual interest in inheritance and the modes of transmission (of goods, of identity, of a literary tradition and of culture).

No longer bound to the form of the written will and literal legal categories, he is nonetheless able to pursue questions of the way one's personal subjectivity takes shape, of the relationship between the testator and the beneficiary, and of the degree of control one has in that process. Moreover, he redirects Trollope's attention to the law itself as an agent of culture and to property as its indicator, to Culture in the abstract as a "possession" not to be owned but on the behalf of which one acts. Margaret Schlegel's manifesto to "struggle against life's daily greyness" echoes Forster's own comments in "Does Culture Matter" that one's commitment to enjoy life can inspire others, not expressly for the sake of pleasure, "but because certain things seem to us unique and priceless and, as it were, push us out into the world on their service" (104).[16] The spirit imbuing Howards End is just such a "unique" and "priceless" thing. It is a historically unified English culture that evokes this sense of mission from legitimate heirs. As Levenson says of this recognition: "the symbolic correspondence on which the novel depends is not given; it must be achieved [...]. Not all characters have the gift of symbolic vision. [The house] is a symbol only to those who live within the symbolic mode" ("Liberalism" 314). The Squire Gregories and Henry Wilcoxes of the world, however, can only take the literal view. They all consider property as conveying personal, private rights, and as testators they seek to enforce their will within the context of a legal horizon of culture.

In the Victorian novel, attempts to circumvent the law (here the laws of illegitimacy) amount to a rejection of cultural, not just personal, values that the rightful heirs in contrast recognize as such. For the empirically-minded realist, these preliminary investigations of the role of the desiring will in shaping subjectivity show it to be a potentially disruptive force that seeks to undermine the legal system when the law runs counter to their wishes. So, although open to the shortcomings

[16] The passage is also quoted in Hoy, 223.

of the legal system and attracted to the idea of the self-defining individual, Trollope cannot do away with Law, with the institutions, however flawed, which are the foundations of culture against which the private self develops. Trollope's novels mainly suggest through his use of the legitimacy/illegitimacy dichotomy that the legitimate property holder is the one who understands its significance beyond its more conventional dimension as a private asset. If Henry Wilcox is Forster's example of this Victorian type, then the Ruths and Margarets exemplify what is presaged by the base-born Ralph Newton: that we should be stewards, as much as critics, of Culture.

Conclusion

> The hidden life is, by definition, hidden. The hidden life that appears in external signs is hidden no longer, has entered the realm of action. And it is the function of the novelist to reveal the hidden life at its source: to tell us more about Queen Victoria than could be known, and thus to produce a character who is not the Queen Victoria of history.
>
> *Homo fictus* is more elusive than his cousin [*homo sapiens*]. He is created in the mind of hundreds of different novelists, who have conflicting methods of gestation, so one must not generalize. Still, one can say a little bit about him. He is generally born off [stage], he is capable of dying on [stage], he wants little food or sleep, he is tirelessly concerned with human relationships. And—most important—we can know more about him than we can about any of our fellow creatures, because his creator and narrator are one. Were we equipped for hyperbole we might exclaim at this point: "If God could tell the story of the Universe, the Universe would become fictitious."
>
> E.M. Forster, *Aspects of the Novel* (1927)

Between the years of 1896 and 1910, a dramatic family drama—a "romance" as the press would come to call it—was playing out in the courts and the papers over the rights of an illegitimate child to his father's title and estate. Henry Edwin Fenn, Senior Reporter in the Probate, Divorce, and Admiralty division of England's High Court, called the Sackville Peerage Case "the most intricate case that has ever been before the Court" (76). Leaders in *The New York Times*, one of many international papers covering the story of Lionel Sackville-West's nearly 20-year relationship with Pepita Duran, the Spanish dancer whom he met on diplomatic assignment to Madrid, sensationalized an already painful and disturbing story: "Fight is on for Sackville Peerage"; "Dancer's Son Claims Sackville Peerage"; "Sackville Romance Detailed in Court"; "Sackville Claimant Rests." Finally, one week after the end of the trial in February 1910, the paper's Sunday Magazine recounted the entire story under the headline "The Romance in the Life of Sackville-West."

Referring to the late Lord Sackville, rather than his son, as "the sorry hero of the romance," the paper took the familiar rhetorical position of supposing that "If the imagination of a novelist had conceived as a romance the true story of the dramatic career of the late Lord Sackville, he would very likely set forth his scenario after the following manner," which, it turns out, is to organize the story into chapters. The seven "chapters" that follow detail the meeting of Lionel, Lord Sackville, and Pepita Duran; the births of their children and, following her death, his diplomatic career in Washington and retirement to Knole with his brother, his daughter, and her eventual husband, Edward Lionel Sackville-West, who was also his nephew and heir presumptive to Knole. The chapters then turn to his son Henry's initial attempts to gain the estate and the title Baron Sackville, including the 1903 petition to have him declared the legitimate heir, followed by Lionel's counter-claim and initiation of the Spanish forgery trial concerning Pepita's marriage to her former dancing instructor Juan Antonio de Oliva. The final chapter confirmed that, although Lord Sackville had wanted to marry Pepita, she was already married to de Oliva who also survived her. And so, concludes the article, "In his great fight for honor, nobility, and wealth, Henry Sackville-West stood alone [...]. He stood alone the innocent victim of man's egotism and passion, and of relentless social conditions against which he and nameless hundreds like him have combated in vain." Although the paper shows sympathy for Henry's plight, there was also much celebrating at Knole over the return of the legitimate family, whose carriage the excited crowds pulled through town up to the doors of the five-acre house.[1]

The story of Henry West and Lionel, his father, provides the kind of plot Trollope might have used in his own depiction of the harms of illegitimacy, but theirs is a variation on his themes in *Ralph the Heir* and *Mr. Scarborough's Family*, a third scenario, in which the illegitimate child lays claim to an estate his father can neither leave him nor thinks to. *Howards End* provided a literary postscript to those novels with its pictures of the Wilcox ethos fulfilling Trollope's prophecy about the dangers of liberal, laissez-faire attitudes towards property. But if Forster couldn't connect with the world being dominated by this type of the contracting individual (one who views property, including the family, as a private asset), even a more feudal model's attractions were limited. Something in between was needed, and in *Howards End*, as Chapter 6 has shown, he bequeaths his England to one who, although "a stranger in blood," was family in spirit.

Just as Forster provided a literary postscript to Trollope's novels, the Sackville-West trials over Knole provide a legal one. Forster began working on the novel in the winter of 1909 as the Spanish case was being prosecuted, and he sent 30 chapters to Edward Arnold for review in March of 1910, just a few weeks after the case had concluded and Henry's petition for legitimacy been dismissed. These observations are not meant to suggest that *Howards End* is symmetrical with the Sackville case, or even that Forster was thinking specifically of it, although it's hard to imagine that he would have been unaware of it given his Cambridge and Bloomsbury connections. Rather, the case in its various stages provides a legal parallel for the kinds of questions Forster was pursuing in his novel, and indeed which all the novels discussed in this book take up. What roles do property and the laws that govern it play in the ways people define themselves, and how they are defined by others? What constitutes a family and a culture? How are intangibles passed from one generation to another, or between people in the same generation?

The trials left a legal legacy as well. Henry petitioned in 1903 to perpetuate testimony, or to gather evidence then, in 1903, as to his parents' marriage that later would be essential to his claims to the peerage but which claims could not be made until after his father's death. (As Justice Kekewich put it, "It is impossible for anyone to say that his right or claim to the estates can be brought to trial

[1] See Susan Mary Alsop, *Lady Sackville* (125–38) for an account of the trial.

before the happening of the event which will bring his title into possession" [*West v. Lord Sackville* 284]).[2] Essentially, he wanted to question witnesses in Spain and in France who had been examined in Gibraltar six years earlier in fulfillment of Lord Sackville's own perpetuation petition. Although Henry's petition was initially granted, Lord Sackville won on appeal on the grounds that the better course of action was for Henry simply to go before the Probate Court and, following the Legitimacy Declaration Act of 1858, seek to have his legitimacy declared, since that would answer both his claims to the "dignity" (the honorific) and the estate.[3]

Six years passed before Henry, now styling himself Henry Sackville-West, went before John Bigham, President of Probate, in October 1909 to petition for a jury trial of his claim for legitimacy.[4] His father had died and Edward Lionel, his sister Victoria Josephine's husband and his own cousin, was now the third Lord Sackville. Henry's counsel pointed to the "serious imputations" made against him as reason to allow a jury to hear his evidence, but Lord Sackville's defense implied that some matters were too delicate and ought to be heard by the judge alone.[5] Bigham took a more practical route: considering the quantity and complexity of the evidence (some 2000 folios and another 150 exhibits, some with photographs) and his doubts "of keeping the attention of twelve men" firmly and clearly upon it, he decided to hear the case himself. He left open the possibility of appeal but none was ever made, and, as the coverage in *The New York Times* shows, the trial came on between the 1st and 7th of February, 1910. Oddly mixing legalistic language with its attempts to humanize and generate sympathy for Henry, the paper reported that,

---

2 The decision on the appeal became precedent: where the question could be decided by going before the Probate judge, then no petition for perpetuation should be granted.

3 Lord Justice Vaughan Williams, although he disagreed with the grounds of Kekewich's ruling, was inclined to uphold his decision in light of new allegations of tampering with the marriage registry. His suggestion went nowhere with Henry who declined to take this route. The Lord Justice's comments imply some misgiving: "The inference I draw is that he [Henry] does not feel much pressed by the disadvantage which I thought might result to his case if a further examination of these witnesses were not allowed to take place, and that at all events, if he does not feel at all pressed by that disadvantage, he is more pressed by the advantage which will accrue to him by postponing the trial of his action till after the death of Lord Sackville, when the only way in which his evidence will be available will be by reading his deposition [...]." (389). The judge expressed the further view that "a party who believes his case to be just and right" will not miss an opportunity to build on its strength by getting "all possible light thrown upon it" and speculated that even the defendants should be open to further examination of their witnesses' evidence since "its value would have been enhanced tenfold." Leaving the decision to the defendants, he concluded, "I do not believe that light is often thrown upon a case by the exclusion of any kind of evidence" (390).

4 See *Sackville-West v. The Attorney-General (Lord Sackville and Others Cited)* (1910).

5 Eldon Bankes, King's Counsel cited *Ricketts v. Ricketts* (1866), a petition "for nullity [of marriage] on the ground of impotence," which J.P. Wilde held was an issue "more fit for a judge alone" to decide (144).

"the petitioner" on the last day "with tears running down his cheeks, acknowledged the overwhelming character of the denials [of the marriage] and withdrew his allegations. His long struggle for birthright, wealth, and a title had failed," and at the bottom of the October trial report is a note saying the petition for legitimacy was dismissed on February 14th of that year.

From a legal point of view, these petitions, depositions, trips abroad, the money borrowed to pay for it all, the family rancor and embarrassment all came down to the question of whether Henry West could be considered legitimate by English law. Could a child whose parents were not legally married actually be entitled to any part of their estate, let alone to a massive estate held by a family whose ancestry dated back to the Conquest and was arguably a foundational part of English history?[6] Shifting the case from Chancery to Probate, however, shifted the question away from one about the estate—which would be preserved no matter whom the rightful heir turned out to be—onto one of legal identity. In effect, it privileged the property over the person and in this regard recalls the conservative notion of ownership as stewardship, as a service rendered to the estate itself and to the family, rather than an object of private gain. But this model of ownership depended on a corresponding notion of legitimacy, and, although Henry West (or Sackville or Sackville-West, as he was variously known) and his siblings had a name by reputation, they could have none by inheritance. Although it is impossible to judge the relative importance of the desire for recognition or even for revenge, or the relief of loneliness or financial need among the many motives one can imagine for pursuing the claim (or for his sisters Amalia and Flora's support), Henry's character, his sense of himself as well as his reputation, was certainly at stake in these proceedings: his father's name and his father's estate were bound up in his own "dignity," which the Court's decision about his legal identity did not support.[7]

Many of the most important laws governing the disposal of property were in a process of change, however. The Administration of Estates Acts was passed in 1925 and, like the Wills Act of 1837, repealed or modified a long list of earlier Statutes (some 45 going back to Edward I). The new act did not abolish already entailed interests and their prejudice against women heirs, as Vita Sackville-West knew only too well when her father Edward Lionel, who had defended his title to the estate against Henry's claims for so long, died and the estate passed to his brother, Vita's Uncle Charlie.[8] However, it did provide a schedule for payment of the estate's debts and legacies along with a more equitable model for distributing the residuary estate. Similarly, it replaced the laws of primogeniture, curtesy, and dower with a "uniform table of descent and distribution" (Ritchie 21). Instead of giving preference to the oldest male heir, a testator's real and personal estate would

6 See Alsop, 88 for the Sackville lineage.

7 He was not heard of after the trial and committed suicide in 1914 (Alsop 138).

8 The three-day period between her father's death and his funeral was "the first and last time [Knole] belonged wholly to Vita, which Vita, writing much later to her son, described as 'a turning-point in my life'" (Glendinning 189).

now pass, first, to his surviving spouse or it would be divided equally among all children, followed by the testator's siblings, aunts and uncles, parents, and so on in a specified order.

While these changes offered a more consistent mode of disposing of property that could benefit heirs and was certainly a desirable change in that respect, its very freedom from the testator's potential caprices or mercurial moods completed the will's transformation from the "speaking likeness" of the testator's personal character to a uniform and utilitarian legal text of his social identity. Looked at from this perspective, the 1925 Act provides a boundary between a class of rights that obtained up to and including the nineteenth and early twentieth centuries and those that better resemble contemporary assumptions and practices and, with them, a change in conceptions of personhood. Many of these changes in patterns of inheritance were anticipated before 1925: the table of descent and distribution, for instance, had been included in the 1922 Law of Property Act but postponed; married women had been enabled effectively to own and bequeath their property in 1893, but in the 1925 act husbands and wives were to be "treated as two persons" instead of the Pauline unity of "one person" adopted by Blackstone and carried through the nineteenth century. In short, the Act of 1925 was a formalization of already circulating legal principles and their attendant conception of legal subjectivity that complements the modernist formalization of literary principles towards which the Edwardians were already tending.

In his Clark lectures on the novel, delivered just two years following passage of the act, E.M. Forster discussed some of these principles. Citing character as just one of several aspects of the novel, Forster nevertheless devoted two meetings to its discussion, thereby inverting Artistotle's emphasis on plot and making character the most important element of poetics.[9] The means of bringing *homo fictus* to life vary, he observes in the epigraph to this conclusion, but in the end the goal of all novelists is to make visible and vibrant the "hidden life" of people. Words and language are the most obvious "external signs" through which the novelist reveals life and draws it into the "realm of action," and as I have argued throughout this study, the hidden life, a sense of individual subjectivity and personal volition, can also be made visible through the legal will. By writing a will, the lawyer or the testator, like the novelist, uses the external signs of language to document possessions, the external signs of social identity. And in all this the inner life of one person is put into action, transmitted along with his property to another generation.

The hidden life of private people also contributes to the larger, hidden life of a culture to which the wills and novels discussed here give later generations insight. If we can know a fictional character better than we know our "fellow creatures" because his author and narrator are one, then to know another culture, we must turn to those who made and wrote about it, who saw, in another of Forster's terms, "certain things" about it that were "unique and priceless" and that "pushed" these writers "out into the world on their service" ("Does Culture Matter?" 104).

---

[9] See Aristotle *Poetics* 85.

The previous six chapters have explained how Victorian and Edwardian novelists sought to bring these characters and cultures to life by specific reference to the last will and testament and to the themes of inheritance. Here I want to look at the purported modernist break with a legal, social, and literary culture their forbears passed on to them by considering finally how Lytton Strachey, in his biography of Queen Victoria, and Virginia Woolf, in her two most famous novels, both tried to move beyond the woman who gave her name to the cultural values—and the literature—of the old generation.

In *Howards End* (1910), Forster followed principles later set out in *Aspects of the Novel* by attempting to transmit the "hidden life" not just of a person's character but also of a country's, England's. In the figure of the monarch, however, these are united. Lytton Strachey shared Forster's interest in the hidden life and, although admittedly not writing a novel, his biography *Queen Victoria* (1921) anticipated Forster's admonition that fiction at least "should tell us more about Queen Victoria than could be known, and thus to produce a character who is not the Queen Victoria of history" (45). Confident in his own method, Strachey described it as shining a "revealing searchlight into obscure recesses, hitherto undivined," but the woman revealed by his probing proved so powerful that even he believed her will to survive was greater than his initial attempts to lay her to rest.[10] Indeed, in his final chapter on Victoria's "Old Age," Strachey makes so many references to her will that he seems to have reverted to a Victorian mode of writing. He describes her as a woman of "innumerable possessions," whose "collecting instinct" was propelled by her "dominating impulses": "the intense sense of her own personality," paired with a yearning "for fixity, for solidity, for the setting up of palpable barriers against the outrages of change and time" (398). Strachey draws a direct line from the essence and continuity of Victoria's personality to the continuity of her personal goods in which "she saw herself reflected in a million facets" (399). Anxious to have them before her all the time, he writes, she commissioned photographs of each item to be placed in an album, so that as she perused the volumes she could look through "things" and "thoughts" and "states of mind and ways of living as well" (401–2).

Strachey suggests that Victoria established the collection for her own benefit, as a way to preserve her memories, if not others' memory of her. One of the greatest satisfactions she derived from the project, he muses, is the sense it gave her "that the transitoriness of this world had been arrested by her might" (401). But with the crown of England to bequeath and with 37 great grandchildren living at the time of her death, Victoria's legacy had been carefully preserved. Even apart from her familial dynasty, there would be plenty of empirical evidence of her, as Virginia Woolf in a twist of language transforms her from a willing agent to an attested document: "no one," she writes, "[had] ever been more closely verified and exactly authenticated than Queen Victoria" ("The Art of Biography" 191). What

[10] Strachey's letters describe his inability to finish the job. Writing to Maynard Keynes in November of 1920, he wonders, "whether I shall kill Victoria or Victoria me" (qtd. in Dickson 34–5).

seems to have surprised Strachey, however, is that the force of her personality, her desire to "impose her will" (411) should have worked itself on him 20 years after her death. Although he describes her fixation with material things in properly Victorian terms, that is, as an expression of her will, his portrait of her accentuates her desire and volition and uses the concrete examples merely to illustrate how powerful that will was.

His final chapter functions in effect as an apology for his having done more to further mythologize than demystify her, and, as Jay Dickson observes, Strachey essentially gives her the last word (42). He seeks to enter "the secret chambers of consciousness" by imagining her dream-state in which "shadows of the past" troop by in reverse order from the latest to her earliest memories (Strachey 423). As an example of stream-of-consciousness, the final sentence ends by drawing back into nothingness, into the time before she was, so that the queen's passage is delivered paradoxically *by her* in "the very form that most famously distinguishes the succeeding literary generation" (Dickson 42). Strachey's method gives the appearance that Victoria invented modernism. By creating Victoria in their own image, however, as Dickson suggests, the modernists could no more deny her than they could deny themselves.

Looked at together, both Forster and Strachey created women whose lives represent a culture and a sensibility each one sought to preserve. Ruth Wilcox looked forward in search of the best heir to her kingdom, while Strachey's Victoria looked backwards, towards her origins, as Strachey himself and the modernists routinely did in their attempts to shake off or redefine their heritage. Virginia Woolf shared in each of these projects. Like Forster, she described the novelist's task as an attempt "to convey this varying, this unknown and uncircumscribed spirit" that for lack of better terms we lamely call Life, Truth, or Reality ("Modern Fiction" 154). Where he pursued the complex task of preserving yet revising cultural values and of establishing a conscious connection from one generation to the next—but also between the disparate strands of a single generation as well—Woolf's *Mrs. Dalloway* (1925) attempts to convey this spirit by focusing on the present and the (frequently unconscious) connections that exist between people by virtue of their shared place within the "semi-transparent envelope" she calls Life. And like Strachey's Queen organizing beautiful things and reviewing the past, Woolf's Mrs. Dalloway puts all her will towards creating the beautiful moment. When viewed as the formalization of theories expressed in "Modern Fiction," *Mrs. Dalloway* fictionalizes the process, as well as the problem, of repudiating the past in order to focus on the current generation with which the modernists were most engaged.

Woolf's novel was also published in the same year the Administration of Estates Act was passed which, as I have suggested, consolidated and formalized legal principles and procedures that had been moving away from Victorian ideas of unlimited testamentary control. However, the salutary effects of these changes were purchased at the cost of character, as efficient, bureaucratized identities were fitted into schedules that could not have compassed the robust and sometimes messy testator of the nineteenth century. In the relationship between law and literature, this rationalizing of the laws of inheritance and their management by a professional class was offset by a literature, as Woolf's essays and novels demonstrate, that became still more committed to the inner workings of character.[11]

As Chapter 2 explained, the Victorian novel created a world in which all its readers could participate. It used a shared language. It created a time and a place for action. It focused primarily on a single character with which the reader could identify, and yet it used his engagement with and absorption into a community as a basis for determining his successful development. By inviting readers to see this character and themselves as part of a larger whole, the realist novel brought them out of their isolation and into a new community. But unlike the non-fictional world, the novel's alternative community was a closed environment, one with boundaries that in essence shut out or contained the variables of lived experience that made it so hard to understand. Within the novel's "horizon of meaning," knowledge developed from the repetition of experience in a variety of cases (Ermarth 16–17). By duplicating a view, the object of which was itself unchanging, the realist novel promoted the possibility that the same meaning was available to all who read it and thus invoked and created consensus among them.

Mrs. Dalloway, surprisingly, shares many of these traits. As the novel opens, Big Ben's "leaden circles" "dissolve" in the London air (4); "greatness" passes (16); and a skywriting airplane breathes out messages in the sky (20). Out of these material events of a single day, Woolf constructs a recurring motif that unites her narrative and her characters. That is, Woolf's narrative moves through her characters' subjective responses to the same material prompt as if to say we are individuals united almost in spite of ourselves and even without our conscious knowledge. We are Peter Walsh waking from his nap on a bench in Regent's Park and watching a child run "full tilt into a lady's legs" (65); we are Lucrezia Warren Smith who kisses the child and watches her run back to her nurse and the "kind-looking man" sitting with her; we are the Warren Smiths who "walked down Harley Street" to meet Sir William Bradshaw, and we are Clarissa Dalloway laying out her dress for the party the doctor will attend that evening—all as the twelve "leaden circles dissolved in the air" (94). In *Mrs. Dalloway*, then, we have a very specific time and a place: London, one day, middle of June, after the war. We have a primary character and a host of others whose paths continually traverse the same

---

[11] To say the laws of inheritance were rationalized (which really only means they were simplified, ordered, legislated) sets up the tantalizing comparison that fiction must be irrational, and certainly any discussion of the modernists has to acknowledge the impact of Freudian psychoanalytic theories on the novel, as well as the potential to view this novelistic penetration of private consciousness as an invasion, rather than a celebration, of personal subjectivity. However, this "irrationality" is just the reason so many modernist writers (and authors of gothic and sensation fiction) feature in the canon of law and literature scholarship since they depart from the apparent rationality of realism and certainly from law's rejection (begun with English and American jurists in the eighteenth century) of its romantic side. See Maria Aristodemou on the English tradition in *From Her to Eternity* and Robert Ferguson on the American in *Law and Letters in American Culture*—on the Anglo-American tradition at least.

ground, bound within the circle of the bells and the circularity of the narrative, and in this Woolf shows her own realist tendencies. However, the shared world, the horizontal relationship, and the preoccupation with memory or memorialization each suggest a peculiar relationship with realism itself.

Unlike the Victorians who in their testamentary novels constantly looked forward for ways to cross generations and to establish a vertical continuum, Woolf's plot focuses exclusively on horizontal relationships played out in the present, in a single day. However, even as the novel draws characters together into a shared world, the depiction of their missed connections heightens the effect of each one's isolation. For example, by repeating the images of the clock, the plane, and the passing greatness, Woolf, like the realists, makes the same object available to all her characters, but those objects no longer mean "one thing understood by all" (Green-Lewis 30), so that the possibility of consensus is withdrawn. And if divided from one another even in their present, physical proximity, the intrusion of memories throughout the novel further separates them. Indeed, the events of the present throw peoples' minds back to past experience, which becomes further remote with each peal of the clock.

Woolf responds to the sense of isolation and flux in her characters, and in her post-war audience, by showing them a world in which they, too, would be part of a community if only they would realize it, and, indeed, most of her characters are poised to make a connection that ultimately fails. The notable exception is Clarissa's response to Septimus's suicide, and the connection between them is unwelcome. All Clarissa's will is being directed towards the creation of a beautiful moment in which all her guests can share.[12] However, this moment is disrupted by news, forced on Clarissa's attention by the doctor Bradshaw, of Septimus's suicide. Clarissa's ability to enact her desire, to will a shared moment of beauty into being, is disappointed by the intrusion of a controlling, institutional presence into the private sphere (it is no accident, surely, that Bradshaw is a psychiatrist, modeled on Woolf's own doctor George Savage whom her father hired), and she can regain only a partial, inconclusive control.

The relationship between Clarissa and Septimus illustrates a further point of Woolf's ambivalence by giving two competing evaluations of memory: Clarissa's idealization of her youth at Bourton, and Septimus Warren Smith's horror of the war. For Clarissa Dalloway, as for Ruth Wilcox in *Howards End*, memory is the chief means of preserving her sense of self, her continuity over time, within the midst of tremendous change. Even if her memories are faulty, idealized visions unshared by Peter Walsh or Sally, they are the fictions by which she sustains herself. While her

---

[12] Woolf shies from the "alien and external" because it trivializes the spirit; this was her complaint in the debates with Bennett and what in her view was the general Edwardian fixation on mundane, material things as a method of representation. The best form to accommodate this spirit is one she herself describes as "difficult [...] to grasp" (157), and if Woolf were a less deliberate artist, one could find Clarissa Dalloway's fuss over a party a hugely ironic way of going about it.

search for connection may be fundamentally flawed by these potentially inauthentic versions of the past and herself in it—and this is no small problem—an inability to escape memory is also personally and interpersonally debilitating. Septimus Warren Smith's vision of the present (of the beauty of small things, for example) is in some ways clearer because of his experience in the war, but his inability to escape the all-too present reality of that experience leaves him no recourse but to defy it through death. It is difficult, to say the least, to know whether Woolf's vision here is optimistic or pessimistic: should we see the cohesion of the novel as granting a unity lacking in the outer world? Does its horizon, bounded as it is by a single day and by certain key events, create the possibility for shared meaning? Or do the endless incursions of memory blur that horizon, that day, and with it secure meaning? How does a modernist sense of immediacy (of experience, of present-time) work when the novel constantly looks backward, rarely forward?

As the party and the novel reach their end, Peter Walsh tells Sally that he will make his goodbyes with her, but, goes the narrative, "he sat on for a moment," suspended by ill-defined feelings of "terror" and "ecstasy" (194). "What is it that fills me with extraordinary excitement?" he asks himself. In answer, Clarissa appears. Amidst the flux and uncertainty, the passage of time, Clarissa's presence is a stabilizing influence. Her solidity literally stops time as it concludes the narrative. There is no moving on from her, "For there she was" (194). The past tense of the final word implies a narrative time beyond the frame of the novel and, therefore, the sense that Clarissa and the queen she obliquely represents are not in fact able to stop time. Still, for Peter and for a length of time we are not permitted to measure—just as we cannot know whether his experience of their connection is more ecstasy than terror—Clarissa's presence stops him.

Mrs. Dalloway's inability to control the moments of connection and the novel's abrupt ending make it an equivocal response to Victorian culture and literary realism. However, Woolf was more decisive in *To the Lighthouse*, published two years later, and with her portrait of Mrs. Ramsay revised Mrs. Dalloway, completing her own task of laying Victoria to rest, just as Lily Briscoe lays down her brush. Clarissa Dalloway's party becomes Mrs. Ramsay's dinner party, but unlike Clarissa, Mrs. Ramsay is able to bring people together in a moment of beauty, to supersede the social insecurities that threaten to divide the group, transforming malaise into a communal, aesthetic experience. Mrs. Ramsay begins the dinner herself feeling outside of the "eddy" of life, left with nothing but a long expanse of dinner table, a "shabby," unbeautiful room, and a hope that someone will make something happen. But she quickly concedes that "the whole of the effort of merging and flowing and creating rested on her [...] if she did not do it, nobody would do it" (83), and so, like the pulse of life and the tick of the clock—metaphors for both the process of creation and its culmination in the moment of beauty—she begins.

Out of William Bankes's letters and Charles Tansley's discomfort over his flannel trousers (both worried about the wasted time spent away from their work), Mrs. Ramsay, with Lily Briscoe's tacit and reluctant agreement to "be nice," orchestrates conversations and relationships among her guests. But these miniature moments of connection overlie their private neuroses, bouts of bad conscience, and reflections on one another. The question raised by this scene is a revised version of the one posed by *Mrs. Dalloway*: are or can these connections be authentic? Do physical proximity and mutual recognition—the effort to acknowledge one another—count for more than private, mental "betrayals" in the calculus of human relationships? Certainly, they are better, in Mrs. Ramsay's view, than her husband's inability to conceal his feelings. Even so, each character, the narrator reveals, is bored by it all and feels the lack of something, but what that something is remains elusive.

When the candles are placed, however, the group itself comes into focus: "some change at once went through them all [...] and they were all conscious of making a party together" (97). Although herself bemused by the change, Mrs. Ramsay wills Paul and Minta to appear—and they do—arriving with the Boeuf en Daube and the return of talk and affection. Lily has scrutinized Mrs. Ramsay throughout (usually faring badly by the comparison that reveals her own preoccupations), but she also sees Mrs. Ramsay's uncanny ability to bring people together as an act of will. "Always she got her own way in the end," she says; "she put a spell on them all by wishing, so simply, so directly" (101). Mrs. Ramsay knows better than Lily how much of this will derives from her and how much belongs to the connective impulse itself. (In her moment of "security," she surveys the table and thinks, "there is a coherence in things, a stability; something, she meant, is immune from change and shines out [...] so that again tonight she had the feeling she had had once today, already, of peace, of rest. Of such moments, she thought, the thing is made that endures" [105].) However, she has come nearer to that "something" by initiating and guiding the dinner party, on the one hand, and by recognizing when to follow its momentum, on the other. As she starts to think about leaving the table, she is arrested by the sound of her husband's and Mr. Carmichael's and even her own voice reciting the same poem. Bound together by its music, their voices become "the voice" of a communal aesthetic experience.

As Mrs. Ramsay pauses on the threshold, the liminal space marks a passing time as well, as she "waited a moment longer, in a scene which was vanishing even as she looked" (111). But her sensitivity to this passage as a scene highlights the way she works with it and precipitates the change she knows is coming. Having just remarked and sympathized with Charles Tansley's inability to find the right opportunity to assert himself, Mrs. Ramsay takes hers, with Minta's arm, and leaves. The scene "changed, it shaped itself differently; it had become, she knew, giving one last look at it over her shoulder, the past" (168).

Lily comments as she watches Mrs. Ramsay go up the stairs: "And directly she left a sort of disintegration set in [...] thus giving a turn to the whole poise of the evening, making the weight fall in a different direction" (112). "Time Passes" corroborates Lily's sense of disintegration as the house decays and Mrs. Ramsay, Prue, and Andrew all die in parentheses. (Mr. Carmichael's success is the only good news delivered there, the war having "revived" public "interest in poetry" [134].) The maternal figure so essential to their cohesion becomes a narrative aside, which signals her inability to stop time more pointedly than Clarissa Dalloway's;

the narrative, like life, moves on without her. However, if she can't stop it, those parentheses nevertheless show the way she periodically interrupts it, too. Mrs. Ramsay's passing becomes shorthand in Woolf—like that other matriarch's, the queen's passing, did for the modernists generally—for a way of being that is no longer possible and perhaps no longer desirable, but which is also undeniable.

At the end of the novel, Mr. Ramsay reaches the lighthouse and Lily Briscoe completes her portrait. She thinks to herself, "I have had my vision" (310). As in *Mrs. Dalloway*, here again is that past tense, the moment of vision that cannot last for more than a second, and, even then, only "*as if* for a second" (209). And this is a single, isolated vision, not one that Lily shares with anyone (or expects to interest anyone, at any rate) and not even one that necessarily brings her closer to her subject. For all her study of Mrs. Ramsay, in recollection as in life, Lily has been looking for a vision, but "a" vision implies neutral insight, any insight, more than a desire to learn something about Mrs. Ramsay herself, who becomes an instrument of that vision without even having to be physically present. While Lily could not complete her portrait in Mrs. Ramsay's presence, the sight of now empty steps frees even Lily's mental vision, her memory. Freed from its source, that is, and from the pull of fidelity exerted by the literal, external form, the Mrs. Ramsay of memory can be manipulated and give to Lily, as Victoria did to the modernists, her vision.

Woolf suggested that "in time to come, Lytton Strachey's Queen Victoria will be Queen Victoria just as Boswell's Johnson is now Dr. Johnson" ("Biography" 191). If the modernist break with social history required its reinvention—in other words, if it is through the modernists that we have come to know Victoria and her era—then their break with literary history suggests that the version of realism we have inherited is also largely an image conjured by them for their own purposes. They willed themselves into existence through their lectures and essays, biographies and novels as much as the Victorians did through the images in their novels of the legal will. The realist writers of the nineteenth century gave their Edwardian heirs a rhetorical model for understanding how culture could be formed and transmitted. In possession of that inheritance, writers of the early twentieth century acknowledged the bequest, but adapted it to the uses of a new cultural and literary outlook, one in which their own consciousness was foregrounded through stylistic developments such as the interior monologue and stream of consciousness, and the general thematic interest in inheritance. Like their Edwardian "Uncles," however, the modernists confronted this past with a certain amount of ambivalence. On the one hand, there could be no further nods to realistic mechanisms such as the legal will, nor false equations of interiority with external things; the modernist writers would grant each character their own subjective experience of a reality that could be felt, if no longer seen. On the other hand, the spirit with which that document was imbued, the force to determine one's own character for the present and for posterity, is surely a trait the modernists inherited as well, transmitting a new literature, a new law, and a new culture through their own novel bequests.

Works Cited

Abbott v. Middleton (1855) 52 Eng. Rep. 813. Print.

Abbs, Peter. Introduction. *Father and Son*. By Edmund Gosse. New York: Penguin, 1989. 9–31. Print.

Allen, Roger. "Sir Edmund Gosse and His Modern Readers: The Continued Appeal of *Father and Son*." *ELH* 55 (1988): 487–503. Print.

Allen v. Maddock (1858) 14 Eng. Rep. 757. Print.

Allnut, George S. *The Practice of Wills and Administrations*. London: John Crockford, 1860. Print.

Alsop, Susan Mary. *Lady Sackville*. New York: Doubleday, 1978. Print.

Altick, Richard D. *The English Common Reader: A Social History of the Mass Reading Public, 1800–1900*. Columbus: Ohio State University Press, 1957. Print.

Anderson, Benedict. *Imagined Communities: Reflections on the Origins and Spread of Nationalism*. London: Verso, 1983. Print.

Anderson, Linda. *Bennett, Wells, and Conrad: Narrative in Transition*. New York: St. Martin's, 1988. Print.

Andrew v. Motley (1862) 12 C.B. (N.S.) 513. Print.

Anonymous. "Recent Works of Fiction." 1853. Eigner: 222–47. Print.

Aristodemou, Maria. *Law and Literature: Journeys from Her to Eternity*. Oxford: Oxford UP, 2000. Print.

Aristotle. *Poetics*. Ed. Kenneth A. Telford. Chicago: Henry Regnery, 1967. Print.

Arnold, Matthew. *Heinrich Heine*. Philadelphia: Leypoldt, 1863. 7–8. Google Book Search. Web. 6 Aug. 2009.

Atkinson v. Anderson (1882) 21 Ch.D. 100

Bailey, Alfred. "Novelists' Law." *The Gentleman's Magazine* 37 (1886): 23–35. Print.

Bakhtin, M.M. *The Dialogic Imagination*. Ed. Michael Holquist. Trans. Caryl Emerson and Michael Holquist. Austin: U of Texas P, 1981. Print.

Banks v. Goodfellow (1870) LR 5 QB 549. Print.

Baring-Gould, S. "Strange Wills." *Once a Week* 21 Feb. 1863: 232–6. Print.

Baron, Jane. "Law, Literature, and the Problems of Interdisciplinarity." *Yale Law Journal* 108 (1999): 1059–82. Print.

Barrell, John. *The Birth of Pandora and the Division of Knowledge*. Philadelphia: U of Pennsylvania P, 1992. Print.

Batchelor, John. *The Edwardian Novelists*. New York: St. Martin's, 1982. Print.

Beer, Gillian. "Origins and Oblivion in Victorian Narrative." *Sex, Politics, and Science in the Nineteenth-Century Novel*. Ed. Ruth Bernard Yeazell. Baltimore: Johns Hopkins UP, 1986. 63–87. Print.

Belsey, Catherine. *Critical Practice*. London: Methuen, 1980. Print.

Bennett, Arnold. *The Author's Craft and Other Critical Writings of Arnold Bennett.* Ed. Samuel Hynes. Lincoln: U of Nebraska P, 1968. Print.
———. *Clayhanger*. 1910. London: Penguin, 1989. Print.
———. *The Journals of Arnold Bennett*. Ed. Newman Flower. 3 vols. London: Cassell, 1932–33. Print.
———. Last Will and Testament. Mar. 18, 1902. Public Records Office, London. Print.
———. *These Twain*. New York: Doran, 1915. Print.
Bennett, J.F.C. *The Practitioners Guide to the Duties of Executors and Administrators*. London: Waterlow Bros. and Layton, 1899. Print.
Bentham, Jeremy. *The Works of Jeremy Bentham, published under the superintendence of his executor, John Bowring*. 1838–43. 11 vols. Rpt. New York: Russell and Russell, 1962. Print.
Bergonzi, Bernard. *The Myth of Modernism and Twentieth-Century Literature*. Brighton: Harvester, 1986. Print.
Best, G.F.A. "The Road to Hiram's Hospital." *Victorian Studies* 5 (1961): 135–50. Print.
Binder, Guyora and Robert Weisberg. *Literary Criticisms of the Law*. Princeton: Princeton UP, 2000. Print.
"A Bitter Legacy." *Times Literary Supplement* 22 May 1903: 158. Print.
Blackstone, William. *Commentaries on the Laws of England*. 1765. Ed. Stanley N. Katz. Chicago: U of Chicago P, 1979. Print.
Blamires, Harry. *Twentieth-Century English Literature*. London: MacMillan, 1986. Print.
Bloom, Harold. *The Anxiety of Influence: A Theory of Poetry*. New York: Oxford UP, 1973. Print.
Bodichon, Barbara Leigh Smith. *A Brief Summary, in Plain Language, of the Most Important Laws Concerning Women*. 1856. Rpt. in T. Dolin: 123–33. Print.
Bogert, George Gleason. *The Law of Trusts and Trustees: A Treatise Covering the Law Relating to Trusts and Allied Subjects Affecting Trust Creation and Administration*. Rev. 2nd ed. St. Paul: West Law, 1991. Print.
Brenchley v. Still (1850) 2 Rob. Eccl. 176. Print.
Bronte, Emily. *Wuthering Heights*. 1847. New York: Norton, 1990. Print.
Browne, Irving. *Law and Lawyers in Literature*. 1882. Rpt. Colorado: Rothman and Co., 1982. Print.
Brunt v. Brunt (1873) LR 3 P&D 37. Print.
Buckley, Jerome. "Towards Early-Modern Autobiography: The Roles of Oscar Wilde, George Moore, Edmund Gosse, and Henry Adams." *Modernism Reconsidered*. Ed. Robert Kiely. Cambridge: Harvard UP, 1983: 1–15. Print.
Bullock v. Bennett (1855) 7 De G.M. & G. 285. Print.
Bulwer-Lytton, Edward. "On Art in Fiction." 1838. Eigner: 22–38. Print.
Burke, Richard C. "Accommodation and Transcendence: Last Wills In Trollope's Novels." *Dickens Studies Annual* 15 (1996): 291–307. Print.

Butler, Samuel. Last Will and Testament. July 30, 1902. Public Records Office, London. Print.

———. *The Way of All Flesh.* 1903. New York: Random House, 1998. Print.

Campbell, Allan R. "The Law as Treated in Fiction." *The Green Bag: A Useless but Entertaining Magazine for Lawyers* 14 (1902): 364–7. Print.

Carroll, David. *George Eliot: The Critical Heritage.* London: Routledge, 1971. Print.

———. "Notes." *Felix Holt.* Ed. Felicia Bonaparte. Oxford: Oxford UP, 1998. Print.

Carson, T.H. *Carson's Real Property Statutes.* London: Sweet, 1902. Print.

Casson v. Dade (1781) 1 Bro. C.C. 99. Print.

Cheese v. Lovejoy (1876) 2 PD 251. Print.

Christie, James Traill. *Concise Precedents of Wills.* London: Maxwell, 1857. Print.

Claflin, Tennessee C. ("Lady Cook"). "Law Regarding Wills and Inheritance." *Westminster Review* 143 (1894): 184–203. Print.

Clarke, William M. *The Secret Life of Wilkie Collins.* London: W.H. Allen, 1988. Print.

Cobbe, Frances Power. "Criminals, Idiots, Women, and Minors." *Criminals, Idiots, Women, and Minors: Victorian Writing by Women on Women.* Ed. Susan Hamilton. Peterborough, Ont: Broadview P, 2004. Print.

Collins, Wilkie. Last Will and Testament. Nov. 11, 1889. Public Records Office, London. Print.

———. *The Moonstone.* 1868. New York: Signet, 1984. Print.

———. *No Name.* 1862. New York: Dover, 1978. Print.

———. *The Woman in White.* 1860. Ed. Frederick Karl. New York: Signet, 1985. Print.

Conrad, Joseph. *Heart of Darkness.* 1899. New York: Norton, 1988. Print.

Cover, Robert. "Nomos and Narrative." *Narrative, Violence, and the Law: The Essays of Robert Cover.* Eds Martha Minow, Michael Ryan, and Austin Sarat. Ann Arbor: U of Michigan P, 1992: 95–173. Print.

Cox, Jane. *"Affection Defying the Power of Death": Wills, Probate, and Death Duty Records.* Birmingham: Federation of Family History Societies, 1993. Print.

Cross, Mary Ann. Last Will and Testament. Feb. 9, 1881. Public Records Office, London. Print.

Cutler, Charles G. "Curious Wills of Curious People." *The English Illustrated Magazine* April–Sept. 1897: 171–3. Print.

"Dancer's Son Claims Sackville Peerage." *New York Times* 2 Mar. 1909: 4. *The New York Times Article Archive.* Web. 14 Nov. 2008.

Dannenberg, Lutz and Hans-Harald Mueller. "On Justifying the Choice of Interpretive Theories," *Journal of Aesthetics and Art Criticism* 43 (1984): 7–16. Print.

David, Deirdre. *Fictions of Resolution in Three Victorian Novels.* New York: Columbia UP, 1981. Print.

Davis v. Angel (1862) 45 Eng. Rep. 1287. Print.

"The Degeneracy of Wills." *The Spectator* 12 Jan.1900: 46–7. Print.

Dicey, Albert Venn. *Lectures on the Relation Between Law and Public Opinion During the Nineteenth Century*. 2nd ed. London: MacMillan, 1914. Ed. And with an introduction by Richard vandeWetering. Indianapolis, IN: The Liberty Fund, 2008. Web. 25 June 2008. <http:oll.libertyfund.org>.

Dickens, Charles. *Dombey and Son*. 1848. New York: Penguin, 1985. Print.

———. Last Will and Testament. July 19, 1870. Public Records Office, London. Print.

———. *Little Dorrit*. 1857. Ed. Stephen Wall. New York: Penguin, 1998. Print.

———. *Martin Chuzzlewit*. 1844. Oxford: Oxford UP, 1995. Print.

———. *Our Mutual Friend*. 1865. Oxford: Oxford UP, 1997. Print.

Dickens, Charles and W.H. Wills. "The Doom of English Wills." *Household Words* 28 Sept. 1850: 1–4. Print.

Dickson, Jay. "Surviving Victoria." *High and Low Moderns: Literature and Culture, 1889–1939*. Eds. Maria DiBattista and Lucy McDiarmid. New York: Oxford UP, 1996. Print.

"Disposal of Property by Will." *The Edinburgh Review* July 1824: 350–75. Print.

Dolin, Kieran. *Fiction and the Law: Legal Discourse in Victorian and Modernist Literature*. Cambridge: Cambridge UP, 1999. Print.

Dolin, Tim. *Mistress of the House: Women of Property in the Victorian Novel*. Aldershot: Ashgate, 1997. Print.

Draycott, Charles. "Whimsical Will-Making." *Temple Bar* 110 (1897): 66–71. Print.

Eigner, Edwin and George J. Worth, eds. *The Metaphysical Novel in England and America: Dickens, Bulwer, Melville, and Hawthorne*. Los Angeles: U of California P, 1978. Print.

———. *Victorian Criticism of the Novel*. Cambridge UP, 1985. Print.

Eliot, Felix. "A Mummy's Bequest." *Belgravia* 69 (1889): 474–83. Print.

Eliot, George. *Felix Holt: The Radical*. 1866. Ed. Lynda Mugglestone. New York: Penguin, 1995. Print.

———. *Middlemarch*. 1872. Ed. Felicia Bonaparte. Oxford: Oxford UP, 1998. Print.

———. *Selections from George Eliot's Letters*. Ed. Gordon S. Haight. New Haven: Yale UP, 1985. Print.

———. "Silly Novels by Lady Novelists." *Westminster Review* 10 (Oct. 1856): 442–61. Print.

Eliot, T.S. "Tradition and the Individual Talent." *The Sacred Wood*. London: Methune, [1919]. Web. 1996. <http://www.Bartleby.com>. 19 Nov. 2008. <http://www.Bartleby.com/200/>.

Ermarth, Elizabeth. *Realism and Consensus in the English Novel*. Princeton: Princeton UP, 1983. Print.

"Extraordinary Wills." *The Green Bag: A Useless but Entertaining Magazine for Lawyers* 10 (1898): 162–4. Print.

Farr, D. Paul. "The Edwardian Golden Age and Nostalgic Truth." *Dalhousie Review* 50 (1970): 378–93. Print.

Fenn, Henry Edwin. *35 Years in the Divorce Court*. London: T. Werner Levine, 1911. Google Book Search. Web. 15 July 2009.

Ferguson, Robert. *Law and Letters in American Culture*. Cambridge: Harvard UP, 1984. Print.

"Fight is On for Sackville Peerage." *The New York Times* 20 Dec. 1908: C4. *The New York Times Article Archive*. Web. 14 Nov. 2008. Print.

Fish, Stanley. *Doing What Comes Naturally: Change, Rhetoric, and the Practice of Theory in Literary and Legal Studies*. Durham: Duke UP, 1989. Print.

———. "What Makes an Interpretation Acceptable?" Keesey 347–56. Print.

Forster, E.M. *Aspects of the Novel*. 1927. New York: Harcourt, 1985. Print.

———. "Does Culture Matter?" in *Two Cheers for Democracy*. vol. 3. Ed. Oliver Stallybrass. London: Edward Arnold, 1972. Print.

———. *Howards End*. 1910. New York: Bantam, 1985. Print.

"The Forsyte Aga." *Times Literary Supplement* 22 June 1922: 411. Print.

Frank, Cathrine O. "Of Testaments and Tattoos: the Wills Act of 1837 and *Mr. Meeson's Will* (1888)." *Law and Literature* 18 (2006): 323–41. Print.

Frechét, Alec. *John Galsworthy: A Reassessment*. Totowa: Barnes and Noble, 1982. Print.

Freeman, Michael and Andrew D. Lewis, eds. *Law and Literature*. Oxford: Oxford UP, 1999. Print.

Fried, Charles. *Contract as Promise: A Theory of Contractual Obligation*. Cambridge: Harvard UP, 1981. Print.

Fry, Thomas Charles. "The Ethics of Wills." *The Economic Review* April 1893: 190–200. Print.

Furst, Lillian. *All is True: The Claims and Strategies of Realist Fiction*. Durham: Duke UP, 1995. Print.

Galsworthy, John. *The Forsyte Saga*. 1922. New York: Oxford UP, 1995. Print.

Galsworthy, John III. Last Will and Testament. Jan. 10, 1905. Public Records Office, London. Print.

Gardner, Phillip. "E.M. Forster and 'The Possession of England.'" *Modern Language Quarterly* 42 (1981): 166–83. Print.

Gaughan, Richard T. "Prospecting for Meaning in *Our Mutual Friend*." *Dickens Studies Annual* 19 (1990): 231–46. Print.

Giles and Clark v. Warren (1872) LR 2 P&D 401. Print.

Gilmour, Robin. Introduction. *The Warden*. By Anthony Trollope. New York: Penguin, 1984. Print.

Gissing, George. "The Place of Realism in Fiction." 1895. *Nineteenth-Century British Novelists on the Novel*. Ed. George L. Barnett. Appleton, 1971. Print.

Glendinning, Victoria. *Vita: The Life of V. Sackville-West*. New York: Quill. 1985. Print.

Gordley, James. *The Philosophical Origins of Modern Contract Law*. Oxford: Clarendon, 1991. Print.

Gosse, Edmund. *Father and Son*. 1907. Ed. Peter Abbs. New York: Penguin, 1989. Print.

———. *Some Diversions of a Man of Letters*. London: Heinemann, 1919. Print.

Gosse, Philip. Last Will and Testament. Oct. 12, 1888. Public Records Office, London. Print.

Great Britain. Administration of Estates Act. 9 April 1925. 15 Geo. 5. c. 23. Print.

———. Bastardy Act of 1845. 8 May 1845. Stat. 8 & 9 Vict. c. 10. Print.

———. Bastardy Act, 1923. 31 July 1923. Stat. 13 & 14 Geo. 5 c. 24. Print.

———. Bastardy Laws Amendment Act of 1872. 10 Aug. 1872. Stat. 35 & 36 Vict. c. 65. Print.

———. Bastardy Laws Amendment Act of 1873. 24 April 1873. Stat. 36 Vict. c. 9. Print.

———. Court of Probate Act of 1857. 25 August 1857. Stat. 20 & 21 Vict. c. 77. Print.

———. Divorce and Matrimonial Causes Act of 1857. 28 August 1857. Stat. 20 & 21 Vict. c. 85. Print.

———. House of Commons Debate. 15 July 1857. vol. 146. cc 1515–23. *Hansards, 1803–2005*. Web. 19 Nov. 2008. <hansard.millbanksystems.com>.

———. House of Commons Debate. 28 Nov. 1958. v. 596 cc 741–91. *Hansards, 1803–2005*. Web. 19 Nov. 2008. <hansard.millbanksystems.com>.

———. House of Commons Debate. 8 May 1959. v 605. cc 781–818. *Hansards, 1803–2005*. Web. 19 Nov. 2008. <hansard.millbanksystems.com>.

———. House of Lords Debate. 13 February 1857. vol. 144. cc 605–19. *Hansards, 1803–2005*. Web. 19 Nov. 2008. <hansard.millbanksystems.com>.

———. House of Lords Debate. 30 July 1869 vol. 198 cc 979–87.

———. House of Lords Debate. 21 June 1870 vol. 202 cc 600–22.

———. Married Women's Property Act, 1870. 9 August 1870. Stat. 33 & 34 Vict. c. 93 s. 1. Print.

———. Married Women's Property Act, 1882. 18 August 1882. Stat. 45 & 46 Vict. c. 75. s. 1. Print.

———. Wills Act of 1837. 3 July 1837. Stat. 7 Will & 1 Vict. c. 26. Print.

———. The Wills Amendment Act of 1852. 17 June 1852. 15 & 16 Vict. c. 23. Print.

Green-Lewis, Jennifer. *Framing the Victorians: Photography and the Culture of Realism*. Cornell UP, 1997. Print.

Grossman, Jonathan H. *The Art of Alibi: English Law Courts and the Novel*. Baltimore: Johns Hopkins UP, 2002. Print.

Haggard. H. Rider. *Mr. Meeson's Will*. Pastime Ser. 16. Chicago: Laird and Lee, 1888. Print.

Halsbury, Earl of. *The Laws of England: Being a Complete Statement of the Whole Law of England*. London: Butterworths, 1908. Print.

———. *Halsbury's Laws of England*. Ed. Lord Symonds. 3rd ed. London: Butterworths, 1953. Print.

———. *Halsbury's Statutes of England and Wales*. 4th ed. 2006 reissue. London: Butterworths, 1989. Print.

Hamilton, J.A. "Sir Cresswell Cresswell." *Dictionary of National Biography* vol. 13. London: Smith, Elder & Co., 1888, 72–3. New York Public Library. July 19 2008. Google Book Search. Web. 12 Aug. 2009.

Hardy, Thomas. "The Profitable Reading of Fiction." 1888. *The Selected Writings of Thomas Hardy: Stories, Poems and Essays*. Ed. Irving Howe. Greenwich: Fawcett, 1966. 138–50. Print.

———. "The Science of Fiction." *Thomas Hardy: Selected Poetry and Non-Fiction Prose*. Ed. Peter Widdowson. London: MacMillan, 1997. 260–64. Print.

Harpham, Geoffrey. "Time Running Out: The Edwardian Sense of Cultural Degeneration." *Clio* 5 (1976): 283–301. Print.

Harris, Virgil. *Ancient, Curious, and Famous Wills*. Boston: Little Brown and Co., 1911. Print.

Harris, Wendell. *Literary Meaning: Reclaiming the Study of Literature*. New York: New York UP, 1996. Print.

Harvey, Geoffrey. "A Parable of Justice: Drama and Rhetoric in *Mr. Scarborough's Family*." *Nineteenth-Century Fiction* 37 (1982): 419–29. Print.

Hastilow v. Stobie (1865) 1 P&D 64. Print.

Hayward, A. "Wills and Will-Making: Ancient and Modern." *Quarterly Review* 108 (1860): 425–69. Print.

Hazlitt, William. "On Will-Making." *Table-Talk: Essays on Men and Manners*. 1821–22. Rpt. Darby, PA: Arden, 1982. Print.

Hepburn, James, ed. *Arnold Bennett: The Critical Heritage*. London: Routledge and Kegan, 1981. Print.

Hewitt, Douglas. *English Fiction of the Early Modern Period, 1890–1940*. London: Longman, 1988. Print.

Hill and Simmonds v. Crook (1871) L.R. 6 H.L. 265. Print.

Hirsch, E.D. "Meaning and Significance Reinterpreted." *Critical Inquiry* 11 (1984): 202–25. Print.

———. "Objective Interpretation." Keesey 26–38. Print.

Hirsch, Pam. *Barbara Leigh Smith Bodichon: Feminist, Artist, and Rebel*. London: Chatto and Windus, 1998. Print.

Holcombe, Lee. *Wives and Property: Reform of the Married Women's Property Laws in Nineteenth-Century England*. Oxford: Martin Robertson, 1983. Print.

"How to Prove a Will." *Chambers's Journal* 8 May 1886: 299–301. Print.

Hoy, Pat C. II "The Narrow, Rich Staircase in Forster's *Howards End*." *Twentieth-Century Literature* 31 (1985): 221–35. Print.

Huffcut, Ernest W. "The Literature of Law." *The Green Bag: A Useless but Entertaining Magazine for Lawyers* 4 (1892): 52–4. Print.

Hynes, Samuel. *Edwardian Occasions: Essays on Writing in the Early Twentieth Century*. New York: Oxford UP, 1972. Print.

———. *The Edwardian Turn of Mind*. Princeton: Princeton UP, 1968. Print.

"I Give and Bequeath." *Household Words* 5 Mar.1853: 22–4. Print.
Iseminger, Gary. *Intention and Interpretation*. Philadelphia: Temple UP, 1992. Print.
James, Henry. "The Art of Fiction." 1884. *The Art of Fiction and Other Essays*. Ed. Morris Roberts. New York: Oxford UP, 1948. 3–23. Print.
———. "The Younger Generation." *Times Literary Supplement* 19 Mar. 1914: 133–5. Print.
Jenner v. Finch (1879) 5 PD 111. Print.
Jenner v. Turner (1880) 16 Ch.D. 188. Print.
Kaplan, Carola M. and Anne B. Simpson, eds. *Seeing Double: Revisioning Edwardian and Modernist Literature*. New York: St. Martin's, 1996. Print.
Kaplan, Fred. *Dickens: A Biography*. New York: William Morrow, 1988. Print.
Keesey, Donald, ed. *Contexts for Criticism*. Palo Alto: Mayfield, 1987. Print.
Kern, Stephen. *The Culture of Time and Space, 1880–1918*. Cambridge: Harvard UP, 1983. Print.
Kiely, Robert. "Plotting and Scheming: The Design of Design in *Our Mutual Friend*." *Dickens Studies Annual* 12 (1983): 267–83. Print.
Knapp, Steven and Walter Benn Michaels. "Against Theory." *Critical Inquiry* 8 (1982): 723–42. Print.
———. "Reply to John Searle." 669–75. *New Literary History* 25 (1994): 637–67. Print.
Knight, H.B. Finlay. *A Girl with a Temper: A Romance of the Wills Act*. London: Bentley, 1892. Print.
"Lady Cook Dies in London at 77." *New York Times*. 20 Jan. 1923:13. *The New York Times Article Archive*. Web. 15 Oct. 2008.
"Lady Cook in Naples." *New York Times*. 3 July 1910: n. pag. *The New York Times Article Archive*. Web. 15 Oct. 2008.
LaFourcade, Georges. *Arnold Bennett: A Study*. New York: Haskell House, 1971. Print.
Lansbury, Coral. *The Reasonable Man: Trollope's Legal Fiction*. Princeton: Princeton UP, 1981. Print.
"Law and Lawyers in Literature." By Irving Browne. Boston: Soule and Bugbee, 1882. Reviewed in *The Atlantic Monthly* April 1882: 545–8. Print.
"Law in Romance." *American Law Review* 1.2 (1867): 477–94. Print.
Lawrence, D.H. "John Galsworthy." 1927. *D.H. Lawrence: Selected Critical Writings*. Ed. Michael Herbert. Oxford: Oxford UP, 1998. 210–22. Print.
———. "To Edward Garnett." 1 Feb. 1913. Letter 544 of *The Letters of D.H. Lawrence*. Ed. James T. Boulton. vol. 1. Cambridge: Cambridge UP, 1979. 509. Print.
Law Amendment Society. "Report of the Personal Laws Committee (of the Law Amendment Society) on the Laws Relating to the Property of Married Women." *Westminster Review* 10 (July 1856): 331–60. Print.
Leadam, Isaac Saunders. "Freedom of Bequest." *Contemporary Review* 53 (1888): 116–28. Print.

Leddy, Michael "Validity and Reinterpretation." *Critical Inquiry* 12 (1986): 616–26. Print.

LeFanu, Sheridan. "Squire Toby's Will." *Temple Bar* 22 (1868): 212–36. Print.

Levenson, Michael. *A Genealogy of Modernism: A Study of English Literary Doctrine 1908–1922*. New York: Cambridge UP, 1984. Print.

———. "Liberalism and Symbolism in *Howards End*." *Papers on Language and Literature* 21 (1985): 295–316. Print.

Levine, George. *The Realistic Imagination: English Literature from Frankenstein to Lady Chatterley*. Chicago: Chicago UP, 1981. Print.

Lewes, G.H. "Realism in Art: Recent German Fiction." 1858. Eigner: 130. Print.

Lewis v. Mathews (1866) LR 2 Eq. 177. Print.

Lewis, L.S. "Some Peculiar Wills." *The Strand Magazine* 14 (1897): 441–7. Print.

Lincoln, Andrew. "The Sociology of Bennett's *Clayhanger*." *English Literature in Transition* 27.3 (1984): 188–200. Print.

Lister v. Smith (1863) 3 Ww. & Tr. 282. Print.

Lloyd v. Lloyd (1852) 61 Eng Rep 338. Print.

Locke, John. *Second Treatise of Government*. 1689. Ed. Richard Cox. Wheeling: Harlan Davidson, 1882. Print.

Lodge, David. *The Modes of Modern Writing*. New York: Cornell UP, 1977. Print.

Longley, Katherine M. "Charles Dickens and the 'Doom' of English Wills." *Journal of the Society of Archivists* 14.1 (1993): 25–38. Print.

"Lord St. Leonards' *Handy Book on Property Law*." By Edward Burtenshaw Sugden, Lord St. Leonards. Reviewed in *Blackwoods Edinburgh Magazine* Feb. 1858: 190–99. Print.

Maas v. Sheffield (1845) 1 Rob. Eccl. 364, 163 Eng. Rep. 1068. Print.

Maine, Sir Henry Sumner. *Ancient Law: Its Connection with the Early History of Society and Its Relation to Modern Ideas*. 1861. Ed. Sir Frederick Pollock. 4th Amer. ed. New York: Henry Holt, 1906. Print.

Majendie, Margaret. "Uncle George's Will: Part I." *Temple Bar* 68 (May 1883): 48–67. Print.

———. "Uncle George's Will: Part II." *Temple Bar* 68 (June 1883): 224–38. Print.

Malone, Cynthia Northcutt. "The Struggle of *Father and Son*: Edmund Gosse's Polemical Autobiography." *a/b: Autobiography Studies* 8 (1993): 16–32. Print.

"The Man of Property." *Times Literary Supplement* 30 Mar. 1906: 116. Print.

Marks, Patricia. "Storytelling as Mimesis in *Our Mutual Friend*." *Dickens Quarterly* 5 (1988): 23–30. Print.

Marrot, H.V. *The Life and Letters of John Galsworthy*. London: Heinemann, 1935. Print.

Marshall, William H. "*The Way of All Flesh*: The Dual Function of Edward Overton." *Texas Studies in Literature and Language* 4 (1963): 583–90. Print.

Martin, Robert B. *Enter Rumour: Four Early Victorian Scandals*. London: Faber, 1962. Print.

Masson, David. “British Novelists Since Scott.” 1859. Eigner: 148–57. Print.
McCulloch, J.R. “Disposal of Property by Will—Entails—French Law of Succession.” *The Edinburgh Review* 40 (July 1824): 350–75. Print.
McGowan, John P. *Representation and Revelation: Victorian Realism from Carlyle to Yeats*. Columbia: U of Missouri P, 1986. Print.
McMaster, R.D. *Trollope and the Law*. New York: St. Martin’s, 1986. Print.
———. “Trollope and the Terrible Meshes of the Law: *Mr. Scarborough’s Family*.” *Nineteenth-Century Fiction* 36 (1981): 135–56. Print.
Meale, Alfred R. and Paisley Livingston. “Intentions and Interpretations,” *Modern Language Notes* 107 (1992): 931–49. Print.
Mill, John Stuart. *Principles of Political Economy and Chapters on Socialism*. Ed. Jonathan Riley. New York: Oxford UP, 1994. Print.
Miller, David A. *Narrative and Its Discontents: Problems of Closure in the Traditional Novel*. Princeton: Princeton UP, 1981. Print.
Miller, Jane Eldridge. *Rebel Women: Feminism, Modernism and the Edwardian Novel*. London: Virago, 1994. Print.
Mills v. Farmer (1815) 1 Meriv. 55. Print.
Milton, John. *Paradise Lost*. 1674. *Norton Anthology of English Literature*. Ed. M.H. Abrams et al. 7th ed. vol. 1. New York: Norton, 2000. Print.
Milton, Paul. “Inheritance as the Key to all Mythologies: George Eliot and Legal Practice.” *Mosaic* 28 (1995): 49–68. Print.
Moggridge v. Thackwell (1792) 1 Ves. Jun. 464. Print.
Morris, Anne and Susan Nott. *All My Worldly Goods: A Feminist Perspective on the Legal Regulation of Wealth*. Aldershot: Ashgate, 1995. Print.
Murfin, Ross C. “The Gap in Trollope’s Fiction: *The Warden* as Example.” *Studies in the Novel* 14 (1982): 17–30. Print.
Murray, E.C. Grenville. “Old Joquelin’s Bequest: A Tale about Women.” *The Cornhill Magazine* June 1879: 681–711. Print.
Newmark, Nathan. “Wills in Fiction.” *The Green Bag*: *A Useless but Entertaining Magazine for Lawyers* 1 (1889): 467–9. Print.
Nunokawa, Jeff. *The Afterlife of Property: Domestic Security and the Victorian Novel*. Princeton: Princeton UP, 1994. Print.
Ogden, C.K. *Bentham’s Theory of Fictions*. London: Kegan Paul, Trench, Trubner & Co., 1932. Print.
Olsen, Stein Haugom. “Authorial Intention.” *British Journal of Aesthetics* 13 (1973): 219–31. Print.
Palmer and Brown v. Dent (1850) 2 Rob. Eccl. 284. Print.
Parkinson, R.N. “The Inheritors; or A Single Ticket for *HE*.” *E.M. Forster: A Human Exploration*. Eds G.K. Das and John Beer. New York: New York UP, 1979. 55–68. Print.
Pascal, Roy. “Narrative Fictions and Reality: a Comment on Frank Kermode’s *A Sense of an Ending*.” *Why the Novel Matters: a Postmodern Perplex*. Eds Caroline McCracken and Mark Spilka. Bloomington: Indiana UP, 1990. Print.

Peters, Julie Stone. "Law, Literature and the Vanishing Real: On the Future of an Interdisciplinary Illusion." *PMLA* 120 (2005): 442–53. Print.
Peterson, Linda. *Victorian Autobiography: The Tradition of Self-Interpretation.* New Haven: Yale UP, 1986. Print.
Philpott v. St. George's Hospital (1855) 21 Beav. 134. Print.
———. (1857) VI H.L.C. 338. Print.
———. (1859) 27 Beav. 107. Print.
Pinchbeck, Iva and Margaret Hewitt, eds. *Children in English Society, volume 2.* London: Routledge, 1973. Print.
Pollock, Frederick. "Notes." *Ancient Law*. By Henry Maine. 4th Amer. ed. New York: Henry Holt, 1906. Print.
Polloczek, Dieter. *Literature and Legal Discourse: Equity and Ethics from Sterne to Conrad.* Cambridge: Cambridge UP, 1999. Print.
Porter, Roger J. "Edmund Gosse's *Father and Son*: Between Form and Flexibility." *Journal of Narrative Technique* 5 (1975): 174–95. Print.
Posner, Richard. *Law and Literature: A Misunderstood Relation.* Cambridge: Harvard UP, 1998. Print.
Powell v. Powell (1866) LR 1 P&D 209. Print.
"Queen Victoria's Descendants." *The Times*. 24 Jan. 1901: 11. *The Times Digital Archive 1785–1985*. Web. 30 July 2009.
Re Gunstan's Goods, Blake v. Blake (1882) 7 PD 102. Print.
Re Overhill's Trust (1853) 1 Sm. & Giff. 362. Print.
Reed, John. *Victorian Will*. Athens: Ohio UP, 1989. Print.
Reid v. Reid (1858) 25 Beav. 468. Print.
Ritchie, John, Neill H. Alford, and Richard Effland, eds. *Decedents' Trusts and Estates: Cases and Materials*. Mineola: Foundation P, 1971. Print.
Rodensky, Lisa. *The Crime in Mind: Criminal Responsibility and the Victorian Novel*. Oxford: Oxford UP, 2003. Print.
"The Romance in the Life of Sackville-West." *New York Times* 13 Feb. 1910: SM12. *The New York Times Article Archive*. Web. 14 Nov. 2008.
Rubinstein, Jill. "'Business in Business': The Money Ethic of Samuel Butler." *English Literature in Transition (1880–1920)* 19.4 (1976): 237–47. Print.
S., J.C. "Law and Literature." *The St. James Magazine* 14 (1865): 194–8. Print.
"Sackville Claimant Rests." *New York Times* 5 Feb. 1910: 3. *The New York Times Article Archive*. Web. 14 Nov. 2008.
"Sackville Romance Detailed in Court." *New York Times* 2 Feb. 1910. *The New York Times Article Archive*. Web. 14 Nov. 2008.
Sackville-West v. The Attorney-General (1910) P. 143. Print.
Sadrin, Anny. *Parentage and Inheritance in the Novels of Charles Dickens.* Cambridge: Cambridge UP, 1994. Print.
Sala, George Augustus. "Wills and Bequests." *Belgravia* 27 (1875): 327–37. Print.
Schor, Hilary. *Dickens and the Daughter of the House*. Cambridge: Cambridge UP, 1999. Print.

Schramm, Jan-Melissa. *Testimony and Advocacy in Victorian Law, Literature, and Theology*. Cambridge: Cambridge UP, 2000. Print.
Searle, John. "Literary Theory and Its Discontents." *New Literary History* 25 (1994): 637–67. Print.
Sefton v. Hopwood (1855) 1 Fost. & F. 578. Print.
Sennett, Richard. *The Fall of Public Man*. New York: Vintage, 1978. Print.
Shanley, Mary Lyndon. *Feminism, Marriage, and the Law in Victorian England*. Princeton: Princeton UP, 1993. Print.
Shires, Linda. "The Aesthetics of the Victorian Novel: Form, Subjectivity, Ideology." *The Cambridge Companion to the Victorian Novel*. Ed. Deirdre David. Cambridge: Cambridge UP, 2001. Print.
Siebenschuh, William R. *Fictional Techniques and Factual Works*. Athens: U of Ohio P, 1983. Print.
Smith and Smith v. Smith (1866) LR 1 P&D 143. Print.
Solomon, J. Fisher. "Realism, Rhetoric, and Reification: Or the Case of the Missing Detective in *Our Mutual Friend*." *Modern Philology* 86 (1988): 34–45. Print.
Squillace, Robert. *Modernism, Modernity, and Arnold Bennett*. Lewisburg: Bucknell UP, 1997. Print.
Stebbings, Chantal. *The Private Trustee in Victorian England*. Cambridge: Cambridge UP, 2002. Print.
Stephen, James Fitzjames. "The Relation of Novels to Life." 1855. Eigner: 161–2. Print.
Sternlicht, Sanford. *John Galsworthy*. Boston: Twayne, 1987. Print.
Stone, Marjorie. "Dickens, Bentham, and the Fictions of the Law: a Victorian Controversy and Its Consequences." *Victorian Studies* 29 (1985): 125–54. Print.
Strachey, Lytton. *Queen Victoria*. London: Harvest, 1921. Print.
Sugden, Edward Burtenshaw, Lord St. Leonards. *A Handy Book on Property Law: In a Series of Letters*. 2nd ed. London: Blackwood and Sons, 1858. Print.
Sutherland, John. *Victorian Fiction*. London: MacMillan, 1995. Print.
Sutphen, Joseph W. "Last Wills and Testaments." *The Popular Science Monthly* 24 (1883): 520–30. Print.
Swinburne, Henry. *A Treatise of Testaments and Last Wills*. 7th ed. Dublin, 1793. Google Book Search. Web. 11 June 2009.
Taylor, Jenny Bourne. "Nobody's Secret: Illegitimate Inheritance and the Uncertainties of Memory." *Nineteenth-Century Contexts* 21 (2000): 565–92. Print.
———. "Representing Illegitimacy in Victorian Culture." *Victorian Identities: Social and Cultural Formations in Nineteenth-Century Literature*. Eds Ruth Robbins and Julian Wolfreys. London: MacMillan, 1996. Print.
Teichman, Jenny. *Illegitimacy: An Examination of Bastardy*. Ithaca: Cornell UP, 1982. Print.
"Testament." *Oxford English Dictionary*. 2nd ed. 1989. Web.
"Testamentary Curiosities." *Chambers's Journal of Popular Literature, Science, and the Arts* n.d. 1872: 421–6. Print.
Thale, Jerome. "The Making of an Edwardian Age." *Mosaic* 7 (1974): 25–43. Print.

Thomas, Ronald R. *Detective Fiction and the Rise of Forensic Science*. Cambridge: Cambridge UP, 1999. Print.
Thomas, Syd. "'Pretty Woman, Elegantly Framed': The Fate of Bella Wilfer in Dickens's *Our Mutual Friend*." *Dickens Quarterly* 14 (1997): 3–23. Print.
Thornton v. Bright (1836) 2 My. & Cr. 229. Print.
Trodd, Anthea. *A Reader's Guide to Edwardian Literature*. Calgary: U of Calgary P, 1991. Print.
Trollope, Anthony. *An Autobiography*. 1883. Ed. David Skilton. New York: Penguin, 1996. Print.
———. *Dr. Thorne*. 1858. Ware: Wordsworth, 1994. Print.
———. Last Will and Testament. Jan. 23, 1883. Public Records Office, London. Print.
———. *Mr. Scarborough's Family*. 1883. New York: Penguin, 1993. Print.
———. *Ralph the Heir*. 1871. Ed. John Sunderland. Oxford: Oxford UP, 1990. Print.
———. *The Warden*. 1855. Ed. Robin Gilmour. New York: Penguin, 1984. Print.
———. *The Way We Live Now*. 1875. New York: Penguin, 1994. Print.
Tucker, Irene. *A Probable State: The Novel, The Contract, and the Jews*. Chicago: U of Chicago P, 2000. Print.
Tudor, Owen D. *Tudor on Charities: A Practical Treatise on the Law Relating to Gifts and Trusts for Charitable Purposes*. Eds H.G. Carter and F.M. Crashaw. London: Sweet and Maxwell, 1929. Print.
Veeser, H. Aram, ed. *The New Historicism*. New York: Routledge, 1989. Print.
Walker v. Tipping (1852) 68 Eng. Rep. 740. Print.
Watt, Ian. *The Rise of the Novel: Studies in Defoe, Richardson, and Fielding*. Berkeley: U of California P, 1959. Print.
"The Way of All Flesh." Rev. *Times Literary Supplement* 26 June 1919: 347. Print.
Weisberg, Richard. *The Failure of the Word: The Protagonist as Lawyer in Modern Fiction*. New Haven: Yale UP, 1989. Print.
———. *Poethics*. New York: Columbia UP, 1992. Print.
———. "Wigmore's Legal Novels Revisited." *Northwestern Law Review* 71 (1976): 17–28. Print.
Weisberg, Richard and Jean-Pierre Barricelli. "Literature and Law." *Interrelations of Literature*. Eds Jean-Pierre Barricelli and Joseph Gibaldi. New York: MLA, 1982. Print.
Weisberg, Robert. "The Law-Literature Enterprise." *Yale Journal of Law and Humanities* 1.1 (1988): 1–67. Print.
Welsh, Alexander. *Strong Representations: Narrative and Circumstantial Evidence in England*. Baltimore: Johns Hopkins UP, 1992. Print.
West v. Lord Sackville (1903) 2 Ch. D.C.A. 378. Print.
West, B.B. *Wills and How Not to Make Them*. London: Longman, 1893. Print.
West, Robin. "Communities, Texts, and Law: Reflections on the Law and Literature Movement." *Yale Journal of Law and Humanities* 1.1 (1988): 129–56. Print.
———. *Narrative, Authority, Law*. Ann Arbor: U of Michigan P, 1993. Print.

White, James Boyd. *Heracles' Bow: Essays on the Rhetoric and Poetics of the Law*. Madison: U of Wisconsin P, 1985. Print.

———. *Justice as Translation: an Essay in Cultural and Legal Criticism*. Chicago: Chicago UP, 1990. Print.

———. *The Legal Imagination: Studies in the Nature of Legal Thought and Expression*. Boston: Little Brown, 1973. Print.

Wiener, Martin J. *Reconstructing the Criminal Character: Culture, Law, and Policy in England, 1830–1914*. Cambridge: Cambridge UP, 1990. Print.

Wigmore, John H. "A List of Legal Novels." *The Brief* 2 Jan. 1900. *Law in Popular Culture Collection*. Tarleton Law Library, Austin, TX. Web. 17 July 2005. <http://tarlton.law.utexas.edu/lpop/etext/wigmorebrief.htm>.

Wilkinson, A.E. "Law and Literature." *The American Law Review* 39 (1905): 204–21. Print.

Williams, Raymond. *The English Novel from Dickens to Lawrence*. New York: Oxford UP, 1970. Print.

"Wills." *Temple Bar* 105 (1894): 410–21. Print.

"Wills and Testaments." *Chambers's Journal of Popular Literature, Science, and the Arts* 18 Nov. 1865: 721–4. Print.

"Wills and Will-Making." *The Leisure Hour* 14 (1865): 6–8. Print.

"Wills: Old and New." *All The Year Round* 23 Aug. 1890: 178–81. Print.

Wimsatt, W.K. Jr., and M.C. Beardsley. "The Intentional Fallacy." *Sewanee Review* 54 (1946): 466–88. Print.

Wisenthal, J.L. "Samuel Butler's Epistle to the Victorians: *The Way of All Flesh* and Unlovely Paul." *Mosaic* 13.1 (1979): 17–19. Print.

Wood, Ellen. "A Last Will and Testament." *Bentley's Miscellany* Oct. 1858: 340–54. Print.

Woolf, Virginia. "The Art of Biography." *The Death of the Moth and Other Essays*. London: Harvest, 1942. Print.

———. "Modern Fiction." 1925. *The Common Reader*. New York: Harvest, 1953. 150–58. Print.

———. "Mr. Bennett and Mrs. Brown." 1924. *The Captain's Deathbed and Other Essays*. New York: Harvest, 1950. 94–119. Print.

———. *Mrs. Dalloway*. London: Harvest, 1925. Print.

———. *To the Lighthouse*. 1927. New York: Harvest, 1981. Print.

Index

For Product Safety Concerns and Information please contact our EU representative GPSR@taylorandfrancis.com
Taylor & Francis Verlag GmbH, Kaufingerstraße 24, 80331 München, Germany

www.ingramcontent.com/pod-product-compliance
Ingram Content Group UK Ltd.
Pitfield, Milton Keynes, MK11 3LW, UK
UKHW021722240926
475702UK00029BA/1810

* 9 7 8 1 1 3 8 2 6 0 5 5 9 *